Junkers Ju 87
Stuka

Junkers Ju 87
Stuka

MANFRED GRIEHL

Airlife
England

First published in the UK in 2001
by Airlife Publishing Ltd

First published in Germany in 1998 by
Motorbuch Verlag, Stuttgart

Translated from the original German text by Tom Morrison

British Library Cataloguing-in-Publication Data
A catalogue record for this book
is available from the British Library

ISBN 1 84037 198 6

This book contains rare photographs and the publishers have made every endeavour to reproduce them to the highest quality. Some, however, have been technically impossible to reproduce to the standard we normally demand, but have been included because of their rarity and interest value.

The information in this book is true and complete to the best of our knowledge. All recommendations are made without any guarantee on the part of the Publisher, who also disclaims any liability incurred in connection with the use of this data or specific details.

Typeset by Celtic Publishing Services, Wrexham
Printed in England by Butler & Tanner Ltd., Frome and London

Airlife Publishing Ltd
101 Longden Road, Shrewsbury, SY3 9EB, England
E-mail: airlife@airlifebooks.com
Website: www.airlifebook.com

Foreword and Acknowledgements

Among the German military aircraft which won particular fame in the *Blitzkrieg* of 1939–40, was without doubt, the Junkers Ju 87, the legendary 'Stuka'.

Like the Bf 109, the Ju 52 or the He 111, the 'Stuka' still has an incomparable attraction for aviation enthusiasts and model builders alike. This may be due to the Ju 87's robustness of construction, and also to its successful engagement on every front and to its pilots, who are still known today.

After the works on the Do 217, He 177 and He 111 bombers were published a monograph on the Ju 87 had to join their ranks. Like the He 111, this Junkers machine was actually conceived only as an interim solution until a more effective twin-engined dive bomber, the Messerschmitt Bf 210, was produced. The result was a dive bomber and ground attack aircraft for the close support of the army; beyond that nothing else was considered. Its application as a cannon-armed, flying tank hunter brought about notable success during the defensive battles on the eastern front in spite of enemy air superiority.

The resulting work, produced after many years of research, and ultimately longer than expected, explains for the first time the course of its development, from the first prototype, the Ju 87 V1 to the last night ground attack aircraft which went into action in 1945. The individual versions are described from both the technical and tactical viewpoints.

Unfortunately however, not all the details of the Ju 87 story could be presented here: the scope of the work set its own boundaries. The overall development of the 'Stuka', as well as the history of the dive bomber and ground attack *Geschwader* that were equipped with it, had of necessity to occupy the foreground.

In the material on the Ju 87 available hitherto the technical literature differs on many points from the historical facts. I have been able to fill in some gaps and correct some errors, but much remains patchy in spite of my efforts. Some hobby-historians – fortunately only a few – did not want to make 'their' information available.

Needless to say, much new pictorial material and many vital documents were found in state and private archives in and outside Germany as well as in company records.

My thanks are due, above all, to the generous support of the Daimler-Benz Co. (DASA), of the state archives in Freiburg/Breisgau, and of the picture archive in Koblenz and, further, of the Airport Co. at Frankfurt/Main as well as the employees of the special collections at the German Museum in Munich. With their help much could be brought to light. The employees of the NASM in Washington, DC, together with the members of the Working Group on Defence Research and the DGLR Lilienthal-Obert were also a powerful source of help. Besides these, the Information Departments of the German Aero Club and the State Bureau of Defence Technology and Procurement (BWB), the German Office (WAST) in Berlin, the study collection of the BWB in Koblenz and the German Aviation Study Office in Frankfurt/ Main supported the work. Furthermore, thanks are due to the German Army Garrison Library in Mainz for their extremely efficient help in procuring literature.

Apart from these, help came from many aviation enthusiasts, especially from Messrs Achs, Arena, Balke, Bekker, Bernád, Borzutzki, Creek, Crow, Dabrowski, Damann, Dressel, Duda, Emiliani, Emmerling, Evans, Filley, Forsyth, Franzke, Haberfellner, Heck, Herwig, Höfling, Jarski, Jayne, Kalinke, Knobloch, König, Dr Koos, Krieg, Lang, Lange, Langheinrich, Leppkes, Lommel, Lutz jr, Marchand, Martinez, Matthiesen, Meier, Menke, Michulec, Müller, Müller-Romminger Nowarra, Obert, Petrick,

Punka, Radinger, Dr Rapp, Ransom, Regel, Dr Reitinger, Ricco, Redemann, Reisinger, Riedinger, Roba, Rohrbach, Rosch, Dr Ruff, Salonen, Salvati, Sauer, Scheibert, Schenk, Schlaug, Schliephake, Schmitt, Schmidt, Schröder, Selinger, Sengfelder, Silva, Smith, Soppa, Stapfer, Staufer, Thiele, Trümper, Turba, Vajda, Valtonen, Vetter, Vogt, Wagner, Walter, Weber, Weinholz, Wetter, Wilczk, Wittigayer, and Zazonil – they all placed their knowledge, photographs and information resources generously at my disposal. Without their selfless contribution this work would not have been possible in its present scope.

Only through the support of these and other people and organisations was it possible – in almost all areas – to shed further light on the history of the Ju 87. As I have said, some information remained patchy, and had to remain so. At the end of the war the Ju 87 had already become 'old iron'. The documentation was at that time already out of date or had fallen victim to the events of war. A quantity of important photographs and information was presumed lost, carelessly destroyed or thrown away by uninterested descendants. As with every other type of German aircraft, much documentation inessential to aviation research, especially photographs, were not lost until long after the war, when they quite simply 'disappeared' from archives and collections. The present owners naturally have no interest in making these resources accessible to anyone.

Many events could also be established only thanks to contemporary witnesses.

As I did in the foreword to my work on the He 111, I would like to to speak to the very hearts of all aviation enthusiasts: aviation history must be regarded as an indispensable part of our technological history and preserved for the future. For the continuation of the research into the German *Luftwaffe* which has already begun, more help is still needed from those who are willing to loan their photographs, log-books and documents of all kinds. It would be gratifying if a number of enthusiasts would help with the archiving and hence with the rescue of our irreplaceable aviation history.

I am always grateful for any comments, corrections, suggestions or encouragement from readers.

I am especially grateful to Mrs Monica Müller for reviewing the manuscript.

Finally, my special thanks are due to Dr Scholten of the Pietsch Publishing Group for her willingness to publish this work.

Manfred Griehl
*Postfach 2162
55011 Mainz

Contents

Translator's Note

German words that do not have precise English equivalents, such as *Geschwader*, or which are well known to English speakers and are more evocative untranslated, such as *Luftwaffe* or *Wehrmacht*, are left untranslated and are printed in italics. This practice, if excessive, can be irritating to the English-speaking reader and has therefore been kept to a minimum. Abbreviations, such as RLM (for *Reichsluftfahrtministerium*), are neither translated nor italicized.

Military ranks are translated, either directly, e.g. *Reichsmarschall* to Imperial Marshal, or to their British equivalent, e.g. *Feldwebel* to Sergeant, as has seemed best to the translator. *Luftwaffe* rank titles were the same as those for the German Army and are therefore translated to their British Army rather than RAF equivalents. Officer cadet ranks are somewhat more obscure and are translated as follows: *Fahnenjunker*: Cadet; *Fahnenjunker-Gefreiter*: Cadet Lance-Corporal; *FahnenjunkerUnter-offizier*: Cadet Corporal; *Fähnrich*: Junior Under Officer; *Oberfähnrich*: Senior Under Officer. *Leutnant* and *Oberleutnant* are translated as 2nd Lieutenant and Lieutenant respectively.

Luftwaffe flying units did not have exact RAF equivalents. They were, approximately:

- *Kette, Rotte, Schwarm* (plurals *Ketten, Rotten, Schwärme*): a sub-unit of two to four aircraft
- *Staffel* (plural *Staffeln*): a unit of about nine aircraft, equivalent to an RAF squadron; numbered in Arabic numerals
- *Gruppe* (plural *Gruppen*): a unit of three *Staffeln* and a staff *Staffel*, about thirty aircraft, numbered in Roman numerals, abbreviated 'Gr' when used independently
- *Geschwader* (plural *Geschwader*): a unit of three *Gruppen* and a staff *Staffel*, about 100 aircraft, abbreviated 'G', and prefixed with letters indicating role – thus 'StG', = *Sturzkampfgeschwader*= Dive Bomber *Geschwader*, 'SG' = *Schlachtgeschwader*, translated here as Ground Attack *Geschwader*, 'JG' = *Jagdgeschwader* = Fighter *Geschwader*, 'KG' = *Kampfgeschwader* = Bomber *Geschwader*. The unit number followed the abbreviation, thus StG 3 = *Sturzkampfgeschwader* 3. The component *Gruppen* of StG 3 would be numbered I/StG 3, II/StG 3 and III/StG 3. The I *Gruppe* comprised *Staffeln* 1–3, the II *Gruppe* comprised *Staffeln* 4–6, the III *Gruppe* comprised *Staffeln* 7–9. Thus 7/StG 3 meant 7th *Staffel*, III *Gruppe*, Dive Bomber *Geschwader* 3.
- *Fliegerkorps/Fliegerdivision*: operational command comprising an unspecified number of *Geschwader* and other units.
- *Luftflotte*: the largest operational command outside the Air Ministry, controlling a variable number of *Fliegerkorps*.

I have made extensive use of the legitimate but unusual English word 'battleworthy'. The author makes a distinction between 'airworthy', i.e. capable of flight, and a condition of full readiness for combat, here translated as 'battleworthy'.

Where there is one common English form of a geographical name, I have used it, e.g. Cologne, Munich, Pomerania, Silesia. Where there are two well-known forms, e.g. Breslau/Wroclaw, and I am aware of both, I have used whichever form seems to be the most easily recognisable to English-speaking readers. Where the name is obscure and/or I am not aware of any other form, I have given the name, as far as possible, in English phonetic spelling; this applies in particular to Russian names.

Overview

1 Introduction

Luftwaffe Service Directive L.Dv.16 *Conduct of Air Warfare*, put together from 1935 onwards by Major-General Walther Wever and Major-General Helmuth Wilberg – both basically protagonists of continental military thinking – set the scene for future air warfare policy.

The directive was based on an earlier one of 1926 and its main objective, was to provide the most efficient possible support of army operations. Only from the spring of 1939 onwards was 'operative air warfare' given greater attention. Besides the tactical employment of fighter units (albeit in the area of their own army operations), this envisaged, for the first time, attacks on 'distant targets', supported by offensive equipment.

This idea was then developed by Herhudt von Rohden, General Hans Geisler's Chief of Staff and leader of the naval air forces until 1939.

General Geisler believed that the *Luftwaffe* should free itself from the operational support of the army and navy and take as the centre-point of its future operations attacks on the key industries and, above all, the air forces of the enemy.

On 1 November 1935, however, Major-General Wever expressed the opinion that the effective support of ground troops and cooperation with the army were among the essential tasks of the *Luftwaffe*. Indeed, he believed that the *Reichsluftwaffe* (later the *Luftwaffe*) should form a self-sufficient part of the *Wehrmacht* but for the time being should have no operational tasks of its own.

The army connection of these early thinkers on modern air war strategy was also plain to see in the case of Major (General Staff) Paul Deichmann, at that time leader of the LA1 group in the *Luftwaffe* General Staff.

Even so, for a long time no strategic air warfare was possible beyond the assignment of combat-ready units of the *Luftwaffe* to all the points of conflict in a future war. The existing equipment in any case limited its actions to neighbouring areas of the European mainland. In the absence of the necessary economic resources, only single-engined fighters and, especially, fast bombers and dive bombers could be produced quickly and – what seemed still more important – in large numbers.

As a consequence of the aircraft chosen, the strategic heavy bomber, envisaged in the teachings of General Douhet, was replaced by an aircraft designed for medium ranges. From this Dr Ing. Manfred von Richthofen, Hans Jeschonnek and others, developed the idea of a highly mobile army support weapon which could intervene effectively in the land battle at any time. The powerful bomber units proposed by Giulio Douhet in his work *Il dominio dell' aria*, purpose-built for a wide-ranging and hence strategic aerial war, lost their significance, at least in Germany. Only between the end of 1930 and February 1932 did Douhet's ideas influence German planning in the Army Weapons Bureau.

At the beginning of 1934 aircraft development was still far from the production of strategic weapons. The idea of the bomber purely as an army support weapon was dominant. Even Walther Wever, who was always known as the proponent of the four-engined bomber, saw that at that time, because of the army's weakness in equipment – heavy weapons were lacking in practically all areas – effective close air support was necessary. This meant, at any rate initially, forgetting about four-engined bombers, such as the planned Do 19, the Hs P 26 or the Ju 89; the desire for such bombers, however, even if in small numbers, still remained.

The dominance of planes suitable as 'ground attack aircraft' became unmistakable. Machines like the Ju 87 were soon to come off the production lines in large numbers. From 1935 at the earliest – but at the latest on the occasion of

These two corporals and the lance-corporal decorated with the Iron Cross, Second Class, belong to 11 (St)/LG 1. In the summer of 1941 the Staffel *was at Rovaniemi in northern Finland.*

the 1936 planning exercise at Bad Salzbrunn – two core areas of aerial warfare were regarded as especially important: first, the establishment of air superiority over the battlefield by means of a superior fighter force, and secondly, the application of effective close air support.

Especially in breaking through enemy positions and lines of fortifications, massed air forces were to create a corridor for the army divisions. In the summer of 1935, for the first time, an air attack exercise was carried out against *Wehrmacht* armoured units on the Münster training area. More than ten years previously, in the winter of 1923–4, the *Reichswehr* had secretly worked on army–air force cooperation, but without reaching any satisfactory solution.

This did not, however, mean that Major-General Wever let the *Luftwaffe* be downgraded to a mere army support weapon at that time. Further-more, throughout his career he exerted himself to break up encrusted leadership structures which were too closely connected with army support and to put forward a well-thought-out strategic and tactical plan for the application of air weapons.

However, the lack of any increase in resources left no room for the use of air weapons on a wide-ranging, strategic scale. Walther Wever's early death on 3 June 1936 prevented the establishment of a lasting, carefully considered balance of strategic and tactical possibilities.

Thus, contrary to Douhet's teaching, the decisive wartime role did not go to the strategic bomber but to an offensive air force used for close support. Indeed *Luftwaffe* Service Directive L.Dv.16, in its later form, foresaw that a decisive result in war would be possible only through the well-directed cooperation of army, navy and air force, yet the *Luftwaffe* General Staff, as well as its subordinate staffs, remained locked in a

Machines such as this Ju 87 R-2 (A5+BL) of 3/StG 1 became the essence of the 'Stuka'.

traditional way of thought which, broadly speaking, was borrowed from the leadership of the First World War.

A static war appeared entirely conceivable and was not to be excluded in a new conflict.

Only a strong air force, according to the German leadership, could provide a reliable means of breaking open solid front lines and setting the German forces in forward motion once more. Moreover, everything must be done, in the event of a static war, to protect the troops from bleeding slowly to death in endless struggles for a few metres of ground.

Although it was already clear by the time of the final phase of the First World War that massive attacks on the infrastructure and military potential of the enemy could bring relief to one's own troops, even in the mid-1930s attacks on the enemy's aircraft industry far inside his hinterland were not given any special consideration. To hit such targets effectively – and put them out of action for a long time – appeared worthwhile but had no priority in the list of targets to be attacked.

By contrast, attacks on the enemy air force – and this comprised the core of L.Dv.16 – was top of the list. More urgent than attacks on mostly distant armaments targets were assaults on naval forces and their bases from the air.

The directive to weaken, and as far as possible cripple, the enemy's aircraft production by means of air attacks only came relatively late. Continuous attacks on the enemy's air force were to weaken his fighting ability permanently and facilitate the rapid advance of one's own ground troops. The continual pressure of attack would take the initiative from the enemy and remove his freedom of action. This, however, in no way precluded strategic options, such as attacks on important armaments targets in the enemy hinterland, at least not in the guidelines of L.Dv.16.

This task was, however, severely limited by the lack of strategic aircraft. Although the productive capacity of the German aircraft industry increased rapidly from 1933–4 onwards, for reasons already outlined, strategic bombers were still lacking in noteworthy quantities.

The most important goal of the air war remained 'intervention in the operations and actions of war on land and sea', which led to the aim of 'attack on enemy air forces'. Major-General Carl von Clausewitz had already seen the greatest military potential 'in the combination of weapons'. Basically, the trend-setting L.Dv.16 formed the consensus for the application of air weapons between the thoughts of Giulio Douhet and a very close cooperation between army and air force.

As a result of the restrictions on German raw materials and production capacity, new compromises had continually to be made between the production goals set by the leadership and industry's productive capability. The ideal way of conducting quick, localised conflicts (Poland, France or the Balkans) was with numerous fighters and dive bombers, which were relatively easy to produce, and with medium bombers. The term '*Blitzkrieg*' was coined, but even the German leadership was surprised by the rapid advance of the *Wehrmacht*; the unexpected fortunes of war contributed to the rapid victories of 1939–41.

The possibilities that the application of air weapons opened up for army support led inevitably to the army continually calling for more and more support and this task of the *Luftwaffe* was considered increasingly urgent.

There was no room for even the most necessary strategic attacks, as industry did not have the capacity to deal with the demand. Even the *Luftwaffe* bomber squadrons were regarded by the army leadership only as an extra-long-range artillery component. The air warfare schools ensured that this belief was perpetuated. Lieutenant-General Erich Quade, who from the beginning of 1938 was commander of the Higher *Luftwaffe* School in Berlin, also advocated the tactical application of air weapons as vital in all phases of the land battle.

As late as 1938 numerous theoretical dissertations and lengthy discussions on what was ultimately the most effective doctrine for the application of the *Luftwaffe* always came back to the view that, against all neighbouring countries on which an attack was contemplated, only short- and medium-range bombers were needed.

This was basically how the situation was seen a few years before at the great *Wehrmacht* planning exercise in 1935, except for minor nuances, without, however, following the conclusions up with action. The war exercise 'Thuringia', which took place in 1938, demonstrated again that close support of the army should come before any deployment against the enemy armaments industry. That was also the belief of the Chief of the General Staff at the time, Ludwig Beck, whose views coincided closely with those of General Erich Ludendorff. In his dissertation *Total War* he wrote: 'The conduct of operations against the enemy war economy will occupy the phase of war in which the air forces are not shackled to the combat tasks of obtaining supremacy in the air or to direct cooperation with army and fleet.'

The *Luftwaffe* leadership nevertheless tried to limit the dominance of the army over the use of air weapons as far as possible, although above all the older officers, who had experienced the First World War, always disagreed: to them it seemed – through painful experience in the trenches – all too obvious that static warfare was to be avoided at any price and that the rapid advance of their own army, with the minimum of bloodshed was to be expedited. The opinion that this option was less important than the early and comprehensive bombardment of hostile armament targets, received scarcely any attention.

The 'manoeuvre of fast-moving troops' which was derived from the teaching staff for army tactics in June 1939 read: 'The closely interlocked cooperation by motorised units of the *Wehrmacht*, supported by close support air units, revealed itself as extremely promising for success.'

Moreover, in *Guidelines for the Application of the Air Force to Direct Support of the Army*, a close cooperation between army and *Luftwaffe* was naturally emphasised. This also applied to effective attacks on enemy field positions and well-protected bunkers which could persistently delay the advance.

The experience gained by the Condor Legion during the Spanish Civil War, not least the low-level attacks by the He 50 and He 51 as well as the new Ju 87, led to a renewed over-emphasis on the close air support concept which had become deeply entrenched, since air weapons were not used strategically.

As long as they were concerned with

On 4 February 1938 Hermann Göring was promoted General Field Marshal.

less-well-armed states in continental Europe which were relatively easy to overrun, the leadership's planning seemed fine – at least in the medium term. For attacks on more distant targets, the intention was to prepare appropriate *Luftwaffe* units with heavy bombers by 1942. This would, according to the *Luftwaffe* leadership, also make possible a quick defeat of Britain, in which the Ju 88 bomber, which was capable of dive bombing, as well as the potent He 177, were to be applied at the critical points.

The planning exercise of *Luftflotte* 2 in May 1939, however, surprisingly resulted in not particularly good prospects of success: the German forces were reckoned to be far too weakly equipped to strike at the British war economy successfully – and, above all, for any length of time – and to bring about a sustained loss of production in the British Isles.

The planning exercise held in 1939 in the presence of the Chief of the *Luftwaffe* General Staff, Hans Jeschonnek, also did not advance the leadership's thinking, as there was no reliable understanding of the massive application of the *Luftwaffe*; neither in the First World War nor in Spain had it been possible to gather sufficient knowledge.

Two possibilities emerged: overwhelming attacks on the enemy air forces or widespread cooperation between army and *Luftwaffe*.

At the beginning of the war Major-General Hans Jeschonnek's opinion was that the *Luftwaffe* must destroy the enemy air forces on the ground and in the air in a surprise attack, in order to ensure continuous air superiority above the army operations area. For this reason, according to the Chief of the General Staff, the rapid defeat of the whole enemy fighter potential was the primary focus. Next, the units were to be applied in indirect support of the army by destroying the enemy infrastructure, especially lines of communication, from the air. Only third in importance for Jeschonnek was the tactical value of short-range fighting units or units taken from the bomber force for that purpose. All these ideas were appropriate only in central Europe, not in an escalating global conflict with economically powerful nations, against which the German *Reich* had nothing (or little) to use.

Only when several of Germany's neighbouring states had been occupied in rapid attacks and sufficient new materials were available from the east were heavy bombers to be produced in quantity.

The various prototypes and project studies for a four-engined heavy bomber that had had some influence under Wever increasingly gave way to the familiar – but initially planned as unarmed – fast, medium-range bombers. Already, on 29 April 1937, Colonel-General Hermann Göring and Lieutenant-General Albert Kesselring had agreed on the dismantling of big bomber development without Ernst Udet (Chief of the Technical Bureau of the Imperial Aviation Ministry – *Reichsluftfahrtministerium*, RLM) or Erhard Milch (Secretary of State and representative of Göring) making any

The combat value of the 'Stuka' was continually increased. This is a Ju 87 B of 5/StG 77 during checking of the weapons installation.

strong protest. It may have been clear to them too that at the end of the 1930s Germany had neither the means to produce a strong fleet of four-engined bombers nor the big forward air bases with correspondingly long runways and extensive dispersal areas to accommodate such bombers effectively.

For this reason it was soon agreed that further work on long-range bombers would only be a 'development measure'. This work, which on the one hand led in the direction of the Ju 290, but also to the He 177 with four high-altitude engines, produced effective bombers during the war, but their numbers were insufficient for offensive action. It was the same with the Me 264, of which only one prototype could be tested.

At the end of December 1937 it was already established, 'in the framework of a concentrated aircraft prototype programme', that the number of different types had to be very quickly reduced. The performance data on the Ju 87, which had meanwhile become available and which was not very satisfactory, strengthened the opinion of the *Luftwaffe* leadership, especially the General Staff, that the Ju 87 'heavy dive bomber' could only be an interim solution. On 26 October 1938 General Field Marshal Hermann Göring approved the recommendations of the *Luftwaffe* General Staff to form eight dive bomber *Geschwader* with the Ju 87 B with the intention that these units would soon be re-equipped with the more effective Bf 210. This aircraft was also to replace the Bf 110s of the destroyer *Geschwader*.

This machine was slow to appear, however. The first flight of the twin-engined Bf 210 V1 did not take place until 2 September 1939. Problem followed problem; the whole development

Ju 87 operations often took place under unfavourable conditions as with I/StG 1 at Vaernes, Norway.

process, after much premature congratulation, became a disaster. The machine, which was ordered in enormous quantities far too soon, could only partly fulfill the role which was expected of it, in spite of numerous construction changes. Thus, the Ju 87 remained as the interim solution until the summer of 1944 with the Ju 87 D. Some of the technical problems were hushed up, but some were never understood.

At the end of the 1930s new objectives appeared: Adolf Hitler made it ever clearer that, beyond the central European countries, the Soviet Union could become the objective of an incomparably bigger (and also far more dangerous) war. Bigger theatres of war would pose new tactical tasks for the combat units of the *Luftwaffe* in the future. They could be faced with attacking an extremely diverse range of targets from the air; the tasks ranged from attacks on single tanks to the destruction of entire mechanised units – at the time, bombing from level flight seemed to be ill-suited to the destruction of such targets.

For this reason light and heavy dive bombers, as well as armoured ground attack aircraft and medium bombers, were still to be a part of operations over the battlefield and its links to the rear. This time the dive bomber forces of the *Luftwaffe* again stood at centre stage.

This led to the perpetuation of the over-regarded idea of pinpoint attack at any price, a tactic which could continue to be successful only as long as the enemy did not gain even partial control of the air.

When the Allies succeeded in doing this over the southern British Isles, the Ju 87 *Geschwader* learned this lesson for the first time, painfully in costly battles. The turning point came with the enormous war of attrition in the east, with losses that could no longer be replaced – or only incompletely – by German industry. Lasting air superiority could no longer be maintained over the Soviet Union. An enemy that regained its strength quickly, soon succeeded in reversing the fortunes of war and going on the offensive again.

After many years of struggle, the dive bomber forces of the *Luftwaffe*, and the ground attack *Geschwader* that were derived from them, lost the chance of victory.

On all fronts the material superiority of the enemy meant that, even though good hits were still scored by individual crews or units, decisive success was no longer obtainable. The costly attacks, especially those of the Ju 87 units, hurt considerably but in spite of all personal valour they could no longer lead to any change in the course of the war.

2 From Artillery Flyer to Tank Hunter

The introduction of dive bombers into the *Luftwaffe* was not a reaction to the American Curtiss Hawk biplane, which was capable of steeply diving flight. The dive bomber – *Sturzkampfbomber*, shortened to the pregnant abbreviation 'Stuka' – had a far longer prehistory than is generally accepted.

As early as the First World War, but also during the *Reichswehr* era, the idea of the diving attack as well as pinpoint bombing was pursued intensively in theory and practice.

Starting in August 1915 the first 'A' ('artillery flyer') units were formed and from the beginning of 1916 were given the task of 'infantry flyers' (Ifl); they eventually became an effective weapon within the first German air forces. Within a year units numbered 201–240 and 101–103 (Bavarian) went into action. The forty-three artillery flying units formed up to that time were reorganised from 29 November 1916 onwards so that their number – with a few newly formed units – increased to fifty-five (Nos. 201–255) with six (later nine) machines each.

For the protection of these units, from 1 January 1917 onwards, protection *Staffeln* (*Schutzstaffeln* – '*Schusta*') of six machines each were formed. The first ground attack operations took place on 24 April 1917 at Graville on the Somme battlefield. Besides protecting the 'infantry flyers' from enemy single-engined fighters, their main task was to suppress anti-aircraft defences by low-level attacks.

The *Schusta* were renamed *Schlachtstaffeln* ('*Schlasta*'), ground attack *Staffeln*, on 27 May

Among the early artillery aircraft was the LVG C VI, a braced biplane with two machine-guns as armament.

The Halberstadt CIV was developed from the CL II and was equipped with two fixed MG 08/15 machine-guns and a movable Parabellum machine-gun.

The Ju J 4, whose testing began on 3 May 1917, was one of the best ground attack aircraft at the end of the First World War.

1918; at the same time they took over the low-level attacks and ground attack operations immediately behind the enemy front line. During attacks by German ground troops these units were used in low-level attacks in front of their own troops. During the Allied push at St Quentin, massed ground attack aircraft, flying by day and night, succeeded in stabilising the front and preventing a breakthrough in that sector.

In scarcely a year thirty ground attack *Staffeln* came into being; by the autumn of 1918 their number had increased to thirty-eight. The formation of ground attack *Staffeln* Nos. 39 and 40 had already been ordered when the war ended. The ground attack school, opened at Saultain on 1 September 1918, began to cater for recruits for this type of armament.

During the battles along the Somme the army High Command had combined the ground attack *Staffeln*, which had been operating individually, into groups and allocated them to the armies as direct support. By the autumn of 1918 the *Staffel* strength was increased to eight aircraft each. The creation of the first ground attack *Geschwader*, of which each army was supposed to have one, was interrupted by the Armistice which was announced soon afterwards.

One thing was certain in the autumn of 1918; in future close air support was not to be left out of consideration and would gain in importance with more effective equipment.

The introduction of the cantilever-winged, armoured, all-metal biplane Ju J 4, of which 189 were delivered before the end of the war, brought a significant increase in fighting power compared to the Halberstadt CL IV.

The last ground attack aircraft of the First World War to see significant action was the Junkers Ju 10 (army designation CL I). With these machines sorties were flown in 1919 against the Red Army in Latvia by Volunteer Air Unit 431. By the end of the war a total of six Ju 10s were built, and a further thirty-seven followed.

On 21 January 1919 the commanding general of the air forces, Cavalry General Ernst von Hoeppner, informed the front-line units of the dissolution of the German air forces, which took place on 26 January. Many units had already disbanded themselves independently before this; some, however, had pulled back from the front in good order with their equipment. Further flying seemed to pilots and ground crews to be a distant prospect for the time being.

Colonel-General Hans von Seeckt, the chief of the Military Personnel Office – the General Staff in disguise – held fast, even after the end of the war, to the conviction that modern air formations must be a part of future armed forces.

Von Seeckt, who had received the Oak Leaves to the Pour Le Mérite on 27 November 1918, was promoted between 1920 and 1922 to the position of Chief of the Army Command and named the young Captain Kurt Student as leader of the Air Technical Group of the Imperial Ministry of Defence. It was thanks to him that the Rhön competitions, which developed from 1920 onwards, were effectively supported and *Reichswehr* officers received flight training.

Anything more than a theoretical interest in military flying was at first hardly possible. This was primarily because of the peace treaty of 28 June 1919 between Germany and the Allies. Among its conditions, was Part V, Articles 198–202, which required the complete demobilisation of the German air forces.

The Interallied Military Control Commission (IMCC), which entered Germany a little later, on 16 September 1919, and started work on 22 February 1920, was required to supervise German disarmament under Articles 203–10. The Interallied Aviation Supervisory Commission, which, like the IMCC, was subordinate to the ambassadors' standing conference in London, controlled flying. On the German side an Army Peace Commission and an Air Peace Commission (run by Major Wagenführ) were put into action, both connected to the Military Personnel Office, and had to work under the instructions of the IMCC.

In the Allies' opinion, the destruction of aviation equipment was going too slowly, so on 22 June 1922 a temporary ban on the renewal of German aviation was agreed upon and in addition the dissolution of police air forces was enforced.

In spite of initial difficulties, the dissolution of the first German air forces took place relatively quickly because of persistent pressure from the Allies. By the end of January 1922 about 15,000 aircraft, 28,000 aero engines and

1,000,000 square metres of hangar space were delivered to the Allies or destroyed under supervision. On 9 February 1922 the disarmament of Germany was confirmed at the ambassadors' conference, whereupon the three-month ban prescribed in the Treaty of Versailles began, according to which aircraft construction was not permitted again until the beginning of May 1922. In any case, the so-called Conceptual Provisions of 14 April 1922 placed such severe restrictions on what was allowed under the treaty that exceedingly narrow limits were set, even to civil air traffic. For example the permissible ceiling height was only 4,000 metres, the maximum range was 300 kilometres and the maximum permitted speed was 170 kph.

The Conceptual Provisions, as well as the continuing ban on building armed or armoured aircraft, continued to cripple the German aviation industry. Only in the Paris Aviation Agreement of 1926 were the Conceptual Provisions cancelled.

It was plain to all that military aviation had been shattered to its very foundations by the Treaty of Versailles. Until the beginning of 1922 the aviation advisors within the *Reichswehr* and *Reichsmarine* were confined to a theoretical preoccupation with military flying matters. The Treaty of Rapallo of 16 February 1922, according to which economic relations between Germany and Soviet Russia were intensified, brought the first progress. It led to military contacts between the two states.

As a result of the unfavourable economic situation, it was not until the end of 1922 that Heinkel and Junkers became more intensively involved with military aircraft projects and even then in secret or outside Germany. Cooperation with their eastern partner had also begun to bear its first fruits. In February 1923 this progressed to conversations between the Imperial Defence Ministry and the Red Army. Captain Kurt Student took part as advisor for aviation technology. The objective of the contacts was the establishment of a training and research base in Russia, outside Allied supervision, something that was achieved as early as 1924; the *Reichswehr* was able to begin training pilots and observers at the Lipetsk airfield south-east of Moscow.

From about 1928 the technical testing of bombers began there – especially those produced in Germany.

Powerful machines capable of diving flight, such as this Ju A 20 (works no. 1044), were among the forerunners of the Ju 87 at the beginning of the 1930s.

The Ju F 48 fi (D-2185, later D-ENER) were among the machines with which dive testing took place.

In the mid-1920s the construction of combat aircraft began under cover designations or at companies set up in neutral foreign countries. A few that were not developed in foreign countries, went in the course of time to service testing at Lipetsk. In Germany pilot training as well as experimental programmes were carried out under cover of a number of private organisations.

The first four-year plan for building up an effective aviation industry, which the Imperial Trade Ministry had set up (in secret agreement with the Imperial Defence Ministry) was for the period between 1925 and 1929. The development advisor in the Army Weapons Bureau, Captain Kurt Student, had channelled the technical and tactical requirements of the Military Personnel Office (Air) and formulated appropriate directives for industry from them. For the flight testing of prototypes, purely as to their flying qualities, the former experimental site at Rechlin on the Müritz was chosen. Weapons testing followed, if the 'test centre of the Imperial Association of the German Aviation Industry' at Rechlin established their suitability, at Lipetsk.

Initially the concern could only be to build up an 'emergency armament', so as not to be left completely unarmed in the event of a conflict. The Ju F 13, the Ju G 24 or the various Dornier developments Do C, F and N were not suitable for offensive use. The performance testing of these aircraft – by the flying advisor or Department T2 III (L) of the Army Organisation – was unsatisfactory.

On 1 February 1928 all bureaux concerned with military aviation were combined into Group Wa (L) of the Army Weapons Bureau; it was led by Captain Volkmann. Because of the peace treaty, however, the far more effective 'Air Inspectorate' suggested by Major Albert Kesselring could not initially be considered. Even so, work on the equipment of future air forces made successful progress in secret.

By the turn of the year 1928–9 German industry had to some extent recovered. Advances had been made in the development of aircraft suitable for civil and military purposes. On 1 October 1929 Captain Wilhelm Wimmer

This Ju A 48 was used by the Luftwaffe *for the training of dive bomber pilots.*

took over the Aviation Technical Group of the Army Weapons Bureau, which had been renamed to conceal its purpose from Wa (L) to (WaPrw 8) in the Statistical Group of the Testing Department. The main aim remained the creation of an emergency defence force, which was to contain some air forces equipped with whatever equipment was necessary.

In this context the equipping of six fighter, three night bomber and thirteen long-range reconnaissance *Staffeln* was considered. In total the *Reichswehr* was to have 150 machines and 50 reserve aircraft at its disposal for 'Plan A'.

Meanwhile, however, the world economic crisis which followed the collapse of the New York Stock Exchange on 24 October 1929 caused numerous bankruptcies and an extremely high rate of inflation. Naturally, the second four-year plan for aviation lagged far behind the first, but it was nevertheless assigned an astonishingly large budget.

The tactical requirements of the 1927–32 armament period now indicated, for the first time, a dive bomber. This originated with Hellmuth Felmy, who had been promoted to Lieutenant-Colonel, and who on 19 May 1930 had compiled a projection of the required air armaments for the calendar years 1931 and 1932 as well as for the coming air armaments period – 1933–7.

Lieutenant-Colonel Felmy's evaluation predicted a decisive increase in aircraft equipment within the next eight years. This entailed the creation of eighty *Staffeln,* together with the necessary infrastructure. Accordingly 1,056 machines of all kinds would have to be equipped in order to make possible an effective air support for the *Reichswehr*. On 24 February 1932 the Chief of the Army High Command, General Kurt *Freiherr* von Hammerstein-Equard, explained in a directive that future air defence and air combat forces were solely 'auxiliary weapons of the army and navy'. In his eyes there was to be no thought of an independent *Reichsluftwaffe*.

Almost at the same time the ambitious Lieutenant-Colonel Hellmuth Felmy produced a memorandum which envisaged as a major priority the development of a bomber force that could be used offensively in order to be able to

Ernst Udet at the controls of the Curtiss Hawk which he regarded so highly.

annihilate enemy air forces. In general, however, according to the later Air Generals Hellmuth Felmy and Wilhelm Speidel, the new air forces were to have a defensive character.

In the Imperial Trade Ministry, meanwhile, the well-known wartime pilot and holder of the Pour le Mérite, Assistant Secretary Ernst Brandenburg, provided not only for a rapid development of civil freight and passenger machines, but tried in secret to find a way of using them as bombers in the future.

The current – second – four-year programme envisaged for the first time several aircraft that could be used offensively. Meanwhile the thesis that a preventive annihilation of the air forces and aviation industry of the enemy by heavy air attacks would increase the chances of victory in a future war was an important aspect of air warfare planning. This idea took hold among the *Luftwaffe* leadership in the next several years.

The later formation of the Air Defence Bureau under the leadership of General Wilhelm Adam was a first and supportive step towards this.

As the means for developing heavy bombers was limited from the outset, until the end of 1932 only light combat types, such as the Ar 64 and Ar 65, the He 51, the He 45 and He 46 reconnaissance aircraft as well as the long-range reconnaissance aircraft and night bomber Do 11,

Hermann Göring at the inspection of the Travemünde Test Centre, where part of the Ju 87 testing took place.

stood a chance of being produced in significant quantities.

All in all it seemed that the externally braced biplane without a retractable undercarriage and with an open cockpit was still being encouraged by numerous decision makers.

The K 47 two-seat fighter of the Junkers Works, which was produced without an order from the Imperial Defence Ministry, was too expensive according to Lieutenant-Colonel Hellmuth Felmy, while Cavalry Captain Wilhelm Speidel rejected the back-to-back seating of the crew as inappropriate. The massive Heinkel He 50 biplane, which was intended to be built as a maritime dive bomber, stood a better chance.

For the time being, however – on 14 July 1932 – the Imperial Defence Minister, General (retired) Kurt von Schleicher, in agreement with Chief of the Army High Command, General Kurt *Freiherr* von Hammerstein-Equard, spoke of the intensification of crew training for the future 'peace army'.

On 16 February 1933 Adolf Hitler stated at a ministers' conference that the setting up of a powerful air force, which had hitherto been denied to him under the terms of the Treaty of Versailles, was to be begun in secret.

No particular significance was to be given – at least overtly – to the ground attack and short-range bombing familiar from the last years of the First World War. The problems of setting up the four fighter, three bomber-type and eight long-range reconnaissance *Staffeln*, which were supposed to be available by 31 March 1933, were too urgent. Except for the bomber plans, the defensive concept remained in force.

The 'offensive components' of the new air force were based at first on the ill-suited Do 11 as well as various other appropriate types (Ju 52). As insufficient production capacity was available for heavy bombers, the construction of conventional biplane fighters remained the main focus for the time being. The memorandum presented by Dr Robert Kraus, Traffic Manager of *Deutsche Lufthansa*, to Secretary of State for Aviation Erhard Milch envisaged the heavy bomber as a decisive part of air armament; Milch could at first only 'basically agree' with this memorandum – for the time being he was concerned with more easily achievable goals.

On 19 June 1933 a discussion took place between the Secretary of State for Aviation, Erhard Milch, and Colonel Walther von Reichenau, in which a more continuous build-up of air power was discussed. As early as the autumn of 1935 the first 600 *Luftwaffe* aircraft were supposed to be ready for flight. In addition, from May 1933 onwards a still more ambitious plan was being worked on. This envisaged 1,000 combat machines in a short time. At that time the Imperial Army possessed just 500 officer pilots, including newly inducted officer candidates. As this number would not be sufficient for long, work went ahead feverishly on the expansion and construction of flying schools.

On the tactical side too, efforts were made to develop guidelines for the means of attack. However, the results of the secret bombing trials were not met with much enthusiasm, either in the Army Weapons Bureau or in the Air Defence Bureau, which was formed on 1 April 1933, and from which only a little later – on 15 May 1933 – the Imperial Aviation Ministry (*Reichsluftfahrtministerium* – RLM) arose. In spite of the use of so-called elite crews, good hits by

Ernst Udet in animated discussion with the world aerobatics champion, Hermann Köhl, and an unknown pilot.

bombs released in horizontal flight were generally the exception. To attack pinpoint targets with any prospect of success other means had to be found. The dive bomber had long offered itself as a means of destroying such targets. For this reason the desire to create an effective dive bomber force, expressed long before Adolf Hitler seized power, was renewed in the summer of 1933.

Captain Hans Jeschonnek, who served as command staff officer with Secretary of State for Aviation Erhard Milch, and who was installed as the liaison officer between the RLM and the Imperial Defence Ministry, was more in favour than others of the dive bombing attack, but he was less able to put his ideas into effect with his current rank. To identify him as the one who was decisive in putting the idea of the diving attack into effect in the *Luftwaffe* may therefore be wrong. As the aspects of the future conduct of aerial warfare were still not adequately established, it made sense to keep all conceivable options open. The formation of the first dive bomber group was begun on 12 October 1933. A few weeks previously Ernst Udet had visited the United States, but it cannot be said that he was the driving force behind the build-up of the dive bomber units: even before his entry into the *Luftwaffe* – at the beginning of 1934 – the first practical progress in the diving attack was made in the 'Schwerin flying group'.

On the other hand, it is true that, even before his appointment as Lieutenant-Colonel in the new German air force on 1 June 1936, Ernst Udet had, as a world champion aerobatic pilot many times over, concerned himself with the problem of diving flight. It is also true that from time to time he had worked as a pilot on the flight testing of aircraft capable of diving flight, or had at least been active as an advisor.

The use of the dive bomber – at first only by the *Reichsmarine* – had, however, been decided on long before Udet's entry into the *Luftwaffe*. In the first formative phase, even in *Luftwaffe* fighter units, dive bombing attacks were intensively practised in Ar 65s and He 51s. Great significance was given to this method of attack as a result of experience in the First World War.

As naval dive bombing could initially not even be discussed because of the lack of appropriate formations, the further development of this form of weapon fell to the *Luftwaffe*.

On 10 February 1934 Ernst Udet was appointed as Inspector General of Fighter and Dive Bomber Pilots. He thus achieved a position that was perfect for him: he could put more weight behind the introduction of dive bombers and induce an awareness of their elite character into the units that were to be formed.

There was much to be said for his endeavour to knock out important pinpoint targets permanently with dive bombers on the first day of a conflict. Even small but tactically important targets in the hinterland of a potential enemy could be located and successfully attacked, as long as they were within medium range. And attacks on pinpoint targets would lead to rapid victory.

Hans Jeschonnek, as Captain and *Staffelkapitän* of the Greifswald training *Geschwader*, was already enthusiastic about the dive bombing idea and continued to be so later as its Commodore. Fortunately he was close to the tactical concepts of Major-General Walther Wever, who had also espoused the dive bombing idea. And he believed that not only tactical but also economic arguments were in favour of the 'Stuka'.

The marked enthusiasm with which Ernst Udet devoted himself to this tactic suited the offensive spirit in which the new *Luftwaffe* was formed. In the face of the proven advantages of the dive bomber it is not surprising that many, even older, officers were afraid to utter open criticism of the 'Stuka' idea: they did not want to fall into disfavour with the *Luftwaffe* leadership.

The concept was well-established but in 1935 not only were there no modern dive bombers, but also no heavy, armour-piercing bombs and, not least, no suitable dive bombing sight. The Görz 219 sight, which had been used hitherto, could only be applied with severe restrictions, as experience at the training *Geschwader* at Greifswald had demonstrated unequivocally.

These uncertainties also brought out the doubters. The dive bombing idea not only had its glowing advocates. In the opinion of several *Luftwaffe* officers dive bombing attacks were effective without restriction only on occasional pinpoint targets. The machines that were envisaged for the purpose, for example the light He 51 A or the heavy He 50, seemed to be applicable only to narrowly limited conflict situations. For more widespread conflicts these aircraft could receive only limited consideration.

The main opponent of the dive bombing concept was the development advisor for free-fall ordnance and bomb release arrangements at the RLM, the Chief Aviation Staff Engineer, Dipl.-Ing. Ernst Marquardt. Between him and the subsequent Chief of the Technical Bureau and Chief of Development and Testing, Ernst Udet, there were storm signals. This was true also for Marquardt's relationship with the man who was later to be Chief of the *Luftwaffe* General Staff, Colonel-General Hans Jeschonnek, at that time a colleague of Erhard Milch. In particular, Dipl.-Ing. Marquardt put forward the idea that precise attacks on pinpoint targets were only to be expected from 'elite crews'; with the majority of pilots only chance hits – for example on a crossroads – were likely.

On 9 June 1936 Lieutenant-Colonel Dr-Ing. Wolfram von Richthofen, leader of the Testing Department (LC) of the RLM, also expressed doubts about dive bomber

Close-up of the cockpit of the Ju 87 B-1. The machine (S2+HK) was in the inventory of 2/StG 77.

development hitherto. The aircraft envisaged for that purpose – such as the He 50 developed for Japanese naval aviation, but also the Hs 123 – had shown themselves to be suitable only under certain conditions. His criticism, however, was not of the dive bombing concept itself. He was only concerned with the improvement of the aircraft envisaged for the dive bombing groups.

As Dr -Ing. von Richthofen did not have sufficient authority to remove an aircraft from the development programme – this would have needed permission from the Chief of the Technical Bureau. It cannot be said, as has often been asserted, that he wished to halt the development of the Ju 87. The development deficiencies had already shown themselves in the first Ju 87 prototypes. It was established by Wolfram von Richthofen, in the experience reports from 1 January 1936 to 15 January 1937, that a far more powerful engine would have to be built into the Ju 87. The main reason lay in the climb performance of the machine, which was categorised as too slight.

In addition, everything possible should be done to improve the leak-proofing of the Jumo 210 powerplant. Continually leaking engine oil spread itself as a film over the whole cockpit canopy and affected the pilot's view of his target.

The experience of the Spanish Civil War led, from the second half of the 1930s onwards, to a fundamental reconsideration of the future air warfare picture. Cooperation between the army and the *Luftwaffe* was intensified, and the material requirements for future conflicts were defined.

The trend-setting *Luftwaffe* Service Directive L.Dv.16 of 1936, which over the years was extended and improved, as well as the *Luftwaffe* General Staff directive of 20 July 1937, also regarded the 'Stuka' as an excellent means of attacking pinpoint targets. This view was linked with the hope that attacks could be limited as far as possible to military installations or to the enemy on the battlefield and thus avoid losses among the civilian population as far as possible – so at any rate went the initial theory. It was also expected that bombs placed with pinpoint accuracy – in contrast to the sticks of bombs dropped by the Ju 86 or He 111 – would be essentially more economical in ordnance.

One factor which was not acknowledged, or was pushed to one side as unimportant, was that, for a successful diving attack, a lengthy training of crews was necessary.

The dive bombing of the higher-performance Ju 88 A-1 was decisively successful in only a few cases. Often the bomb loads landed from 250 metres to over 1,000 metres from the target. Precise drops on the target remained the exception. Even before the beginning of the war, Lieutenant-Colonel (later Air General) Maximilian *Ritter* von Pohl warned against over-confidence in the pinpoint target method because it required a great amount of flying practice. In his opinion – and this was borne out in the course of the Second World War – the front-line units had increasingly to make do with pilots and crews who had received a shorter and hence poorer training; for this reason, according to *Ritter* von Pohl, even towards the beginning of a war, targets would have to be approached in shallow-dive or horizontal attacks.

In the Technical Bureau of the RLM, by contrast, the dive bombing concept was firmly accepted and it was believed that, in the conversion of the Ju 88 high-speed bomber into a dive bomber, a reliable means had been found to overcome the poor range of the Ju 87. Now, even over longer ranges, heavy free-fall ordnance was to be transported and dropped from diving flight. The Do 19 and Ju 89, hitherto planned as heavy bombers but not particularly effective because of their low-powered engines, were used only as prototypes and – as no conversion was successful – were finally scrapped.

In 1938 the offensive components of the *Luftwaffe* were given stronger emphasis than hitherto, with the initial formation of five ground attack *Gruppen*. Limited resources, however, meant that this intention was not fully carried out. On 1 February 1939 the dive bomber units were taken out of the jurisdiction of the Inspector of Fighter and Dive Bomber Pilots and assigned to that of the Inspector of Bomber and Reconnaissance Pilots.

Only seven months later, on 25 September 1939 – after the successes of the Polish campaign – the Staff of the Special Purpose Flying Division was formed out of the Staff of the Special Purpose Flying Leader under the leadership of Major-General Dipl.-Ing. Wolfram *Freiherr* von Richthofen.

Because of its higher performance, the Ju 87 B quickly displaced the A version in the operational units. This is a machine of the carrier Gruppe *186 (later I/StG 1).*

Only a few days later, on 5 October 1939, the existing units were formed into the VIII Close Combat *Fliegerkorps* in order to ensure the future direct support of the ground battle over wider areas.

All warnings from those with practical experience that the Ju 87 was too slow and needed continuous fighter cover were pushed aside, as were, for example, the arguments of Colonel (later General of Pilots) Paul Deichmann, who had even warned strongly against the use of the essentially more potent Ju 88 over the enemy hinterland without corresponding fighter protection.

With German air superiority, machines such as the Ju 87 B-1 were hardly endangered at all – mostly by the enemy ground defences during the actual attack. The so-called 'Jericho trumpets', which are supposed to have been brought into play by Ernst Udet, were also greatly overestimated in the long run. Although panic could be produced in those under attack in the Polish and French campaigns by means of these noise-making devices, the effect did not continue for long. In the course of time the enemy became accustomed to them, so that in the end their installation was completely dispensed with.

The first operations near and along the south coast of England quickly showed that not only the tactical range but also the current maximum speed were in the long run insufficient to push through against enemy fighters. As early as the summer of 1941 there was not always sufficient fighter protection and losses grew continually. The massive 'Stuka' attack, which had always been presented in German propaganda as the unbeatable weapon, had quickly found its limits in actual operations.

The move towards 'living space in the east', and the consequent attack on the Soviet Union on 22 June 1941, changed the situation fundamentally. Initially during the tumultuous advance, overwhelming victories were won again and again. Even though these were battles of encirclement, notable bombing results were achieved. The dive bomber units which were sent into action, to which the Ju 87 B had been issued as the standard aircraft, distinguished themselves in the autumn of 1941, as they facilitated the advance of three army groups. A decisive victory in the campaign was not, however, to be won with single-engined dive bombers.

The robustness of the Ju 87 meant that the machine could be sent into action, even in unfavourable climatic conditions, without further ado.

The attack on Moscow, which began on 2 October 1941, failed, not only because of the sudden onset of winter, but much more because of the physical exhaustion of the German forces and not least because of the counter-offensive with rested Siberian divisions, which took place from 5 December 1941 onwards. The struggle in the east developed into a campaign of attrition, in which the German side held a poor hand of cards.

On 18 September 1941, three months after the start of 'Plan Barbarossa' – the attack on the Soviet Union – the Secretary of State for Aviation made a comprehensive presentation before Imperial Marshal Hermann Göring. In view of the successful advance in the east, said Erhard Milch, not only could Bf 110 and He 111 production be cancelled as early as 1942, but also all Ju 87 production.

The losses of the *Luftwaffe* units, however,

In spite of hard service for crews and maintenance personnel, the events of war from time to time also offered quieter times, as this groundcrew member of I/StG 1 in Libya shows.

and not only the dive bomber *Geschwader*, rose far more rapidly than expected. Ever longer lines of communication, an insufficient stock of spare parts, lack of fuel and much else meant that there could be no further talk of an optimal progress of close air support. The stiffening resistance of the Soviet forces caused ever higher losses among the ground troops. Equally, stronger ground defences, as well as the resurrected fighter forces from the end of 1941 onwards, resulted in increasing losses in the 'Stuka' units. It quickly became clear to the *Luftwaffe* High Command that the forecast Ju 87 production would not suffice to cover the needs of the front-line units in the 1942 calendar year and hence must be increased as quickly as possible.

The last weeks of 1941 had already shown that a rival to the *Wehrmacht* had developed which, both on the ground and in the air, continually became stronger. Under the chairmanship of Colonel (General Staff) Wolfgang Vorwald (RLM LC), some of the leading minds of the *Luftwaffe* leadership staff, of the RLM and of the Test Centre Command came together to work out a new production programme. The engine question was the main focus, as the more powerful version of the Jumo 211, with which the Ju 87 D had been equipped, was much too low-powered for its planned successor types. For this reason Majors Walter Storp and Edgar Petersen suggested the widespread introduction of the Jumo 213 as quickly as possible. For the Ju 87 the conversion to the more powerful engine should take place, if possible, in 1942, but in the short term provision should be made for more machines to be produced than hitherto – for the time being with Jumo 211 J-type engines, in order to compensate, at least to some extent, for front-line losses.

The leadership staff of the *Luftwaffe* (FüSt Abt. I T) agreed to an increase in production and from the beginning of 1942 onwards worked out new guidelines for the future equipment of the operational *Luftwaffe* Ju 87 units.

By 23 January 1942 the Secretary of State for Aviation and Inspector General of the *Luftwaffe*, Erhard Milch, had had his basic requirements for the aircraft procurement programme compiled.

In the area of dive bombing and ground attack, in his opinion, it was a matter of meeting the powerful Soviet enemy better equipped, not

A Ju 87 (T6+FM) of 7/StG 2 on the return flight from a dive bombing attack over North Africa. (Federal Archives)

This photograph of the road to Leningrad (St Petersburg) in the northern sector of the eastern front shows the destructive effect of well-conducted Ju 87 attacks.

only quantitatively but also qualitatively; a Ju 87 with increased performance had its place, but at the same time he was still undecided about a successor type. The Imperial Marshal therefore ordered on 12 May 1942 that the Ju 87 D, incidentally like all other low-level attack aircraft, should receive a more powerful fixed armament (at least 20-mm weapons). Because only wing installation could be considered in the Ju 87 D-1, the calibre of any heavier offensive armament was naturally restricted within narrow limits. From the Ju 87 D-5 onwards two MG 151/20 cannon were to be installed. Heavier weapons could only be carried under the wings, as the wing cross-section was too small. A little later, in June 1942, General Field Marshal Erhard Milch advocated the replacement of the Ju 87 in the near future. The projected Ju 187, successor to the Ju 87, was to be purely a carrier-based bomber with a total of 120 machines. The actual decision to proceed was put off from month to month as no one wanted to commit themselves and, after various failures in armaments production, they were averse to any risk.

The Chief of the *Luftwaffe* General Staff, with his comprehensive report to the Chief of Development and Testing on 14 July 1942, compiled his own requirements and suggestions for the future aircraft procurement programme. In the area of close air support attention was given to the fact that only a fundamentally more effective and more mobile defence could defeat enemy ground operations. For this reason Ju 87 production was now to run on until the end of 1943 and indeed be progressively increased to 165 machines a month – front-line losses left no other choice. In addition, according to the planners' programme, the Fw 190 was to go into action in greater numbers as a ground attack aircraft and as a replacement for the Ju 87.

From 1944 onwards, according to the planning in the summer of 1942, a production rate of 150 (instead of 165) Ju 87s, equipped with the Jumo 213 engine, was estimated to be sufficient. At the same time, an essentially more modern ground attack aircraft than the Ju 87 D, with a retractable undercarriage, was to be developed, based as far as possible on the 'Stuka'.

According to the guidelines (RLM GL/C g.Kdos. Nr. 500/42) of 20 October 1942, future aircraft development should at first be directed towards the war in the east and should ensure that the units were at last equipped with superior flying equipment. In detail the following operational goals were outlined:

Dive Bombers
The light dive bomber will still have to be an aircraft of the robust and stable type as the Ju 87. Outstanding performance can be dispensed with in favour of suitability for forward airfields and dive capability, as long as operations only take place under fighter protection. The fastest possible climb away after the dive recovery is the only performance-related demand on this class. The front-line units, according to experience hitherto, would rather do without armour plating than this characteristic.

Ground Attack or Armoured Aircraft
As an aircraft expressly for low-level attack, the ground attack or armoured aircraft is to be perfected further, progressing from the existing Hs 129. The application of weapons of larger calibre and the strengthening of its own protection are the factors which determine the layout of the aircraft. It is already clear that in this area in the very near future a replacement of the current Hs 129 must take place.

In spite of this explanation, which at first sight is pregnant with meaning, it could only partially be put into effect by the end of 1943.There could hardly be any talk of *Luftwaffe* superiority in the eastern theatre of war after the winter of 1942–3. Because of the limited options open to the Germans, the execution of these directives remained extensively with the Ju 87 ground attack aircraft and the Hs 129 tank hunter. Only the small splinter and hollow-charge bombs (SD 2 to SD 4 HL), also mentioned in the guildelines of 20 October 1942, brought tactical success.

As a result of the immense deliveries of armaments by the western Allies, as well as the rapid increase of Soviet home production, the Red Army was more and more successful in wresting the initiative from the *Wehrmacht*. Any approach was acceptable if it would hinder the enemy armies in their rapid advance to the west.

Notwithstanding the tense situation, it had

This Ju 87 B-2 loaded with cement bombs flew with 'Stuka' School 1 at Wertheim.

proved impossible to make lasting improvements to the equipment of the ground attack units. The innovations in the tactical field were mostly only a series of improvements to the free-fall ordnance. Thus, the Technical Bureau (Department GL/C) reported on 8 March 1943, in a secret command report (g.Kdos. Nr. 6129/43), on the new possibilities of attacking tanks from the air. The operational equipment demanded could certainly have led to a successful defence against the enemy had it been available in sufficient quantities. However, the amount of equipment produced hitherto, compared with the capabilities of the Soviets, had as much effect as a troop trial. Thus, only twenty-five Ju 87 G-1s with the BK 3.7 cannon, were equipped by mid-March 1943. Problems occurred in the spring of 1943 in the production of tungsten-cored ammunition. Owing to the needs of the army, which were assessed as urgent, bottlenecks were also foreseeable in the future.

In this context it was recognised, absolutely correctly, that from the summer of 1943 onwards air attacks on tanks would grow still further in importance and that from the winter of 1943–4 – because of the further increased tank production of the enemy – they would have to reckon with massed attacks by Soviet tank armies. To the Ju 87 D-5 fell the role of supporting German tank hunters as far as possible by dropping splinter and high-explosive bombs and of attempting to suppress enemy flak by low-level attacks on their firing positions. The use of small but effective hollow-charge bombs (SD 4 HL) was supposed to succeed above all against tank assembly areas, where they could be dropped from both ground attack aircraft and dive bombers. Attacks on enemy tanks that had broken through were, by contrast, the direct task of flying tank hunters equipped with heavy cannon.

German production capacity certainly prevented the manufacture of tank hunters in quantities that would have sufficed for an effective attack on the enemy tank masses. Basically, because of this, only 'fire-fighting' operations over individual sectors of the front were possible.

Nothing deterred the abandonment of Ju 87 production in favour of the fast Fw 190 fighter bomber, which was decided on on 10 September 1943. Even the conversion of the existing dive bomber *Geschwader* into ground attack *Geschwader*, which began in the autumn of 1943, could only be of value in the medium term. Sending a few newly formed units into action could, in view of the enormous length of the front, bring only partial relief to the ground troops.

With retreat on all fronts, the close air support of German ground troops became more important than ever from 1943 onwards. The collapse of the eastern front also led, in the summer of 1944, to a lack of oil. This loss, as well as the Allied air attacks on refineries and lines of communication, enforced a simultaneous and rapid decline in both the production and the delivery of fuel. This resulted in a further restriction of flying activity in the *Luftwaffe* day and night ground attack units.

Scarcely any further effective help could therefore come from the air to the defeated divisions on collapsing fronts, caused by the ever-intensifying assault of the enemy.

Although the anti-tank units, consisting of 'cannon birds' (Ju 87 G-2s) and Fw 190 A-8s equipped with 'Tank Lightning' (*Panzerblitz*) or 'Tank Terror' (*Panzerschreck*), achieved surprisingly high scores from the end of 1944 onwards, the overwhelming enemy could no longer be brought to a standstill.

A Russian T-28 tank near Pleskau after a direct hit by an SC 50 bomb.

3 The Ju 87 from 'Anton' to 'Dora'

3.1 The Ju 87 'Anton'

3.1.1 Development Guidelines

In the summer of 1933 secret bomb drops were made over the Jüterbog North artillery range from Ju 52s, Do 13s and He 70s with makeshift equipment.

The results were not promising, in view of the available equipment but also as a result of insufficient practice for the crews. A few things suggested that, instead of attacking from horizontal flight, the target should be attacked from closer to.

Hermann Pohlmann's first sketches and preliminary projections for a suitable dive bomber were made in the autumn of 1933. A former First World War combat pilot, Dipl.-Ing. Pohlmann entered the construction office at Junkers in August 1921 and by the end of 1929 was among the leading lights in the development department. He considered a military variant of the Ju G 24 and was engaged in studies for the Ju G 38 and Ju 52, to mention only some of his work here.

In his opinion, the projected dive bomber should be a 'pilot's aircraft', which should be constructed as simply as possible and robustly designed. For this reason a complicated retractable undercarriage was dropped from the design from the outset. The machine was to be of proven aerodynamic form and was to be entirely of smooth plate construction.

The new development built on the work of Professor Hugo Junkers' assistant, Dipl.-Ing. Karl Plauth, who lost his life in November 1927. His ideas, further developed by Dipl.-Ing. Pohlmann, led to the Ju A 48, whose testing began on 29 September 1928. The Ju A 48 (registration D-ITOR), equipped with a BMW Hornet engine of 440 kW (600 hp), was fitted experimentally with dive brakes. At Lipetsk another Ju A 48 fi (works no. 1057, D-IPOS) was tested and judged excellent. The machine exhibited very good flying characteristics and, thanks to its construction layout as a 'two-seat bomber', became the direct forerunner of the dive bomber'. In the course of the following years it

Dipl.-Ing. Ernst Zindel was decisively involved early on in the construction of powerful Junkers machines and was finally nominated as Chief Construction Engineer of the Junkers Aircraft and Engine Works Co. Ltd (JFM).

would become apparent that the wing construction of the Ju K 47 (the military version of the Ju A 48) was not always strong enough for the increasing loads and had to be strengthened. In spite of everything, however, the way was shown to an effective operational aircraft for the *Luftwaffe*.

The immense stresses imposed in diving flight, and especially during the recovery, led to the plating of the Ju K 47 being wrinkled in some instances, and small tears resulted.

As a result of the diving trials carried out with the Ju K 47 ba (=Ju A 48 be) at Breslau in 1932, Dipl.-Ing. Hermann Pohlmann at first considered the use of a double fin, in order to give a better rearward field of fire to the radio operator (and gunner) sitting back to back with the pilot. The main identifying feature of his design was a double-spar gull wing of cantilever construction with two massive sprung undercarriage legs.

At the end of 1933 a two-seat bomber, in all respects capable of diving and aerobatic flight, was at the preliminary project stage. In 1934, when the order was placed for a heavy dive bomber, the project took on an essentially greater significance.

The technical and tactical guidelines of the Air Weapons Command Bureau (LA, the camouflaged *Luftwaffe* General Staff) were forwarded at the beginning of 1934 to the Technical Bureau (LC), in order to be written up as a call for tenders. In April 1934 these were issued to the German aviation industry.

When the Curtiss Hawk, imported from the USA, was demonstrated by Ernst Udet in the presence of Erhard Milch, Walther Wever and Robert *Ritter* von Greim at the Jüterbog airfield a month later, in May 1934, this led immediately to serious doubts about the dive bomber concept. In the course of the bombing experiments at the Jüterbog North artillery range, practice dive bombing attacks, authorised by the army command, took place in 1934. In these, small bombs weighing only 1 kg, with a teardrop-shaped cast body ('dwarf bombs'), were dropped, of which six were hung on release mechanisms under the wings outside the propeller arc. Ernst Udet entered the dive at a height of 1,000 metres, released the bombs at barely 100 metres and recovered at the last minute.

Demonstrations such as this aroused significant doubts, both with the Secretary of State for Aviation, Erhard Milch, and with Major-General Walther Wever, the Chief of the Air Weapons Command Bureau, as to whether such achievements could be expected of 'average pilots' in the *Luftwaffe*.

3.1.2 Development and Construction

Building on the work done hitherto, the development department of the Junkers works at Dessau was able to adapt to the guidelines of the call for tenders in a remarkably short time and to start building a mock-up only a few weeks later. By the summer of 1934 the 1:1 scale wooden mock-up of the desired heavy dive bomber had come into being in a small workshop.

The monoplane with gull wings and double fins was inspected by several employees of the Imperial Aviation Ministry in September 1934. Although a firm order was still awaited, the construction of three prototypes was prepared at the Junkers works and more work was done on the concept of the future Ju 87.

The first heavy dive bomber was originally to have been completed in April 1935, but the need for strengthening of the airframe soon led – in spite of a continually increasing number of construction and design engineers – to significant delays.

In October 1934 the preconstruction of cockpit, fuselage and tail began. From November onwards the work progressed into the area of the wings, undercarriage and powerplant. By 31 December 1934 sixteen construction engineers were occupied on the new type. A total of 3,460 working hours was spent on the project. In early 1935 the detailed construction of all individual parts and assemblies began, for which the number of construction bureau employees working on this task rose to about fifty. For the construction of the first three machines 12,993 hours were spent on preparation work and 48,896 hours on the main construction. In addition, 10,600 hours were necessary for structural design. Between mid-July and the end of October 1935 the work was nearly completed in all essential areas.

The Aircraft Development Programme dated

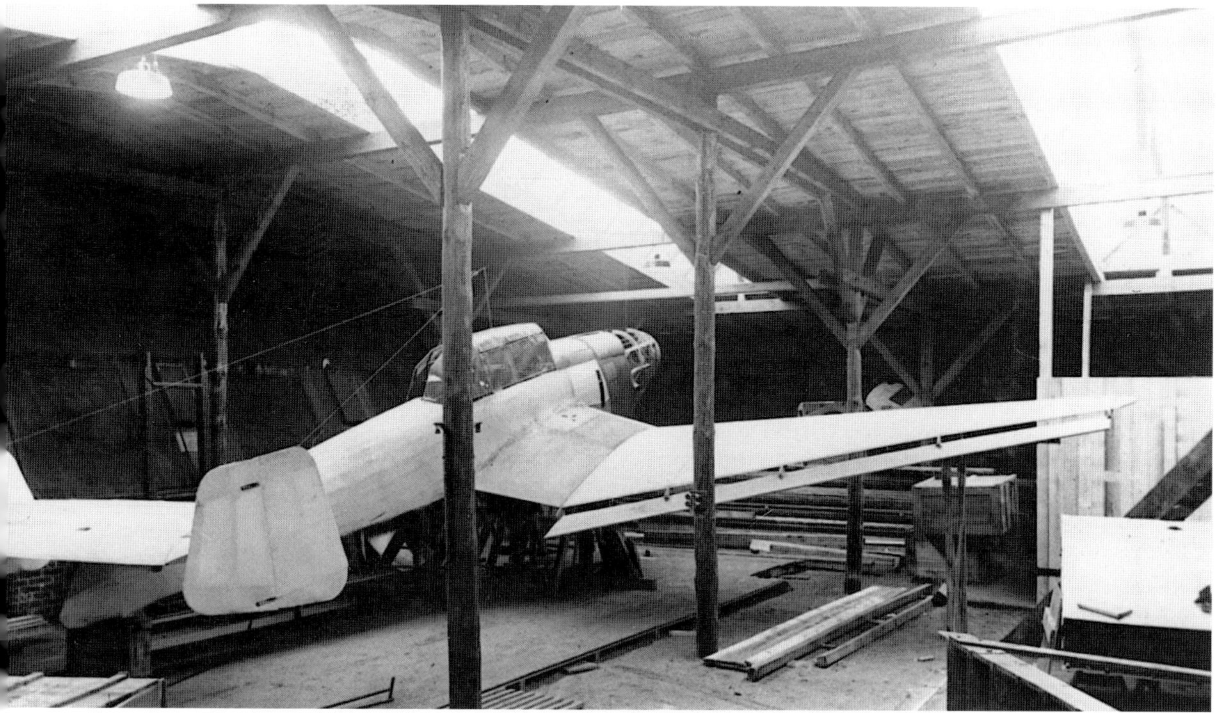

Mock-up of the future Ju 87, for which a double fin was still envisaged.

The tail of the Ju 87 V1 under construction in the works at Dessau.

1 February 1935 set the new flight clearance date for the first prototype at 1 July 1935 instead of 1 April 1935, as the first date could not be met. The construction work on a few small parts which were not immediately essential could not be completed until October 1935.

The planned Jumo 10 in-line engine (later designated the Jumo 210) was still not available at the time; it was therefore necessary at first to install a British Rolls-Royce Kestrel V.

3.1.3 Prototypes

On 7 August 1935 came the inspection of the rough-built airframe of the Ju 87 V1 (V – *Versuchsmuster* = experimental type) by representatives of the Imperial Aviation Ministry. Meanwhile, the flight clearance date (1 July 1935), already postponed once, had to be postponed again – to September 1935.

On 17 September the first flight of the Ju 87 V1 (works no. 4921) took place successfully at Dessau with Flight Captain Willi Neuenhofen at the controls. The machine flew at first without registration and later carried the identification D-UBYR. Only slight stability problems appeared in the autumn of 1935 with the prototype equipped with double fins. In spite of its truly massive appearance, the two-seat Ju 87 V1 exhibited astonishingly good flying qualities, to which the arrangement of rudders and landing flaps chosen by Junkers certainly contributed.

Apparently the only major problem lay in the cooler, which was somewhat too small. As a result the British 385-kW (525-hp) in-line engine overheated easily.

The first prototype of the Ju 87 was therefore

The Ju 87 V1 (D-UBYR) was originally to be equipped with a DB 600 in-line engine.

The Ju 87 V1 (works no. 4921) undertook its first flight on 17 September 1935.

equipped with a new and larger oil cooler within a few days.

As the RLM showed no interest in procuring a bomber equipped with a Rolls-Royce engine, consideration was given at the end of 1935 to whether the Ju 87 V1 could be equipped with a DB 600 in-line engine. This suggestion was accepted by the RLM, whereupon the Aircraft Development Programme of 1 January 1936 included the installation of this engine in the short term. This did not take place, however, as the machine crashed on 24 January 1936 at Kleutsch, east of Dresden. According to the accident report, it went into an inverted spin during testing of the terminal dynamic pressure in a vertical dive. Flight Captain Willi Neuenhofen and the engineer, Heinrich Kreft, who was accompanying him, had no chance to save themselves.

The flight clearance date for the second prototype, the Ju 87 V2, was originally set for 15 May 1935. The prototype was equipped as in the parts list established up to 28 January 1936. Like the Ju 87 V1, the V2 was also unarmed. In contrast to the first prototype, however, the central fin shape had been taken over from the Ju K 47, as doubts existed about the stability of the current double fin.

As the originally planned Jumo 210 was not available, the machine was to be equipped with a BMW Hornet engine. As a result of delays, on 8 July 1935 the original flight clearance date was put back to 1 October 1935. One month later came the rough-construction inspection of the Ju 87 V2 at Dessau. Because of the results of this, and in light of the introduction of a new fin and construction improvements in the stability of the flying surfaces, the start date for flight testing was set on 1 November 1935 for the end of that month. It did not happen, however, as there were doubts about the flight safety of the prototype.

The Aircraft Development Programme of 1 January 1936 contains the remark that 'with the Ju 87 V2 for the time being only systems tests can be carried out'. The first flight of the Ju 87 V2 (works no. 4922, D-IDQR) could not take place until 25 February 1936.

In March 1936 the machine was at Rechlin, after a meticulous entry inspection, to establish

The Ju 87 V2 (works no. 4922, D-IDQR, later D-UHUH) undertook its first flight at Dessau on 25 February 1936.

the flight behaviour as well as for performance testing. After the endurance testing had been given priority in April 1936, the machine was demonstrated over the Rechlin airfield on 26 May 1936 with an underslung 500-kg load, by Flight Captain Hesselbach.

The machine was at first equipped with a Jumo 210 Aa engine, which was exchanged for a Jumo 210 G (works no. 19310) at the beginning of 1937.

Although it was officially returned to the Junkers works on 4 April 1936, the prototype initially stayed at Rechlin and at the beginning of July took part in a comparison flight there. This performance comparison was intended to determine which of the three heavy dive bombers – Ar 81, Ju 87 and He 118 – was the most useful type for this application.

The flying comparison of the three machines was preceded by a meeting between the current chief of the Testing Department LC of the RLM, Lieutenant-Colonel Wolfram *Freiherr* von Richthofen, the brother of the 'Red Baron' Manfred von Richthofen, and Dipl.-Ing. Ernst Zindel. Ernst Zindel was the leader of the construction office of the Junkers works until the end of the war and played a decisive part in the development of the Ju 88 as well as many other Junkers bombers.

In the course of the conversation Dr-Ing. von Richthofen told the Junkers representative confidentially that the Ju 87 would probably have little chance. The final decision would lie with Colonel Ernst Udet, Chief of the Technical Bureau from 9 June 1936 onwards; according to von Richthofen, Udet had already decided in favour of the Ar 81 biplane. Because of his great experience with manoeuvrable biplanes during the First World War and his time as an aerobatic pilot after the war, Ernst Udet settled for the Arado construction team, who were especially accommodating to him. In his opinion, better manoeuvrability in the approach flight to a diving attack was a decisive advantage. The trials with the imported American biplanes had also led him to this conclusion.

If the Ar 81 V3 proved to be unsuitable, Ernst Udet wanted to fall back on one of the low-wing aircraft being offered. Here, however, the He 113 V3, with its 60 per cent more powerful Daimler-Benz DB 600 C (30-litre) in-line engine, was unmistakably in the lead.

As the Ju 87 had had to be equipped with a less-powerful 20-litre powerplant on the instructions of the Bureau, its future chances seemed very slight. Under these negative signs, Dipl.-Ing. Hermann Pohlmann as leader of the Ju 87 development, Dipl.-Ing. Hesselbach as works flight test pilot and demonstration pilot of the Junkers flight test group and Dipl.-Ing. Ernst Zindel as construction chief with overall responsibility, presented themselves at the *Luftwaffe* test centre at Rechlin.

When the Junkers team arrived in Mecklenburg, Works Pilot I. von Schönebeck, the Arado works test pilot, had already demonstrated the prototype of the Ar 81 before Colonel Ernst Udet and stood before the Chief of the *Luftwaffe* Technical Bureau, full of confidence in victory.

The demonstration of the He 113 V3 (works no. 1295, D-UHUR) was next. As the prototype still did not have dive brakes, steep dives were omitted. Only a bomb drop from a shallow dive – and that at a great height – was simulated, but this made absolutely no impression on Ernst Udet.

Only later were a few prototypes as well as the zero series aircraft of the He 118 A-0 equipped with the necessary dive flaps.

Next it was the turn of Dipl.-Ing. Hesselbach from the Junkers works. He made his dive with dive flaps fully extended. Ernst Zindel thought the approach flight went well, but he could have wished for a more daring dive recovery, in order to leave a more lasting impression on the risk-loving Ernst Udet.

A firm decision was still awaited. Zindel went to Berlin for an important meeting while Pohlmann and Hesselbach stayed at Rechlin. They were there when the Arado test pilot I. von Schönebeck pressed Colonel Ernst Udet to take a seat in the cockpit of the Ar 81 (D-UDIX). After a flight of only a few minutes, however, Udet returned to Rechlin. Even during the landing roll it could be seen that he was not at all pleased with the machine's flying behaviour, although he had previously favoured it highly (probably on the grounds of its biplane configuration).

Thereupon Pohlmann was able to persuade

Because of the increase in its flying weight the Ju 87 V2 received a new registration.

The tail of the Ju 87 V4 (works no. 4924, D-UBIP), which had minor construction improvements in comparison with the V3.

Udet to take a flight in the Ju 87 V2. Unwillingly the Colonel went to what in his eyes was a completely underpowered machine. The instructions of the RLM had been the only known reason for its being equipped with a 20 litre engine, although the Bureau chief did not seem to be aware of this. He seemed fairly impressed with its performance and benign flying behaviour. The decision was, in any event, again put off.

The third prototype, the He 118, was also in Ernst Udet's flying plans. The testing of its flying characteristics – including aerobatic flight – took place successfully on 14 July 1936. His judgement was: 'Airframe good; poor control surface qualities cancel out all other positive characteristics!'

Colonel Udet, however, wanted to gain a better picture of the machine for himself a little later. On 27 July 1936 he went into the Heinkel works at Marienehe, near Rostock, in order to fly the He 118 V1 again. On that day the famous American pilot, Colonel Charles Lindbergh, was visiting Ernst Heinkel, so Dr Heinkel was able to speak to Ernst Udet only by telephone, but he expressly warned him that he must be extremely careful with the propeller adjustment. Whether Ernst Udet forgot this advice or thought it unimportant will probably never be clear, but the engine oversped in a dive so that the propeller failed and broke away. The Bureau chief landed safely by parachute.

With that the decision was taken: the heavy dive bomber would be the Junkers Ju 87.

In August 1936 the second prototype returned to Dessau in good condition and took part in various test programmes there. On 8 February 1940 the Ju 87 V2 (D-UHUH) was transferred to the Junkers works as a testbed according to the loan contract for *Reich* property aircraft. On 7 September 1940 the German Aviation Experimental Institute (DVL – *Deutsche Versuchsanstalt für Luftfahrt*) received the machine with the new registration D-IDQR. After a modified radio was installed, the machine was next transferred to the German Imperial Post Office, which it served as an experimental carrier at least until November 1940. The machine finally received a new Jumo 210 G, engine number 21034. The subsequent disposition of the engine testbed is unknown.

The third prototype, the Ju 87 V3 (works no. 4923, D-UKYQ), corresponded to the construction specifications of the Ju 87 V2 and had a simple fin from the outset. In contrast to the second prototype, the elevator was fitted with balance weights and the undercarriage fairing was slightly altered for reasons to do with the centre of gravity.

According to the Aircraft Development Programme of 1 February 1935, the machine was supposed to begin flight testing on

1 August 1935 and to be available for testing by the Rechlin Test Centre by 1 November 1935. The date for the completion of flight testing and the acceptance of prototype testing was set as 1 June 1936. As with the two previous prototypes, significant delays occurred. The flight clearance date had first to be postponed to December 1935 and then to January 1936. Thus, according to Junkers, the testing by the Test Centre Command would be delayed by at least six months.

The first flight at Dessau did not take place until 27 March 1936. After a relatively short time at the works, the machine, equipped with a Jumo 210 Aa in-line engine, went to Rechlin. In October 1936 its performance was assessed with various drop loads.

From 1 March 1937 onwards the Ju 87 V3 flew as a *Reich* property loaned aircraft at Junkers and was there subjected to various systems tests.

At the beginning of 1940, the aircraft was finally transferred as D-IBXF to the Junkers propaganda film studio and was still there on 15 October 1940. The subsequent whereabouts of the prototype is unknown.

In November 1935 an order was issued for the Ju 87 V4 and V5. The Ju 87 V4 (works no. 4924, D-UBIP) followed the first three prototypes as a production prototype for the zero series Ju 87 A-0. Because of the test results, Colonel Wilhelm Wimmer, Chief of the Technical Bureau of the RLM, had had an extensive list of requirements compiled for the manufacturer in the late summer of 1935, in which changes to the airframe were required, some of which were expensive. At the same time, the flight clearance date of the first production prototype to be altered was set for April 1936. Accordingly, the machine was to be tested thoroughly at the Test Centre between July and October 1936.

The Ju 87 V4 built by Junkers had, in comparison to its three predecessors, a somewhat enlarged fin and a rebuilt tail. An improved and somewhat flatter engine cowling additionally gave the pilot a better forward view, and the wing had a straight leading edge. In the left wing, moreover, a fixed MG 17 machine-gun could be installed.

The Ju 87 V4 together with another prototype during maintenance at the flight testing operation at Dessau.

The Ju 87 V4 was equipped with a braking parachute for dive testing at steep angles.

In the Aircraft Development Programme of 1 January 1936 it was therefore remarked: 'The Ju 87 V4 corresponds to the series version with the Jumo 10.' The Jumo 10 was finally renamed the well-known Jumo 210, with the help of which the first flight took place successfully on 20 June 1936. In October 1936 dive brakes were installed under the wings of the V4, the first Ju 87 to have them, which caused a further delay in the progress of testing. In November 1936 the machine was at Rechlin for a few days. Next, the prototype went to Spain by ship. There the Ju 87 V4 flew about forty hours between 1 December 1936 and 15 January 1937 with the Bomber Experimental Command VK/88 of the Condor Legion, for the first time under service conditions.

In mid-January 1937 Lieutenant-Colonel Dr-Ing. Wolfram *Freiherr* von Richthofen produced an experience report on operations with the Ju 87 V4. During the operations of the fourth prototype there were six drops of an SC 250 bomb. In these, and in a few experimental dives, it was shown that a perfect view of the target was not possible as the sight window in the floor completely oiled over after a short period, so that the Junkers sight became unusable. The Stuvi A3 sight which had originally been planned was not delivered at all.

The experimental operations as a reconnaissance and ground attack aircraft also did not go satisfactorily, as neither the operation of a hand camera by the observer nor shooting at ground targets from the observer's position could be done in any sensible way.

The flight characteristics were still regarded as only just satisfactory from the point of view of the Experimental Command. Some of the stated performance figures could, however, be observed in practice. With full tanks and an SC 250 bomb, the Ju 87 V4 took off after about 250 metres. The time taken to climb to an operating altitude of 3,000 metres was only eight minutes. The horizontal speed with an engine speed of 2,700 rpm and 1.26 bar pressure was given as 250 kph.

The performance overall was insufficient, in von Richthofen's view, to send the machine over enemy-controlled territory without fighter protection. In order to be able to climb faster in combat, according to the Colonel, a more powerful aero engine was urgently needed.

In nearly vertical dives from 3,500 metres to

The Ju 87 A-0 (29-4) was tested for a time in Spain with 5/J88 by 2nd Lieutenant Haas and Sergeant Kramer.

1,000 metres, the dive brakes led to a stable terminal speed of 450 kph. Compared to the He 50, which was capable of diving flight, the acceleration forces in the recovery were estimated as lower by the pilots. For von Richthofen a higher engine performance was also necessary for a rapid departure after recovering from the dive, in order to be able to leave the area of the enemy defences faster than was currently possible. The maximum speed should, as far as possible, not be lower than 350 kph, the speed of enemy piston-engined fighters. The possibility of any defence against enemy fighter attacks from behind was also limited because of the slit gun mounting initially installed.

The existing instrument panel, which could not be scanned, particularly in action, was also a cause for complaint, as navigation and powerplant control instruments were mixed together.

By contrast, the flawless quality of the machine was praised, which in the prototypes was already so good that it was unaffected by being parked in the open, even in unfavourable weather.

Basically, all the weak points were thus already recognised, and they would also appear in combat with the production machines.

The fourth prototype then went back to Germany and flew until at least October 1937 at the Junkers works, in order to resolve the points of criticism as quickly as possible, and also to improve the dive brakes.

The Ju 87 V5 (works no. 4925) was intended to be produced in May 1936 as a production prototype with the DB 600, after the Ju 87 V1 envisaged for this powerplant crashed on 24 January 1936. The decision to install the Daimler-Benz in-line engine was taken in October 1935, whereupon in November Junkers was instructed to equip the fifth Ju 87 accordingly.

After flight testing at the works, the

Preparation for operations with the Condor Legion in the spring of 1938.

prototype was transferred to Rechlin and tested there between August and November 1936.

By the summer of 1936 it was still not clear when the availability of the DB 600 could be relied upon, so the RLM ordered that the machine was now to be prepared with a Jumo 210 Da in-line engine. Because of increasingly serious engine problems, the work was advancing only slowly in July 1936. In particular, the reworking of the engine cowling, as well as the cooler, demanded much more work than expected, so that the first flight – after a few taxi trials – did not take place until 14 August 1936. As a result, testing by the Test Centre Command was delayed until about October 1937. Before that the machine was 'called away for a special purpose': like the Ju 87 V4, the prototype flew in troop trials (with VK/88) in the Spanish Civil War.

The Aircraft Development Programme next envisaged its use at Rechlin with the Division GL/C-E5, where the installation of a course controller in the Ju 87 A-0, whose construction corresponded to the V5, was to be tested.

3.1.4 Production Versions

3.1.4.1 The Ju 87 A-0

In the Aircraft Development Programme of 1 November 1935 a zero series (A-0) of seven Ju 87 A machines was ordered, which were to be equipped with the Jumo 210 A engine, which was at first still designated Jumo 10. The Junkers

Prototypes of the Ju 87

Number	Registration	Works no.	First Reference	Remarks and Construction Series
Ju 87 V1	D-UBYR	4921	17/9/35	First flight, prototype
Ju 87 V2	D-IDQR	4922	25/2/36	First flight, prototype
	D-UHUH		4/6/37	New reg. as lease aircraft
Ju 87 V3	D-IBXF	4923	27/3/36	First flight, prototype
Ju 87 V4	D-UBIP	4924	20/6/36	First flight, A-0 version
Ju 87 V5	Unknown	4925	14/8/36	First flight, A-0 version
Ju 87 V6	Unknown	087 0027	14/6/37	First flight, A-0 to B-0
Ju 87 V7	Unknown	087 0028	23/8/37	First flight, A-0 to B-0
Ju 87 V8	Unknown	4926	11/11/37	First flight, B-0 version
Ju 87 V9	D-IELZ	4927	16/2/38	First flight, B-0 to B-1
	WL-IELZ		16/10/39	Service trials
Ju 87 V10	D-IHFH	4928	17/3/38	First flight, C-0 version
	TK+HD			Carrier trials
Ju 87 V11	D-ILGM	4929	12/5/38	First flight, B-0 to C-1
	TL+OV			Carrier trials
Ju 87 V15	D-IGDK	087 0321?	25/3/39	A-1 to B-2
Ju 87 V16	GT+AX	087 0279	31/8/40	A-1 to B-2
Ju 87 V17	–	–	–	No reference
Ju 87 V18	–	–	–	No reference
Ju 87 V19	VN+EN	4930	3/2/40	C-1 version
Ju 87 V21	D-INRF	087 0536	1/3/41	B-1 to D-1
Ju 87 V22	SF+TY	087 0540	1/3/41	B-1 to D-1
Ju 87 V23	PB+UB	087 0542	1/3/41	B-1 to D-1
Ju 87 V24	BK+EE	087 0544	1/3/41	B-1 to D-1 to D-4
Ju 87 V25	BK+EF	087 0530	1/3/41	B-1 to D-1/trop.
Ju 87 V26	–	–	–	No reference
Ju 87 V27	–	–	–	No reference
Ju 87 V28	–	–	–	No reference
Ju 87 V29	Unknown	087 0321?	1/11/42	A-1 to B
Ju 87 V30	Unknown	2296	20/6/43	D-5 version
Ju 87 V31	–	–	–	No reference
Ju 87 V42				
Ju 87 V43	NI+VZ	Unknown		May 1943, Junkers works photo J. 43600
Ju 87 V44	–	–	–	No reference
Ju 87 V46				
Ju 87 V47	CE+EJ	2246	9/5/42	Use unknown

works received an appropriate preliminary notice for this in December 1935, according to which it was expected that the Ju 87 would soon be approved in Berlin for introduction. The first of these zero series aircraft was supposed to be delivered in May 1936, but the test results of the Ju 87 V4 were still awaited. Thus, neither the acceptance date for the last of the seven Ju 87 A-0s in August 1936, nor the completion date for its testing in November 1936 could be met. By April 1936, the flight testing of the prototypes, and also that of the first zero series aircraft, had taken so long that even the RLM no longer reckoned on dates being met before the end of 1936.

ABOVE AND BELOW: *Costly construction gave the main undercarriage of the Ju 87 A great strength.*

Several of the Development Programmes, which were adapted to the actual situation, took this into account and pushed the test dates for the zero series ever further back. The final delivery date was finally postponed until May 1937.

In September 1936 the RLM decided that, instead of seven Ju 87 A-0s, eleven zero series aircraft should be produced. Next, they were to be tested in service units until July 1937. The acceptance date by the Construction Acceptance, Air (*Bauabnahme Luft* – BAL) for the first Ju 87 A-0 was set as October 1936, and for the last machine as 31 December 1936. Two variants of the Ju 87 A-0 (as well as the A-1) were planned:

- a heavy, land-based dive bomber with one MG 17 machine-gun, a bomb of 250 kg, an observer and a movable MG 15 machine-gun
- a heavy, land-based dive bomber with one MG 17 and a bomb of 500 kg, but without an observer or a movable MG 15

The machine was a cantilever, low-wing aircraft in all-metal construction with an enclosed cabin. The fuselage up to the level of the observer's seat was built of duralumin and the rear fuselage segment was of stressed skin construction. To facilitate later serial production, the Ju 87 A-0 series had a straight wing leading edge. The ailerons were in two aerofoil sections with smooth leading and trailing edges. The tailplane was adjustable and connected inseparably with the landing flaps. The elevator and rudder trim tabs could be adjusted by the pilot. The landing flaps were in two parts and lay between the fuselage and the ailerons.

Because of the repeatedly delayed development, the first seven Ju 87 A-0s left the assembly shops of the Junkers Aircraft and Engine Works (JFM) at Dessau by March 1937. The delivery of the remaining machines was not to be expected until the end of April 1937. The planned A-0 machines differed from the first three Ju 87 prototypes above all in the flatter engine cowling, which provided a better view during taxiing, as the powerplant had been set lower by 0.25 metre. In addition, the fuselage aft of the rear-facing defence position, equipped with an MG 15, was set lower. This resulted in better tactical possibilities for the use of defensive weapons.

The tactical testing of the first Ju 87 A-0s

Fuelling of Ju 87 A training aircraft on the airfield at Schweinfurt in 1938.

began slowly in December 1936. Up to April 1937, extensive flight testing was carried out, including performance measurements and take-off and load tests with the most varied loads.

Numerous surveyed bomb drops followed. In these the limited tactical possibilities, which were caused by the engine being insufficiently powerful for the gross weight, were revealed. For this reason several prototypes, as well as the machines of the Ju 87 A-0 series, received the somewhat more powerful Jumo 210 D in-line engine instead of the Jumo 210 Aa. The oil circulation was also improved and a bigger oil cooler inlet was created. Because of the construction improvements required in recent months, the number of Ju 87 A-0s available for testing remained small.

A few of the early A-series aircraft were tested by the Rechlin Test Centre from 1937 onwards in order, on the one hand, to evaluate the production version and, on the other hand, to gain ideas for further developments. It also served to translate a number of diverse development and testing intentions into fact. In the course of this work Dipl.-Ing. Heinrich Beauvais flew Ju 87 A-1s with the registrations D-IFMP, D-IEUB, D-IDYD and D-IDHD at Rechlin until June 1937. With the last machine he carried out numerous experiments in the field of propeller development. Between April and July 1938 there followed flights with D-IFUB and D-IBNQ. Also, with D-IMFV, testing focused on an improved variable-pitch propeller adjustment manufactured by VDM.

Another Ju 87 A-1 (D-IEAO) was transferred to Rechlin on 14 February 1938 and was brought in for cold starting experiments, together with the He 118 (D-OQYF), until March 1938. The endurance tests with the Jumo 210 Da followed in the spring of 1938. In the winter of 1938–9 cold start testing was continued and, from 15 June 1939 onwards, several cross-country flights followed in order to obtain new engine data for the development of the Jumo 210.

Of the eleven zero series machines to be manufactured (works nos. 087 0001 – 087 0011), only three survived testing and flew until 1940. The first of these (works no. 087 0002, NG+TL) was transferred to the Reinforcements Bureau of the *Luftwaffe* on 15 May 1942. One (works no. 087 0009) crashed at 'Stuka' School 2 at Graz-Thalerhof. The pilot, Corporal Sebastian Hage, was able to parachute to safety.

The last of the three, works no. 087 0004, was still flying in 1941, and was lost on 24 October 1943 at Training *Geschwader* StG 101 at Lyon North airfield. In this accident the pilot, Corporal August Breme, died, while his Ju 87 A-0 had to be written off as a total (90 per cent) loss. The pilot of the second machine involved in the collision (Ju 87 A-1, works no. 087 0045) survived the accident uninjured.

View from the radio operator's seat towards the pilot.

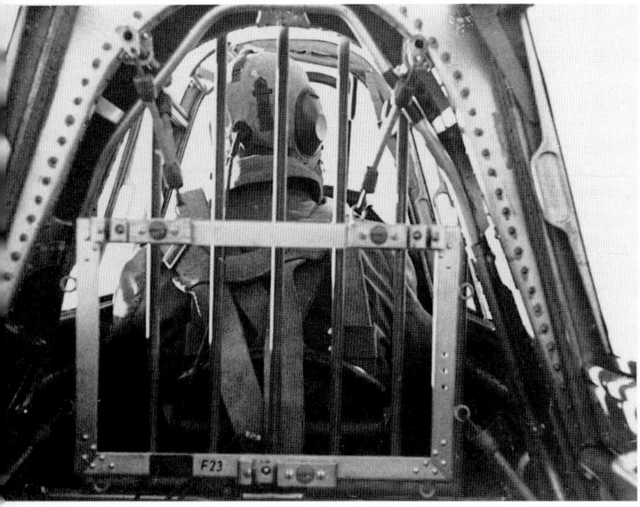

3.1.4.2 The Ju 87 A-1

The early production version, the Ju 87 A-1, differed only slightly from the eleven zero series machines. The new version had the more powerful Jumo 210 D engine with a two-position, adjustable Junkers H-PA-10° propeller of 3.3 metres diameter. The two 220-litre fuel tanks built into the inner wings were still not protected against gunfire. Only the 47-litre oil tank was leak-proofed. Oil cooling was by means of two Junkers pipe coolers which could only be switched on on the ground. The layout of the airframe and the rudder installation corresponded in every respect to that of the Ju 87 A-0. The A-1 machines also fell into the H5 airframe stress group (airframe stress categories ranged from H1, light, to H5, heavy and capable of aerobatics) and were instrumented for night and blind flying but were not capable of blind landing. The maximum permissible speeds of the operational units were 320 kph in level flight and 450 kph in a dive.

The Ju 87 A-1 generally had only one MG 17 as wing armament. The planned second weapon had to be omitted as a rule for reasons of weight. The fixed machine-gun was mounted in a Junkers gun mount in the bend of the right wing. The ammunition supply consisted of 500 rounds and was housed in the undercarriage cowling. A Revi C 12C gunsight, manufactured by the firm Zeiss-Jena, served as a sight for the fixed armament. The rearward-pointing, movable MG 15 was still mounted in a so-called slit mounting, also a Junkers development. With this the gunner could aim the MG 15, which was mounted on a rail, along the direction of flight towards the rear and had to be content with a small firing angle to each side. The ammunition supply for this gun in the Ju 87 A-1 consisted of 14 drum magazines with 75 rounds each. Thus a total of 1,050 rounds of ammunition was carried for the defensive position (instead of 900 in the Ju 87 A-0).

The bomb release mechanism of the A-1 (and later the A-2) consisted of an ETC 500/A bomb release (with a 500 XI B lock) by Siemens, which could take a maximum load of 500 kg. The bomb load consisted initially of either a 250-kg or a 500-kg bomb. In order to bring the bomb load outside the propeller arc, a movable fork was used.

W. Aretz prepares for the next training flight with D-IDHD at the Dive Bomber School at Insterburg.

Carrying a 500-kg drop load was only possible in the Ju 87 A by doing without the radio operator. Besides the second crew member and his personal equipment, the whole defensive armament including its ammunition supply was also naturally left behind, which led to a weight saving of 180 kg. With a two-man crew the bomb load had to be restricted to 250 kg because the aero engine was not powerful enough. An automatic dive recovery system assisted the pilot. This device enabled the control surfaces, trim and dive brakes to ensure the recovery of the machine in all circumstances. With an improved device, which was installed next, the bomb was released automatically 500 metres above ground and the recovery was also begun automatically. The necessary dive bombing sight – *Sturzkampfvisier*, known as a '*Stuvi*' for short – was a proprietary development of the Junkers works at Dessau.

The following flight performance figures were established, according to the performance tables of German military aircraft of 1 June 1937, for the Ju 87 A with 250-kg to 500-kg bomb load and Jumo 210 D powerplant:

Maximum speed at ground level	280 kph
Maximum speed at 4,000 metres operational altitude	290 kph
Range at ground level	525 km
Range at 4,000 metres operational altitude	600 km
Time to climb to 4,000 metres operational altitude	16 minutes
Time to climb to 5,000 metres operational altitude	21 minutes
Time to climb to 6,000 metres operational altitude	31 minutes
Service ceiling	7,000 metres

For the numbers and equipment planned for the *Geschwader* authorised by General Field

Crews of the Insterburg Dive Bomber School in front of their training machines.

Marshal Hermann Göring on 26 October 1938, the Ju 87 A-1, even in its improved version the A-2, no longer stood a chance. Meanwhile, the essentially more effective Ju 87 B became available for that purpose.

This also arose from the Concentrated Aircraft Type Programme in which the *Luftwaffe* General Staff had decided on equipping eight dive bomber *Geschwader* with the Ju 87. These were intended to be only an interim solution until the delivery of the twin-engined Me 210 A-1, which was specifically planned for these units.

3.1.4.3 The Ju 87 A-2

From the Ju 87 A-1 originated the slightly improved A-2 version, which differed mainly in an extended radio telegraphy (*Funktelegraphie* – FT) installation. Besides an intercom (*Eigenverständigungs-Anlage* – EiV) between the pilot and radio operator/gunner, both voice and Morse transmission were now possible from the pilot's seat.

With the start of serial production of the more powerful Jumo 210 Da, both the Ju 87 A-1 and the A-2 were retrofitted with this engine. The powerplant was equipped with a two-stage supercharger and drove a two-position, adjustable Junkers H-PA-III propeller. The record of *Luftwaffe* aircraft types and construction series dated 1 August 1941 emphasises the new propeller, which was adjustable manually in flight, as the essential distinguishing feature between the A-1 and A-2. Externally, the A-2 was chiefly recognisable by its fin, which was rounded off at the top. Some of the machines were retrofitted for training purposes with two or four ETC 50 bomb racks under the wings, in order to be able to carry up to four 50-kg cement practice bombs.

At Junkers, Works Pilot Harder test flew several Ju 87 A-2s from the beginning of June 1939 onwards, which had been retrofitted from A-1 standards. The machines carried the works

This photograph of a Ju 87 A-1 was taken on an airfield in Franconia in the winter of 1938–9.

numbers 087 0420, 087 0423 and 087 0427 to 087 0429. The last Ju 87 A-2 was probably works number 087 0429, which flew on 9 June 1939.

3.1.5 Production of the Ju 87 A

After the satisfactory completion of the testing of the Ju 87 V4 prototype, which already had the equipment specifications of the A-0, nothing stood in the way of the construction of zero series machines. At first seven, then eleven Ju 87 A-0s were envisaged, of which the majority were delivered to the operational units by the end of 1937.

As the RLM did not want any more unpleasant surprises with the planned Ju 87 A-1 production version, 216 production aircraft of this version were ordered at once in October 1936. These machines were mostly assembled in the Junkers Dessau home plant and were delivered from spring 1937 onwards.

In March 1937 the order was reduced to 187 Ju 87 A-1s, and, taking into account delays to date, the last machines were expected from Dessau in March 1938. The order quantity then shrank to twenty-nine, mainly because of the flying performance, which was categorised as seriously inadequate.

Because of numerous development and production commitments at Junkers, capacity at Dessau became limited. Therefore the RLM, together with the management of JFM, had to find a suitable licensed manufacturer for the further serial production of the Ju 87 as quickly as possible.

Both Blohm & Voss and Henschel, however, where some Do 17 and Ju 86 production had already been transferred, were out of the picture for mass production of the Ju 87 A-1 because of lack of assembly capacity. For that reason, the RLM decided on the Weser Aircraft Co. Ltd, known as Weser or WFG for short.

The licensed construction of the first machines was written into Delivery Plan (*Lieferplan* – LP) 4 of the RLM in November 1936. At WFG, thirty-five Ju 87 A-1s were planned from October 1937 onwards, which were to be

This Ju 87 A-2 (works no. 0152, NG+RL) had just arrived at 'Stuka' School 2 and was still unarmed.

completed by March 1938 at the latest. As this date was impossible to meet from the outset, the Bremen works was finally given until May 1938 to fulfill the whole order.

In the next Delivery Plan, LP 5 of 7 April 1937, the number of Ju 87s to be produced was raised to seventy. Of these ten per month were assigned to WFG. WFG received the necessary production preparation – initially also pre-built assemblies – directly from Dessau. However, the manufacture of the necessary assemblies for Ju 87 production began surprisingly quickly at WFG. As with all aircraft manufacturers, the necessary equipment (instruments, armament, radios and the like) was obtained from various sub-suppliers.

Since the Junkers works, situated in central Germany, had to devote itself to increased Ju 52 and Ju 88 production, widespread bottlenecks occurred, and the RLM put heavy pressure on WFG increasingly to remove the whole assembly of the Ju 87 to Bremen and its surroundings. The individual parts were manufactured in a newly built plant there and final assembly took place at the WFG home plant. The Ju 87 tails were made by the Delmenhorst works. The Karman firm at Osnabrück delivered the outer skin of the fuselage. The assembled Ju 87 As, later also the Ju 87 Bs to Ds, were finally taken by ship to Lemwerder, west of Bremen. Acceptance took place there in Shop 210.

At a company parade on 15 December 1937, the first Ju 87 A-1 finally assembled at the Bremen works was presented before the employees and a small number of Junkers representatives who had travelled from Dessau.

Originally the first Ju 87 A-1 should have been cleared for flight at WFG in October. However, it made its first flight on 26 February 1938 and from March 1938 onwards was tested at Bremen.

The second machine followed at Lemwerder on 31 March 1938. By the end of April a further four machines were completed at WFG. Since the Ju 87 A-1 was essentially poorer in performance than the Ju 87 B-1 envisaged for mass production, the current order for seventy A-1s was cancelled; accordingly only thirty-five more were ordered from WFG, as well as the first forty Ju 87 B-1s. Shortly thereafter, the order suddenly increased to 112 machines, of which the component of A-1 aircraft remained at thirty-five. The production of twenty-six Ju 87 A-1s per month, which was the aim for the end of 1937, therefore became invalid.

Up to the end of March 1938, 165 Ju 87 A-0s and A-1s were delivered from Dessau production alone. Ju 87 A production there ended after the final assembly of the last twenty-seven A-1s, which were delivered by June 1938.

Ju 87 A production also came to an end at Weser in August 1938, although slightly longer was needed at Lemwerder to fully equip and flight test the last A series machines.

Up to the summer of 1938, a total of 262 Ju 87 As was assembled. Of these 192 came from Dessau and the remaining seventy from Bremen. The number of machines retrofitted to A-2 standards can have affected only a part of the A-1 production. Because of the debut of the higher-performance Ju 87 B-1 version, the conversion to Ju 87 A-2 standards was prematurely abandoned in the summer of 1939.

3.1.6 Operational Use

Dive bomber training began on 1 April 1934 at JG 132, formed at Döberitz, in which unit fighter pilots were also trained. As a suitable combat type was still lacking, He 50 biplanes were used for this purpose. Later, in the spring of 1936, the first He 51s were added.

The first 'Stuka' unit was formed from parts of JG 131 on 28 March 1935. I (St.)/162 was formed first as a part of the Schwerin flying group. On 1 April 1936 II/162 at Lübeck-Blankensee, as well as I/165 at Kitzingen, originated out of the staff and I *Gruppe* at Schwerin. At first hardly anyone knew about the future Ju 87, which was still in the testing arena at this time.

The operational testing of the Ju 87 took place under the strictest secrecy from late autumn 1936 onwards, during the Spanish Civil War. Flying operations were conducted there, at first with a single prototype, the Ju 87 V4, from December 1936 onwards. Starting in the spring of 1937, further operations followed with the Ju 87 V5, which had been brought to Spain in the meantime. Next, both prototypes were replaced by three Ju 87 A-0s.

Initially the aim was only to try out every conceivable technical and tactical possibility of the heavy Junkers dive bomber. Accordingly, the *Luftwaffe* tried to obtain the first tactical experience in service conditions for the widest possible circle of crews in the Condor Legion. For this reason pilots and radio operators were exchanged for new crews after a short time.

The service application of the Ju 87 dive bomber took place in Germany from the Ju 87 A-0 onwards. The first zero series machines

A Ju 87 A-2 after transfer at Graz-Thalerhof, July 1939.

Somersault by a Ju 87 A-1, which belonged to the Radio Operators' School at Halle an der Saale.

entered the 1st *Staffel* of 162 'Immelmann' dive bomber *Geschwader* in the spring of 1938. By mid-1938, a few of the first Ju 87 A-1s, some of which initially had the engine equipment of the A-0, were also delivered there.

The first of the Ju 87 A-1s delivered to the combat unit was D-IEAU. From 1/StG 162 finally came the IV ('Stuka')/Training *Geschwader* 1. At least three Ju 87 A-1s were with 2 (Maritime)/Training *Geschwader* 2 and served various training purposes there along with Ar 196, Do 18, He 60, He 114 and He 111 aircraft. The Ju 87s assigned to the training *Geschwader* bore the identification signs 6L+M18, 6L+L24 and L2+L41.

The funeral of four pilots killed in an accident at the Garz airfield on the island of Usedom.

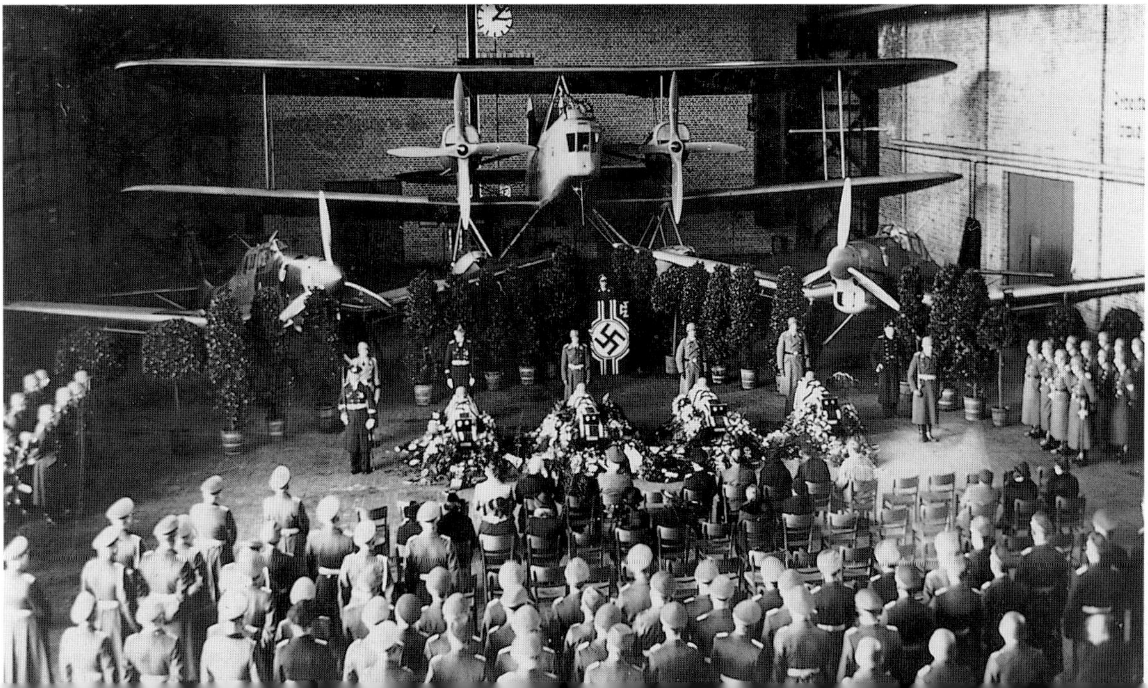

Somersault accident to TR+NF, a Ju 87 A-1. The machine belonged to the Radio Operators' School at Halle.

The Ju 87 A-2s in service with the dive bomber pilot schools were mostly flown without fixed armament. The photograph was taken on an airfield in Franconia at the beginning of 1940. In the background is a Ju 87 B-1.

The A-1 machines, which basically were grossly ineffective, served more and more for the induction of new 'Stuka' crews and were replaced by Ju 87 B-1s as soon as possible.

In the early summer of 1938, Ju 87 A-1s (and A-2s) were mainly flying as training aircraft at the 'Stuka' schools at Insterburg in East Prussia, at Schweinfurt and in the Wertheim area.

The Ju 87 A was still used for crew training until 1943. Besides the 'Stuka' Initial School (at Aibling and Mühldorf), Dive Bomber Pilot Schools 1 (at Wertheim and Kitzingen) and 2 (at Graz-Thalerhof and Foggia), numerous Ju 87 As flew with Training *Geschwader* StG 101 (at Cuers and St Raphael), StG 102 (at Graz) and StG 103 (at Metz).

A few Ju 87 As still flew with Ground Attack Training *Geschwader* SG 101 to 103, which had developed from the units mentioned above, even as late as the early summer of 1944.

Ju 87 As were also found at flying schools, but only in ones and twos. Solely as individual aircraft, early Ju 87s flew with Flying Technical School 6, Air Fleet Signals School 5 (at Erfurt) and the *Luftwaffe* Medical School.

The last Ju 87 A-1s and A-2s were captured by Allied troops in Germany at the beginning of 1945 – some of them in heavily damaged condition.

3.2 The Ju 87 'Berta'

3.2.1 Development Guidelines

After the initial testing of the Ju 87 V2 at the Rechlin Test Centre and of the Ju 87 V4 in Spain had shown that there were not sufficient reserves of power in the Jumo 210 Aa aero engine, the need for it to be replaced in the near future by a more effective version of the heavy dive bomber became obvious from the late autumn of 1936 onwards.

Given that the airframe was to be retained as far as possible, this meant installing a more powerful 30-litre engine instead of the 20-litre powerplant, to ensure that two crew members could be carried, as well as the full drop load: 1 × 500 kg or 1 × 250 kg and 2–4 × 50 kg.

However, not until the second half of 1936 did the fuel-injected powerplant which was installed instead of the Jumo 211 Aa (carburetted version) demonstrate the necessary operational safety to be used in production machines. With the Jumo 210 Da, the emergency power increased from 735 kW (1,000 hp) to 885 kW (1,200 hp).

By means of a redesigned, three-bladed, adjustable propeller it was possible, with a governor (which had its limitations) to maintain a

The Ju 87 V9 (works no. 4927, D-IELX) served as the production prototype for the Ju 87 B-0 version.

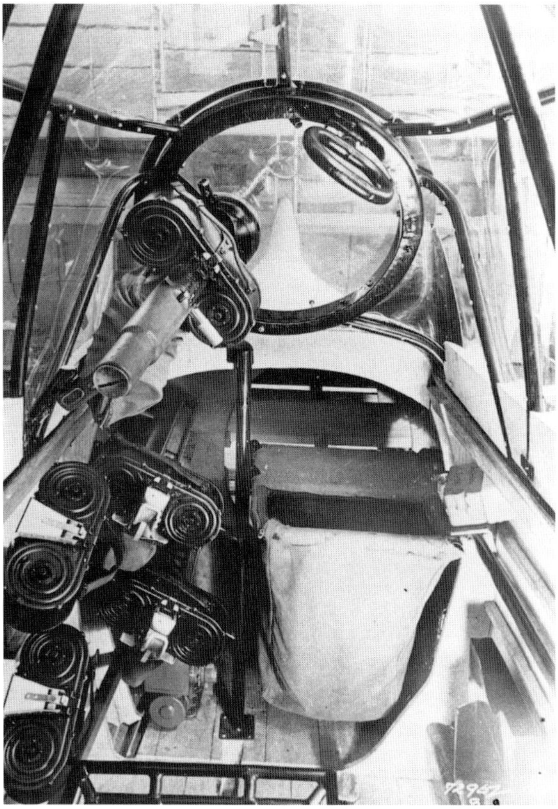

Mock-up of the gun position which was obligatory for all Ju 87 Bs and Rs.

constant propeller rpm and, in addition, to prevent overspeeding of the in-line engine in diving flight. Because of the higher powerplant weight, the airframe of the Ju 87 B had to be altered in comparison with the A version. In order to maintain a stable centre of gravity in the dive bomber, the already altered 'trouser legs' – as the voluminous undercarriage main legs of the Ju 87 A were known – had to be reduced to the shape well known from the Ju 87 B onwards. The closer-fitting fairing, with the altered spring struts, not only had greater strength but was also easier to maintain.

The changes were not confined to the higher-performance powerplant. The cockpit, whose layout had been prepared as a mock-up by June 1936 and had been inspected by the RLM and the Test Centre Command (*Kommando der Erprobungsstellen* – KdE), went through a comprehensive reconfiguration. The new, two-piece, sliding canopy made possible an easier entry and exit; at its rear end was a lenticular gun mounting with a movable MG 15.

By means of the dive brakes under each wing, the speed of the machine was held constant between 500 and 600 kph, so that not only was the diving attack safer, but also a steady-state dive became possible and hence a sure aim with the machine.

The diving attack was initiated by the pilot moving the dive lever to the rear; this limited the throw of the joystick. An automatic device deactivated the two dive brakes, as well as the trim tabs. In the dive, the pilot next released his drop load by pressing a knob on the joystick grip. Thanks to the dive automation, the trim tabs were withdrawn after the drop load was released, and the machine was recovered from the dive. Thereafter the dive lever was moved forward again, whereupon the automatic device retracted the two dive brakes and completely released the joystick.

Thanks to the construction changes incorporated from the Ju 87 B-1 version onwards, a fully battleworthy, two-seat dive bomber was available to the *Luftwaffe* from the summer of 1938 onwards; its production sufficed to equip the first combat units envisaged for dive bombing operations.

At the beginning of the attack on Poland in September 1939, according to the report of the Quartermaster General dated 31 August 1939, a total of 366 Ju 87 As and Bs was available.

3.2.2 Prototypes

In January 1937 the Junkers works received the order to submit to the RLM suggestions for a more effective version of the Ju 87 A. According to the Aircraft Development Programme of 1 May 1937, a production prototype was supposed to start its flight testing by June 1937 at the latest. As an initial experiment, the Ju 87 A-1 (works no. 087 0027) was modified and received a 30-litre Jumo 211 A engine instead of a Jumo 210 Da, with a Junkers H-PA or H-PC propeller.

On 14 June 1937 the first B prototype took off as the Ju 87 V6 for a successful first flight after ground testing. The machine was originally

This photograph of the Ju 87 V11 was taken in the winter of 1937–8; in the background is the parked Ju 88 V3 (D-AREN) in a shed of the home plant at Dessau.

supposed to be tested at the Rechlin Test Centre between August and September 1937, but no records of this test are available. By September 1937 at the latest, the Ju 87 V6 was at Dessau and was tested there until 28 February 1938 with a Jumo VS-5 adjustable propeller. From March onwards, according to an RLM decision, the machine was available to Junkers for propeller testing.

The Ju 87 V6 was followed on 23 August 1937 by the seventh prototype (works no. 087 0028), which also developed from the modification of a Ju 87 A-1 and was also fitted experimentally with a Jumo 211 A engine. Otherwise the airframe of the V7 resembled the A-1 series. According to an RLM guideline, the second Ju 87 to be equipped with the Jumo 211 A in-line engine served as a preliminary experiment for the development of the Ju 87 B, which had progressed well in the meantime. The machine was also ordered at the beginning of 1937 so that a flight clearance date in September 1937 could be assumed.

Before that, between 12 and 16 June 1937, a vibration investigation was carried out on the Ju 87 V7 with the engine cowling removed. After an evaluation of the results at the beginning of July 1937, no doubts remained about the installation of oil and water coolers to complete the installation of the Jumo 211 A in the series production of the Ju 87 B.

The first flight of the Ju 87 V7 took place on 23 August 1937, earlier than planned. Next, it was established in September 1937 that the machine should go into service at the test centre at Rechlin from December 1937 onwards. Another machine was ordered in April 1937 (V8) as the first production prototype equipped to Ju 87 B series standards. This was to be completed by the end of 1937 and to be delivered at the Rechlin Test Centre by December 1937 at the latest. There the flight testing as well as the whole performance evaluation was to take place by February 1938.

The first flight of the Ju 87 V8 (works no. 4928) was undertaken as early as 11 November 1937, although still without

The early Ju 87 Bs received the three-tone paint scheme which was more striking than the later standard camouflage.

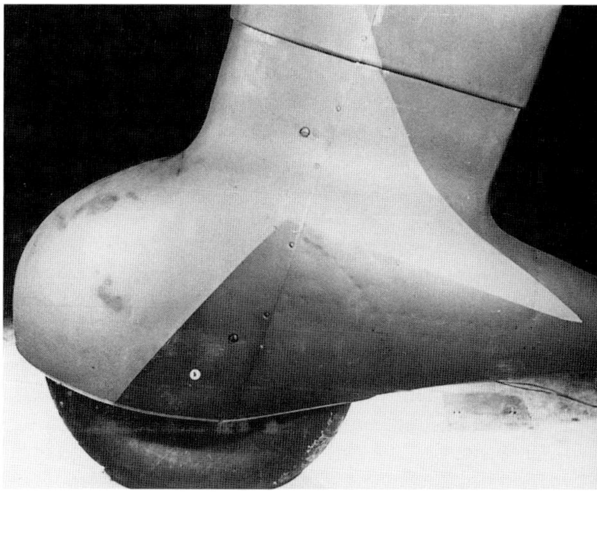

complete equipment, which was to comply with the parts list of 22 September 1937. By the beginning of December the equipment was mostly complete. According to log-book entries by Works Pilot Hotopf, the machine was still flying at Junkers as the production prototype for the Ju 87 B-1 at least until 14 May 1938.

As the next production prototype of the future B series, the Ju 87 V9 (works no. 4927, D-IELX), was similarly tested as a zero series (B-0) machine. The machine was supposed to have been flight tested at Junkers in December 1937, but because equipment was not delivered on schedule, it was not cleared for testing until the beginning of 1938.

The first flight took place at Dessau on 16 February 1938. After testing at Rechlin, the machine was at Dessau again on 16 October 1938 and was flown there by Flight Captain Wilhelm Zimmermann. With the registration WL-IELZ, the Ju 87 V9 was next sent for service testing.

The next two Ju 87 B-0s (works nos. 4928 and 4929) served, however, not for the further testing of the B version, but for the preparation of the C series (carrier-borne aircraft) which was developed from it.

In order to widen the testing of the B version, the further conversion of the Ju 87 A-0, works no. 087 0005, was ordered. The machine was converted at Junkers, starting in October 1937, and was envisaged as a production prototype for Rechlin, starting in November. From February 1938 onwards further detailed investigations at the manufacturer were planned. The machine corresponded to the Ju 87 B-1 standard.

Further testing of the Ju 87 B-1 was with a converted Ju 87 A-1 (works no. 087 0309, D-ICZR). After the removal of the Jumo 210 Da and the installation of a Jumo 211 D (with VS-II propeller), this aircraft flew with Junkers at Dessau from the end of October 1941. It was a *Reich* property loan aircraft, which was placed at the disposal of the Junkers works.

The next construction series was designated Ju 87 B-2. Two production prototypes were built, the Ju 87 V15 (works no. 087 0321, D-IGDK) and V16 (works no. 087 0279, GT+AX). The machines were flying from 25 March 1939 onwards. The V15 went into service with Junkers as a test machine in March 1941 and was lost in a crash at Rechlin in 1942. The V16 was taken from Dessau to Rechlin on 31 August 1940 by Flight Captain Wilhelm Zimmermann and from there went to the Tarnewitz Test Centre for weapons testing on 23 November 1940.

Whether the Ju 87 V17 and V18 were ever manufactured could not be established as, in principle, the existing production prototypes were quite sufficient for testing. The Ju 87 V19 (works no. 4930, VN+EN), a B-0 machine, was available from the beginning of 1940 onwards and served for preliminary experiments to do with the Ju 87 E carrier-based aircraft. The next prototypes V21 to V25 were converted from B-1 standards as prototypes for the D-1 and D-1/trop. series.

3.2.3 Production Versions

Other than the A-0s converted to Ju 87 B-0s, only two standard production series of the B version were developed and built in large numbers, mostly at the Weser aircraft works. At Junkers, after the arrangement of licensed production through Weser, only the manufacture or conversion of a few prototypes and small series took place, particularly for powerplant and equipment testing.

3.2.3.1 The Ju 87 B-0

A total of six zero series Ju 87 B-0 aircraft were manufactured from Ju 87 A airframes that were already available. These began flight testing from the summer of 1938 onwards. In the process of development, at least three B-0s were converted to the C and E versions and served for the testing of future carrier-based aircraft.

3.2.3.2 The Ju 87 B-1

The Ju 87 B-1 version differed from its predecessors mainly in the use of the Jumo 211 A engine instead of the less powerful Jumo 210 Da which had powered the Ju 87 A-1 (and some of the A-2). As a propeller, Junkers had chosen a fully automatic Ju-H-PA metal propeller, adjustable infinitely through 20°.

An early Ju 87 B-2 on the Junkers works airfield. Flight Captain Konrad Beyer (left) discusses experimental results with Technical Representative Schneider from Siemens.

This Ju 87 B airframe served as a testbed which was available to the Baehr company for cooler tests.

The various versions of the B-1 series can be distinguished by the exhaust installation used. While the first production blocks still displayed simple exhaust openings, the later Ju 87 B-1s had modern exhaust pipes. The same was true for the cowl flaps, which were installed in different layouts, and finally in an enlarged form.

The bomb rack under the fuselage, consisting of a 500 XI B lock, was taken over from the Ju 87 A-1, which restricted the bomb load to 500 kg. However, the aircraft could in all cases be flown with a two-man crew.

As a reflector sight, a Revi 12C with an SP 1 swivelling plate from the firm Zeiss-Jena was installed in the Ju 87 B-1 (as well as the B-2) at the height of the massive front windscreen.

The Ju 87 B received noise-making propellers with a diameter of 0.7 metres, developed by the German Aviation Experimental Institute (*Deutsche Versuchsanstalt für Luftfahrt* – DVL), installed on the upper part of the main undercarriage legs to enhance the intimidating effect of the dive bombing attack. After the attack the noise-makers were blocked by means of an oil-pressure device. Once the enemy had become used to dive bombing attacks, the noise-makers were removed, not least because of the speed loss of 20–25 kph which they caused. Instead, some of the free-fall weapons were equipped

Close-up of the Ju 87 V16 (works no. 0279, GT+AX) which was among the first Ju 87s equipped to the standards of the B-2 construction series.

Dipl.-Ing. Hermann Pohlmann in front of a Ju 87 B-2 at Dessau in conversation with Konrad Beyer and some men from the flight operations division.

with so-called 'Jericho trumpets' – small whistles – which were fixed to the guide fins of the bombs (SC 50 to SC 500) and produced a corresponding noise after release.

The defensive armament still consisted of a movable Rheinmetall-Borsig MG 17 machine-gun, which was operated by the radio operator and usually had an ammunition supply of 900 rounds. As fixed armament the choice fell back on the proven MG 17; instead of only one, however, one was now built into each wing. The ammunition supply amounted to 500 rounds per gun. Later the muzzles of the fixed weapons were fitted with simple flash suppressors, introduced in the B-2 or retrofitted. Beside the MG 17 was placed a remote-controlled camera for recording bombing results.

At 480 litres, the fuel capacity was slight in comparison to the 780 litres in the Ju 87 D-1 version, and significantly restricted the operating radius with a full bomb load. Unlike later versions, the machine was designed without special armour. The operation of both the dive brakes and the horizontal stabiliser was by means of an oil-hydraulic system.

As for the radio, the FuG VII with EiV Ia intercom was mostly replaced by the improved FuG VIIa radio with EiV V intercom.

As optional equipment, the Ju 87 B-1 could be fitted with a ski undercarriage instead of wheels.

3.2.3.3 The Ju 87 B-2

The zero series programme of 26 April 1939 already foresaw the manufacture of two production prototypes of the B-2 version, which were later built from A-1 airframes. February and March 1939 were named as the flight clearance dates. It was possible to complete the V15 and V16 roughly on time and they started testing at the beginning of 1939.

The Ju 87 B-2 differed from the B-1 mainly in

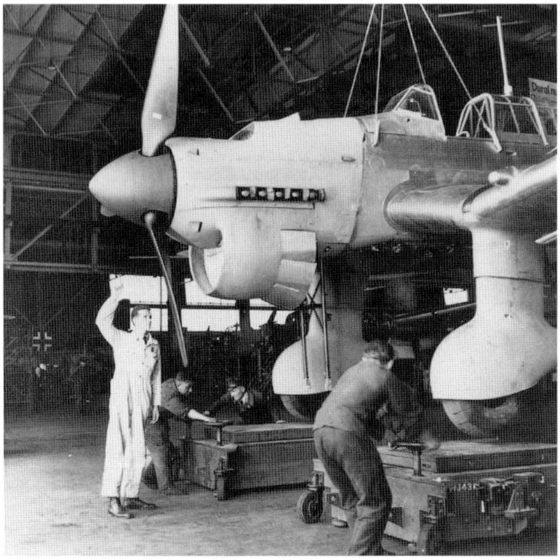

A newly completed, early Ju 87 B-2 hangs on an overhead crane in a Dessau works hall.

having the more powerful Jumo 211 D aero engine. A few of the first machines were still fitted with the less powerful Jumo 211 A as an interim measure, as neither the originally planned H powerplant nor sufficient Jumo 211 D engines were available. With the Jumo 211 H engines, either a VS5 or a V11 adjustable propeller would have been installed.

The cowl flaps could be closed by an oil-hydraulic system from the Ju 87 B-2 version onwards. Only with the more powerful engine (Jumo 211 D) was it possible to increase the maximum possible bomb load to 1,000 kg. For this, instead of the XIB bomb lock, the machines were equipped with a bomb rack carrying the 1000/500 XIB lock. Under the wings were two ETC 50 VIIIa bomb racks, on which bundled small bombs or SC 50s could be carried. Because of the heavier bomb load, the Junkers works had adjusted the undercarriage of the B-2 version to the higher gross weight and had strengthened it accordingly.

In contrast to the B-1, however, it could not be used with skis.

As the B versions in their standard form were unarmoured, their crews were seriously endangered by the enemy ground defences.

Detailed view of the bomb lock and diverter fork which ensured that the free-fall load did not collide with the propeller.

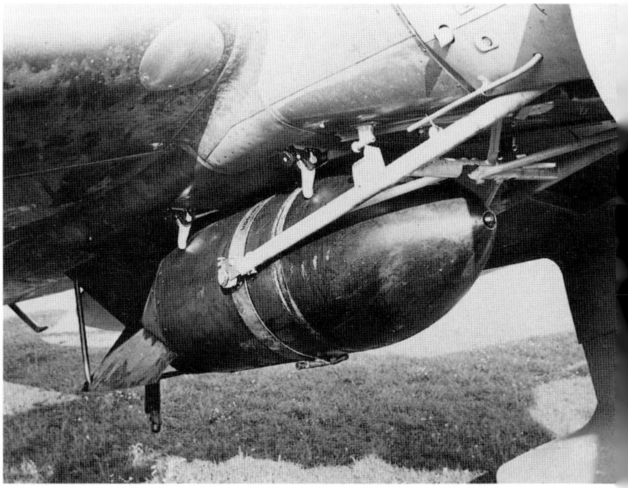

Close-up of the diverter fork of the Ju 87 B loaded with an SC 500 bombload in a loading exercise at the works.

Test flying at Junkers: an engine technician works on the fine adjustment of the Jumo 211 in-line engine.

A Ju 87 B-1 (works no. 0206) ready for delivery at Dessau.

This danger was later at least slightly reduced with optional equipment.

According to the Junkers information and data sheets, the Ju 87 B-1 performed as follows compared to the Ju 87 R-2 and Ju 87 D-1:

Series	Ju 87 B-1	Ju 87 R-2	Ju 87 D-1
Basic weight (kg)	2750	3450	3900
Gross weight (kg)	4300	5600	6450
Maximum speed (kph)	340	320	350
Climb to 3,000 metres (minutes)	7	16	22
Service ceiling (m)	7200	5800	4200
Range (km)	850	1210	800

This table shows clearly that, as a result of the more powerful and heavier powerplants, the gross weight rose continually, but the speed did not increase significantly, and the service ceiling and range were greatly reduced. This was, above all, because of the tactical measure of equipping the machines with improved armour, so as to be able to use them in a second role as low-flying ground attack aircraft. The first step away from the dive bomber was thus taken.

3.2.4 Production of the Ju 87 B

In November 1936, because of the planned series production at Dessau of a new, twin-engined dive bomber, the Ju 88 A-1, the RLM had decided that the production of the Ju 87 B-1 would, as far as possible, be licensed out.

As production in the Bremen area could not be started in a matter of a month, initial production had to take place at Dessau as well.

In March 1937 ninety-eight Ju 87 B-1s were ordered from the Junkers home plant at Dessau. These were to be manufactured between February and July 1937, together with forty Ju 87 B-1s at the Weser aircraft works. Production aircraft were to be manufactured at Weser from April 1938 onwards. The last of these Ju 87 B-1s was supposed to come off the production line by the end of July 1938, but before the end of this procurement process, the delivery of another 352 Ju 87 B-1s at JFM and 740 at Weser was arranged for the period from August 1938 to March 1940. Aircraft Procurement Programme

This Ju 87 B-1 is an example of an early construction type from the summer of 1938, which can be recognised by the exhaust system.

From October 1938 a few Ju 87 B-1s were put through rigorous operational testing in Spain.

No. 11 of the RLM C Bureau, dated 1 April 1939, envisaged the manufacture of 964 Ju 87 Bs by July 1940. Of these, 187 had already been completed by 31 March 1939.

After the delivery of 311 B-1s from Dessau, in June 1940 came an order for twenty-nine Ju 87 B-2s. The machines were to leave final assembly and be test flown at JFM between July and September 1940. Then came the procurement of another 100 Ju 87 B-2s which were to be manufactured at Weser between July and October 1940. Next an order was issued for the production of ninety-eight B-2s. Their production, however, could not be completed, as in the summer of 1941 the production of the new D series began. The last order may have been placed as a result of the non-appearance of the Ju 87 D-1, to fill gaps in the front-line units.

In total about 700 Ju 87 B-1s and about 230 Ju 87 B-2s were delivered, of which nearly 550 originated at Junkers, all the others at WFG.

A substantial proportion of the earlier B-1s were in any event brought up to the same equipment standard as the B-2s that were produced from 1940 onwards, by retrofitting the Jumo 211 D as well as by installing improved bomb release and radio equipment. This mostly happened when the machines were in the workshop as a result of battle damage or technical faults. Some of the work was done by the Metal and Aircraft Works at Wels; after reacceptance the machines were directed to front-line or training units.

3.2.5 Troop Trials and Retrofits

Other than testing at Rechlin, which was chiefly concerned with performance and free-fall ordnance under practice conditions, the first operational trials of the Ju 87 B took place in the Spanish Civil War.

In October 1938 three Ju 87 A-1s were withdrawn from Spain and replaced by five Ju 87 B-1s. From 17 November to 1 December

Loading of a Ju 87 B-1 with high-explosive bombs in September 1939.

1938 the combat units of the Condor Legion had the opportunity to pause for rest, to reorganise their *Staffeln* and to be ready for the decisive offensive which lay ahead.

After the battle on the Ebro, *Generalissimo* Francisco Franco initially gave up the attack on Madrid in favour of an offensive in Catalonia. On 23 December 1938 the new dive bombers successfully attacked an ammunition dump near Mayals, when the cloud cover broke up for a short time. From mid-January 1939 onwards, the machines assigned to 5.K/88 (29th) took part in operations intended to support the advance on Tarragona. One of the dive bombers is said to have been shot down. On 4 March 1939 three Ju 87s attacked the road bridge at Salvacanete without success. The heavy high-explosive bombs detonated far away.

On 16 March 1938 twenty He 111s, together with two of the dive bombers, were sent into action against bridges at Meco and Fuentiduena de Tajo as well as road installations at Los Santos. The last attacks took place on 27 March 1939 and served as direct support of the advance on Madrid. As early as April the remaining Ju 87 Bs were withdrawn and transported back to Germany by ship. The machines were part of the small amount of air equipment that was not transferred to the newly founded Spanish air force. Even at the great victory parade on 12 May 1939, the Ju 87 Bs took no part – probably for reasons of secrecy.

A little later, on 22 May 1939, Francisco Franco took leave of the members of the Condor Legion in Leon; a few days later they began their homeward journey to Germany from Vigo on the *Wilhelm Gustloff*.

Meanwhile, the equipment of new 'Stuka' *Staffeln* with the Ju 87 B, together with numerous training flights and movement exercises, continued undiminished. Even training demanded its sacrifices of 'Stuka' pilots, although these were of necessity accepted as the price of the tumultuous build-up of the units.

A particularly heavy loss struck the *Luftwaffe* shortly before the beginning of the war – on 15 August 1939 – during a demonstration by Ju 87s equipped with practice bombs. When the crews dived on their prescribed target on the Neuhammer training area in Silesia, a catastrophe occurred.

The unit of thirty Ju 87s had made its approach flight at an altitude of 5,000 metres

Preparation for the next operation over Poland. Several mechanics are working with a lifting dolly to attach the main load under the fuselage of a Ju 87 B-1.

and had begun the practice diving attack. After penetrating the cloud cover (cloud was reported between 900 and 2,800 metres), the crews should have released their target marker bombs at about 300 metres and recovered from the dive.

Ground fog which had formed suddenly, of which the unit was, through an oversight, not informed, caused thirteen of the thirty crews to fly to their deaths, together with their unit leader, because they did not have time to pull out.

In spite of this unmitigated catastrophe, the idea of dive bombing operations was maintained. At the end of August 1939 the *Luftwaffe* had the following units equipped with Ju 87 Bs, which were intensively prepared for conflict in the summer of 1939:

I/StG 1	at Insterburg
I/StG 2	at Cottbus
II/StG 2	at Stolp-Reitz
III/StG 2	at Langensalza
III/StG 51	at Wertheim
I/StG 76	at Graz
I/StG 77	at Brieg
II/StG 77	at Breslau
IV('Stuka')/KG 1	at Barth

With this aircraft's equipment, all current drop loads up to the SC 500 bomb could be carried, as with the Ju 87 A. From the Ju 87 B-2 onwards, according to regulations, 1,000-kg bomb loads were added, such as, for example, the SC 1000 bomb but, most importantly, the armour-piercing SD 1000.

Except for the last named drop loads, complete free-fall ordnance testing was unnecessary, as this had taken place sufficiently with the testing of the Ju 87 A. Basically the concern was only to evaluate the higher performance expected as a result of the new powerplant installation, and to produce appropriate operating data tables. The newly added heavy-calibre bomb was an exception.

By 1 February 1940 a deflection fork had been specially built for the SD 1000 armour-piercing bomb and, after a few initial experiments, was soon tested at Rechlin. In April 1940 the take-off performance of the Ju 87 B was assessed up to a gross weight of 5,500 kg. A simplified one-piece fork was also studied practically and a new loading instruction was produced for the Ju 87 B-1/B-2. At the same time, extensive take-off and landing experiments were undertaken with an underslung SC 1000 bomb.

By the beginning of 1941, the bomb release mechanism of the Ju 87 B, together with that of the long-range R version, had been tested for subsequent use with SD 2 ground attack bombs. Attacks on dispersed positions were investigated, using this type of bomb, which developed an extreme splintering effect in low-level attacks.

ABOVE: *This Ju 87 B of 6/StG 77 can look back on operations in many countries, as the removable pennant shows.*

BELOW: *Three pilots of 3/StG 1 at Oslo-Fornebu on 9 April 1940 in front of one of their Ju 87 B-2s.*

This Ju 87 B-2 was in service with Dive Bomber Pilot School 1 for bombing training. Under the wings are 50-kg cement bombs.

The SD 2 bombs were hung on two racks (Rost 24 SD 2/XII) under the wings. The total of forty-eight SD 2s carried could be released with impact or time fusing. The small bombs could not, however, be released while they were still 'at safe'. In the case of hung-up SD 2s, this led to some losses among the crews. For the release of these offensive loads an optimal flight altitude of between 25 and 40 metres was fixed. As soon as the release altitude was below 10 metres, the danger of bombs failing to explode was particularly great. The load was released by the push button on the KG 12A stick grip.

Although the 'Stuka' *Gruppen* equipped with the Ju 87 B achieved impressive results during the initial phase of the Second World War, it became clear that the equipment needed improvement.

Among the changes needed to ensure the tactical capability of the Ju 87 B-1 and B-2 were, for example, the improvement of the radio installation. The installation of the FuG 25a transponder was investigated, with testing in September 1941. Official approval for installation followed.

In addition, changing operating conditions were taken into account with four conversion packages which went into effect with the Ju 87 B-1 and B-2:

U1	Tropical emergency equipment (later: Ju 87 B-2/trop.)
U2	Improved intercom
U3	Strengthened passive protection behind the pilot's seat and rear armour for the radio operator
U4	Ski undercarriage (only with the Ju 87 B-1)

Of these conversion packages, the additional tropical equipment and the additional armour around the crew space were the most requested. With the additional armouring of the rear position, a lenticular gun mount with a small pane of armoured glass was used instead of the usual

Ju 87 D und G
Bed.Vorschr.-Fl

Flugbetrieb **II 37**

Motor Jumo 211 J
Luftschraube VS 11
3,46 m

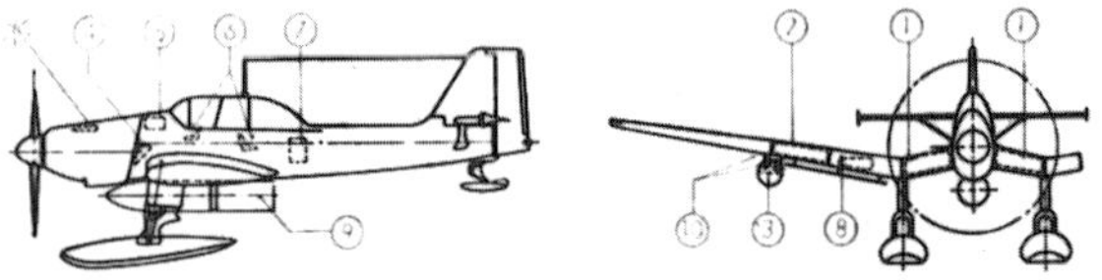

†) Für Abflüge mit Überlast nur gültig auf besonderen Einsatzbefehl vom RLM — GL 6

Dieser Ladeplan hat nur Gültigkeit für das seinem Verwendungszweck entsprechend ausgerüstete Flugzeug.
Die Maschine kann mit 1 oder 2 Mann geflogen werden.
Die Bombe hängt ungefähr im Schwerpunkt.
Vor Notlandung sind Bomben blind und Kraftstoffzusatzbeh. abzuwerfen.
Höchstzulässiges Landegewicht normal 5000 kg, in Ausnahmefällen 5500 kg.

[1]) Restmenge im Rüstgewicht enthalten.
[2]) Mit 8 kg Kraftstoff für Kaltstart.
[3]) Bei Verwendung von 4 x 50 bzw. 8 x 50 kg Bomben verringerts sich das Fluggewicht um 60 bzw. 120 kg (Schwerpunkt hierdurch unverändert).
[5]) Klammerwerte gelten nach Abwurf der Tf-Lasten.
[6]) Abwerfbare Zusatzbehälter beim Abfangen leer. 1/3 gefüllt für Sturzflug zulässig.
[7]) Durch Einbau nachstehender Rüstsätze erhöht sich das jeweilige Rüstgewicht um folgende Werte:
Rüstsatz S = Schleppkupplung 7 kg
„ FLA = Flammenvernichter 20 kg
„ = Winterbordnotausrüstung 40 kg
*) Zusatzbehälter bis Werk-Nr. 130 970 (siehe Beladevorschrift)

Verwendungsgruppe: H
Beanspruchungsgruppe: 5 (abgemindertes Lastvielfache)
Höchstzul. Fluggewicht: Normal 6300 kg; Überlastfall 6500 kg

Schwerpunktslagen hinter Tm — Vorderkante für: Rüstgewicht: 0,575 m … 0,595 m; höchstzul. Vorlage: 0,550 m; höchstzul. Rücklage: 0,712 m

Rüstzustand „C"			1	2	3	4	5	6	7	8	9	10 †)	11	12	13 †)	14
Rüstsätze			M1	M1, M2	M1	M1, M2	M1, M2	M1, M3	M1, M2	M1, M3	M1	M1, M2	M1, B	M1, B	M1, B	
Bomben Anzahl und Größe			1 x 250	1x 250 4 x 65	1 x 500	1x 500 4 x 65	1 x 250 2x 250	1 x 250 8x 65	1x500 2x250	1x500 8x 65	1x1000	1x1000 4x 65	1x250	1x500	1x1000	
Leergewicht		kg	3780	3860	3780	3860	3860	3940	3860	3940	3780	3860	3860	3860	3860	
Zusätzliche Ausrüstung		kg	400	400	400	400	400	400	400	400	400	400	400	400	400	
Rüstgewicht [7])		kg	4180	4260	4180	4260	4260	4340	4260	4340	4180	4260	4260	4260	4260	
Zuladung 1 Kraftstoff	in den Tm-Behältern Inhalt 480 l	kg	15[1]) … 355	15[1]) … 580									15[1]) … 355	15" … 580		
2	in den Tf-Behältern " 300 l	kg	0 … 225										0 … 225			
3	in den abw. Behältern " 590 l	kg											0 … 435	0 … 435	0 … 250	
4/5 Schmierstoff	im Entnahmebehälter / im Behälter a.d. Steuerbr. Inhalt 85 l	kg	13[1]) … 75[2])	13" … 75"									13" … 75"	13" … 75"		
6 Besatzung	2 Mann	kg	140 … 200	140 … 306									140 … 200	140 … 306		
7 Munition	für MG 81Z 1400 Schuß	kg	0 … 36										0 … 36			
8 Munition	für MG 151 360 Schuß	kg	0 … 70										0 … 70			
9 Bomben	am Rumpf 250 … 1000	kg	0 … 250	0 … 250	0 … 500	0 … 500	0 … 250	0 … 250	0 … 500	0 … 500	0 … 1000	0 … 1000	0 … 250	0 … 500	0 … 1000	
10	an den Tragfl. je 1x250 oder 2 bzw. 4x65	kg		0 … 260		0 … 260	0 … 500	0 … 520	0 … 500	0 … 520		0 … 260				
Abfluggewicht		kg	5363	5703[3])	5613	5953[3])	5843	6043[3])	6193	6293[3])	6113	6453[3])	5878	6128	6453	
Sichere Lastvielfache [4]) [5])			5,40	5,8 (5,4)	4,85	5,35 (5,0)	5,85 (5,25)	5,80 (5,25)	5,45 (5,0)	5,50 (5,00)	4,60	4,85 (4,6)	5,40 [6])	5,15 [6])	4,75 [6])	

Hierzu gehört Beladevorschrift S 8700—5118

Ladeplan Ju 87 D-5 (Rüstzustand C) S 8700-5117 c

15

Data table for the use of Ju 87s with skis.

Two Ju 87 Bs and several Ds were equipped with skis. The following registrations are known: DJ+FU, DP+KA, GP+YA and TN+ZT. (Federal Archives)

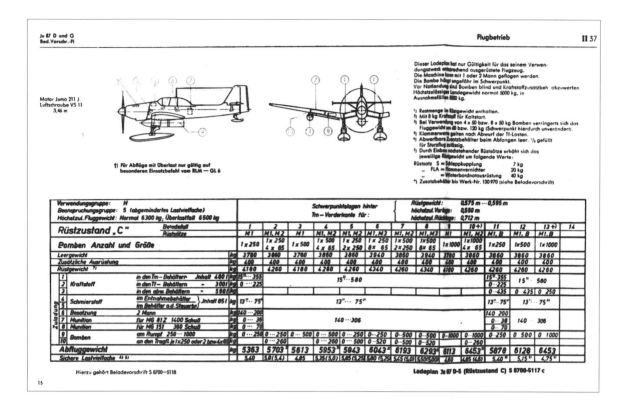

The Ju 87 V21 (D-INRF) was used as a production prototype with ski undercarriage.

lenticular gun mount, as well as side armour plates. Some of the machines, however, were also equipped with the rear position which was familiar from the Ju 88, with an LLK lenticular gun mount, but with the MG 15 machine-gun retained instead of the MG 81 I which was standard with that mounting.

Instead of the designations Ju 87 B-1/U1 and B-2/U1, the designations Ju 87 B-1/trop. and B-2/trop. finally came into use. The series thus equipped differed (as did the tropical versions of the Ju 87 R) by having a rectangular air intake with a dust filter instead of the usual half-round intake in the normal version.

A weak point of Ju 87 B development was the initially very weak fixed armament. Even during operations in the west, it had been shown that the forward-firing armament of only two fixed MG 17s had no great combat value. On the weapons-technical side, therefore, installation investigations were carried out with the object of using two 20-mm cannon in the wings. At first, two production Ju 87 Bs were converted for this purpose.

The new weapons installation consisted of two MG 151/20 cannon, in accordance with the requirements of the *Luftwaffe* leadership. The basic testing took place at the works in 1941, after which the production prototypes were taken to Africa and flown there under service conditions. As the armament showed itself to be far superior to the previous type, its introduction in one of the next production versions was encouraged. Because MG 151/20 production could hardly meet demand, the first of these weapons was not installed until the start of Ju 87 D-5 production, which was somewhat delayed.

With the Ju 87 B-1 and B-2, testing other than in the areas of guns and powerplant was basically complete by 1941. Service under the hard conditions of the Russian winter produced a problem, however. The production version of a ski undercarriage for the Ju 87 B-1 was manufactured from the winter of 1941–2 onwards. In the course of the experiments there were two breakages in slight dives, as the ski springing was insufficient for the forces that developed.

The use of the skis was, however, disputed in the front-line units from the beginning. From the point of view of the Commanding General of the VIII *Fliegerkorps*, the use of fighters, dive bombers or bombers with skis was not regarded as particularly important at the beginning of 1942. In his opinion, the rolled snow runways were completely sufficient for the Ju 87s provided they were kept in good order by snow graders – as did the Russian enemy – after the new snow had been removed by rotary snow ploughs or ground crews.

In March 1942 155 sets of skis were ordered for the Ju 87s for the winter of 1942–3, but they were soon cancelled after the *Luftwaffe* leadership reported that it was not required. The Ju 87 Bs also retained their wheeled undercarriages because of the unavoidable reduction in performance caused by the skis. The front-line units quickly took to removing the lower undercarriage fairings from their Ju 87 Bs, ensuring the safe use of the normal wheel undercarriage on snow and ice to some extent.

The front-line units considered it more important, as was recognised at a meeting on 7 April 1942 chaired by General Field Marshal Erhard Milch, that improved winter clothing should be made ready as fast as possible for the *Luftwaffe* units operating over the eastern theatre of war, so as not to lose crews after forced landings because of the low temperatures.

In spite of numerous retroactive improvements, the Ju 87 B-1 and B-2 basically remained suitable only for narrowly restricted theatres of war, as these versions lacked the necessary range, but above all the necessary firepower. In the meantime the front-line units had to be content with the obsolete version of the 'Stuka'.

Replacement by the first of the more effective Ju 87 Ds took place from September 1941 onwards.

3.3 Ju 87 R 'Long-Range Stuka'

3.3.1 Development Guidelines

Operations with the Ju 87 over Poland and western Europe had shown that the range of the Ju 87 B-1 and B-2 barely met the demands of

An early Ju 87 R-2 during an intermediate landing on transit to Italy.

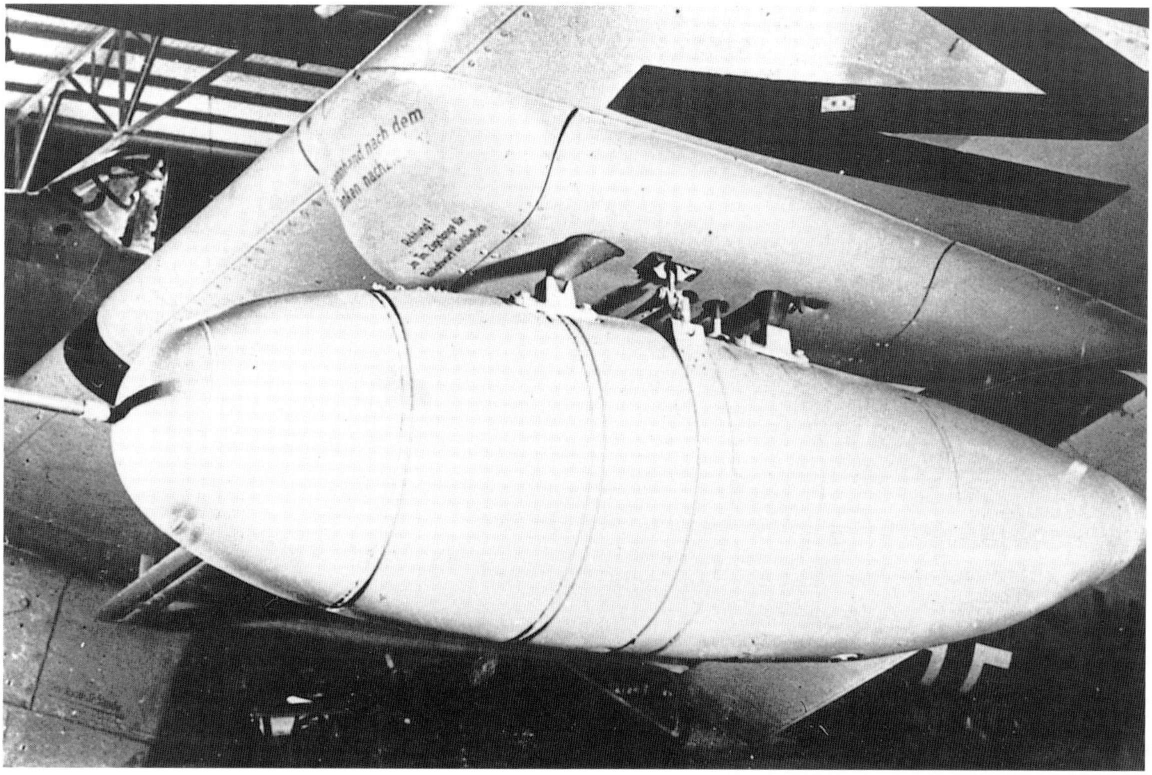

Detailed view of the Ju 87 R-1 production prototype with its 300-litre drop tanks hung under the wings, which decisively increased the penetration range.

the theatres of war, with the sole exception of direct air support close to the front line. Dive bombing attacks on shipping targets farther from the coast could not be undertaken because of the limited tactical radius of the B versions (250–300 km).

In order to extend the range of the Ju 87, the fuel and oil installation was expanded – building on the B-1 and B-2 versions. By means of two 300-litre drop tanks under the wings, the total range could be extended to a maximum of 1,255 km (at 4,000 metres altitude). With that the penetration radius increased to more than 500 km. The new tankage consisted of two 240-litre tanks in the inner wings, as well as the external tanks mentioned, and thus had a capacity of 1,080 litres of fuel.

The first production prototype for the planned Ju 87 R-1 ('R' for *Reichweitenausführung* – 'Long-Range Version') was equipped with an enlarged tank installation at Junkers at the beginning of 1940. After flight testing at the works, the machine went to Rechlin and went through the entry inspection. In April 1940 the performance measurement of the Ju 87 B-1, provisionally converted to Ju 87 R-1 standards, took place. Here, besides the maximum range, the whole performance spectrum of the two-seater machine was ascertained during many flying experiments with and without two 300-litre drop tanks as well as with and without additional loads under the fuselage bomb rack. The R-1 machine transferred for the purpose was equipped with a Jumo 211 A engine. A Ju 87 R-1 (works no. 5554, PC+XV) was tested in the autumn of 1940, but was wrecked on 20 December 1940 at Schwarzenmoor after a crash from inverted flight.

The first Ju 87 R-2 was lost at the airfield at Jüterbog. Sergeant Walter Reks crashed fatally with machine no. 5912 at Delmenhorst; the Ju 87 R-2 was almost completely destroyed.

In transit equipment and tools were carried in the under-slung wooden box. This Ju 87 R-2 of 2/StG 2 landed at Fornebu near Oslo in April 1940.

After testing one of the first production aircraft of the R-2 series, the Rechlin Test Centre produced the customary operating data table on 14 January 1941.

The testing of the Ju 87 R-4 (TJ+FP) with the Jumo 211 D-1 engine also took place at Rechlin. Between 17 April 1941 and 8 May 1942 more than thirty flights were undertaken there.

3.3.2 Production Versions

The four versions of the Ju 87 R series could be equipped with a Jumo 211 A, D or J engine. The essential distinguishing feature from the 'Berta' was the enlarged fuel installation. The following versions are noted in the Registers of Aircraft Types of the RLM:

Ju 87 R-1	Jumo 211 A
Ju 87 R-2	Jumo 211 D
Ju 87 R-2/trop.	Jumo 211 D
Ju 87 R-3	Jumo 211 D
Ju 87 R-4	Jumo 211 J

The Ju 87 R-1 had the airframe of the Ju 87 B-1 and, because of the two additional 300-litre drop tanks, had a fuel and oil capacity of 1,370 litres in total. As a result of the increased range, the installation of an additional oil tank in the fuselage had become necessary.

These Ju 87 R-2s were either in transit or at a school in 1940.

The machines driven by a Jumo 211 A or D-1 had, as a rule, a radio installation of the type that was standard in the Ju 87 B-1. This consisted in the R-1 and R-2 (as also in the D-1/trop.) of the following sets:

- radio set FuG VIIa
- intercom EiV 1a
- homing set Peil G IV
- transponder FuG 25

It should also be noted that the FuG 25 transponder was envisaged, but was actually installed only in a few machines. With the FuG VIIa, radio traffic was possible between individual machines (air-to-air) as well as with the unit's ground radio station (air-to-ground) at any time. The EiV 1 installation made possible telephonic communication between the two crew members. The Peil G IV allowed homing by reference to an instrument or audio signal to any voice or Morse transmitter of sufficient strength. In addition, broadcasts could be received non-directionally on the Peil G IV.

The machines could be put into service with or without armour. If the armour was omitted, the range naturally increased. As with the Ju 87 B-1, the R-1 could be used with wheel or ski undercarriage.

The Ju 87 R-2 was built on the airframe of the Ju 87 B-2 and had a Jumo 211 D in-line engine with the VS 5/VS 11 adjustable propeller. According to the operating data table for the Ju 87 R-2 with the Jumo 211 D, the airframe was designed to be strong enough for dives at speeds up to 600 kph. Because this was the maximum officially authorised speed, a certain degree of safety was naturally assured at even higher speeds.

As a rule, the Ju 87 R-2 reached a speed of

In an emergency the Ju 87 crew could save themselves with a two-seat rubber boat until machines of an air-sea rescue Staffel *appeared.*

With a tow coupling as stable as this the 'Stuka' Staffeln *could bring their DFS 230 freight gliders into action on a move.*

285–305 kph near the surface and 320–350 kph at 5,000 metres operating altitude. The total flight endurance near the surface was only 3 hours 45 minutes and was a good 4 hours 15 minutes maximum at 4,000 metres altitude. The total flight range was between 1,120 and 1,255 km, according to altitude.

In contrast to the Ju 87 R-1, the possibility of changing between land and snow undercarriages was not considered, as the machines were intended mostly to be used over the sea and in the southern theatre of war. For this reason a tropical version, the R-2/trop., was manufactured as a convertible aircraft. These machines received a dust filter with a larger, rectangular inlet, in order to avoid engine damage by dust and desert sand, as well as a comprehensive equipment supplement to give the crew a certain degree of safety in the event of a forced landing.

The tropical emergency equipment of the Ju 87 R-2/trop. version (and all other trop. versions) was designed for the two-man crew and was stowed in the fuselage as well as in both wings.

It consisted of two tropical emergency equipment rucksacks in the left wing. In the right wing were two sleeping bags, two mosquito nets and a tent packed with all accessories. Near the ammunition boxes were two rubber mattresses. In addition, a double- or triple-barrelled shotgun, as well as a 98k carbine, were part of the emergency equipment, and were carried behind the pilot's seat. On the left, beside the radio panel, was a flare pistol for shooting white, red and green flare ammunition. An additional flare pistol was also a part of the emergency equipment. In linen bags were a folding shovel, a box of emergency rations, a tropical medical package, a petrol cooker, cooking utensils, a marching compass, sunglasses, two bush knives, a torch and other useful items. In the left wing was a crank-driven emergency transmitter. Four bottles of drinking water completed the emergency equipment, along with a small, screw-top tin with 250 grammes of salt, which was supposed to be used for barter in Africa! Instead of the tropical emergency equipment, a winter emergency kit of two light rucksacks with appropriate contents could be carried.

The Ju 87 R-3 involved an experimental conversion of the Jumo 211 D-equipped Ju 87 R-2. This version, which was usable as a tug, arose through redesignation after the installation of an expanded set of radio equipment. This was necessary when towing load-carrying gliders, so that communication with the glider crew would be available by way of the tow rope. The series was manufactured only in limited numbers as a retrofit.

The last of the R series was the Ju 87 R-4. These machines differed from the R-2 in having the more powerful Jumo 211 J engine, which was also installed subsequently in the Ju 87 D-1.

The machines received altered wing mid-sections, corresponding to those of the Ju 87 D-1, so that the protected (self-sealing) fuel tanks could be used without problems.

3.3.3 Production of the Ju 87 R

In June 1940 a first order was placed for the manufacture of a total of 105 Ju 87 R-1s, as well as seven Ju 87 R-2s initially, at the Weser Aircraft Co. Ltd. These Ju 87 Rs, as well as all later R-4s, were to be built by Weser without exception, according to the C Bureau programme of 15 March 1941.

The first R-1 machines were intended to leave the plant there between July 1940 and August 1941. In total, the directives of the RLM Development Bureau, dated 1 February 1941, envisaged the production of 1,582 Ju 87s of the series R-1 (Jumo 211 A), R-2 (Jumo 211 D), R-4 (Jumo 211 J) and D-1 (Jumo 211 J).

By 30 October 1940 all 105 R-1s had been delivered. Already, while the R-1 was in production, the number of Ju 87 R-2s to be delivered was increased to 471 machines. Of the R-2s, by the autumn of 1940 the first 123 had been accepted. Thus at that time 348 machines were still to be delivered.

The completion of these R-2s was supposed to take place from November 1940 to April 1941. After the supply of sufficient Jumo 211 D in-line engines was assured, the order was increased in June 1940 by 138 aircraft to a new total of 609 R-2s. Because of the start-up of production of the R-4, however, this order was reduced a little later and then partly cancelled.

The order for the series production of the R-4 on 15 March 1941 comprised only 145 operational machines. Production start-up was considered for April 1941 at the latest, with five aircraft in that month. As a result of the necessary removal of a part of the Weser production

A Luftwaffe *war reporter shot this photograph of Ju 87 R-2s of 3/StG 2 during a move. In the foreground is works no. 5473 (T6+CL) with under-slung auxiliary tanks.* (Federal Archives)

Inspection of the 1st Staffel *of StG 1 at Oslo by General Field Marshal Milch.*

to Berlin-Tempelhof, various start-up difficulties occurred, as was to be expected – in particular because of a lack of resources and machine tools that were not delivered. Moreover, numerous changes that had subsequently become necessary at the same time as production started up meant that, at some expense, the equipment had to be altered and installation work had to be carried out on the airframe. Therefore, a total of only seven R-4s and fifteen R-2s left the Tempelhof works in May. As completion started much more slowly than expected, it could be foreseen that by August 1941 deliveries would fall far short of the 145 ordered. A delay also occurred with the delivery of three Ju 87 R-4s for conversion, which were to be equipped with a course controller at Junkers. The retrofit put forward in the C Bureau Conversion Programme of 1 March 1941 was designated 'Axis Conversion'. ('Axis Conversion' referred to aircraft for the Italian air force.)

By 31 May 1941 the production shortfall had increased to forty-six Ju 87 R-4s; an attempt was made to deliver fifty-five machines in July in order to reduce the shortfall. In the event, only forty-two were completed. The monthly quota of fifty machines was unachievable as already numerous workers were needed to prepare for the production of the D-1 series.

In May 1941, moreover, preparations began for the conversion of twenty-six Ju 87 Bs to the tropical version of the R-2. In the early summer of 1941 six Ju 87 R-2/trop. were be converted for tropical service by the *Luftwaffe* at Paderborn and a further twenty Ju 87 Bs at Mönchengladbach, which, at the same time, required equipment with the supplementary fuel installation.

The Weser Aircraft Works delivered the last of a total of 471 Ju 87 R-2s at the end of June 1941. At the same time, fifty-three of the 110 Ju 87 R-4s produced there were completed in June. In July 1941 bombing meant that the production of the Ju 87 R-4 could not be completed on time, and new delays affected the D while the production lines were still blocked with the older version of the Ju 87.

Only after Ju 87 B production was completely ended were all further efforts concentrated on the production of the Ju 87 D-1 from the summer of 1941 onwards as well as – to a limited extent – the final assembly of the remaining 145 R-4 machines still on order. Of the latter, thirty-eight of the 105 machines manufactured so far were delivered in July 1941. In August 1941 the production of the last Ju 87 R series reached twenty-six units. By now 131 R-4s had come off the assembly line at Weser.

In the following month eight Ju 87 R-4s, and in October the last two machines of this version, were completed. Two machines were destroyed in production test flying, so that only 143 of the 145 machines ordered could be transferred to the *Luftwaffe*. The last Ju 87 R-4s were test flown and were then delivered to the front-line units.

3.3.4 Ju 87 R Operations

The first dive bomber *Gruppe* to be equipped with the Ju 87 R-1, albeit with only a few aircraft, was I/StG 1, where the first 'long-range Stukas' appeared in the summer of 1940. The Staff *Kette* as well as two *Staffeln* of this unit had previously flown their first operations with the Ju 87 B from April 1940 onwards over Denmark and Norway. The leader of the unit was Captain Paul-Werner Hozzel. Apart from over Poland, long flights were now necessary, so that the call for an increase in range became ever louder among the units. On 19 April 1940 the 'Stuka' unit was received on the well-built airport at Stavanger.

An evening news report on 28 April 1940 misreported an unsuccessful 'Stuka' attack against seven transport ships off Namsos. In an operation on 2 May 1940 one Ju 87 B went missing. On 10 May 1940 I/StG 1 was at

A Ju 87 B-2 (works no. 5248) which crash-landed in France became an object of astonishment to soldiers.

Two members of the Todt Organisation view a Ju 87 B of 10 (St)/LG 1 at Rovaniemi in Finland. Note the improved defensive position with an MG 15 machine-gun.

Trondheim-Vaernes. One month later, on 10 June 1940, the Norwegian armed forces capitulated after a resistance which was fierce at times.

Only after the conclusion of the battles did the first Ju 87 R-1s go into service with I *Gruppe* of StG 1, so that its service could begin with a short induction of the crews. After the unit, partly equipped with the Ju 87 R, had taken part in the French campaign, it was now faced with attacks on the British Isles. For these operations the following eleven dive bomber units were ready with about 400 Ju 87s:

IV(St)/LG 1 with Ju 87 B-2s
I to III/StG 1 with Ju 87 B-2s and R-1s
I to III/StG 2 with Ju 87 B-2s
I/StG 3 with Ju 87 B-2s
I to III/StG 77 with Ju 87 B-2s

In the short but all too costly operations against Britain with the 'Stuka', losses initially occurred only with the Ju 87 B-1 and B-2 versions. The first two Ju 87s were lost on 14 July 1940; by the end of July, fifteen dive bombers were lost. In August the German units paid the price of forty-six Ju 87s recorded as crashed, shot down or missing. Others were wrecked in territory occupied by the *Wehrmacht*. In attacks on British fighter airfields and radar stations along the Channel coast alone the *Luftwaffe* lost nineteen Ju 87 Bs. In September the set-piece battles of the Battle of Britain reached their peak. As the operations of the *Luftwaffe* had been moved to Greater London, the Ju 87s could not be used any more. During the bombing attacks by Do 17s, Ju 88s and He 111s in the summer of 1940, a Ju 87 R (works no. 5461) of I/StG 1 was lost in a crash landing in German-occupied territory on 25 September 1940.

The heavy German losses over the British Isles meant that the battles faded out from October 1940 onwards. Once again it came back

It was mostly Ju 87 R-2s which went into action with III/StG 2. T6+HG is equipped with a VS 11 adjustable propeller.

to attacks on Allied ships in the area of the Thames estuary. On 9 October 1940 a Ju 87 R-1 (works no. 5291) was lost in the course of these operations, following a crash landing at the Evrecy airfield in which it was 15 per cent damaged.

On 17 October 1940, at the western end of the Bristol Channel four German destroyers were caught by two cruisers and several destroyers of the Royal Navy ('Force F'), but, because of the inept tactics of the enemy, were able to get away. Although there was no RAF fighter protection over the British force, the German side adhered to Imperial Marshal Hermann Göring's order

Dummy munitions for the training of armourers. Besides an SC 500 Ex, SC 250 Ex and SC 50 Ex were also in use for training. (Ex – Exerziermunition*)*

The arms of IV (St)/LG 1 – a devil riding on a bomb.

that Ju 87s were to take off only with their own fighter protection. Rigid adherence to orders may thus have prevented a tactical success: the Ju 87 R-1s remained at their dispersals.

On 30 October 1940 a crew belonging to I/StG 1 rammed a parked Do 215 B on Brest airfield, and the Ju 87 R-1 (works no. 5541) was 20 per cent damaged. In November and December there were no further Ju 87 R losses in the west. Besides I/StG 1, Ju 87 R-1s and, increasingly from January1941, the new Ju 87 R-2 with the Jumo 211 D engine, went to III/StG 2. The first accident happened on 4 January 1941 on Ernes airfield, where a Ju 87 R-2 (works no. 5692) was damaged. The crew got away with a fright; the machine could be rebuilt without great expense, as it was only 15 per cent damaged. The first R-2 losses were with StG 2 in February 1941. Various kinds of taxiing and landing damage led to seven operational machines being out of action in a short time with the I *Gruppe* of the unit. During the air battles for Britain between 19 July 1940 and 31 October 1940 a total of sixty-five out of 400 Ju 87s were lost or damaged.

After the Ju 87 B and R could no longer be used in the west, the Balkans and the Mediterranean became the new area of operations for the 'Stuka' units. In the operations over the Balkans there were probably no Ju 87 R-equipped units in action.

The attacks on British positions in the Mediterranean and air support over North Africa led to the first widespread operations with the Ju 87 R.

From the summer of 1941 onwards the 'long-range Stukas' were also to be found over the eastern front. Thanks to their greater operating radius, bombing attacks on the retreating Red Army and its supply centres up to November 1941 were of particular significance for the German advance. With IV ('Stuka')/Training *Geschwader* (LG) 1, which went into action over Finland, there were a few losses and crashes in the winter of 1941–2, in which personal injuries were to be regretted. The unit was mostly equipped with the R-2 and the R-4, but still had some Ju 87 B-2s as well. Further Ju 87 R-2s and R-4s flew in the late summer of 1942 with I/StG 5, which was created out of IV('Stuka')/LG 1, as well as with the reinforcement *Staffel* of the unit.

After the more effective Ju 87 D version came into service with the units, the Ju 87 R was used increasingly as a tug for the DFS 230 (DFS – *Deutsche Forschungsanstalt für Segelflug* = German Gliding Research Institute) load-carrying glider.

A few Ju 87 Rs were also occasionally to be found with flying units as well as with various air service commands as liaison aircraft, but because of their small numbers they played scarcely any part.

For the bulk of the Ju 87 Rs which were still available, another use was found. After most Ju 87 Bs and Rs had been replaced in the 'Stuka' *Gruppen* by the D-1 version or its successors, the Ju 87 R-1s, R-2s and R-4s that were still available after the costly combat operations went into service with a few schools as training aircraft. As the machines belonged to the previous generation of Ju 87s used on operations, there was an additional use for them with the training *Geschwader* (StG 101–103).

At first a few machines were assigned to StG 101. From the late summer of 1943 onwards these training *Geschwader* provided practical operations training for the newly trained crews with Ju 87 Bs, Rs and Ds. The dive bomber training units, which had turned into ground attack training *Geschwader*, still had Ju 87 R-1s, R-2s and R-4s in significant quantities as late as the spring of 1944. With SG 101 to SG 103 the new crews, as previously, received their final training before being sent into battle. In any event, the execution of low-level attacks was given an ever greater importance.

Most of the training *Gruppen* equipped with Ju 87s were at that time stationed at Deutsch-Brod (between Prague and Brno) as well as in France (Metz-Frescaty, Diedenhofen/Thionville and St Rafael). In one air attack on Frescaty airfield alone on 25 April 1944 six Ju 87 R-1s, R-2s and R-4s were damaged or destroyed.

After the retreat from France the remaining Ju 87 Rs went to Biblis near Worms, where training was continued from June 1944 onwards. By the end of the war almost all the Ju 87 Rs there had been replaced by the plentiful Ju 87 D-1s and their successors which were also no longer battleworthy and basically obsolete. The remaining Ju 87 Rs were then scrapped, as Ju 87s were needed for operational training in only limited quantities; meanwhile the Fw 190 had found an ever wider application with the units as a fighter bomber and ground attack aircraft.

3.4 The Ju 87 'Dora'

3.4.1 Development Guidelines

As an imminent replacement for the Ju 87 B and R, series production of the Ju 87 D was considered from the end of 1940 onwards. Because of the inadequate performance of the obsolete versions, the conversion of production to the Ju 87 D was promising, as its Jumo 211 J offered a higher speed and a greater reserve of performance.

In June 1941 Junkers was given an official order for five production prototypes of the D series, Ju 87 V21–V25. The accounts could thus be settled for work performed hitherto by Junkers on its own account. The transition to an improved version of the 'Stuka' was foreseeable after the experience over Britain. Besides a more powerful powerplant, the Jumo 211 J (P), the following changes were regarded as necessary by the *Luftwaffe* High Command (OKL).

An extensively simplified bomb release mechanism designed for all current offensive loads, and also exceedingly easy to maintain, was a basic requirement for operations that also had to be carried out under unfavourable field conditions. At the same time, the intended installation of two MG 151/20 cannon in the wings – compared to the the MG 17s installed hitherto – led to a fundamentally greater firepower. And finally, the use of the DB 603 engine instead of the Jumo 211 was intended to circumvent the bottlenecks caused by equipping the Ju 88 with the Jumo 211.

In August 1941 discussions took place concerning the use of the Daimler-Benz DB 603 in-line engine in the Ju 87 D-1 airframe. In September studies were begun because of the change in the powerplant equipment and the installation of the MG 151/20, which was also required by the RLM. In October the work was in full progress. Other than the DB powerplant and the desired cannon armament, the Junkers development department had to establish whether a Rost 24 bomb rack, which made possible the use of light SD free-fall weapons, was to be installed.

The tactical aim of the demands made by the *Luftwaffe* was ground attack operations against so-called 'mass targets' and enemy tanks from low altitude.

As early as November 1941 it became clear, however, that the use of the DB 603 powerplant did not need to be pursued further because

The Ju 87 V15 (D-IGDK) was among the later B prototypes for testing of the D series.

Close-up of the Ju 87 V22 (works no. 087 0540, SF+TY), March 1941.

The Ju 87 V21 (D-INRF) was tested with a ski undercarriage. The machine was damaged after one of the undercarriage legs broke.

testing had shown that it performed poorly, compared to the more powerful versions of the Jumo 211.

For this reason a new series of tests was ordered by the Technical Bureau to ascertain whether a Jumo 213 could be installed as a replacement for the DB 603. The Ju 87 F version originated later from this. In December 1941 the monthly report 12/41 indicated that work was still going on at Junkers to install the DB 603, as the Jumo 211 J was still not ready for series production.

3.4.2 Prototypes

The flight clearance date for the first Ju 87 D prototype was supposed to be December 1940 but, because of difficulties with the powerplant, it was delayed until the beginning of 1941.

According to the quarterly report for the period October–December 1940, the flight testing of the Ju 87 B (works no. 0321), which was supposed to serve as a preliminary trial of the Jumo 211 J planned for the D series, had been significantly affected by numerous engine defects.

The practical testing of the D series therefore first began in March 1941. The first prototype

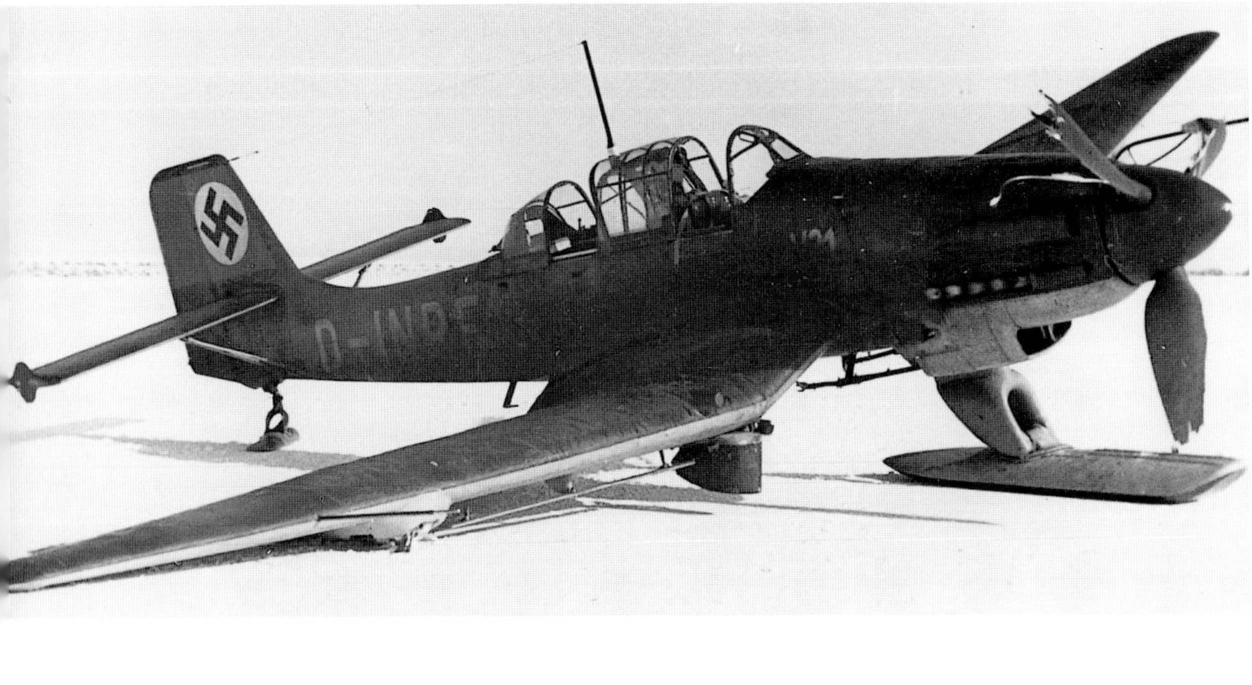

From the Ju 87 D-1 series the defensive power of the machine was significantly increased by the installation of the MG 81 Z twin machine-guns.

was the Ju 87 V21 (works no. 0536, D-INRF).

Between March and August 1941 the machine, at first powered by a Jumo 211 J, was at the Dessau home plant, where it served mainly for characteristics and performance testing. In August 1941, a propeller of hybrid construction broke up there. The Jumo 211 J of the V21 had been exchanged for a still more powerful version, the Jumo 211 F, and as soon as testing started the propeller broke up at a speed of 1,420 rpm.

From 30 September 1941 onwards, weapons testing with the Ju 87 V21 took place at Rechlin. The final transfer followed there after a comprehensive examination by the Construction Acceptance, Air (BAL) of the Test Centre on 16 October 1941. Next the machine was put into service for cooler and powerplant testing. At the beginning of February 1942 at the latest, the machine was again at the disposal of Junkers, where it served for the testing of new cowl flaps. In November 1941 it was under repair before the testing programme was continued.

After this, Junkers received a so-called 'war order' on 14 September 1943, whereby the Ju 87 V21 had to be given up to the front-line units. As a replacement the Junkers works received the Ju 87 C-1 with the works number 2552 at the end of 1942, in order to carry out the testing of take-off assistance devices.

The second Ju 87 D-1 prototype, the V22 (works no. 0540, SF+TY), was supposed to be cleared for flight at the end of 1940, but it was still parked in an unready condition at the manufacturer in March 1941 and only from May 1941 onwards did it serve for performance and equipment testing. The Ju 87 V22 was at the works on 1 October 1941 and at that time was mainly used in powerplant testing.

On 10 November 1941 the Ju 87 V22 was taken over by the BAL. The machine was, however, initially placed at the disposal of the works for further testing programmes. The flight behaviour of the second D prototype fulfilled the expectations of both the Junkers works and the Test Centre. In spite of unfavourable weather in November, cold starting was possible at all times without much trouble; even in intense cold, complete engine failures did not occur.

At the beginning of 1942 vibration measurements were carried out with the Ju 87 V22 at Junkers; otherwise the machine was put into service briefly between February and April 1942 at Dessau for examination of the changes to the Jumo 211 J and was then transferred to Rechlin.

On 20 August 1942 Sergeant Hermann Ruthard crashed into the Müritz lake near Rechlin with a civilian employee of the test centre, probably as a result of carbon monoxide poisoning. Both crew members lost their lives.

The Ju 87 V23 (works no. 542, PB+UB), like the two previous prototypes, was supposed to begin testing by 31 December 1940, but it was still not ready for flight at the end of February 1941, as the powerplant had not been delivered on time. Even by 1 March 1941 the Jumo 211 J was still missing. The production prototype of the Ju 87 D-1 version was not completed until April and hence could not be transferred to the Rechlin Test Centre before May 1941.

One of the early D-1s, the Ju 87 V24, works no. 544, BK+EE, was to have served as an experimental carrier-borne aircraft from the beginning of 1941. A flight clearance date of 15 March 1941 was forecast in the C Bureau

Works no. 2291, assembled as a production prototype airframe, served various purposes, among them a full-size simulation of changes to the cockpit.

programme of 1 February 1941. It could not, however, be equipped with the Jumo 211 J on time in the spring of 1941 and from May 1941 onwards had to remain parked at Junkers for several weeks without a powerplant. Acceptance by the BAL could not, therefore, take place until August 1941. The Ju 87 V24 was damaged in the fuselage during its testing at Rechlin. After repair at Dessau, it was again transported to the Test Centre in November 1941. Later it was brought up to the construction standards of a Ju 87 R and transferred to a front-line unit.

The Ju 87 V25 (works no. 0530, BK+EF) was the production prototype for the tropical version of the Ju 87 D-1. The machine was also supposed to be equipped with a Jumo 211 J, and its flight clearance date was planned for April 1941, but it was still parked at the works on 1 March 1941, as the engine had not arrived. The date for flight testing had, therefore, to be put back to May 1941 and then to July 1941. Only in the summer of 1941 could the machine be finally completed and then tested in detail for its service suitability as the first Ju 87 D-1/trop. After the machine was transferred to the Rechlin Test Centre on 12 September 1941, it went through the usual entry checks, in which a few small defects were found. The machine was equipped with a Delbag sand filter especially in order to handle operations in areas with a hot, dusty environment, such as the Mediterranean, without problems.

The second production prototype with tropical equipment was the Ju 87 D-1/trop., works no. 5706. By October 1941 at the latest both tropical aircraft had been supplied to the Test Centre Command.

At the end of June 1943 the Ju 87 V30 (works

no. 2296) was under construction at Junkers. The machine served as the production prototype for the D-5 series, one of the later standard D versions. On 26 June 1943 the V30 was at the Rechlin Test Centre for type testing. In August 1943 the aircraft was put into service at the Travemünde Test Centre in order to determine the best location for the FuG 16 radio set, together with the control loop of the FuG 1. The installation was next tested at Rechlin, but was regarded as too prone to break down for service use.

With another Ju 87 D, whose works number is not known, a main undercarriage that could be blown off in the event of a forced landing was built as a prototype and then tested in practice. An order for the concept of a jettisonable undercarriage for the Ju 87 D had already arrived at the Junkers works in May 1942. However, because the construction office was fully occupied with other programmes, this work progressed only slowly.

It was therefore not until the summer of 1943 that the first Ju 87 D-5 served – not entirely without danger – for testing a device to blow off the undercarriage, which often failed during workshop trials. Until a completely satisfactory solution was found, blowing off the undercarriage, a facility which the front-line crews wanted, had to be forbidden. Not until December 1943 was it established that a solution would be possible in the Ju 87 D-5 to D-8 by using a new kind of explosive bolt. Only a few weeks later, in January 1944, after installation at Rechlin, an experiment was carried out successfully to blow off an undercarriage in flight.

In order to increase the performance of all Ju 87 D series, several machines were equipped with improved powerplants and tested in daily operations. On 24 June 1944, during this endurance testing, the Ju 87 D-5 (BG+LW, works no. 130523) was lost at Kemijärvi in the far north of Finland. The Rechlin Test Centre crew crashed with their production prototype because of an operating error.

The aims behind the Ju 87 V43 (NI+VZ) and V47 (works no. 2246, CE+EJ), which were at Junkers at the beginning of 1942, have not been clarified. The V47 was still referred to as a prototype on 31 January 1945 in the monthly report 1/45, but its purpose at that time was not indicated.

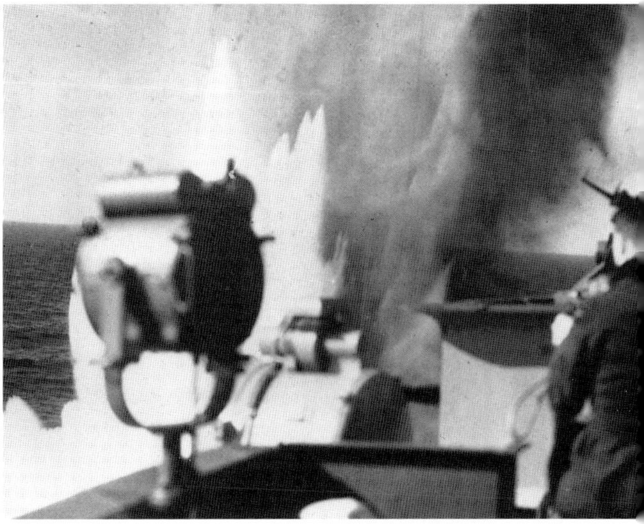

In attacks on Allied warships – here bombing on a dummy carrier in January 1941 – it became clear that the performance of the Ju 87 R was no longer adequate.

3.4.3 Service Trials

In the autumn of 1941, in addition to some of the above prototypes, eight production prototypes of the Ju 87 D-1 version were at Rechlin. The machines bore the works numbers 2005, 2008, 2010, 2014, 2019, 2022, 2023 and 2035. In the course of several weeks 295 take-offs and 236 flying hours were completed with them.

The service endurance testing of the Ju 87 D-1 resulted in the Rechlin Test Centre establishing at the end of November 1941 that there were no difficulties in its operation. Equally few were the criticisms of its in-flight safety. The only recommendation was that the sliding canopy be opened on the approach to an emergency landing (as in aircraft of comparable construction). When works no. 2019 overturned on a soft field, the pilot in the closed cockpit almost suffocated because, rather as in the Ju 87 B, he could not climb out through the side window.

The crews found the behaviour of the Ju 87 D-1, in taxiing as well as on take-off and landing, completely faultless. Even in take-offs in a crosswind up to 5 metres per second (18 kph), the machine could be kept straight with nothing more than rudder and ailerons.

View into the clearly arranged cockpit of the Ju 87 D. Note the bomb release electrical system with a modern control panel (lower right).

With regard to performance and range, the data provided by Junkers was fully confirmed.

During testing with free-fall ordnance, load tests were carried out with one SC 250 bomb, one SC 250 and four SC 50s; one SC 500, three SC 250s and two drop tanks; one SC 500 and two drop tanks; and one 1,000-kg bomb.

Although the machines still had the undercarriage of the Ju 87 B-2, even take-offs with heavy loads were problem-free. Bomb release was without difficulty; even without much practice, bombing accuracy was relatively good. Only the electric gear of the release mechanism initially showed a few, easily remedied, deficiencies.

In a dive with a medium-weight bomb hung under the fuselage as well as four SC 50s or SD 50s under the wings only the heavy load was released first and, as a rule, the recovery was made with the four smaller bombs still in place.

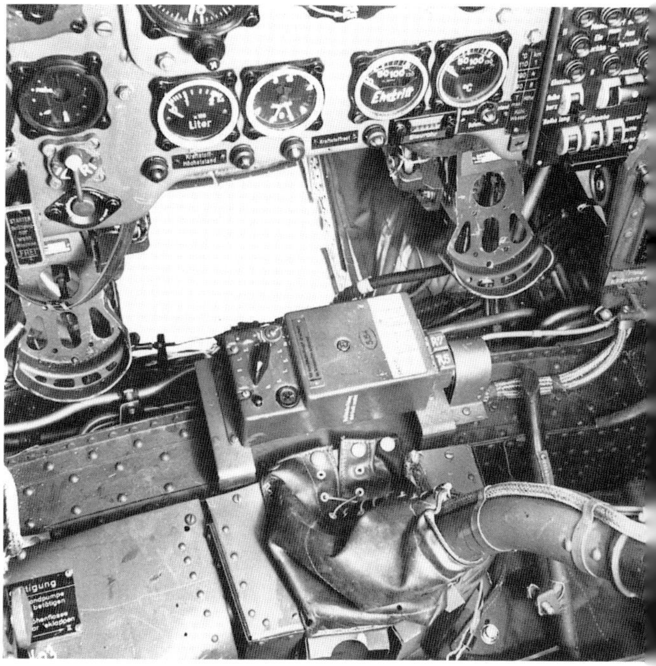

With a window that could be closed off in flight, the Ju 87 D-5 pilot could observe the ground and pick out targets for attack.

With a load of three SC 250s, neither the recovery from the dive nor the dive itself led to any problems. A longer flight with a load not released from one side, however, naturally tired the pilot.

The conversion from drop tank shackles to bomb racks could be carried out in only three hours by four trained ground crew.

The fixed armament was also investigated by the Travemünde Test Centre and, as with the Ju 87 B/R, noted as operationally capable. This was true both for the fixed machine-guns and for the defensive armament, which, thanks to the MG 81 Z twin machine-guns now used, was decisively strengthened.

The operational possibilities at night were, however, restricted. The comprehensive assessment of the night flying characteristics was, therefore, not good. Because of the instrumentation and the radio installation used hitherto, operations were possible only in bright moonlight with any prospect of success. The radio installation had an air-to-air range of about 70 km. The intercom functioned faultlessly during the tests.

Following this test phase, the majority of the machines were given to front-line units, while a few were used for various on-going testing programmes at the works or at the test centre.

The Ju 87 D-1 (works no. 2008) was equipped with a different weapons installation at the beginning of 1942. In October 1942 the machine was tested at the works with instrumentation which had been installed in the cooler area. The tests mainly concerned the altered temperature regulator and the cooler shut-off valves. Works number 2013 served as a series-equipped production prototype with MG 151/20 cannon armament and, further, for testing with improved cowl flaps; in addition it had a few changes to the airframe and powerplant.

On 1 July 1943 the Ju 87 D-1 (works no. 2019, BK+ES) was lost during engine testing at Neustrelitz when it overturned after an emergency landing caused by an engine failure; the pilot was Heinrich Bewerbung.

One disadvantage became apparent in service trials; during steep practice dives a slight vibration occurred in the aileron area. Slight installation changes cured this problem.

When the front-line units again reported noticeable vibrations at the beginning of July 1943, with their new Ju 87 D-5s equipped with the large wings, one of the machines was again investigated at JFM. As a result of the continued flutter of the ailerons, a noticeable vibration was set up in the airframe at speeds of 500 kph. Investigations of this phenomenon were therefore begun in mid-month at JFM at Dessau, in order to establish its cause. The tests led to a reduction of the disturbing influences by the installation of new aileron hinges. A check flight at Rechlin up to 650 kph in diving flight then went faultlessly. The changes suggested by Junkers were authorised by the BAL at Rechlin, so that nothing stood in the way of the introduction of the new hinges. They could be installed by the front-line units themselves.

All in all, the Ju 87 D – in spite of its low performance compared to enemy fighter aircraft – was a good weapons platform.

This was, however, a relatively expensively equipped machine. In wartime conditions, ways were soon sought to simplify the equipment of operational types from the D-5 series onwards as soon as possible. A series Ju 87 D was, for example, fitted with a simplified lubrication system as a forerunner of the planned 'rationalised version', the D-6. The Rechlin Test Centre carried out the function testing of a production machine. As no difficulties occurred in this area, the more easily manufactured lubrication system was released for service use.

In the aircraft's electrical system and the radio installation, systems that could be manufactured more quickly were also suggested, but only some of the numerous suggestions became reality as prototypes and were tested by the Test Centre Command. In December 1943 a Ju 87 D was equipped with a unit hydraulic system and flight tested. As this was safe in operation, the testing at the Rechlin Test Centre was positive, apart from minor criticisms.

Only in the cooler installation did problems occasionally arise in very low temperatures. In an attempt to improve the installation without great expense, numerous, often time-consuming, detailed investigations were carried out up to the end of 1943. The work in this area was still going on in the summer of 1944. One of the Ju 87 D-3s being used crashed at Hamburg during range testing as a result of an engine failure, in spite of the improved cooler.

3.4.4 Production Versions

The following eight versions of the Ju 87 D were developed as ground attack aircraft and torpedo bombers, according to information in the Aircraft Production Series sheets dating from 19 August 1944.

3.4.4.1 The Ju 87 D-1

The new basic D-1 version differed externally from the previous A, B and R versions, and not

Two Ju 87 D-3s were first tested with 300-litre drop tanks before this possibility was considered for the series.

only in the aerodynamic improvement in the area of the cockpit canopy. Above all, it was equipped with an essentially more powerful engine, the Jumo 211 J or the Jumo 211 P, both equipped with supercharger intercoolers. The fuel consumption was 310 litres per hour near the ground, 305 litres per hour at a flight altitude of 2,500 metres and about 320 litres per hour at 5,000 metres. The VS 11 adjustable propeller was used mainly, with a maximum permissible speed of 2,250 rpm.

The radio installation corresponded to the Ju 87 B, in which as a rule the FuG VII a or c radio with EiV 1a or V intercom was installed, except for the additional FuG 25 transponder as well as the Peil G IV, V or VI homing set.

The fuel installation comprised internal tanks with a capacity of 780 litres. In addition, two drop tanks could be carried, whereby the fuel capacity was increased to about 1,370 litres.

According to the results of the Rechlin performance test of December 1941, the fuel supply made possible a flying time of 2 hours 15 minutes or, with two 300-litre drop tanks, a good four hours. This corresponded in the D-1 to D-4 to a range of 750–820 km.

The D-1 version differed from the B-1 and B-2 in the following ways:

- extensive aerodynamic improvements to the cockpit with MG 81 Z twin machine-guns as radio operator's position armament with 1,000 rounds per gun
- strengthened undercarriage legs which made possible the alternative use of a wheel or ski undercarriage; the undercarriage was supposed to be jettisonable from the outset, but, as we have seen, this became possible only after an extensive rework of the explosive device

As additional equipment the machines could be equipped with a flame damper installation for dusk and night operations, especially for night ground attack. As a tug, the D-1 version, like the majority of the subsequent D versions, could be equipped with a tow coupling. The bomb release installation consisted of a locking rack with a 1000/500 XI B, 1000 XI or 2000 XIII lock. Under both wings in the series two ETC 50 VIII e electric release racks were installed. The SC 1800 bomb was envisaged as the maximum permissible drop load, if it was carried, however, other loads could not be carried under the wing electric release racks.

As a fixed offensive armament in the D-1, two fixed MG 17 machine-guns were built into the left and right wings. They were operated by the pilot. The Revi C/12C or the improved C/12D served as a reflector sight. The firing of the on-board weapons was electro-pneumatic with the EPAD 17 trigger and loading mechanism; electrical safety was assured by the ESi 17 safety device. Five hundred rounds of ammunition could be carried per gun.

Because of its multifarious operational possibilities, the D-1 version – after the Ju 87 B-2 and R-2 – quickly became the new standard type of the *Luftwaffe* dive bomber *Geschwader*.

Only with the delivery of the more effective Ju 87 D-5 was this machine given over to diverse training and reinforcement units.

3.4.4.2 The Ju 87 D-2

The Ju 87 D-2 was intended to serve as the tropical version of the Ju 87 D-1. For this, as with previous tropical versions, appropriate emergency equipment (emergency rations, water containers, hunting weapons and the like) would have been necessary, as well as the installation of a dust filter. The D-2/trop. would have differed from its predecessors above all in using the Ju 87 B-2 undercarriage, as well as an extended fuel system with two 300-litre drop tanks under the wings from the outset. Further, it was supposed to receive the wings used in the earlier Ju 87 B-2, of which enough were still available. This, however, did not happen.

Instead of the Ju 87 D-2/trop., a better armoured version of the D series was demanded, on the grounds of significant losses to enemy ground defences.

The ground attack aircraft armour of the Ju 87 D-2 was supposed to provide a permanent reduction in the danger to the crew from ground fire. As flight trials with an appropriately converted prototype, equipped with this fundamentally increased passive protection, resulted in a noticeable reduction in performance and ceiling, however, the OKL henceforth placed no particular value on the production of the D-2 in the layout that was planned.

The NSU tracked vehicle had become an essential supply vehicle with many Luftwaffe *units in the east. In the background is the Ju 87 D-1 prototype (DP+KA) which was tested with a ski undercarriage.*

Nevertheless, the work led to a reconsideration of supplementary armour. After acceptance of the altered mock-up by the Technical Bureau and the Test Centre Command, no further doubts remained about the installation of the new armour.

The drawings and the prototype manufactured by Junkers were delivered to WFG at Bremen in February 1942, together with the similarly manufactured patterns. The armour was in part retrofitted in the D-1, as well as being built in from the D-5 onwards, and led to an improvement in the passive protection of both crew and machine.

The further alteration to the armour of the Ju 87 D required by the Chief of Development and Testing on 12 June 1942, which involved installing an armoured seat for the pilot, took place from the early summer of 1943 onwards in the context of a retrofit or in the course of repairs in the field workshops or in the repair facility at Graz.

3.4.4.3 The Ju 87 D-3

The D-3 was also a version of the Ju 87 D-1, with an extended basic armour as well as the option of building on extra armour protection, above all in the armoured underpart of the fuselage and armoured coolant pipes. In order to obviate any significant increase in weight, in May 1943 the omission of the noise devices was authorised by the RLM for the D-3 also; instead two armour plates were attached to the sides of the fuselage, in order better to protect the crew against shots and splinter effect. The work was

This D-3 machine was experimentally equipped with the weapons installation of the future D-5. In addition, strengthened fuselage armour and two drop tanks were added.

accepted by the Rechlin Test Centre in May and June 1943, whereupon a corresponding change order was issued on 12 June 1943.

The Jumo 211 J-equipped version of the D-3 started as part of a conversion programme, and then as newly built aircraft (works nos. 100001 ff, 110001 ff and 131001 ff) in significant numbers. From the Ju 87 D-3 series onwards it was planned to install a mass-balanced aileron, but this was only first introduced in the D-5.

Together with its predecessor the D-1 and its successor the D-5, the D-3 was among the standard versions of the 'Dora' construction series. A proportion of the machines was assembled as Ju 87 D-3 'N' with the night ground attack supplementary equipment, or as a tropical version (Ju 87 D-3/trop.).

3.4.4.4 The Ju 87 D-4

The fuselage of the Ju 87 D-1 served as a point of origin for the development of the Ju 87 D-4 torpedo bomber, on which a 750-kg or 905-kg aerial torpedo could be carried on a PVC 1006 B rack. The machines were also intended to operate from aircraft carriers. It was thought that the D-4 machines would be converted from existing Ju 87 D-3 fuselages.

Other than the release mechanism necessary for torpedo operations, the urgent work needed in this version was the development and practical testing of an improved arrester hook. Although the experiments began in December 1941, a really reliable version was not found until 1942.

Operation as a dive bomber was a secondary role for the Ju 87 D-4. In this case the release mechanism would have corresponded in all respects to that of the Ju 87 D-1. The majority of the D-4 machines were intended to be equipped with a flame eliminator and, in contrast to the three previous D versions, possessed a fixed,

As a further production prototype, this Ju 87 D-1 received stronger armour. As a result of the heavy weight and the resultant deterioration in performance, often only some of the armour plates were often installed.

forward-firing armament of two MG 151/20 cannon. For these an ammunition supply of 180 rounds per gun could be carried.

The production prototype was the Ju 87 D-1, works no. 2013. The machine was taken to Tarnewitz in March 1943 and subjected to a comprehensive weapons testing there. A further change was the increase of the ammunition supply for the radio operator's armament from 1,000 to 2,000 rounds.

As with the D-1 and D-3, the use of extra armour as well as the omission of the noise devices on the undercarriage legs was planned.

Further details of the development of the torpedo bomber are found in Chapter 7.

3.4.4.5 The Ju 87 D-5

The Ju 87 D-5 was based on the D-3 and was the first version to have the new, lengthened wings. Enlarged by 0.6 metres each, these led to a slight increase in performance compared to the D-1 and D-3.

The flight testing was carried out mainly with two Ju 87 D-5s (works nos. 130502 and 130504), equipped with Jumo 211 P in-line engines with supercharger intercoolers. The first of these powerplants was tested at Rechlin in August 1943 and was intended to replace the Jumo 211 J-1 in the Ju 87 D. During flight testing an improvement in the rate of climb to about 15 metres per second was established. As the conversion to the Jumo 213 was also possible with the Ju 87 in the late summer of 1943, the Jumo 211 P was dispensed with in order to make better use of the company's development capability, with the result that development stopped with the Jumo 211 J and the lengthened wings.

Thanks to the new mass-balanced ailerons,

which now had four aileron hinges instead of three, as well as the strengthened floor window, higher diving speeds with dive brakes retracted were permitted for the D-5. The permitted indicated airspeed at altitudes up to 2,000 metres was now up to 650 kph. The longest flying time at 370 kph at 5,000 metres was 2 hours, 15 minutes. The range, according to tests at Rechlin at the beginning of 1944, was between 715 km near the surface and 835 km at 5,000 metres.

Fuel was carried in a 480-litre fuselage tank and two wing tanks of 150 litres each. As with the D-1, two 300-litre drop tanks could also be carried. According to the Operating Instructions (Loading Plan) for the Ju 87 D-5, this resulted in a take-off weight of between 5,150 and 6,480 kg. The increased gross weight took into account an undercarriage with strengthened, easily removable fairings, which were thus more easily maintained under field conditions.

In response to wartime conditions, the equipment of the D-5 was 'rationalised'. The fuel consumption indicator was thus omitted, as was mixture control through the propeller speed selector. From the D-5 onwards, the lubrication system was also changed; the supplementary oil tank on the engine was omitted and a connection was made to the bigger oil tank on the control column frame.

As extra equipment, the tow coupling behind the tailwheel (designation 'S'), a flame eliminator (designation 'N') or a winter emergency kit could be carried. The ammunition for the MG 81 Z twin machine-guns, operated by the radio operator, was usually reduced to 1,400 rounds (instead of 2,000). The ammunition supply for the two fixed MG 151/20s comprised two magazines of 180 rounds of 20 mm, which were usually belted in a 2:2:2 sequence of different shell types. The MG 151 armament corresponded to the production prototype completed on 15 March 1943, which was tested at the Tarnewitz Test Centre from the early summer of 1943 onwards.

As free-fall ordnance, the following combinations were possible with the Ju 87 D-5, as tested with works no. 130523:

- 1 × 250 kg
- 1 × 250 kg and 4 × 65 kg
- 1 × 500 kg
- 1 × 500 kg and 4 × 65 kg
- 3 × 250 kg
- 1 × 1,000 kg
- 1 × 1,000 kg and 4 × 65 kg
- 1 × 1,400 kg
- 1 × 1,800 kg

Although maximum loads, such as the SC 1800 bomb, were transportable, as a rule only drop loads (bombs or scatter-bomb containers) weighing between 250 kg and 500 kg, as well as SC/SD 50 or SC 70 loads, were hung under the wing racks. The much bigger SD 1000, SD 1400 or SC 1800 bombs were tested with the Ju 87 B and D, but proved themselves too

A Ju 87 production prototype in which additional coolers had been built into the inner wings.

In all construction series the weapons in the wings had to be zeroed in order to maintain the prescribed point of impact.

awkward and too heavy for single-engined ground attack aircraft. As a result of the sharply increased gross weight, only short-range operations were possible.

Further, the switch gear of the existing release mechanism was reworked with the Ju 87 D-5. While in the Ju 87 D-1 the bomb release installation and automatic dive recovery were both activated by a common push button, from the D-5 onwards these two functions were once again separated. Separate push buttons on the control column were now envisaged for bomb release and for retrimming the machine after the diving attack.

As protection against ground fire, two side armour plates could be built into the Ju 87 D-5 without great expense. Further, the 5-mm-thick glass pane in the floor window was extensively exchanged for an 8-mm pane.

Radio testing was carried out with Ju 87 V30 (works no. 2296). This was mainly concerned with the radio-technical examination of the prototype installation of the FuG 16 Z, which meant homing flight could be carried out.

Notable quantities of the Ju 87 D-5 were manufactured in the context of new construction (works nos. 131000 ff, 132000 ff, 140000 ff, 141000 ff and 142000 ff) and thereby the Ju 87 D-1 and D-3 were replaced. As previously with the Ju 87 D-3, a proportion of the machines were converted as night ground attack aircraft and next carried the type designation Ju 87 D-5 'N'.

Ju 87 D und G
Bed.Vorschr.-Fl

Flugbetrieb **II** 39

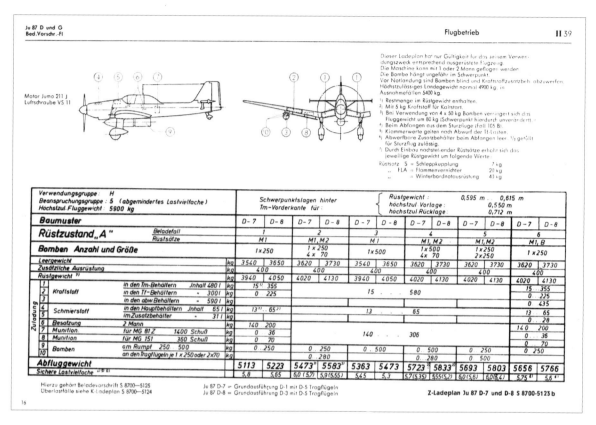

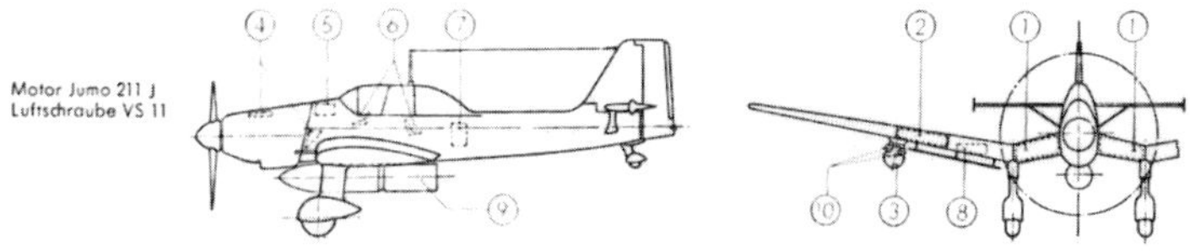

Dieser Ladeplan hat nur Gültigkeit für das seinem Verwendungszweck entsprechend ausgerüstete Flugzeug.
Die Maschine kann mit 1 oder 2 Mann geflogen werden.
Die Bombe hängt ungefähr im Schwerpunkt.
Vor Notlandung sind Bomben blind und Kraftstoffzusatzbeh. abzuwerfen.
Höchstzulässiges Landegewicht normal 4900 kg, in Ausnahmefällen 5400 kg.

1) Restmenge im Rüstgewicht enthalten.
2) Mit 5 kg Kraftstoff für Kaltstart.
3) Bei Verwendung von 4 x 50 kg Bomben verringert sich das Fluggewicht um 80 kg (Schwerpunkt hierdurch unverändert).
4) Beim Abfangen aus dem Sturzfluge (Fall 105 B).
5) Klammerwerte gelten nach Abwurf der Tf-Lasten.
6) Abwerfbare Zusatzbehälter beim Abfangen leer, 1/3 gefüllt für Sturzflug zulässig.
7) Durch Einbau nachstehender Rüstsätze erhöht sich das jeweilige Rüstgewicht um folgende Werte:

Rüstsatz S = Schleppkupplung 7 kg
„ FLA = Flammenvernichter 20 kg
„ = Winterbordnotausrüstung 40 kg

Verwendungsgruppe: H
Beanspruchungsgruppe: 5 (abgemindertes Lastvielfache)
Höchstzul. Fluggewicht: 5900 kg

Schwerpunktslagen hinter Tm-Vorderkante für: Rüstgewicht: 0,595 m ... 0,615 m; höchstzul. Vorlage: 0,550 m; höchstzul. Rücklage: 0,712 m

Baumuster		D-7	D-8	D-7	D-8	D-7	D-8	D-7	D-8	D-7	D-8	D-7	D-8
Rüstzustand „A" Beladefall		1		2		3		4		5		6	
Rüstsätze		M1		M1, M2		M1		M1, M2		M1, M2		M1, B	
Bomben Anzahl und Größe		1x250		1 x 250 4 x 70		1x500		1x500 4x 70		1x250 2x250		1 x 250	
Leergewicht	kg	3540	3650	3620	3730	3540	3650	3620	3730	3620	3730	3620	3730
Zusätzliche Ausrüstung	kg	400		400		400		400		400		400	
Rüstgewicht 7)	kg	3940	4050	4020	4130	3940	4050	4020	4130	4020	4130	4020	4130
Zuladung 1 Kraftstoff in den Tm-Behältern Jnhalt 480 l	kg	15 1) ... 355		15 . . . 580								15 ... 355	
2 in den Tf-Behältern " 300 l	kg	0 ... 225										0 ... 225	
3 in den abw. Behältern " 590 l	kg											0 ... 435	
4 Schmierstoff in den Hauptbehältern Jnhalt 65 l	kg	13 1) .. 65 2)		13 . . . 65								13 ... 65	
5 im Zusatzbehälter " 31 l	kg											0 ... 28	
6 Besatzung 2 Mann	kg	140 ... 200		140 . . . 306								140 ... 200	
7 Munition für MG 81 Z 1400 Schuß	kg	0 ... 36										0 ... 36	
8 Munition für MG 151 360 Schuß	kg	0 ... 70										0 ... 70	
9 Bomben am Rumpf 250 ... 500	kg	0 ... 250		0 ... 250		0 ... 500		0 ... 500		0 ... 250		0 ... 250	
10 an den Tragflügeln je 1 x 250 oder 2x70	kg			0 ... 280				0 ... 280		0 ... 500			
Abfluggewicht		5113	5223	5473 3)	5583 3)	5363	5473	5723 3)	5833 3)	5693	5803	5656	5766
Sichere Lastvielfache 4) 5) 6)		5,8	5,65	6,0 (5,7)	5,9 (5,55)	5,45	5,3	5,7 (5,35)	5,55 (5,2)	6,0 (5,6)	6,0 (5,4)	5,75 6)	5,6 6)

Hierzu gehört Beladevorschrift S 8700—5125
Überlastfälle siehe K-Ladeplan S 8700—5124

Ju 87 D-7 = Grundausführung D-1 mit D-5 Tragflügeln
Ju 87 D-8 = Grundausführung D-3 mit D-5 Tragflügeln

Z-Ladeplan Ju 87 D-7 und D-8 S 8700-5123 b

16

Loading plan for the Ju 87 D-7 and D-8 conversion aircraft which were equipped with Jumo 211 J powerplants and the larger wings of the Ju 87 D-5.

3.4.4.6 The Ju 87 D-6

The Ju 87 D-6 originated solely as a 'rationalised version' of the Ju 87 D-5. It was a simplified version of the existing standard D-5, brought about by the tight raw materials situation: with the D-6 series, the electrical system, bomb release switching and similar equipment was significantly simplified.

The work on the simplified version was still far from complete at the end of 1943. According to the Operating Instructions (works document 2097) of February 1944, only limited numbers of this machine were produced in order to gather experience with the 'rationalised version'. Because of the not insignificant cost of the changes, it did not go into series production.

3.4.4.7 The Ju 87 D-7

The Ju 87 D-7 involved equipping conversion aircraft of the Ju 87 D-1 version with the bigger wings of the D-5 so as to increase their performance. The fire power was also changed as it was now possible to use two MG 151/20 cannon.

It was planned to retrofit the Ju 87 D-7 – as with the D-3 and D-5 series – with two flame eliminator pipes beside the powerplant, but how far this conversion went cannot be reliably clarified.

3.4.4.8 The Ju 87 D-8

The Ju 87 D-8 version was planned as a second conversion variant. Instead of the D-3 wings, those of the D-5 were again considered. Otherwise, the Ju 87 D-8 was a Ju 87 D-3 from which the extra armour had been omitted.

The installation investigations, as well as the production prototype, were ordered in September 1943. The Ju 87 D-8, like the D-7, could be equipped with either a ski undercarriage or a normal wheeled undercarriage. Like the D-7, too, it could have been used as a night ground attack machine capable of blind flying.

3.4.5 Production of the Ju 87 D

The first production guidelines for the Ju 87 D-1 originated from 1940. Within a short time 495 Ju 87 Ds were ordered, which were to be delivered between May 1941 and March 1942. The revised production guidelines of the RLM (C-Bureau), as early as the beginning of February 1941, envisaged the construction of 832 Ju 87 Ds. All these machines were to be manufactured by Weser. A production start-up was estimated for the beginning of June 1941; from September 1941 the construction of forty Ju 87 Ds per month was expected; later production was to be increased to ninety machines or more per month.

The start of series production was delayed, as with the other versions. First the conversion from B production did not take place on time, then there were still deficiencies in part of the new production equipment which brought the exactness of fit of the assemblies into question.

Thus, in June 1941, neither of the two planned Ju 87 Ds could be delivered, as work at the Karman firm on the upper fuselage skin had not advanced quickly enough. Only with great effort was the first production prototype rough-finished by 30 June 1941.

Numerous changes also led to work on the new version advancing slowly at first. Optimists at the RLM, as previously in similar cases, still hoped for final assembly of forty-eight machines in July and twenty-five more in August 1941.

Of the forty-eight Ju 87 D-1s planned for July 1941, only the first production machine could finally be made ready for flight. This was destroyed in the works and no more machines were delivered until the end of July. At Junkers, the grantor of the production licence, and in the RLM Division LC 2, there was, however, still optimism and it was believed that it was possible to recover the shortfall by the end of September 1941 at the latest.

However, in August no Ju 87 Ds were

Close-up of the exhaust system and supercharger inlet of the Ju 87 D.

Ju 87 D und G
Bed.-Vorschr.-Fl. **Flugbetrieb** **II 27**

Beanspruchungsgruppe	H 5 mit abgeminderten Lastvielfachen			
Motor-Belastungsgrenzen				
	Zul. Zeit	Ladedruck	Drehzahl bis 6,5 km	Drehzahl über 6,5 km
Stand	—	1,4	n = ca. 2500 s. B.-V.-Fl. Teil I	
Abflug normal	1'	1,4	2600	—
Abflug Uberlast	1'	1,4	2600	—
Flug	—	—	—	—
Flug Steig Kampfl.	30'	1,25	2400	2400
Flug Hochstzul. Dauerleist.		1,15	2250	2400
Laderumschalthöhe	Automatik		2500 m ± 300	
Gleit- und Sturzflug	n_{max} = 2250			

Flugzeit und Flugstrecke bei höchstzulässiger Dauerleistung

Flughöhe m	300	2500	5000
Laderschaltung	BL	BL	HL
Ladedruck ata	1,15	1,06 Vg	1,11 Vg
Drehzahl U/min	2250	2250	2250
Kraftstoffverbrauch l/h	310	295	305
Für 770 l Kraftstoff ohne Abwurfbehälter und ohne Lasten			
Wahre mittlere Geschwindigkeit in km/h	320	340	370
Gesamtflugzeit h'	2h 15'	2h 25'	2h 25'
Reichweiten km	715	800	835

Muster	Ju 87 D-5 bis D-8 Ju 87 H-5 bis H-8 mit Ladeluftkühler	
Zulassung		
Werk-Nr.		
Motor	Jumo 211 J mit Ladeluftkühler	
Luftschraube	Muster VS 11 Grundeinstellung: 25°	

Höchstzulässige angezeigte Geschwindigk. bei Bahnneigungsflug (Fahrtmesser)

Höhe (km)	Va (km/h) mit Sturzflug-Bremse	Va (km/h) ohne Sturzflug-Bremse
0 2	600	650 *)
über 2	550	600 *)

*) Fur alle Flugzeuge D-5 bis D-8, die nicht 4 Querruderlager, Querruder-Massenausgleich sowie verstärktes Bodensichtfenster haben, gelten die Werte „mit Sturzflugbremse"

Triebwerks-Überwachungsgeräte

Kühlstofftemperatur max 120°

Höhe	Normale Höchsttemp.
1	110°
4	100°
8	90°

Schmierstoff-Temperatur

	Eintritt	
min	30°	
max	105°	

Schmierstoffdruck

Am Boden $p_{min} = 5,5$ $p_{max} = 9$

In 5,5 km Höhe $p_{min} = 4,0$

Kraftstoffdruck

1,0 - 2,0

Diese Werte sind durch Marken an den entsprechenden Geräten vor dem Einstecken der Karte zu kennzeichnen

Schmierstoff: Rotring Shell mittel Intava 100	Beschriftung auf Einfülldeckel
Kraftstoff Okt. 87	

Ausgabe 3	Tag: 29. 12. 43	JFM-FTV Dru

Betriebsdatentafel Ju 87 D-5 bis D-8, H-5 bis H-8

Für Einsatzflüge siehe Rechliner Flugstreckentabelle

Operating data table for the Ju 87 D-5 to D-8 and the derivative training versions H-5 to H-8.

delivered. Only in September 1941 did the first two – of the 102 that should have been completed by then – go to Construction Acceptance. The first of these machines was needed for further testing programmes in the Test Centre Command; the second was already earmarked for one of the air equipment testing bureaux.

In spite of the tight personnel situation caused by the removal of part of the production from Bremen to Berlin, the RLM received a forecast of forty-six Ju 87 D-1s to be completed in September 1941. In October the shortfall to be recovered had risen to 165 machines; only twenty-three of the forty Ju 87 D-1s supposed to be produced each month could actually be delivered.

As a result of unfavourable weather, there were, by November and December, massive shortfalls at the production test flying operations at Lemwerder.

Therefore the RLM had to be put off until the end of December 1941: by that time the first eighty-five Ju 87 D-1s were now due to be delivered and on their way to the front-line units.

As was to be expected, however, the first of these production machines still had numerous defects as well as the normal 'teething troubles'. This was revealed when various production aircraft were tranferred from Bremen to Italy. Of the machines that took off, eight had signs of failure or damage at the interim landing at Böblingen near Stuttgart.

The most important fault reported to the works was a sudden tendency for the machines to swerve on landing due to the fact that the undercarriage brakes had been insufficiently run in. There were also various cases of damage to the newly delivered Ju 87 Ds during the following months. The majority of the failures were attributable to manufacturing errors at WFG or to excessive demands on the aircraft.

By 25 March 1942 the majority of the defects that had appeared had been overcome by an immediate action programme by WFG technical representatives. In the process, in April 1942, new protected fuel tanks were installed in the machines that were checked over. After these measures had been carried out, there were only requests for changes from the front-line units, which in part could be introduced through later change orders.

The delivery rate was increased markedly from November 1942 onwards and reached its peak in the spring of 1944 with more than 150 machines per month. Until production ceased, about 3,300 Ju 87 Ds, mostly D-1s, D-3s and D-5s, were manufactured.

The Aircraft Delivery Forecast of 27 January 1944 was the first preview of the progressive phasing out of Ju 87 D production in the medium term. While in January 1944 the manufacture of 125 machines was still expected, between February and April only 120 more Ju 87 Ds could be anticipated, in May 100, in June 85 and in September 45 ground attack aircraft. In spite of these guidelines, the last Ju 87s did not leave final assembly until November 1944. As was to be expected, delivery Study 1023 of 30 March 1944 (gKdos. 15075/44), which was

The ground crews of the Ju 87 Staffeln *had to struggle with difficult conditions, especially in the winter months. Here a Jumo 211 powerplant is being started.*

adapted to the war situation, referred to the slow disappearance of the Ju 87 from March 1945 onwards. In April 1944 Study 1023 already foresaw a ratio between the manufacture of Fw 190s, Hs 129s and Ju 87s of 200:40:135. The days of Ju 87 D production were thus numbered. A premature stoppage of production between September and December 1944 was already a possibility. Meanwhile production went on, in order at least to some extent to replace losses.

In May 1944, besides forty-eight new Ju 87 Ds, a further forty machines were completed as repaired aircraft. Twelve of these ground attack aircraft went to *Luftflotte* 4, which also received fourteen Hs 129s. The General of Training Pilots received four others, while seventy-two were made available for future conversions. Of these fifty-eight were converted as night ground attack aircraft. Four were issued to 15/SG 151, one to Test Command 24 and one to the Pilot Transit *Geschwader*.

In total eighty-three more Ju 87 Ds were available in June 1944. Besides forty-five newly built aircraft, thirty-eight repaired machines were accepted. Of these 15/SG 151 received five machines this time, while the General of Reconnaissance Pilots received one more. Thirty-three of the ground attack aircraft were converted as night ground attack and soon joined the strength of the night ground attack *Gruppen*.

A little later, in July 1944, a ratio of 470 Fw 190s to 40 Hs 129s to 70 Ju 87s was reached in the production of ground attack aircraft.

In August 1944 a total of 140 more Ju 87s stood ready for the *Luftwaffe*. Of these sixty-six originated from Weser production, to which were added another fifty-four repaired aircraft. The remaining twenty Ju 87s originated from the OKL reserve. Besides the seventy-seven machines delivered to front-line units, forty-four were transferred to pilot training. Twelve were assigned to the jurisdiction of the General of Reconnaissance Pilots.

The 105 Ju 87s newly added in September 1944 comprised twenty-four newly built aircraft, forty repaired machines and, again, twenty originated from the OKL reserve. Again, numerous machines were converted for night ground attack. They were mainly intended to go into action with SG 151 as well as with NSGr. 5.

In September 1944 the long-expected cessation of Ju 87 production was ordered. A month later, in October, the production of ground attack aircraft was as follows: 635 Fw 190 Fs and Gs, 40 Hs 129s and 25 Ju 87s.

In December 1944 Ju 87 production finally ceased, after the last fifteen of the exceedingly robust ground attack aircraft had been produced in November. According to the planning guideline of 30 March 1944, the production of the Hs 129 would have lasted somewhat longer, until February 1945. From March 1944 onwards,

A Ju 87 unit departing for an operation in the battle of Kursk, which was known as Operation Citadel. (Federal Archives)

instead, 800 Fw 190 ground attack aircraft were supposed to come off the production lines each month. Delivery Plan 225, however, envisaged a more realistic number of 400 per month. This production was supposed to be valid until March 1946!

3.4.6 Changes in Front-Line Service

3.4.6.1 Free-Fall Weapons

The free-fall loads made available for the Ju 87 consisted extensively of aerial mines with a 50 per cent explosive component as well as, in the second half of the war, various large free-fall containers with the most diverse contents.

In 1937 the *Luftwaffe* is known to have had at its disposal only four types of SC bombs, which weighed 10, 50, 250 and 500 kg. For these, three different fuses were available. The bombs SC 50 and above were used with the Ju 87 A and B as well as with the Ju 87 D. The PC-500-RS armour piercing bomb, which was developed from the spring of 1940 onwards specially for the Ju 87, was intended to be dropped from a dive and was planned specifically for attacking reinforced targets.

Engineer General Dipl.-Ing. Ernst Marquart, the former group leader of the Free-Fall Weapons Division in the Imperial Aviation Ministry and later divisional chief of LC 7/RLM, made an exhaustive presentation before General Field Marshal Erhard Milch. In his opinion, the use of rocket-propelled armour-piercing bombs demanded flying experience which was far above the average performance. Hence, this type of armament could only be used in a very small way by elite crews.

Greater free-fall loads than the usual SC 500 or SD 500 were scarcely used at all operationally. Even the use of the SD 1000 against armoured targets remained the exception with the Ju 87 B and D.

Special measures to modify the Ju 87 for improved, and especially for still heavier, free-fall weapons were thus not necessary with the Ju 87 D. What remained was the effort, already begun in December 1941, to simplify as far as possible the very complicated bomb release mechanism of the planned Ju 87 D-1 and thereby to render it less prone to failures and

Dipl.-Ing. Flight Captain Melitta *Gräfin* von Stauffenberg

Flight Captain Melitta von Stauffenberg, together with Hanna Reitsch, was among those female pilots who undertook hazardous flight testing for the aviation industry. With the Ju 87 and Ju 88 alone, she carried out over 2,000 dives.

Melitta Gräfin *von Stauffenberg at the controls of a Ju 87.*

9 January 1903	Born in Krotoshin in the Province of Poznan as Melitta Schiller
To 1918	State Higher Girls' School at Krotoshin
To 1919	Girls' High School in Poznan
To 1922	School-leaving exam at the High School at Hirschberg, Silesia
From 1922	Studies at the Polytechnic in Munich (in applied physics and aerodynamics)
1927	Diploma examination with partial examination in aeromechanics
1927	Employed by the German Aviation League at Berlin-Adlershof
1 May 1928	Dipl.-Ing. and scientific employee with the German Aviation Union; service in the high-altitude flight section
1 December 1928	Service with the Institute for Aerodynamics
July 1929	Registration as pilot trainee with the German Aviation Co. at Berlin-Staaken
September 1929	Gained the A intermediate licence in a Klemm L 20
To 1930	Gained the A, B, C2 and K2 licences
1931–2	Evaluation of experimental investigations on adjustable propellers
1935–6	Blind flying training with Deutsche Lufthansa at Hannover
1936–7	Continuation of blind flying training at Breslau
31 July 1936	Aerobatic demonstration at Berlin-Tempelhof in an He 70
1 November 1936	Employment with the Askania works as engineer pilot for equipment testing
9 November 1937	Nominated Flight Captain (second woman after Hanna Reitsch)
2 July 1938	Took part in the 'coast flight' from Königsberg to Wyk on Föhr Island
1939	Marriage to Professor Dr Alexander *Graf* Schenk von Stauffenberg
24 October 1939	Military service at the *Luftwaffe* Test Centre at Rechlin (E7); testing of bombs and aiming devices
October 1941	Several aiming dives with BZA 1 switchgear and four SC 250s (to December 1941)
22 January 1943	Decoration with the Iron Cross, Second Class, after 1,500 dives (mostly with Ju 87s and Ju 88s)
9 August 1943	Loss of cockpit canopy during an extreme dive with a Ju 87
16 November 1943	Overturned in a Ju 87 during braking
11 January 1944	Recommended for decoration with the Iron Cross, First Class
6 February 1944	Foundation of a research centre for special air equipment; leadership by Dipl.-Ing. *Gräfin* von Stauffenberg recommended by Imperial Marshal Hermann Göring
12 June 1944	Court registration of the research centre at Berlin-Charlottenburg
27 June 1944	Completion to date of 2,507 dives and 358 night flights
24 July 1944	Arrest after the attempt on Hitler's life
2 September 1944	Release on parole on instructions of the *Reichsführer SS*
November 1944	Continuation of testing of the night landing procedure at the Experimental Centre for Special Air Equipment at the *Luftwaffe* Technical Academy
16 February 1945	Removal of the experimental centre from Berlin-Gatow to the Würzburg area
25 March 1945	Removal of the experimental centre from Würzburg to Weimar-Nohra
8 April 1945	*Gräfin* von Stauffenberg shot down in a Bü 181 (GY+BL) near the community of Stephansposching west of Deggendorf, Bavaria by an Allied fighter aircraft.

Gräfin Stauffenberg carried out the majority of the dives during the testing of the Ju 87 and therefore made an extremely valuable contribution to the development of this bomber aircraft.

easier to maintain than the existing installations. As a result of the testing of the production prototypes – after the conclusion of the various loading exercises as well as all the previous bomb dropping experiments – in February 1942 a comprehensive technical operating instruction was produced for the free-fall armament under the fuselage and wings.

From the beginning of 1943 onwards the task, more and more, was to make massive attacks on enemy positions or to support German attacks from the air, in order to bring relief to divisions in combat with a numerically far superior enemy. For this purpose, according to the bureau chiefs' conference on 12 February 1943, besides the AB 70-4 bomb container (*Abwurfbehälter* – AB) (for fighter bomber operations), the AB 70-5 (SD 2 interrupted release from high altitude), the AB 250-1 (SD 2 from low-level flight) and the AB 250-2 (ballistic launch in low-level flight), as well as the AB 500 and AB 1000 with various contents, should be brought into action as soon as possible.

It was also ordered at the beginning of 1943 that the production of bomb containers filled with small bombs was to be increased from 7,000 to 10,000 a month, above all for the AB 250. The planned AB 1000 could still not be manufactured because by January 1943 its development was still not concluded. In any case, bomb containers larger than the AB 500 proved to be unsuited to the Ju 87.

Bomb Types

Tabulation RLM LC 7 II, Berlin, 27 September 1941

Designation	**Remarks**	**Names**
SD 2		
SD 50	(Pr, L, StG)	Dora
SC 50	(J/A, L)	Ida
SD 250	(StG, J/B, L)	Dolly
SC 250	(J/A, L)	Irma
SD 500		Dagmar
SD 500 A	(StG)	Diana
SD 500 E		Erna
SD 500 J	(L)	Lisa
SC 1000 L2	(formerly SC 1000)	Hermann
PC 1000	(formerly SD 1000)	Esau
PC 1000 nA	(new development)	Esau new type
PC 1400	(formerly SD 1400)	Fritz
PC 1400 II X		Fritz X
SD 1700	(formerly SC 1700)	Dietrich (formerly Siegfried, Sigismund)
SC 1800		Satan
SC 2500		Max
SC 2500	(St)	Steel Max
PC 500 RS	(formerly PC 500)	Pauline
PC 1000 RS	(formerly PC 1000)	Paul
PC 1800 RS	(formerly PC 1700)	Pirate

Note: The use of the SC 2500 was not possible with the Ju 87. Loads beyond the size of the SC 1000 were only used operationally in exceptional cases. Mostly this was done only in loading exercises by the Rechlin Test Centre.

Abbreviations for Free-Fall Ordnance

Abbreviation	Designation	Bomb Group
AB	Bomb container	Bomb dispensers
B	Incendiary bomb (Electron)	Incendiary bombs
Bl C	Cylindrical flash bomb	Illuminator bombs
BT	Torpedo bomb	Torpedo bombs
C	Incendiary bomb	Liquid-filled incendiary bombs
SA	High-explosive bomb	High-charge bombs I
SB	High-explosive bomb	High-charge bombs II
Sbe	Concrete splinter bomb	Mine bombs
SC	Cylindrical high-explosive bomb	Mine bombs
SD	Thick-walled high-explosive bomb	Splinter bombs
KC	Cylindrical chemical bomb	Special munitions
LC	Cylindrical illumination bomb	Illumination bombs
LM	Aerial mine	Aircraft mines
NC	Cylindrical smoke bomb	Smoke bombs
PC	Anti-tank bomb	Cylindrical anti-tank bombs
PD	Armour-piercing bomb	Thick-walled armour-piercing bombs
ZC	Cylindrical cement bomb	Practice bombs

Between March and May 1943, as Captain Haller reported to General Field Marshal Erhard Milch on 4 June 1943, the Ju 87 was mainly employed against field positions and enemy armour. For this SD 1 and SD 2 bombs were preferred.

The majority of the Ju 87 *Gruppen* in action in the *Luftflotte* 4 area were extremely successful in this and had good mechanical availability with their machines. Only in the undercarriage were there still problems; in particular breakages of the sprung legs resulted in various aircraft being out of action in the units. The reason lay in the often badly prepared or completely unprepared forward airfields in the east from which the crews had to operate.

The greater use of the Ju 87 D to support the army against massive enemy tank attacks, as well as cordoning them off, was extremely important to the progress of the war from the end of 1942 onwards. For this purpose, according to Engineer General Ernst Marquardt, the small SD 4 HL hollow-charge bomb was far superior to all large-calibre free-fall weapons. The probability of hits naturally rose with the number of Ju 87 Ds in operation, with which, according to action reports, carpet bombing was particularly effective.

The weapon was still not released for general use by Adolf Hitler, however, who felt that he alone was in charge of the matter. The operations were, therefore, the test phase of the 4-kg hollow-charge bomb against armoured targets. But the official release was not long delayed.

Retrofitting with an electric bomb selector switch (*Bombenziel-Anlage* – BZA), which was ordered on 7 January 1944 at the request of the General of Ground Attack Pilots, was intended to bring about an improvement in the bomb release installation. As the installation was inexpensive, the Test Centre Command was able to accept the prototype installation of a BZA 2 as early as the spring of 1944 and its installation could then be authorised for series production.

Soon afterwards, fifty Ju 87 Ds were ordered to be equipped with the BZA directly at their units on the authority of the General of Ground Attack Pilots, in order to gain the first practical experience quickly.

As there were insufficient numbers of the necessary equipment sets at Weser, the units planned for it were supposed to be retrofitted directly, as soon as BZA production had increased.

However, the cost in time and effort of the production of the BZA was significant and insufficient numbers of these devices were therefore available, so General Field Marshal Milch decided that their first installation would be in a later aircraft series. According to the Field Marshal, the BZA could also be installed in the course of repair work.

3.4.6.2 Fixed Armament

Because of continual requests from the front-line units, from the summer of 1941 onwards the first preliminary consideration was given to installing two fixed MG 151/20 cannon in the wings of the Ju 87. In December 1941 the provisional prototype installation was already well advanced. The first Ju 87 D-1 with full cannon armament (MG 151/20) could not, however, be completed until 15 March 1942.

The prototype construction took place at the Junkers works at Bernburg. The testing of the machine took place at the Tarnewitz Test Centre and went quite smoothly.

On 15 December 1942, following the development conference in Berlin, because of a proposal from the General Staff, 6th Division, consideration was given to whether all Ju 87 Ds for service over the eastern front could be equipped with two MG 151/20s. The wish for a stronger fixed armament, primarily for offensive use, led, from the beginning of 1943 onwards, to the successive strengthening of the weapons installation, beginning with the D-3 series.

Besides being equipped with two 20-mm weapons in the wings, the Ju 87 D series was envisaged for use with two weapons containers (*Waffenbehältern* – WB). The capability to carry

This Ju 87 D-3 was equipped with a flame eliminator and two WB 81 weapons containers and flew on night and dusk operations in the southern sector of the eastern front.

Close-up of the WB 81 as it was used with Ju 87 D-3s in low-level attacks over Transylvania.

this type of additional armament was first required by the RLM on 19 October 1942. After practical testing by the Rechlin Test Centre up to mid-December 1942, by 30 December an appropriate refit instruction had been written at Junkers; on 15 January 1943 it was issued to the front-line units, who then had to provide for retrofitting on their own account.

The weapons containers could be hung from the two wing racks as external loads without further changes. It was only necessary to install a few small parts and electrical cables in the Ju 87 D airframe.

Thus, on the right, under the bomb selection switch, the switch box for the two WB 81s was installed with a selection switch and push button. On the lower right side of the pilot's space was the fusing switch box. From there cables ran inside both wings to the underhung weapons containers. Only seven hours were necessary for installation, as long as two experienced technicians were available.

Because of its high fire density, this additional armament was suited above all to attack on massed targets in low-level flight – troop concentrations or columns of march.

The additional armament was fired through the EPD-FF, the electric-pneumatic actuator valve, by the pilot, aiming with the reflector sight.

Two different versions of the WB 81 weapons container, with three MG 81 Z twin machine-guns each, were introduced:

- WB 81 A, aimed forwards and downwards (15°)
- WB 81 B, aimed parallel to the aircraft's longitudinal axis

Even in the summer of 1947 Ju 87 D wrecks were still to be found on the airfield of Zeltweg in Austria.

In order to spread the fire, the outside machine-guns were installed pointing 0.5° outwards. The containers were 2.5 metres long, with a diameter of only 0.5 metres. Without ammunition, the WB 81 weighed only 140 kg, with about 500 rounds per MG 81 Z, about 180 kg.

In spite of the effect of the weapons, the additional armament was not particularly liked by the crews, as the containers reduced the speed of the Ju 87 Ds attacking in low-level flight, so that the enemy flak had a better chance of hitting the machines.

3.4.7 Undercarriage

The undercarriage of the Ju 87 was altered many times in order to deal with a steadily increasing take-off weight. In the Ju 87 D-1 version, the tailwheel of the Ju 87 B-2 was initially still installed, as the larger tailwheel of the D version was not available in sufficient quantity until the beginning of 1942. The same was true of the complete main undercarriage of the Ju 87 B-2 series which was installed at first.

From March 1943 onwards, a change order was issued by the RLM which envisaged a displacement of the wheel axis to the rear by 90 mm in order to permanently improve the stability on the ground for all current (and future) Ju 87 series.

A second essential change concerned safety in an emergency landing. The explosively jettisonable main undercarriage required by the RLM was first static-tested by the Rechlin Test Centre in a still immature variant in the early summer of 1942. Next, from March 1943 onwards, came the testing of the strength of such an installation. Dropping the undercarriage legs was intended to make possible a belly landing with the Ju 87 D, even on unfavourable terrain, without excessively endangering the crew. For this purpose, one explosive charge was installed for each undercarriage leg. At first, installation only in the D-1 to D-5 was considered, but later, machines up to the D-7 and the G-1 and G-2 tank hunters were added. As the charge initially selected was too big and caused damage to the airframe, in the beginning of 1944

After the Ju 87 R-4, the Ju 87 D-1, D-3 and D-5 construction series became the new standard. The R versions, however, remained in service for some time; here is a machine of I/StG 1 with four bundles of five SC 10 bombs under the wings.

a reduced charge was installed with improved safety. The retrofit could be undertaken by four installers within five hours. Mostly, however, the conversion was undertaken in the repair shop at Wels.

The explosive device could be fired only up to a maximum speed of 250 kph, as otherwise both machine and crew were endangered.

As an alternative to the wheeled undercarriage of the Ju 87 D-1, equipment with skis was possible. On the express instructions of the RLM, a refit instruction was issued by 10 February 1942 and sent to the front-line units. The skis could first be installed on the rearwards-displaced main undercarriage of the Ju 87 D. Besides the movable skis for the main undercarriage, a smaller ski was developed for the tail.

The work led to the manufacture of two production prototypes. The installation of the skis on the faired undercarriage was tested by the Rechlin Test Centre in June 1942 and was authorised by the RLM and released for construction.

4 Large-Scale Production

4.1 Production Guidelines

In April 1934 the main aircraft manufacturers received the guidelines for the development of a heavy dive bomber. In the course of the following year numerous questions of detail were clarified, in order to improve the future equipment of the planned machines.

At the beginning of 1936 the RLM Technical Bureau (LC II) initiated a renewed comparison between the currently available aircraft and the modern military machines which were known to exist in other European countries.

As a result, it was decided on 17 March 1936 to put through 'a thorough qualitative improvement of the air equipment', as it was believed that Germany would fall behind with the guidelines issued to the German aviation industry hitherto. One aspect of this improvement was the effort to create an effective dive bomber as soon as possible.

On 22 March 1936 the chief of the Technical Bureau issued instructions that both the heavy dive bombers, the Ju 87 as well as the He 118, must be manufactured immediately. As an acceptable, and perhaps even better, performance was expected from the Ar 81, a limited series order was issued for this aircraft as well. For this reason another competitor, the Ha 137, a small, solidly built and, in addition, single-seater low-wing aircraft was not to be

Machines such as this Ju 87 A-2 of I/StG 162 were manufactured only in limited quantities because of their low performance.

Under test in Spain the Ju 87 Bs showed themselves to be more powerful than the Ju 87 As which had been in service there previously, and higher production quantities resulted.

developed further and was to be built only as a production prototype. The reason for this decision lay in the bomb releases carried out from diving flight at Rechlin in 1935. As a result, the Technical Bureau had come to the conclusion that low-wing aircraft were completely unsuitable as dive bombers. Only the Ju 87 and He 118 were therefore to be used further for study or as training aircraft.

At the end of October 1935, therefore, planning envisaged the initial construction of seven Ju 87s. Of these the first machine was supposed to be manufactured in May 1936, the last in August 1938.

Even before the comparison flights arranged for July 1936 between the Ar 81, the He 118 and the Ju 87, on 22 May 1936 came the increase in manufacture of the zero series Ju 87 A-0 version from seven to eleven. The machines were to be received by Construction Acceptance, Air (BAL) at the Junkers works between October and December 1936. As a new guideline, the conversion from the Jumo 210 A to the more powerful Jumo 210 F was ordered, although in the early summer of 1936 it was still far from certain at what time the first of these engines would leave the series production line. Compared to the equipment hitherto, the zero series aircraft were supposed to have a FuG VII radio instead of the FuG VI. Further, a homing device, the installation of a better oxygen system and complete interference suppression of the electrical system were prescribed by the Technical Bureau. As a dive bombing sight, an improved Stuvi A2 was required.

Besides the movable MG 15 machine-gun, the machines were to have a fixed MG 17 built into the right wing. A mock-up of the weapons installation had already been completed at Junkers in March 1936. Thereupon, firing trials were to be undertaken as quickly as possible so as to obtain practical results. The dive bomber developed at Junkers was, however, still far from being capable of dive bombing. Numerous technical deficiencies came to light in the flights with the Ju 87 V2 carried out at Rechlin in the spring of 1936. For example the oil system necessary for diving flight was lacking, so that at first steep dives had to be postponed. Without it, the oil circulation was not assured in diving flight.

Only in the summer of 1936 did it become clear that the heavy dive bomber from Dessau would make the running. Neither the Ar 81 nor the He 118 had come through in the comparison flights at Rechlin.

Meanwhile the development work had made further progress. In October 1936 the Ju 87 V4 (works no. 4924, D-UBIP) received the new dive brakes under both wings and thereby became the production prototype for the A series version.

From December onwards the front-line test began, the actual service testing of the first Ju 87 A-0s. Even before its conclusion in April 1937 the current order of Ju 87 A-0s was increased from eleven to thirteen on 15 October 1936. The last of these machines were to be delivered by March 1937 at the latest.

At the same time a first order was placed for 216 Ju 87 A-1s which were intended to leave the workshops at Junkers between January 1936 and March 1938. As the capacity of Junkers was fully occupied, licensing to other production facilities was necessary. An initial order for the manufacture of 35 Ju 87 A-1s was therefore transferred to the Weser Aircraft Co. Ltd.

As the Ju 87 A-1 could only conditionally fulfill the performance demanded of it, the original production volume was reduced again. Instead, the improved Ju 87 A-2 version was ordered, together with the more effective Ju 87 B series. In view of the great importance attached to the Ju 87 dive bomber, it is not surprising that more than 360 Ju 87 As and Bs had been manufactured at two plants alone (Dessau and Bremen) by the beginning of the war on 1 September 1939.

Up to 30 September 1939, according to the annual balance sheet of the Junkers Aircraft and Engine Works (JFM) at Dessau, a total of RM 2,365,196.00 was billed for Ju 87 construction orders. For various development orders in this area a further RM 243,646.00 was billed to the *Reich*.

According to the report of the Audit and Trust AG in Berlin up to the financial year end on 30 September 1941, RM 3,059,000.00 was billed for Ju 87 airframes up to this time. By the end of June 1940 697 Ju 87 B-1s and 129 B-2s had already come off the production lines. Besides these, 105 Ju 87 R-1s and seven R-2s had left

The Ju 87 B-1s (these are machines of IV (St)/LG 1) were soon replaced by the B-2 and R-2 versions.

final assembly. For the Ju 87 B-1 and B-2, there was still an order for ninety-six machines on 1 July 1940. As the range of the Ju 87 B had not satisfied the demands of the front-line units at all, production had inevitably gone over to the long-range versions, the Ju 87 R-1 and R-2. After 105 R-1s, series production was converted to the R-2, of which 616 aircraft were ordered.

At the same time, development work was directed towards a fundamentally improved 'Stuka', the Ju 87 D-1, which was to come off the assembly line as soon as possible. Four hundred and ninety-five of these machines were ordered at once. According to the plan, production was supposed to begin in May 1941 and be completed by March 1942. The immense production quantities could not, however, be completed according to the schedule predicted by the RLM, as a new standard bomber for the *Luftwaffe*, the Ju 88, occupied a large part of the Junkers production capacity. In face of this, shortfalls developed in Ju 87 production at Dessau.

For this reason, on 23 February 1942 General Field Marshal Erhard Milch appeared at Weser (WFG) and demanded that the plant catch up immediately on the Ju 87 production shortfalls which had also occurred there. Moreover, according to Milch, the plant would have to adapt to a new and fundamentally increased delivery programme, starting on 1 May 1942. Should these delivery plans not be met, 'the severest penalties' were threatened.

As the complete fulfilment of his demands would have required at least 700 new workers and numerous skilled workers were eliminated because they had received call-up papers from the *Wehrmacht*, the situation for Weser looked bleak.

Thanks to help from the Junkers works, it was possible to make 300 new employees available immediately and, in the medium term, to obtain Russian prisoners of war as well as Russian civilian workers. By taking some of the skilled workers from every other area of the firm and putting them onto the Ju 87 programme, as well as by countless hours of overtime and extra work, it was possible to catch up the shortfall.

On 2 May 1942 Dipl.-Ing. Feilcke (WFG) reported this gratifying development to the Chief of Testing and Development, whereupon the spirits of the RLM rose and WFG received a highly official commendation.

As a result of the losses which had occurred meanwhile, the *Luftwaffe* demanded ever greater supplies of factory-new Ju 87s. Therefore, in mid-May 1942, as had been intended earlier, Engineer General Walter Hertel, the chief of the procurement bureaux, examined the possibility of an increase in the rate of Ju 87 production. Based on the fact that each new Ju 87 *Geschwader* required 100 machines as initial equipment, as well as a monthly supply of twenty Ju 87s, an immediate increase in the monthly production quota was expected.

The production situation was extremely tight because of wartime conditions, so that the

The Ju 87 B-2, manufactured in large numbers, was the standard version of the 'Stuka' for several years. The machines shown here flew with 7/StG 51.

desired increase in output at first seemed impossible. Not until the period June–December 1942 did sufficient capacity become available to be able to produce eighty Ju 87s a month. In March 1943 an additional ten 'Stukas' a month were to be built, and from April onwards a further twenty, i.e. 100 machines in total. A precondition for this was a reduction in the manufacture of the BV 138 reconnaissance flying boat by Blohm & Voss; besides this, the manufacture of wing outer sections for the Fw 200 four-engined, long-range bomber and reconnaissance aircraft at WFG would have to be abandoned. In addition a further problem became apparent: the delivery of a sufficient quantity of aero engines. Hertel, however, wanted to take these from the current production programme for the Me 323 'Giant' transporter.

By the beginning of June 1942, however, it was apparent that the increase in Ju 87 production would not be achievable until March 1943, but would then increase to 120 machines a month. Once the licence work on the maritime reconnaissance BV 138 had been shut down, little else would stand in the way of fulfilling the new quotas, other than delivery slippages of certain equipment parts and the perennial shortage of personnel.

On 17 August 1942, in spite of all the bottlenecks, it was ordered that production of the Ju 87 was now to increase to 150 machines per month. On the other hand, more and more equipment parts were missing for Ju 87 D airframes that were already partly built. The situation with certain undercarriage parts was the tightest.

Because of the extremely critical situation in the east, from September 1942 onwards General Field Marshal Milch demanded the fastest possible increase in Ju 87 production to 350 machines per month, an output which was, quite simply, not achievable.

Shortly thereafter, on 6 October 1942, he forcefully ordered that the desired construction quantities were to be achieved immediately in order to meet the most urgent needs of the *Luftwaffe* at least halfway. At the very least an output of 300 per month was necessary. With the existing industrial capacity, such an increase could not be engineered. For that reason the GL/A (Defence Economy) department of the RLM as well as the Industry Council were

Ju 87 B-2s were delivered with either the VS 5 adjustable propeller (like the B-2 of 2/StG 2 shown here) or with the VS 11.

supposed to come up with more feasible recommendations. By 20 October 1942, however, only a few reports had been prepared, as the Bureau's task of moving whole plants to the east, especially to Slovakia or Poland, could not be completed in a few days.

First, Engineer Colonel Georg-Bernhard Alpers, department head of GL/C-B2, who was responsible for all aircraft procurement, went to Slovakia in order to assess the possibilities for a partial removal of Ju 87 production. The buildings inspected there made possible the production of only twenty-five Ju 87s per month at most. This was 30 per cent of the machines needed for the fulfilment of the current production requirement. It was hoped, however, that the machine tools needed for production could be procured with relatively few problems from Italy and neutral Switzerland.

The Slovakian administration wanted to provide the 3,500–4,000 craftsmen and labourers necessary; technical management personnel, by contrast, were to be provided by Weser. The Slovakian allies, however, demanded 25 per cent of production for the equipment of their own air forces. The production rate of twenty-five Ju 87s per month seemed too small to the Chief of Testing and Development – he demanded at least fifty machines per month. Later, after the new production plant was completely equipped, General Field Marshal Milch's planning predicted the monthly final assembly of a total of 150 Ju 87s in several decentralised plants.

There was a sudden collapse of production in October 1942. After a warehouse at WFG burned down, there was a shortage of undercarriage halves and tailwheels. It was hoped, however, that the shortfall could be made up by the end of the year through extra work.

On 1 December 1942 Junkers Director Carl Frydag spoke against a third production site in Slovakia.

Up to January 1943 these arrangements sufficed, according to the directives that were in force, to produce another 407 Ju 87s. Director Carl Frydag, as a member of the *Luftwaffe* Industry Council, reported that in the medium term 120 Ju 87s could be manufactured at the Bremen plant and 230 at the Berlin-Tempelhof plant. His main hopes lay in taking over the enormous maintenance hangar of the Berlin-Tempelhof airport. There, in a length of 500 metres, two complete production lines for fuselage and wing construction could be housed. In order to prevent a lengthy production failure, two complete sets of Ju 87 instructions and jigs were to be assembled and housed in a bomb-proof site.

For political reasons and in spite of the doubts of Junkers (JFM) and Weser (WFG), General Field Marshal Milch next ordered that the Slovakian Aircraft Co. was to receive an initial order for 100 machines. The majority of the workers to be assigned there later for Ju 87 production were to be trained at Weser. Because of the unfavourable initial situation – in particular numerous special machines were lacking – a production start-up was reckoned on not earlier than the late summer of 1944.

On 22 December 1942 General Field Marshal Milch issued a new order that production was to be brought up to the required output quantities very quickly in order to assure supplies for the front-line units. As early as the beginning of 1943 it was possible to reach the prescribed production numbers at WFG again, and the most urgent needs of the front-line units were at least in part fulfilled.

The evaluation of numerous operations reports had shown that only with sufficient close air support could Soviet units be brought to a standstill within a short time after a breakthrough. A precondition was, however, regional air superiority. The use of fast fighter bombers, such as the Fw 190, was thus advantageous. The path was set once more to turn away from the Ju 87.

The discussion in Study 1014 of the production programme replaced Study 1013 only a few weeks later. The reworked production planning provided the basis for decision-making for the forthcoming conference with Imperial Marshal Hermann Göring. The essence of this study was a reduction of aircraft production in the dive bomber and ground attack aircraft sectors. Each month only 40 Hs 129s with 14N engines from Gnome & Rhône as well as an additional maximum of 200 Ju 87 Ds with Jumo 211s (or Jumo 213s) were to be manufactured.

The current General of Bomber Pilots also saw at the beginning of 1943 that the further development of the Ju 87 would hardly bring any further tactical value. He therefore favoured a continual reduction of its manufacture as well as a rapid conversion to the single-engined Fw 190 fighter bomber. In contrast, Major-General Adolf Galland held the concept that the robust Ju 87 and Hs 129 should not be rejected prematurely, but that a monthly production of 150 machines was entirely sufficient. The maximum number of units equipped with these ground attack aircraft should not exceed eight *Geschwader*.

Despite some doubts, on 5 February 1943 Ju 87 production was increased from 125 machines per month to 150. The planned production start-up of the Ju 87 F with the Jumo 213 engine had, however, to be postponed as the necessary capacity was not available at the Junkers works. Thus the use of the proven Jumo 211 J in-line engine continued initially.

In order to increase production to more than 125 new machines per month, General Field Marshal Milch demanded the immediate erection of a second production line at Berlin-Tempelhof.

In February 1943 Ju 87 production was therefore once again on the daily orders. Colonel Kurt Kleinrath, chief of Department 6 on the *Luftwaffe* General Staff, regarded the monthly final assembly of 150 Ju 87s as insufficient to ensure a successful coastal defence in the Mediterranean area and a powerful deployment in the east.

As sufficient capacity for yet another increase in the production rate was not available at WFG, the idea of a third final assembly plant in Slovakia came to life again. Although innumerable problems had to be reckoned with, work began on putting the idea into effect. A little later the first Slovakian workers arrived at WFG for training in the construction of metal aircraft.

In March 1943 for the first time 140 machines left the WFG production plant. This corresponded exactly to the quota. Even so, the riveting of more than half of these machines exhibited numerous defects. After the amendment of the riveting procedure, all subsequent machines were in order in this respect and could be accepted without problems. At any rate, no further complaints about this issue came back from the *Geschwader*.

On 11 May 1943, during a Bureau Chiefs' conference in Berlin, the discussion came back again to the problem of a replacement for the Ju 87. As the planned new 'armoured aircraft' (see Chapter 11) had scarcely any chance of becoming reality, the further construction of the Ju 87 remained the only option. It was the only

The conversion of Ju 87 R-4 production to the D-1 construction series brought the units a significant increase in performance in tank hunting. The machine shown here belonged to the 10th Staffel *of StG 77.*

way of satisfying the needs of the operational units with the means currently available.

In order to catch up the shortfalls in the production of the Ju 87, in May 1943, as an exception, 167 machines were supposed to be built. In the event, however, only 155 Ju 87 Ds could be completed.

On 28 July 1943 the guidelines for the setting up of a new air defence programme were issued. The programme, however, seemed practicable only to the extent that the production of all types would be reduced – with the exception of fighters and destroyers, whose numbers were to rise strongly. From the summer of 1943 particular importance was given to the Bf 109 G, the Fw 190 A, F and G, and the Ju 88 C night fighter. But Milch decreed on 3 August 1943 that these directives were not to affect the production of the Ju 87, Ju 188, Ju 288 and Ju 290, in order to maintain offensive possibilities in the conduct of the air war.

This was all the more important as the average life expectancy of the Ju 87s had been reduced since 1941 from 9.5 to 5.5 months. After an average of 100 flying hours (instead of 145) the machine, statistically, was lost. Up to the late summer of 1943 the life expectancy of operational aircraft fell still further as a result of the increased potential of the enemy.

With this the end of the further use of the Ju 87 D over the eastern front came in sight. As early as 26 October 1943 the General of Ground Attack Pilots (*General der Schlachtflieger* – GdS) described the planned withdrawal of the Ju 87 from November 1944 onwards as far too late, as this type would no longer be capable of surviving in operations. The Hs 129, in the opinion of the GdS, would also in the future no longer be successful in attacking tanks, unless the ground attack units received new armaments in the form of a specific anti-tank bomb or some other special weapon.

Hence, the Fighting General of Ground Attack Pilots believed it was absolutely essential to force on the Fw 190 F as quickly as possible as a ground attack aircraft. General Field Marshal Milch shared this opinion and additionally ordered a sufficient reserve of Jumo 211 J powerplants for the Ju 87 D-3 and D-5, so that the use of the 'Stuka' would be assured for a certain transition period, even after its official withdrawal.

On 11 January 1944 Major-General Dipl.-Ing. Wolfgang Vorwald decided that a large proportion of the still available Ju 87 D-3s and D-5s should in future be used as night ground attack aircraft with special equipment. He also saw in the twin-engined Siebel Si 204 transport aircraft, whose production start-up was practically decided, a sure replacement for the Ju 87.

The first two Si 204 production prototypes (V22 and V23), which were to serve experimentally as night ground attackers, were expected for 1 April 1944. From July 1944 onwards the production of the Si 204 E was supposed to begin with twenty to thirty machines per month. The Si 204 E, however, could only partly fulfil what was expected of it.

By 15 February 1944 a shortfall in Ju 87 D production of 178 machines had accumulated. Twenty Ju 87s could not be delivered, as no weapons were available.

In May 1944 seventy-eight new Ju 87 Ds were manufactured; a further sixty-nine machines were cleared for service after repair. In the next six months a further 438 Ju 87 Ds and Gs could be added to the supply circuit as new or repaired aircraft. Whether a few Ju 87s could still be assembled from parts after December 1944 could not be established with certainty. Further information on the production of the later Ju 87 Ds can be found in section 3.3.5.

4.2 Production and Repair Plants

4.2.1 Junkers Ltd

As a result of insufficient production capacity, the series production of the Ju 87 A at Junkers began only slowly. Thus the first five production machines of the Ju 87 A-0 heavy dive bomber only left final assembly at the Junkers Aircraft and Engine Works Ltd (JFM) at Dessau from the end of 1936 onwards; two more took until March 1937.

In October 1936 there was already a far larger order at Junkers, which comprised 210 Ju 87 A-1s, but it was reduced in the spring of 1937 to 187 machines in favour of the improved Ju 87 B-1. Delivery Plan LP 5 of April 1937 forecast an average monthly production of twenty-five Ju 87 A-1s at Junkers up to the conversion to the

Ju 87 B-1. The whole order was completed by the early summer of 1938. The supplement of 3 June 1938 to Aircraft Procurement Programme No. 8 brought an increase from 394 to 2,207 Ju 87 Bs. The drastic increase in the production numbers was supposed to be assured by ten-hour shifts and a 15 per cent increase in the workforce. A check on these directives, however, showed that such production figures were scarcely achievable under the above conditions.

For that reason, apart from the remaining Ju 87 A-1s, ninety-eight Ju 87 B-1s were added, starting in 1938, whose manufacture was to be carried out by 31 July 1938. From August 1938 onwards the production of the series order which had expanded to 352 Ju 87 Bs was the main preoccupation at Junkers. The machines were to be delivered by 31 March 1940 at the latest. Junkers then received a further order which again fundamentally increased the number of Ju 87 B-2s to be produced at the home plant.

By 30 June 1940 the first 311 Ju 87 B-1s and twenty-nine Ju 87 B-2s had been completed at Dessau. The remaining seventeen Ju 87 B-2s were expected by September 1940. The production of the Ju 87 R, as well as the whole of the work on the essentially more powerful Ju 87 D prototypes and production prototypes, were given over to the Weser Aircraft Co. Ltd in the Bremen area.

At the Junkers works about 550 Ju 87 A-0s, A-1s, A-2s, B-1s and B-2s were thus built or converted.

The majority of the approximately 6,500 Ju 87s produced originated from the Weser Aircraft Co. Ltd, with 5,930 machines.

4.2.2 Weser Aircraft Co. Ltd

4.2.2.1 Production in the Bremen Area

The history of the Weser Aircraft Co. Ltd (WFG) began on 1 June 1934 with the take-over in Berlin of the Rohrbach Metal Aircraft Co. Ltd. On 22 September 1934 land was obtained at Deschimag in the Bremen industrial harbour area and, from the end of 1934 onwards, the retraining of personnel as metal aircraft builders and other craftsmen for the Weser Aircraft Co. Ltd, called Weser for short, was started.

Under the leadership of Shipbuilding Director Dipl.-Ing. Fritz Feilcke, an effective

Production of the Ju 87 at the WFG works at Lemwerder.

New Ju 87 D-5s (with MG 151/20 cannon in the wings) leave the production line at Lemwerder. (Federal Archives)

aviation concern with 28,978 employees arose out of part of the shipyard business. The business was based not only in Bremen but also in Delmenhorst, Einswarden, Lemwerder and Nordenham. Together with the production site arranged later at Berlin-Tempelhof, other branch plants as well as various suppliers were merged into the Weser Aircraft Co. Ltd.

Feilcke functioned until the end of the war as the so-called Chief Manager and was at the same time the Technical Director of the concern. Besides the construction of the home plant at Bremen, plants followed next at Delmenhorst as well as Einswarden, where a former shipyard was taken over.

Up to the end of 1935 the plant was occupied with the construction of airframes for the Do 23 twin-engined medium bomber, wings and tails for the Ju W 34 single-engined freight aircraft, and wings for the Ju 86 medium bomber. The licence production of thirty-six Ju W 34(S)s and forty-four He 60 multi-purpose maritime aircraft followed. At the beginning of 1936 the earlier Rohrbach works in Berlin was dissolved, whereupon the concern expanded further in the lower Weser area. At Lemwerder the construction preparations began for a large final assembly works and, from 15 March 1936 onwards, the layout of an airfield. The airfield was at the same time built as an operational facility for the *Luftwaffe* using *Reich* resources. Several larger shops were built, for example a hangar of more than 2,500 square metres and a combined assembly hall of 4,300 square metres floor area. At the same time the construction of workshops, offices and powerplant and several smaller buildings began. Another assembly shop, built by 1940, had an area of almost 10,000 square metres, of which a total of 6,520 square metres could be used for aircraft assembly. The Weser Aircraft Co. Ltd finally consisted of several large main plants:

Plant 1	Bremen (land of Deschimag Co. Ltd, Weser)
Plant 2	Bremen (land in the Bremen industrial harbour)
Plant 3	Delmenhorst (formerly German Linoleum Works Co. Ltd)
Plant 4	Einswarden (formerly land of the Einswarden shipyard)
Plant 5	Lemwerder (formerly marshland at Lemwerder)
Plant 6	Nordenham (former maritime air field at Nordenham)
Plant 7	Berlin-Tempelhof (former hangars of the large airport)

Thanks to intense efforts, parts manufacture for aircraft could begin in a part of the Lemwerder section in October 1936.

To the aircraft already mentioned and twenty Do 18 flying boats were added for the first time thirty-five Ju 87 dive bombers in the framework of a licensed order.

At first Weser received the appropriate tooling from Junkers as well as prefabricated assemblies for the production of the Ju 87. The licensed construction of the Ju 87 was carried out according to Delivery Plan LP 4 of 1 November 1936. From October 1937 onwards the first dive bombers were to leave final assembly and be test flown. The number of Ju 87s was increased on 7 April 1937 in the context of Delivery Plan LP 5 to a total of seventy A-1 machines and a monthly manufacture of ten machines was required from Weser. The RLM soon changed this, cancelling the existing order and issuing an order for thirty-five newly built Ju 87 A-1s and 40 Ju 87 B-1s. Soon afterwards the number of Ju 87 As and Bs to be produced increased to 112 machines, after which an order for the construction of a further thirty-seven Ju 87 B-1s was added in March 1937. Besides Lemwerder, the Delmenhorst plant (tail construction), and the Karman plant at Osnabrück (fuselage construction) were involved in the production of the Ju 87. The latter subsequently manufactured the cockpit canopies, the Jumo powerplant cowlings and the undercarriage fairings.

The first two machines built at Lemwerder, two Ju 87 A-1s, were completed in the late autumn of 1937. The first of these was presented on 15 December 1937 at a so-called company parade of the Weser Aircraft Co. Ltd in the presence of Director Thiedemann. On 26 February 1938 this machine successfully completed its first flight at Lemwerder before representatives of the Junkers works. A month later, on 31 March 1938, the second Ju 87 A built at Weser took off; at least three more followed by the end of April 1938.

As an extensive conversion operation was still run at Lemwerder (among others, for Ju 52s, Ju 86s, Ju 88s and Ju 90s), the workshop capacity was continually fully occupied, so that a significant increase in production quantities was hardly to be considered.

From 1938 onwards, the operation at Lemwerder was led by Dipl.-Ing. Gottfried Loew, to whom the management of the Bremen plant was also assigned four years later. Over the years demands changed continually. The need for dive bombers increased in accordance with the growth of the *Luftwaffe*.

Unusual view of the cockpit of the Ju 87, well protected against gunfire from the front. At the controls sits Junior Under Officer Josef Reitinger.

Delivery Plans 5a, 6 and 7 followed, according to which the production of the Ju 87 was to increase progressively. In March 1938 licence orders were in place for thirty-five Ju 87 A-1s and 740 Ju 87 B-1s. Finally a production rate of eighty machines per month was demanded. LP 8 envisaged only 800 machines, LP 10 more than 1,000, LP 16 only 700, but LP 18 envisaged 1,100, which were to be manufactured by the spring of 1941.

It was thus inevitable that the licensed production operations would have to be reorganised. The production processes were examined and made more efficient, in order to meet the requirement for a higher rate of production. Thus, at the start of Ju 87 A production about 6,000 production items indicated on drawings were in use; by the thousandth machine this was to increase to about 18,000. Only the excellent infrastructure at Weser enabled the licensed production programme to some extent be developed in the framework already laid down.

The conversion work had a disruptive effect on this effort and, because of its high cost in labour, seriously affected the mass production of the Ju 87 B from the outset.

By 31 December 1938, therefore, 136 Ju 87s were delivered from Lemwerder. Together with the seven completed in 1937, this gave a total of 143 dive bombers.

Only with the displacement of the disruptive conversion work to Berlin-Tempelhof was more space made available at Lemwerder for the mass production of the Ju 87 B. In the second assembly hall another production line was installed immediately for the Ju 87, so that fuselage frames delivered from outside could have their whole equipment installed simultaneously.

In 1939 alone 577 Ju 87s were listed in the monthly reports from WFG Bremen-Lemwerder. According to these, a total of 720 dive bombers were assembled in the Bremen area by 31 December 1939. Up to June 1940, however, compilations of the RLM show only 598 Ju 87 B-1s, B-2s, R-1s and R-2s built entirely at Bremen, as at first numerous large parts were delivered by rail from Junkers.

In the summer of 1940 the order volume still comprised sixty-nine Ju 87 B-2s, 609 R-2s and, for the time being, 495 D-1s. The series production of the remaining B and R machines took place from July 1940 onwards and was supposed to last until October 1940 for the B-2s, until August 1941 for the R-2s and for the D-1s at least until March 1942. Because of problems

These dive bomber pilots, who later became well known, seem very pleased with the Ju 87 B. Left to right: Bruno Dilley, Kurt Kuhlmey and Franz Tisch.

with the delivery of items of equipment, however, especially engines, and because of a tight situation with the supply of raw materials, there were numerous delays during subsequent months.

In addition, Allied air attacks or overflights in the greater Bremen area caused production shutdowns as at first air raid warnings were sounded prematurely. It was still believed that the flak defences were adequate, but doubts increased as the incursions of British bombers over the north German centres of industry grew steadily in intensity. As an immediate measure the management of the Weser Aircraft Co. Ltd, together with the state authorities, had dispersed all branches of manufacture in the Bremen area. The risk that all production would come to a halt in the event of a heavy air attack was thereby reduced, but because of the proximity of the individual plants, it was not entirely excluded.

Meanwhile the Bremen production facilities of WFG, as the main producer of the Ju 87, had great significance for the *Luftwaffe*. Production at the Lemwerder final assembly works in 1940 already comprised 579 Ju 87 aircraft, and the total of WFG production there reached 1,299 airframes.

On 27 February 1941 the delivery of the thousandth Ju 87 completed by Weser at the Bremen works took place. Imperial Marshal Hermann Göring sent a congratulatory telegram:

> I give you my special recognition of the outstanding achievements in your aircraft production, with which you have made an essential contribution to the build-up of the German air defence.
>
> Signed: Göring

By the end of August 1939 266 Ju 87s had been delivered. Between 1 September 1939 and 27 February 1941 the production rate climbed steeply; a further 734 machines followed. In addition, in February 1941 another 1,280 Ju 87 Ds were ordered for delivery by 31 March 1942 at the latest. In the event, however, only 763 of these machines were produced, as a large part of the production was displaced to Berlin-Tempelhof.

In total 1,763 Ju 87 As to Ds had originated in the Bremen works up till then. In 1941 more machines than ever before were completed and flight tested at Lemwerder. The monthly reports show a figure of 651. On 31 December 1941 the number of Ju 87s built at Bremen since 1937 stood at 1,950.

Between 1 January 1942 and 31 August 1944, according to information provided by the former plant manager, Dipl.-Ing. Gottfried Loew, 1,409 Ju 87s were made ready and equipped. Of these 102 went through final assembly up to the end of 1942, another 1,001 in 1943 and 306 in the following year.

For the period ending 31 December 1942 a total of 3,530 Ju 87s at Weser appear in the monthly reports on the completion of front-line machines and machines assigned to reserve units. In February 1943 this total reached 3,797 and in April 1943 4,109. General Field Marshal Milch in his capacity as Chief of Testing and Development and Inspector General of the *Luftwaffe* took this as the occasion, on 26 May 1943, to express his thanks to the Weser Aircraft Co. Ltd:

> Dear Mr Feilcke
>
> The deliveries from your Bremen and Berlin works have fulfilled the progress required by me every month and have even exceeded it from month to month.
>
> An even greater value is to be placed on this achievement as, in the face of a steeply rising increase in production, you had to put through extensive removals with great difficulty and had to suffer heavily from enemy action.
>
> In April you and your subordinates were able to bring forth a jubilee machine. The production quantity reached a height that has never before been achieved by a single works in the production of a single type of aircraft.
>
> I ask you to convey to all those involved my recognition and my best congratulations!
>
> Heil Hitler!
>
> Signed: Milch, General Field Marshal

The achievements to date were plain to see: in the first half year of 1943 exactly 145 machines per month had been produced. For the previous years up to the cessation of production, the following total picture thus emerged at Weser:

Year	Total Number	Monthly Average
1937	7	2
1938	136	11
1939	577	48
1940	769	64
1941	1,074	90
1942	967	90
1943	1,629	135
1944	771	96

Between 1938 and 1944 3,172 Ju 87s of Bremen and Lemwerder production left the Lemwerder flight testing operation. To this must be added numerous Ju 87s which had been damaged in crashes or by enemy action and were overhauled or repaired at Weser.

The leadership of the Lemwerder flight testing was in the hands of Flight Captain Gerhard Hubrich, accompanied by works pilots and partly by Flight Captains Vitus Bork, Hellmuth Florich, Bert Langhoff and Rudolf Schoenert. According to Herbert Wenz, the 4,000th flight test at the Weser Aircraft Co. Ltd took place in April 1943.

According to information from the plant, 3,820 of the total of 5,930 Ju 87s were built by the summer of 1944. This figure comes from the monthly reports on completion of front-line machines.

According to these sources, production in the Bremen area ceased in May 1944 with thirty-five machines. For the first five months of 1944 production of 341 Ju 87 Ds was reported.

From the middle of the war, production was sustained, and indeed increased, only by the use of conscripts, prisoners of war and convicts. At Altenesch, Einswarden, Nordenham and Lemwerder there were camps for civilian workers. More than 600 employees were concentrated at WFG in Nordenham. Two hundred workers were housed at Brake near Einswarden. At Altenesch there were more than 800 people who were employed at Lemwerder; at Delmenhorst more than 1,500 workers, some prisoners of war, were available for production in two separate camps.

Instead of Ju 87 D production, from the summer of 1944 onwards the completion of Fw 190 A-8s was begun, and seventy-four machines were delivered by 31 December 1944 and a further 150 by the cessation of production in April 1945. For this task an external command of the Flossenburg concentration camp was lodged in a new branch plant at Rabstein near Böhmisch Kamnitz, in which aircraft parts for WFG were produced between September 1944 and 13 April 1945.

On 25 April 1945 Allied troops occupied Bremen, although there was still weak resistance on the part of the town commandant on the following day.

4.2.2.2 Production at Berlin-Tempelhof

At Berlin-Tempelhof the conversion work of the Weser Aircraft Co. Ltd started up – as already mentioned – in the extensive hangars of the major airport which, due to wartime conditions, were no longer fully used.

This displacement dates back to a conference at the RLM on 25 November 1939, after which the round hangar at Tempelhof was examined for its suitability for aircraft production. On 14 December 1939 the Weser Aircraft Co. Ltd received a written instruction from Chief of Testing and Development Ernst Udet, in which the quickest possible removal of the conversion work to Berlin was ordered.

The first machine to be converted there, an He 111, entered the works on 9 January 1940. From the middle of the month there followed the assembly of Ju 86s from main assemblies that were delivered there; these were converted to training aircraft and at the same time equipped with BMW-132 radial engines.

At the end of April 1940 the setting up of the Tempelhof conversion work was concluded in its basic features according to plan. In hangars 3–7, ramp A and all connected ground floor space, the so-called hall of honour and a few other spaces, final assembly of the Ju 87 was to begin in the medium term as well as production of fuselages.

In the course of Ju 87 production the exhaust system changed in response to the changing powerplants. Here is an early B-1 of 9 (St)/LG 1 (L1+JT).

By the summer of 1941 nearly 1,000 employees were at work in Berlin and had delivered at least 200 converted machines to the *Luftwaffe*.

The so-called Pichon List, which originated in the memoranda of Chief Engineer Pichon, referred to the initial delivery of eighteen Ju 87 Bs from the Berlin-Tempelhof works, starting in June 1940. In July there were twenty and in August 1940 a further twenty-three newly built machines.

The 190 Ju 87 Bs completed in Berlin up to 31 December 1940 according to the Pichon List, may still in part have been airframes delivered in pieces from Bremen, as production originating solely in the Berlin works did not begin until June 1941.

The transfer of a large part of the production is first known to have taken place in the spring of 1941. The call from the front-line units for Ju 87 reinforcements had become louder, as high 'Stuka' combat losses had to be replaced. Ju 87 production hence received far greater attention than hitherto. For this reason the RLM ordered that both production at Lemwerder and the final assembly at Tempelhof of airframes delivered from Bremen must be speeded up.

The RLM therefore considered transferring as much as two-thirds of Ju 87 production to Berlin-Tempelhof. One advantage of such a move was that the north German area could be reached relatively easily by RAF units, and the whole parts production, which was concentrated in a single area, could have been affected by air raids, leading to a complete interruption of Ju 87 manufacture.

The air attacks on Bremen of 1 July 1940 as well as those between 1 and 4 January 1941 demonstrated this; various splinter bombs caused damage to several Ju 87 Bs.

On 10 July 1941 a lengthy conference took place at the Imperial Aviation Ministry between Engineer Colonel Gottfried Reidenbach, divisional leader in the RLM, and the Director General of WFG, Dipl.-Ing. Fritz Feilcke, on an expansion of the transfer of Ju 87 production to Berlin-Tempelhof. Thereupon the RLM, in letters dated 18 July 1941 and 26 August 1941, ordered the relocation of two-thirds of Ju 87 production to the Berlin area.

The objective was that every part of Ju 87

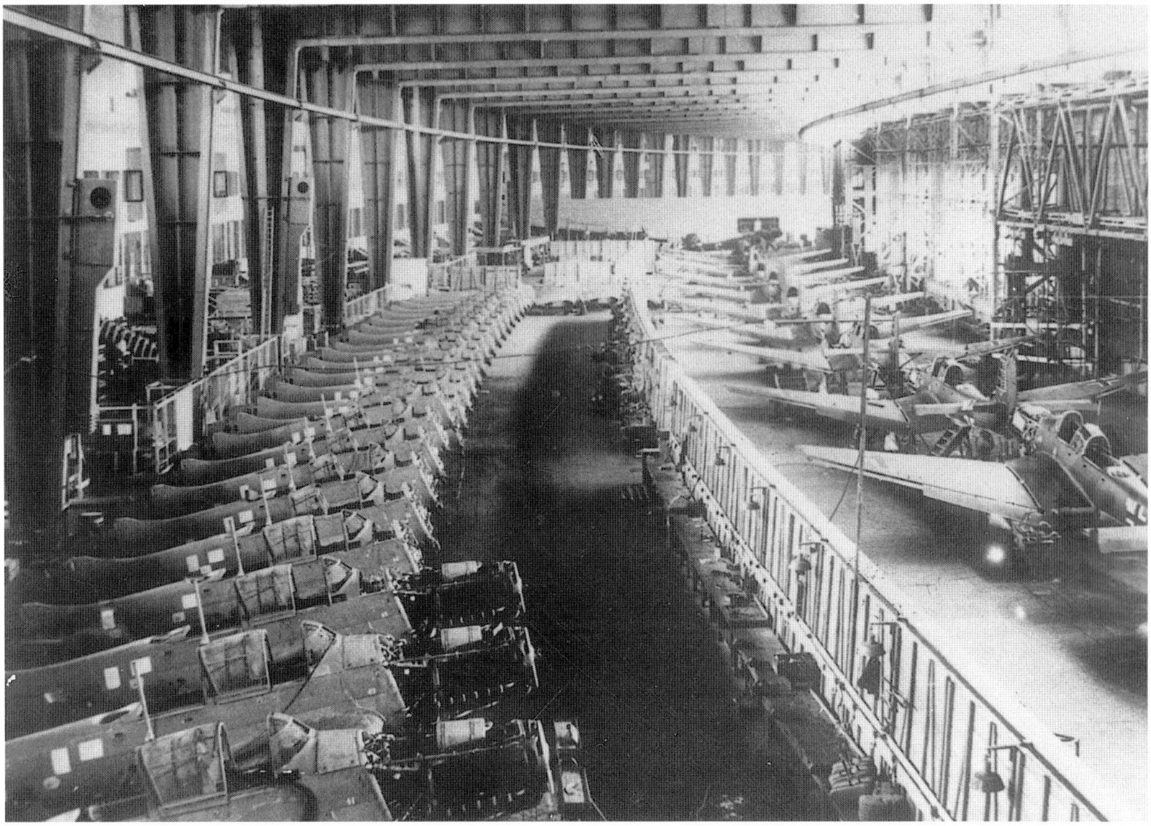

Large-scale production at Berlin-Tempelhof continued almost undisturbed until the end of 1944.

production at WFG be available at least twice over. Particularly costly production tools should as far as possible be made available in triplicate, so as to be able to resume Ju 87 production without major effort after air attacks.

On 31 July 1941 310 employees from Weser were already involved in Berlin Ju 87 production. From late summer onwards work on the transfer to Tempelhof was intensified. A part of this was the provision of adequate accommodation for the roughly 3,000 employees who were to take on large-scale production in Berlin. As insufficient buildings were available in the immediate surroundings, a further twenty-five barrack blocks together with canteens had to be set up at Tempelhof.

In the production halls – to the extent that this had not happened already – massive splinter protection walls were put up to limit the damage as much as possible in the event of enemy air attacks.

Up to the end of 1941 an average of thirty-five Ju 87s left final assembly at Berlin each month. The bulk of the 613 dive bombers received at Tempelhof by Construction Acceptance, Air, by that time were of the Ju 87 B version.

Starting in the spring of 1942, the first Ju 87 D airframes were shipped in main assemblies on German Imperial Railways flat waggons from Lemwerder to Tempelhof, where final assembly began on a production line. It was also the intention to set up an autonomous production line at Berlin for licensed manufacture; this included the manufacture of all the assemblies needed for the Ju 87 D.

Not until the summer of 1942 was the production of individual parts at Berlin so far under way that additional deliveries from Bremen could cease. The first Ju 87 D-1s manufactured and finished entirely at Tempelhof left the series

The maintenance crews with the Luftwaffe *close support units often had to work under difficult conditions in the open air.* (Federal Archives)

production there in July 1942. By the end of 1942 a further 429 Ju 87 Ds were produced; with that, the total number of all WFG machines rose to 3,530.

In April 1943 the highest monthly production rate was reached with 158 Ju 87s. Of that 103 came from WFG Lemwerder and fifty-five from assembly at Tempelhof. By the end of the year the number of machines finally assembled in Berlin stood at 638. For the branch plant there, this resulted in production to date of 1,680 Ju 87s compared to 3,479 at Bremen. In total 5,159 Ju 87s had now been delivered.

From the end of 1943, even the *Reich* capital increasingly became the target of massive Allied air attacks. After bombs had fallen at Tempelhof, two tunnels under the airport, and an underground hangar were assigned for Ju 87 production to Dr Hans Albrecht Caspari, who had been appointed manager of the Berlin works in 1938. Other than that, part of the two-storey Paradestrasse underground station with its underground access ways, was shut off and became a part of the Berlin branch plant.

In 1944 about 5,000–6,000 workers were employed at the WFG Berlin-Tempelhof works, a good 2,000 of them from the Berlin area. About 500 management staff, plant engineers, master craftsmen and lead hands originated mostly from the north German branch plants. More than 2,500 foreign workers, mostly conscripts and prisoners of war, comprised almost a half of the workforce.

The hangars occupied by WFG, with the exception of hangar 5, survived the Allied air attacks for the most part undamaged. The airfield, by contrast, was hit by carpet bombing and was out of action for a time. The hangar floors, originally open to the apron, were equipped with a complete wooden wall as protection against the weather.

The management of the flight testing operation was at first housed in the old airport building, but it fell victim to an aerial mine. Thereafter the flight management was moved to one of the neighbouring buildings.

Between January and July 1944 the monthly production rate was about fifty-four machines. Up to the cessation of new construction a further 430 aircraft were delivered. According to the Pichon List, WFG prepared 2,110 Ju 87s for the *Luftwaffe* at Tempelhof alone. Together with the WFG production at Bremen, this gives a total of 5,930 Ju 87s. This number may, however, not have represented the 'combat-ready machines to be delivered to the *Luftwaffe*', but the accountants' total number of all machines, even when these were available only in the form of disconnected assemblies. A further proportion crashed during flight testing. Others were stored as OKL (OKL – *Oberkommando der Luftwaffe*) reserve or served for the necessary supply of replacement parts, up to complete assemblies

Transport of damaged Ju 87 airframes to a repair plant.

such as wings, tails or replacement fuselages. According to information from former WFG employees, the discrepancy between these and the production figures put together by Junkers could result from this. Other works information gives a total of only 5,126 airframes manufactured at WFG, which were delivered to the *Luftwaffe*.

The last of the Ju 87 Ds assembled in Berlin from available replacement parts were completed in the autumn of 1944. Instead of the Ju 87 D-5, from the end of October 1944 onwards the assembly of Fw 190 A-8 fighters was begun. In total, after the conclusion of the Ju 87 programme at WFG, 244 complete Fw 190s, in addition to 898 fuselages and 415 complete wing sets, were manufactured.

The situation at the Berlin plant from the end of 1944 to the beginning of 1945 bore the imprint of restrictions due to war conditions and instructions, some of which were contradictory, from the RLM which, in spite of the dramatically deteriorating war situation, continually issued new directives.

On the morning of 25 April 1945 Soviet units succeeded in noticeably tightening their ring around the centre of Berlin. Hours later, towards ten o'clock, the enemy pushed forward without interruption onto the Tempelhof airfield. By 26 April 1945 the 28th Guards Corps, supported by the 1st Guards Tank Army, had captured the whole area, and with it the WFG branch plant, into Soviet hands.

4.2.3 Slovakian Aircraft Co. Ltd

In addition to the two Weser plants, the Ju 87 was intended to be produced also at Trencianske Biskupiske in Slovakia, south-west of Brno.

There was general agreement on this in the RLM in the autumn of 1942, even though the Industry Council in October 1942 opposed a fragmentation of Ju 87 production and shied away from the risks involved in setting up a third production area with relatively few and insufficiently trained workers.

In mid-October the Slovakian Aircraft Co. Ltd was established and training of the workers began at WFG from February 1943 onwards. But only at the end of 1943 could the installation of a plant suitable for Ju 87 assembly start in Slovakia.

Up to the late summer of 1944, in the end, only about twenty Ju 87 D-5s were finally assembled at Trencianske Biskupiske from delivered assemblies. Because of many difficulties, their assembly advanced only slowly. The revolt in Slovakia brought all related activities to an end only weeks later.

4.2.4 Wels Aircraft and Metal Fabrication Works

Besides the construction of new Ju 87s in the Bremen area as well as at Dessau, the Aircraft and Metal Fabrication Works at Wels became very important between 1940 and 1944. The firm's headquarters were in Wels-Lichtenegg and originated from the former Hinterschweiger works. By the end of 1944 the metalworking operation had become one of the *Luftwaffe*'s most important repair depots, the Insterburg repair operation being the sole exception.

From the spring of 1940 onwards, the plant was concerned mainly with the repair of Ju 87s. The first three were repaired in May 1940 with the inclusion of all current modifications in order to maintain the combat value of the machines. By the end of 1940 seventy-one airframes had been repaired, with most of the work taking place between September and October 1940.

In the following year there were only eighty-five repair aircraft, of which a monthly average of four could be returned to the front-line units in the first five months. From June onwards, as a rule, this figure was between eight and ten.

In 1942 the repair output was 152 machines. On average about a dozen Ju 87s per month were remanufactured and test flown.

The highest repair output was reached in 1943 with 258 aircraft. Each month at least twenty Ju 87 Bs, but chiefly Ju 87 Ds, were returned to airworthy condition.

In the following year another 180 machines were returned to the front-line units. Because of war conditions there was no output in May and June 1944. In July 1944 fourteen Ju 87 Ds and Gs were again completed.

From 1944 onwards the firm was increasingly required to produce twenty wing sets a month for the Me 262 as well as the construction of more than 1,000 tank covers for this jet fighter. The repair of Ju 87s was no longer important.

4.3 Air Attacks

4.3.1 Attacks on WFG in the Bremen Area

The first aimed air attack on the Bremen region, codenamed 'Salmon' by the RAF, took place at about 00.45 hrs on the night of 1 May 1940.

The first daylight attack on Bremen was undertaken by the RAF on 21 June 1940 at about 10.20 hrs, but caused only slight damage to buildings in the town. Shortly thereafter, on 30 June 1940, the bomb aimer of a single British bomber surprisingly released several high-explosive bombs over assembly hall 12, which was under construction at the time, resulting in three deaths and some severe injuries.

On 1 July 1940 the RAF attacked the Weser Aircraft Co. Ltd, resulting in damage to some Ju 87s in the pre-assembly and fuselage assembly areas. The fire which broke out in shop 210 was, according to a report by the Defence Economy and Armaments Bureau X, which was responsible, 'insignificant and could be doused immediately'.

In the heavy air attacks on the Weser plant between 1 and 4 January 1941 splinter bombs damaged several Ju 87 airframes. On the night of 2 January 1941 the RAF attacked Bremen; Focke-Wulf was hit but not WFG.

On the night of 13 March 1941, fifty-four Wellingtons of the RAF flew again to the Focke-Wulf plant which was categorised as the more important. During the attack two of the British bombers were lost.

The British air attack of 1 July 1940 on the Bremen Ju 87 manufacturing plant …

On the night of 16–17 April 1941 thick cloud cover prevented the RAF crews from releasing their bombs with certainty on industrial targets in the Bremen area. On the following night the attack hit Nordenham on the Weser, where six high-explosive bombs fell, but three failed to explode. Again there were several hits on Focke-Wulf. In the attack on the night of 4 June 1942, the RAF had the good fortune to score some light hits on the Focke-Wulf plant site. At WFG several Ju 87 airframes under construction were damaged by a fire started by four bomb hits.

WFG again escaped major damage. Only shop 2 received a chance hit from a stray bomb.

On the night of 5 September 1942 strong forces attacked the centre of Bremen with 251 machines in three separate waves with support by Pathfinder bombers. The plant installations of WFG received no hits.

A heavy attack by the American Eighth Air Force on 30 August 1944 hit both Kiel harbour and the Bremen aviation industry. This time 327 B-17s, protected by 258 P-51 Mustang fighters, intended to destroy the above industrial targets. From 15.51 hrs onwards there were some individual hits on the Focke-Wulf plant site but not on WFG.

On the night of 7 October 1944 there followed a heavy attack by 246 Avro Lancasters and seven de Havilland Mosquitos of RAF Bomber Command on the Bremen area, in which two aircraft plants, and possibly Focke-Wulf as well, were hit.

Shortly afterwards, on 12 October 1944,

... led to slight interruptions in delivery.

Osnabrück and Bremen were on the USAF target list. The 3rd Air Division of the Eighth Air Force attacked several aircraft production targets without causing major damage.

The attacks on the Bremen area then eased off before several more Mosquito attacks between 18 February 1945 and 22 April 1945.

On 24 February 1945, 11 March 1945 and 30 March 1945 USAF bombs were aimed mainly at U-boat production in the Bremen harbour area.

The last recorded air attack on Bremen was at midday on 25 April 1945 at about 17.00 hrs. In total RAF Bomber Command had released 12,844,000 kg of free-fall ordnance over Bremen, and the Eighth Air Force 12,699,000 kg, and the town lay in eighth place in terms of heavy bombing attacks on major German cities.

In contrast to Focke-Wulf, at WFG between 1940 and 1945 scarcely more than chance hits had been recorded, and these led to no lasting damage to Ju 87 production.

4.3.2 Attacks on WFG at Berlin-Tempelhof

Like the production sites of WFG at Bremen, the second final assembly operation survived the confusion of war almost undamaged.

In spite of a number of air attacks on the centre and outskirts of Berlin, and despite numerous air raid warnings and production disruptions, the workforce did not have to survive massive bombing while they were at work.

The first British bomber, which belonged to 10 Squadron of RAF Bomber Command, appeared in the sky over Berlin on the night of

2 October 1940. Several smaller and larger attacks were to follow.

On the night of 1–2 March 1943 the RAF was over the southern parts of the *Reich* capital with 302 machines. In Tempelhof twenty industrial operations and 875 buildings were hit or damaged. At Telefunken the important British H2S airborne radar device, which had only recently been acquired and was being studied and evaluated there, was destroyed. At WFG the workforce got away with a fright.

A few months later, on the night of 23–4 August 1943, 727 RAF bombers, the majority four-engined Lancasters and Handley Page Halifaxes, attacked targets in Berlin. The attack was not especially successful for Bomber Command; 7.9 per cent of the machines dispatched were lost. The Pathfinder forces could not precisely distinguish the target areas for which they were aiming, so that the majority of the target marking was dropped over the southern parts of the city – and so also over Tempelhof. But even this time WFG got away with only light damage.

On 28 January 1944 between 03.15 and 03.50 hrs a heavy air attack took place over the south and south-east parts of the *Reich* capital, in which the Tempelhof district was especially heavily hit, without major damage to Ju 87 production.

Numerous bombs fell on the airfield during the war, and the flight testing operation was removed to Jüterbog as the danger continually increased and after Allied bombs had hit the building in which the flight testing operation was housed.

Otherwise, only the wooden cladding of the former departure hall was wrecked by the blast effect of high-explosive bombs dropped by the RAF and USAF, and it could be repaired within a relatively short time. Protection walls had been erected against splinter effects – as also in the shops in the Bremen area – so that the air attack damage, which was in any case slight, had hardly any effect in the medium term.

4.3.3 Attacks on JFM at Dessau

The home plant of Junkers Ltd was the target of heavy Allied air attacks several times during the war, but not until Ju 87 production at Dessau had already finished.

4.3.4 Attacks on the Wels Aircraft and Metal Works

The repair operation at Wels was the target of a heavy Allied air attack by the American 15th Air Force on the morning of 30 May 1944, which also attacked targets at Neukirchl, Neunkirchen and Pottendorf. In total 614,000 kg of free-fall ordnance was released over Wels and nearby targets by crews of the Consolidated B-24 Liberators.

The effect of the attack was devastating, as the German defences had hardly anything with which to counter an air attack on such a massive scale.

The number of Ju 87s repaired there monthly had just reached thirty-two machines when the damage from the heavy air attack enforced a shutdown of the works for almost two months. Subsequently, the deliveries following the destruction that took place on 30 May 1944 reached a good ten machines per month, but sank rapidly from the beginning of 1945 onwards, when the work on Me 262 assemblies and parts was considered more important.

4.4 Export of the Ju 87

Numerous Ju 87s of the different series were delivered to states with links to the German *Reich*.

On the delivery list were production prototypes for both Japan and the Soviet Union. Series aircraft were to serve in the setting up of the first dive bomber formation of the Austrian air forces, and during the war Bulgaria, Italy, Croatia, Romania, Hungary and Slovakia received Ju 87-type machines.

The range of machines delivered abroad reached from the Ju 87 A-1, through numerous B and R variants, up to the Ju 87 D-5. By the end of the war even a few G-2s were supposed to be delivered to Hungarian units, but as a result of the military events of early 1945 this intention was not followed through.

4.4.1 Bulgaria

In 1940 the Bulgarian air force consisted of six air regiments with a total of more than 130 machines and nine flak batteries. In the mid-1930s the equipment was relatively obsolete and

The Bulgarian 2 Pulk Szturmovy *possessed two* Jatos *which were equipped with Avia B 534s (2nd* Jato/2*) and Ju 87s (1st* Jato/2*).*

from 1939 onwards they relied mostly on material captured from the Polish campaign as well as on Bf 109 E fighters and Caproni medium bombers. The aircraft equipment of Bulgaria was regarded as modest, but this would change, or so it was hoped in Sofia, after the Three Powers Pact of 1 March 1941 came into force. In his Instruction No. 18 Adolf Hitler had expressly stated: 'The wishes of the Bulgarians for army equipment build-up (weapons and ammunition deliveries) are to be treated sympathetically.'

Bulgaria also played an important role in the attack on Greece in April 1941 to ensure a rapid advance to the south and south-west.

To improve their air force equipment, the country chiefly received used Bf 109 E fighters as well as a few obsolete Do 17 long-range reconnaissance aircraft. More modern equipment was withheld, in spite of numerous requests – as was also the case with Romania. On 13 August 1943 the Bulgarian air force received its first six, albeit used, Ju 87 R-2s and R-4s. On 6 September 1943 a further six Ju 87 Rs followed, which were mainly to serve for crew training.

Of the forty operational Ju 87 D-5s originally designated for Bulgaria, by the end of 1944 only twenty-five machines had been delivered. Of the remaining fifteen, eight followed in May 1944, five in June and two in July 1944.

In the following weeks instruction of the crews designated for combat duty was started. With the Ju 87 Ds three *Jatos* (*Staffeln*) were equipped, which were intended to form the 1st *Shturmovi Orliak* (Ground Attack *Gruppe*).

With this air equipment the operational forces went into action, mainly over 'bandit-infested areas' in Bulgaria and Yugoslavia to support the army in its defensive battles. This included, chiefly, the protection of fortified places but also offensive operations against partisan support points.

On 5 September 1944 the Soviet Union

At various times up to 37 Ju 87 R-2s, R-4s and D-5s flew with the 2 Pulk Szturmovy.

declared war on Bulgaria, whereupon the pro-Western administration under Muraviev was replaced by a pro-Soviet one. Only a day later this regime broke off diplomatic relations with Germany. Three days later war was declared on the German *Reich*. On 16 September 1944 the Red Army occupied the capital, Sofia; on 25 September 1944 the whole Bulgarian army was placed under the Red Army; three days later an armistice was signed in Moscow. All the available Ju 87 Rs and Ds in Bulgarian territory at that time – about thirty – were seized by the Red Army which wanted to bring the aircraft into action again with Bulgarian crews. These machines are supposed to have flown individual ground attack sorties against their former allies at the end of 1944.

4.4.2 Italy

On 10 June 1940 Italy delivered its declaration of war on France and Great Britain. Only a few weeks later the Italian High Command, through its Air Attaché, Colonel Giuseppe Teucci, asked for the delivery of 100 Ju 87 B dive bombers from the German *Reich*.

Although no delivery dates could be established at such short notice, on 9 July 1940 the instruction of the first fifteen crews began, as well as the corresponding ground personnel, under the command of Captain Ercolano Ercolani, at 2 Dive Bomber School at Graz-Thalerhof. As early as 20 July 1940 the first practice dive bombing attack was carried out with a cement bomb. The practice flights were flown at Thalerhof mostly with Ju 87 A-1s and A-2s, but from time to time also with Ju 87 B-1s.

Initially only ten machines destined for the Italian air force were made ready on 15 August 1940. Previously another fifteen Ju 87 B-1s had been announced as the first delivery. The first machines were transferred by Captain Ercolani together with Lieutenants Fernandino Malvezzi and Andrea Brezzi as well as three other pilots from the 236th *Squadriglia* (*Staffel*) together with Captain Giovanni Santinoni, Lieutenant Franco Benato and two other pilots of the 237th *Squadriglia*. From Udine and Forli, south of Ravenna, the crews flew to Rome-Ciampino and from there on 20 August 1940 to Naples-Capodichino. From Naples they went via Catania to Comiso in the south of Sicily. The remaining five Ju 87 Bs of the first delivery were

With German dive bomber pilots allied Italian Squadriglie *also intervened in the battles in North Africa. This Ju 87 B-2 (works no. 5763) was captured by British troops in September 1941.*

transferred on 25 August 1940 by pilots of both squadrons, which belonged to the 96th *Gruppo* (Flying *Gruppe*).

Between August 1940 and July 1941 Italy received a total of fifty-two Ju 87s as arms assistance (nos. MM 7047–98).

The first combat operations of the 96th *Gruppo* BaT (*Bombardemento a Tuffo* = dive bombing attack) with Ju 87 B-2s struck at Malta and shipping targets in the seas surrounding the main island. On 2 September 1940 five Ju 87 Bs of the 236th and 237th *Squadriglia* attacked ships of the Royal Navy about 150 km south of Malta. In the evening attacks began on British fortifications and a large tank park on the island. On 15 September 1940 the operations of the two squadrons, which were carried out from an operational altitude of 6,000 metres, were directed against the airfield of Hal Far on the main island of Malta. CR 42 fighters were provided as escort for the dive bombers to protect the Ju 87 Bs against the Hawker Hurricanes of the RAF. A fierce battle with British fighters ensued. One of the Ju 87 Bs (works no. 5687) returned to its home base in Sicily in spite of damage from gunfire suffered in the air battle. All other machines reached their point of origin without problems.

Although the situation in the African theatre of war at the end of September 1940 was tense – the Italian offensive in western Egypt came to a standstill east of Sidi Barrani – a month later the Italian attack on Greece began.

On 27 October 1940 seventeen Ju 87s of the 96th 'Stuka' *Gruppo* attacked targets in the Balkans from an airfield in the neighbourhood of Lecce. The Ju 87 unit stationed there was led by Captain Ercolano Ercolani.

In the air attack of 2 November 1940 six Ju 87 R-2s of the 96th 'Stuka' *Gruppo* flew an attack on Ioannina in north-western Greece. At the same time ten Cant Z 1007bis three-engined bombers attacked the town. Two days later four Ju 87 R-2 crews devoted their attention to this target again; at the same time a prototype of the Italian SM 86 dive bomber, flown by a works pilot from the Savoia-Marchetti plant, Elio Scarpini, went

Ju 87 R-2s of the 239th Squadriglia *returning from an operation over Yugoslavia, 1941.*

into action for the first time.

In a counter-attack by the II Greek Corps Italy came under increasing pressure in the new theatre of war.

On 14 November 1940 a Ju 87 attack took place, in which enemy airfields were the main target. In the process a PZL 24 was hit. Further, on that day a Greek gun battery was effectively attacked. Even so, the Italian units were soon pushed back to their starting positions in occupied Albania. Their own forces had been unable to force a victory.

From 20 November 1940 onwards the build-up of the 97th 'Stuka' *Gruppo* began at Comiso with Ju 87 B-2s. Two 'Stuka' *Squadriglie*, the 238th and the 239th, were subordinated to the *Gruppo* staff. Here a part of the 96th *Gruppo* was put to work as instruction staff and as the core of those units. Besides the flying personnel, the best of the ground personnel had been trained at Graz-Thalerhof, in order to be able to take over the maintenance of the Ju 87s.

On 28 November 1940 six Ju 87s of the 96th *Gruppo* under the protection of 18 Fiat CR 42s attacked several mostly small warships off the coast of Gozo, an island in the neighbourhood of Malta.

The 97th *Gruppo* was in action over Greece meanwhile. From the beginning of December 1940 the unit was led by Lieutenant-Colonel Antonio Moscatelli. The 238th *Squadriglia*, which consisted of eighteen Ju 87 Bs at that time, was under the command of Captain Domenico Sciaudone.

On 6 December 1940 the 96th *Gruppo* moved from Trapani on Sicily to Lecce, south of Brindisi and from 14 December 1940 stood ready for action there. On that day six machines of the 238th *Squadriglia* attacked Pigerasi successfully with high-explosive and incendiary bombs. Six days later the fortress of Borsch and the Kiepara area were massively attacked by Italian dive bombers in two waves with heavy bomb loads.

On 19 December 1940 combat forces from Italy attacked the harbour of Edda and sank at

The Ju 87 B-2s of the 96th Gruppo *were amalgamated with the 101st* Gruppo. *The machine illustrated here was flying to targets in Greece.*

least one of the small vessels lying there without major opposition.

The first Italian dive bomber to be lost was probably the Ju 87 B, works no. 5769, which was lost two days later. On 21 December 1940 its crew were to have attacked a point target at Malvezzi from an altitude of 1,500 metres. In the process the machine was shot down by a hitherto unrecognised flak battery at Kolonia. Lieutenant Elio Scarpini and his radio operator, Sergeant-Major Gianpetro Crespi, did not return from the operation.

The Ju 87 B-2, works no. 5806, flown by Luigi Stevanato, exploded after its incendiary bomb load had been ignited by a flak hit. On 23 December 1940 several Ju 87 Bs were attacking targets in and around Doliana.

On the morning of 29 December 1940 an incendiary bomb attack was attempted against the temporary bridge at Ioannina, 150 km behind the Greek lines, by nine Ju 87s. At the same time a flak position was attacked at Borsch.

Meanwhile, more personnel trained at Graz-Thalerhof had entered the squadrons, which had a positive effect on their operational condition.

By contrast, the war situation in which Italy found itself looked less promising. British troops had taken Sidi Barrani; the Italian units were pushed further back and the enemy was able to conquer Sollum. In Greece the situation was also confused.

A thoroughly favourable opportunity seemed to offer itself to disrupt supply shipping in *Mare Nostrum* – the Mediterranean.

On 8 January 1941 the groundcrews at Comiso loaded twelve Ju 87 Bs with one 500-kg high-explosive bomb each. Long-range reconnaissance had reported British warships and

This Ju 87 R-2 (works no. 2763) of the 209th Squadriglia *was photographed in the autumn of 1941 at Derna, Libya.*

transports which were under way from Gibraltar in the direction of Alexandria as worthwhile targets. About 50 km south of Pantellaria at least two hits were obtained on enemy freighters. Next, seven Ju 87s of the Italian 236th and 237th 'Stuka' *Squadriglie* attacked the modern aircraft carrier, HMS *Illustrious*, west of Gozo Island at Malta, albeit without success. A few days later, on 10 January 1941, the carrier was bombarded by 43 Ju 87 R-2s of II/StG 2 as well as I/StG 1 and had to be towed to Malta, heavily damaged.

Meanwhile, the Italian 97th 'Stuka' *Gruppo* was involved in further battles over Greece and on 21 January 1941 attacked enemy positions at Permeti with six 250-kg and twenty-five 50-kg bombs. For the 96th 'Stuka' *Gruppo* there began at that time a new chapter in its operations: battles over North Africa.

There British units had, from 9 December 1940 onwards, pushed the Italian troops in Cyrenaica fully onto the defensive and had driven far to the west without major opposition.

From 30 January 1941, the 96th *Gruppo* could be made available in Libya for the support of the Italian units. As the existing 'Stuka' units had shown themselves to be too weak, further combat forces followed in March. They took off from Comiso and landed near Tripoli on the Castel Benito airfield.

By the end of March the Axis forces in Tripolitania were able to consolidate and, from 4 April 1941, to begin the reconquest of Cyrenaica. In order to be able to attack Allied naval forces between Sicily and North Africa, ten Ju 87s of the Italian 238th 'Stuka' *Squadriglia* were transferred from Tirana via Lecce and Puglia to Trapani and then operated from various forward bases in Sicily.

With the 97th *Gruppo* twenty machines were available in the 4th *Squadriglia* area (Bari), which were stationed at Lecce and were under the command of Lieutenant-Colonel Antonio Moscatelli. In particular, they stood ready for future operations over the Balkans. On 6 April 1941 the Balkan campaign began under German command, and the 2nd Italian Army fought its way forward from Istria along the Dalmatian coast.

On 13 April 1941 eight Ju 87s of the Italian 208th 'Stuka' *Squadriglia* flew an attack on Mostar in support of the ground operations. Several targets were also attacked at Vouissa and Perati.

Shortly before that, on 11 April 1941, several dive bombers of the Italian 96th 'Stuka' *Gruppo* attacked Allied shipping targets lying off Tobruk. Further, but only partly effective, operations followed on 13, 14 and 19 April during the battles around the small port, which had been built into a fortress.

Then thirty-seven German Ju 87s, together with three machines of the 236th *Squadriglia*, again attacked the Allied transports off the North African coast as well as freighters anchored in Tobruk harbour. The port was closed in by Axis forces and was besieged between 1 June and 31 December 1941.

Italian dive bombers again and again went into action. On 28 June 1941 the combat forces of the 239th *Squadriglia* succeeded in sinking the Australian destroyer HMS *Waterhen*; a month later another warship sank after a dive bombing attack.

In spite of reinforcements the 'Stuka' forces sent into action in Africa were not enough to intervene in the battles decisively. For this reason the Italian High Command considered it was necessary to set up new dive bomber units. Further crews and ground personnel made their way to Styria.

On 11 July 1941 the first crews intended for the 99th Italian 'Stuka' *Gruppo*, which was in the process of formation, flew from Graz-Thalerhof back to Italy after the conclusion of their training. The 208th 'Stuka' *Squadriglia* was formed at Lecce and the 209th at the Lonate Pozzolo airfield, both of which were later to be sent into action at Tirana in Albania. A condition of the setting up of new Italian 'Stuka' *Squadriglie*, however, was more reinforcement with modern flying equipment, as and when the German *Reich* was prepared to deliver it.

According to a company overview of the Junkers works of 31 July 1941, between December 1940 and June 1941, apart from fifteen machines delivered hitherto, a further thirty-five Ju 87 Bs were given up to Italy from *Luftwaffe* inventory. Besides that, as early as 19 February 1941, according to information from the Junkers management, an additional order

Sergeant Tarantola Cappelli in front of his Ju 87 R-2 which belonged to the 209th Squadriglia.

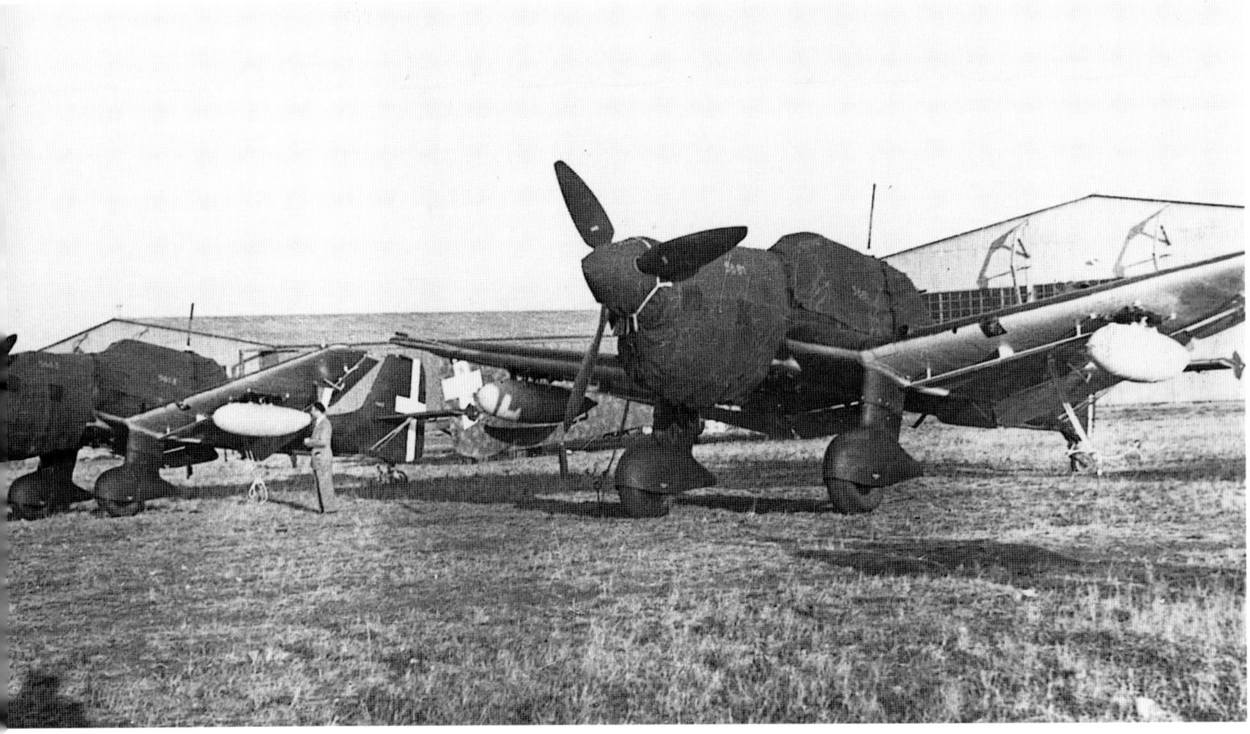

These parked Ju 87 R-2s were on the strength of the 100th Gruppo *which went into action over the Balkans.*

for a further fifty Ju 87s, valued at RM 10,625,000, was charged on the books. The machines were to be diverted directly from *Luftwaffe* inventory, overhauled and delivered to Italy as quickly as possible. The costs were then reckoned up directly with Junkers.

The deliveries between July 1941 and October 1942 comprised fifty Ju 87s (MM 8009–58). The majority of the machines were finally sent into action over the Mediterranean and North Africa. On 15 July 1941 five Italian Ju 87s attacked Allied positions at Marsa Luch. Two days later the 209th *Squadriglia* went to support the forces of the *Regia Aeronautica* in action in Libya. The Italian 236th *Squadriglia* was also transferred from Lonato Pozzolo to the African theatre of war.

In the campaigns that followed the Ju 87 B-2s and R-2s often intervened with German dive bombers in the fierce ground battles or bombarded important enemy reinforcement systems behind the front.

Malta and its capital, Valletta, also became the target of further dive bombing attacks, which were carried out by crews of the 238th and 239th *Squadriglie*. Several spirited operations, with an average of five to seven machines, were carried out between June and November 1941.

Further south, in North Africa, a defensive battle was waged at Sollum, followed between 18 November 1941 and 17 December 1941 by the battle of Marmarica. In order to disrupt the enemy lines of communication, in November Ju 87s of the Italian 208th, 238th and 239th 'Stuka' *Squadriglie* attacked the extensive port installations and reinforcement areas of Valletta on Malta. The last attacks were carried out by crews of the 238th and 239th *Squadriglie* on 9 and 10 November 1941.

There was a new retreat in Cyrenaica by 24 December 1941. The defence of the Mersa Brega position followed until 20 January 1942 before the reconquest of Cyrenaica began; this lasted until the end of February 1942. German and Italian dive bomber pilots took part in these battles too, with decisive effect. In air fighting near Tobruk at midday on 12 February 1942, an

Captain Raul Zucconi in front of a Ju 87 B-2 of the 101st Gruppo Autonomo *on an airfield in Sicily.*

Italian Ju 87 was attacked by several British Hawker Hurricane and Curtiss P-40 Warhawk fighters and was shot down after a short battle. The machine belonged to the 209th *Squadriglia*. In the course of the battle two German Ju 87s and a Bf 109 were lost.

A little later, on the afternoon of 16 February 1942, the exhausted Italian 209th 'Stuka' *Squadriglia* left the North African theatre of war. The need for further units which could be used offensively led to the formation of the Italian 102nd 'Stuka' *Gruppo* from 1 May 1942, which was led by Captain Giuseppe Cenni. Subordinate to him were the nine Ju 87s of the 209th *Squadriglia* of Captain Aldo Stringa and the 239th *Squadriglia* of Lieutenant Giuseppe Tamborra. While the *Squadriglie* were still in training, further changes took shape in North Africa.

The second conquest of the fortress of Tobruk followed in June 1942; battles of pursuit followed as far as western Egypt. On 14 June 1942 seventeen Italian Ju 87s of the 209th *Squadriglia* from Trapini-Chinisia attacked Allied ships without success 50 km north-east of Bizerta with three SD 1000 bombs and two SD 500s. The attack by eleven Ju 87s on freighters 90 km south of Pantellaria on 15 June 1942 also produced no results. The crews of six Ju 87s, which took off two days later from Cagliari-Elmas against maritime targets, could also not score any hits.

Two weeks later, on 29 June 1942, came the conquest of the fortress of Mersa Matruh and in July an extremely fierce struggle for the Alamein position, in which the British had material superiority from the beginning.

In the battles over North Africa the Italian 'Stuka' *Squadriglie* lost several Ju 87s through enemy action and landing accidents on insufficiently prepared airfields. For that reason eight more Ju 87s were delivered to the *Regia Aeronautica* in October 1942 – far too few to provide adequate replacements in the Italian 'Stuka' units.

After the loss of the battle of Alamein by the Axis powers, there came a new retreat to Cyrenaica in November 1942. At that time only the Italian 101st 'Stuka' *Gruppo* was still in North Africa, with few Ju 87s. The 102nd *Gruppo* was stationed in Sicily with twenty-two Ju 87s, although of this unit only two aircraft were battleworthy. With this the number of battleworthy machines had reached rock bottom. Only the German StG 3 still possessed a significant quantity of Ju 87 D-3s.

From mid-April 1943 onwards the first twelve Ju 87 D-3s went to Italy from Graz, where the induction of Italian personnel had again taken place. By 20 April 1943 another six D-3s had followed. Eight days later there was a total of forty-one Ju 87 D-3s on the Siena-Ampugnano airfield; fourteen of these aircraft were transferred to Sicily in the end to support the defence of the island.

Between March and May 1943 the desperate defensive battle in Tunisia ended with the

Machines of the 209th Squadriglia *return undamaged from operations over Libya.*

capitulation of the last defenders and the complete retreat of Axis forces from Africa. The superior Allied forces had forced their way through after hard fighting and had created a springboard for the landing in southern Europe.

At that time a new delivery of Ju 87 D-3s was in progress. The first of these machines was taken over by the *Regia Aeronautica* in April. By June 1943 forty-nine aircraft were delivered. Most of these machines would serve in the defence against Allied attacks on Sicily, Sardinia and southern Italy.

After the previous losses, it was necessary in the summer of 1943 to train new crews as fast as possible. On 9 July eight Ju 87 B-2s were available for that purpose at Lonate Pozzolo and, with the corresponding personnel, formed the *Nucleo Addestramento Tuffatori*, a training centre for future ground attack pilots.

On 10 July 1943 the Allies landed successfully in Sicily. Two days later seven Ju 87 D-3s of the *Regia Aeronautica* attacked several freighters in spite of powerful defences, and a vessel of about 7,000 tons was sunk. Two days later several Ju 87 D-3s of the Italian 207th 'Stuka' *Squadriglia*, together with Macchi MC 200 Saetta single-seat fighters of the 51st Fighter *Squadriglia* as protection, flew an operation in which one of the new Ju 87s was lost.

The days of Germany's southern ally were numbered. On 24–5 July 1943 came the fall of Benito Mussolini. On 8 September Italy capitulated and was then occupied by the *Wehrmacht*.

The last Italian *Gruppo* still in action in the summer of 1943 was the 121st 'Stuka' *Gruppo*, stationed at Chilivani on Sardinia. The unit possessed only eleven machines, of which five Ju 87 Ds were later taken over into the inventory of the new Italian air force.

4.4.3 Japan

As an export version for the Japanese, the Ju 87 K-1 was developed. This was a Ju 87 A-1 with the Jumo 210 D in-line engine. Armament, bomb release mechanism and radio were taken over, unchanged, from the A-1.

4.4.4 Croatia

After the defeat of Yugoslavia in 1941 the former kingdom was divided between the victors and their allies. As early as 10 April 1941 the Ustasha leader Ante Pavelic proclaimed an independent state of Croatia and joined the Three Powers Pact on 15 June 1941. After thousands of volunteers had reported for service in the east, Croatia began to build up its own air forces, which were to go into action over the Soviet Union under the command of the *Luftwaffe*. Both fighter and bomber units were formed.

In January 1944 the Lucko Bomber *Gruppe* was formed within the framework of the Croatian Legion and equipped with a few Ju 87 R-2s as well as Fiat CR 42s. With these the training of Croatian crews began immediately. A month later, in February 1944, the 3(Croat)/KGr 1 arose out of the Lucko Bomber *Gruppe*.

From August 1944 onwards forces of the 3rd *Staffel* took part in ground attack operations against partisans under the leadership of *Luftflotte* 6. In the late summer the 3 (Croat)/KGr 1 possessed a few used Fw 190s as well as several older Ju 87 Ds. The machines of the unit stationed at the former Lubenstadt retained their German markings. In October 1944 the whole Croatian Bomber *Gruppe* was dissolved; the machines, to the extent that they were still usable, went back to the *Luftwaffe*.

4.4.5 Austria

At the beginning of November 1937 Captain Hans Schalk from *Fliegerregiment* No. 2 of the Austrian air forces visited several German aircraft factories over a period of three weeks to test fighter, reconnaissance and dive bomber aircraft for Alpine country. As dive bombers, both the Hs 123 and the Ju 87 were offered to him. Because of the extremely low-powered Jumo 210 in-line engine, it seemed to him that the performance of the two-seat Junkers machine was not very satisfactory. Even so, the Ju 87 A seemed to have an inherently greater development potential than the Hs 123.

The choice fell therefore on the Junkers dive bomber. The purchase of twelve machines for the Austrian air forces was planned by the Ministry of Defence.

By an order dated 21 March 1938, nine people were therefore sent to the Junkers works in central Germany to gather experience with the maintenance of the Jumo 210 Ea. Under the leadership of Engineer First Lieutenant Johann Hoffmann, a master craftsman, Corporal Josef Preuner, as well as two engine fitters, made their way to Dessau and Köthen. Later the military aircraft assistant Karl Jilik was added to the team. The twelve machines to be procured (Nos. 361–372) were to be lodged at the airfield of St Pölten and at the Wörschach air base. The Ministry of Defence wanted the delivery of the Ju 87 As to be complete by 1938 at the latest.

The first two machines were delivered by 31 December 1937; the transfer of the remaining ten was planned to take place by 31 December 1938. The price per machine was RM 149,500. Together with spare parts for the airframes and engines, about RM 310,000 was spent on maintenance materials for the first two aircraft.

With the entry of German troops into Austria, further deliveries were no longer in question. The aircraft equipment of Austria was taken over into the inventory of the German *Luftwaffe*. Thus only two dive bombers were ever delivered.

4.4.6 Romania

The Romanian air forces, the *Forele Aeriene Regale ale Romaniei* (FARR), did not receive their first Ju 87 D-3s and D-5s until August 1943. The reason was that German aircraft production could scarcely satisfy the needs of its own air forces and Germany therefore exported mostly older equipment to its allies. The Romanian air forces were hence, from 1940 onwards – and then only now and again – 'favoured' with captured material from the campaigns in France, Poland and Yugoslavia.

At the beginning of 1943 a slight surplus of newly built aircraft had arisen, as too few trained German crews were available. Romania therefore received, besides Bf 109 G-6s, Ju 88 A-4s and D-1s, ultimately also Hs 129s – and the first Ju 87 D-3s.

The Ju 87 Ds assigned to the *Grupul 3 Bombardement Picaj* (Bomber Group) received the tactical numbers 1–45, in which nine reserve aircraft were also included.

During the operations of the FARR, therefore, only numbers 1–36 went into action. The machines with these tactical numbers flew with the *Escadrila* (*Staffel*) 73 (Nos. 1–12), the *Esc.* 81 (Nos. 13–24) and the *Esc.* 85 (25–36). When the Ju 87 Ds of the *Grupul* 6 joined up with the *Corpul* 1 *Aerian* in 1944, the machines were given the numbers 178–204 and 862–872. The aircraft then belonged to *Esc.* 87 (Nos. 178–192), *Esc.* 74 (Nos. 193–204) and to *Esc.* 86 (Nos. 862–872). All these machines, however, were only loaned aircraft from the inventory of the German *Luftwaffe*.

The operations of the Romanian ground attack forces began in the spring of 1943 with the *Grupul* 3 *Bombardement Picaj* with its *Esc.* 73, 81 and 85; the unit was subordinate to the *Flotia* 3 *Bombardement*, which was a part of the *Corpul* 1 *Aerian*. The conversion training of crews to the Ju 87 D-3/D-5 began from 1 April 1943 onwards at Nicolaev and ended in the middle of June 1943. On 16 June 1943 the unit had twenty-nine battleworthy Ju 87 Ds at its disposal.

During the following weeks, the unit was sent into action against the Mius position and on 6 July 1943 was moved to the Kerch Peninsula (east of the Crimea). There it had the task of giving air support to the German and Romanian divisions (of the 3rd Army) in the Kuban bridgehead with bombs and gunfire. The operations, some of which were flown ruthlessly, were highly praised by the XVII Army, the 97th Infantry Division and, not least, the I *Fliegerkorps*.

Among the operational tasks of the Romanian crews was also the laying of light sea mines and low level attacks on Soviet gun boats as well as enemy coastal vessels.

The operations were regarded as the most potent support that the German ground troops had ever received from allied air forces during the war.

By 9 August 1943 thirty-one of the forty-five

Some of the Romanian groundcrews of Grupul *6 take a short break near their Ju 87 D-3, spring 1943.* (Federal Archives)

The earth walls between which this Romanian Ju 87 D-5 was parked, can only have provided slight protection against splinter bombs.

Ju 87 Ds transferred to the Romanians were damaged, although none of the machines was a 100 per cent loss. Six had damage from fighter attacks and twenty-five from the Soviet air defence units. At the end of October 1943 Soviet units had completely cut off the Crimean Peninsula. After ground attack operations had been interrupted in October 1943 by the rapidly declining availability of operational machines, the attacks were renewed from 4 November 1943 onwards. From Karankut in the Crimea from December 1943 onwards, both the 3rd Romanian Mountain Division and the 6th Romanian Cavalry Division were massively supported from the air in order to give more weight to their counter-attack on the Russian forces that had landed at Eltigen. On 2 April 1944 the ground attack unit possessed seventeen Ju 87 D-3s which – mostly with AB 250 and AB 500 bomb dispensers – intervened in the ground battles.

In mid-April 1944 the Grupul 3 *Bombardement Picaj* had to be withdrawn from the Crimea as the enemy had become active there. During the Soviet spring offensive the German-Romanian southern front was retaken as far as the eastern frontier of Romania. Some of the Ju 87 Ds, which were unserviceable at the time, had to be left behind on the forward airfields or were blown up by their own troops.

Between the end of May and the beginning of June 1944 the squadrons suffered their first heavy losses. Four Ju 87 Ds did not return from just one operational flight over Bessarabia on 30 May 1944. It then became quieter again on this sector of the front, so the crews and ground personnel were able to recover somewhat. The air superiority of the Red Army had an ever more oppressive effect as they were able to put ever stronger fighter units into action.

There was a second ground attack unit equipped with Ju 87 Ds in the FARR. This was the *Grupul 6 Bombardement Picaj*, which was formed from 20 May 1944 and at first had only

The Ju 87 D-3s transferred to the Romanian air force were taken over without changing the camouflage paint. Only the German nationality markings and radio callsigns were provisionally painted over.

two squadrons, *Esc.* 74 and 87, at its disposal. The unit was put under the command of the *Corpul 1 Aerian*, led by the bearer of the Knight's Cross, Major-General Emanoil Ionescu, and went into action on 30 June 1944. Two weeks later, on 16 June 1944, *Esc.* 86 was ready for action as the third squadron and joined the Group in order to fly similar ground attack operations over the weakening eastern front.

Between 16 June 1943 and 23 August 1944 the *Grupul* 3 *Bombardement Picaj* had received a total of 113 Ju 87 D-3s and D-5s; with the exception of one repaired aircraft, these were all of new manufacture. Of these sixteen finally had to be written off as total losses. Ten of them fell to fighters or flak, three went missing in action, and three machines were lost in flying accidents. Other than that, twenty-six aircraft were more or less heavily damaged by enemy defences and a further forty-six in accidents. Altogether, eighty-eight out of 113 Ju 87 Ds were put out of action. On 23 August 1944 only twenty-five machines were still available for operations; of these, however, only eighteen were reported as battleworthy.

The *Grupul* 6 *Bombardement Picaj* lost a total of twenty-eight Ju 87 D-3s out of the fifty-five assigned to it up to 23 August 1944. The majority of these originated with the *Grupul* 3 *Bombardement Picaj*, which thereupon was equipped with new loan aircraft from the *Luftwaffe*. Of these three fell to enemy action. Six went missing in action and had to be written off; a further two were destroyed in flying accidents. Other than that, seventeen Ju 87 D-3s were damaged by the enemy or in flying operations.

In the middle of August 1944 the *Grupul* 6 *Bombardement Picaj* could still summon up twenty-one machines, of which only six were unserviceable. On 20 August 1944 the Soviet offensives at Jassy and Tiraspol began, which led to a retreat to the Carpathian passes. The losses

This Ju 87 D-5 was prepared for ground attack operations at Husi in Moldavia. Note the fuse extensions on the 50-kg bombs.

among the Romanian pilots rose further because of the fighter superiority of the Red Army. For example, on 21 August 1944 three Ju 87s supporting the 1st Panzer Division fell victim to the constantly present fighters and massive anti-aircraft defences of the enemy.

On 23 August 1944 at 22.00 hrs the Romanian King Michael gave notice over the radio that his country would be separated from the Axis powers and that fighting against the Red Army would therefore cease immediately.

Some of the Romanian operational machines on the airfield of Husi in Moldavia on 24 August 1944 were taken over by Hans-Ulrich Rudel's unit and only one day later were sent into action on the German side.

The air attack by German bombers and ground attack aircraft on the centre of Bucharest on 25 August 1944 led to the declaration of war on Germany.

This had serious consequences: in the *Luftflotte* 4 zone, 376 machines were thus lost. The majority stood, unserviceable, at various repair centres in Romania and could not be taken away immediately. Among these were the relatively new twenty-seven Ju 87 D-3s of the *Grupul* 3 *Bombardement Picaj*, which were all taken over, undamaged, by the enemy. Romania now possessed numerous modern combat machines, but few spare parts to keep them battleworthy in the medium term. In the course of further military actions some of the reinforcement organisation of *Luftflotte* 4 became easy booty for their former allies.

The *Grupul* 6 *Bombardement Picaj* was added to the *Grupul* 3 *Bombardement Picaj*; from this a relatively strong ground attack unit, the *Grupul* 3/6, was set up. This could mainly rely on *Escadrila* 74 and 81, which were equipped with the Ju 87 D-5. The first actions, however, were against German troops. The new objective was the liberation of northern Transylvania. Soviet troops entered Bucharest on 31 August 1944

The Ju 87 D-3s of Grupul 3 *attacked Russian troop concentrations with AB 250s and AB50/70s with good effect in the late summer of 1943.*

– except for northern Transylvania, the Red Army had occupied the whole of Romania by the beginning of September 1944. With up to twenty-eight divisions, Romanian troops under the command of the 2nd Ukrainian Front took part in battles in Moravia, Slovakia and Austria. In these attacks the Romanian Ju 87 crews suffered heavy losses from Hungarian flak units. Further machines fell victim to the German fighter pilots in action there.

At the beginning of 1945 one unit, the *Escadrila* 74, was formed from the two squadrons of the *Grupul* 3 and 6 *Bombardement Picaj*, which continued to fly Ju 87 D-5s. Together with the *Esc.* 41, a tank hunter squadron equipped with Hs 129 Bs, it now formed the *Grupul* 8 *Asalt/Picaj*, a mixed tank hunting and ground attack group. The unit was equipped afresh with Ilyushin Il-10s in order to maintain its combat strength.

In total, between April 1943 and August 1944, the FARR had received just ninety Ju 87 D-3s and D-5s, mostly as good as new, and captured a few more. According to other sources, up to 170 Ju 87s are said to have been in service with the Romanian air forces.

4.4.7 Hungary

After Italy, the Hungarian air forces received the greatest number of Ju 87 dive bombers which were delivered to Germany's allies. The Ju 87 B was used extremely successfully during the campaign in Poland, and Hungary made efforts in 1940, within the framework of German military assistance, to obtain at least twenty Ju 87 B-2s. On the German side this request was complied with, but without any definite undertaking as to when delivery could be expected.

At first the Hungarian air forces received two repaired Ju 87 Bs from the *Luftwaffe*, which flew as B.601 and B.602. The 'B' stood for *Bombázó* (Bomber).

A Ju 87 A-1 (B.603) was also delivered for training purposes; by January 1942 four more machines of this version had followed it (B.604ff); these machines also served only for crew training.

The Junkers works order book on 31 August 1941 showed an order for twenty-six Ju 87s, dating from 25 January 1940. The delivery of the remaining Bs, equipped with the 210 Da engine, was at that time still outstanding. The first two Ju 87 B-2s (B.601 and B.602) had gone to Hungary in 1940 specifically as Ju 87 K-2s. After they had been thoroughly tested, they were assigned to the Bomber *Gruppe* 3/1. In March 1942 two K-4s (converted Ju 87 A-1s with Jumo 210 D engines) stood ready for acceptance by Hungary after the completion of a thorough overhaul. Of these at least one was delivered.

According to the monthly report of the Junkers Aircraft Works for May 1942, the order 'Dresden II', which had already been started and which was planned for the Hungarian air force, was cancelled, so the delivery of the twenty-six Ju 87s ordered did not take place.

The crews intended for Ju 87 operations were at first trained on Fiat CR 32s and only thereafter received their training on Ju 87 K-2s(B) and Ju 87 K-4s(A). The two Ju 87 K-2s thus served mainly in the training of Hungarian crews in the diving attack.

The first operational formation which was to be equipped with Ju 87 Ds was the *Zuhanóbombázó-század* 2/2 (2nd Dive Bomber *Staffel*). The unit was originally to have been equipped with thirty Ju 87 D-1s. Instead of these machines, whose production had already ceased, the more modern Ju 87 D-3 and D-5 versions were surprisingly delivered. The Ju 87 D-3 (B.632) and the Ju 87 D-5 (B.631) were the first two of these new machines. In the summer of 1943 there were twelve D-3s or D-5s (B.633ff). One of the aircraft assigned was so heavily damaged in a landing accident that it was not worthwhile repairing and it was scrapped.

The *Staffel* consisted of four flights of three machines each. At the end of May 1943 the unit was moved to Kiev by road and on 1 August 1943 began preparations for its first combat duties. The aircraft consisted at that time of eleven Ju 87 D-3s and one D-5 (B.645). The first combat operation took place on 3 August 1943

This Ju 87 A-2 (B6+04) was parked without a powerplant at Veszprem, Hungary, in the autumn of 1943.

The Ju 87 B-2s with the Hungarian air forces mostly went into service as training aircraft.

against a large partisan encampment in the Bryansk Forest.

Immediately after this operation, the *Staffel* was moved to the Poltava base of II/StG 77 and placed under the tactical command of the German 'Stuka' unit.

By 8 October 1944 the Hungarian squadron had completed its thousandth operation. The service of the ground attack *Staffel* ended on 22 October 1944. By that date about 1,200 missions had been flown over the eastern front, in which 810,000 kg of free-fall ordnance had been dropped. The crews also succeeded in shooting down one attacking P-39 Airacobra fighter and two Lavochkin La 5 fighters.

In these operations six crews and fifteen out of the twenty-one (or twenty-two) Ju 87 D-3s and D-5s delivered were lost. The remaining operational machines were taken back by the *Luftwaffe*. The Hungarian crews, together with their ground personnel, made their way home to Hungary.

On 19 March 1944 the bloodless occupation of Hungary by the German *Wehrmacht* occurred. The formation of new army and air force units began, in order to hold up the Soviet advance in the area of the Carpathians and the Ukraine. A compliant regime carried out the instructions of the Berlin Imperial Chancellery.

In March 1944 training flights began with the newly formed dive bomber *Staffel*, the *Zuhanóbombázó-század* 102/2. Kolosvár (Cluj) in Transylvania had been chosen as its base. Ten thoroughly overhauled Ju 87 B-1s for which the *Luftwaffe* had no further use were transferred there. According to a report of the Junkers works technical sales department, the training machines were ten Ju 87 B-1s (as K-3s). In May 1944 twelve out of twenty Ju 87 D-5s which had been originally promised joined them, so that induction could take place on a current operational type.

The *Staffel* went into action over the eastern front on 16 June 1944 with its movement flight to Kuniow. For operational purposes it was subordinated to III/SG 77 there. An actual combat operation did not take place until 30 June 1944. In July 1944 the squadron was placed under I/SG 77. Up to the end of August 1944 crews of the *Zuhanóbombázó-század* 102/2 flew a total of

Loading of a Ju 87 D-3 in the Hungarian theatre of war.

forty-seven combat operations and in the process dropped 150,000 kg of bombs. In July 1944 the squadron operated from Hordynia and Starzawa (Poland).

At the end of August 1944 the remaining machines – four were lost during the previous operations – were transferred to the *Zuhanóbombázó-század* 102/1. After retraining of the unit with the help of staff from the 'Stuka' *Zuhanóbombázó-század* 102/2, it moved in September 1944 to Hajduszoboszlò in Hungary. Next it was moved to Börgönd, where the majority of the Ju 87 Ds (ZB+01ff) were destroyed on 12 October 1944 in a low-level attack by American piston-engined fighters.

On 11 October 1944 a provisional armistice was signed between the *Reich* regent, Admiral Miklós von Horthy, and the representatives of the USSR. This did not last, however, as, after the announcement of the armistice, the regent was forced to withdraw this declaration and the Arrow Cross (a Fascist paramilitary organisation) seized power. The centre of administration, the fortress of Budapest, was then occupied by units of the SS *Sturmbannführer* Otto Skorzeny; Admiral Horthy was taken to Germany.

Parts of the army and other paramilitary formations (the Arrow Cross) resumed the battle on the German side, others with the Red Army.

Remnants of the Hungarian 'Stuka' *Staffeln* flew low-level attacks against Soviet armoured units with German operational forces from autumn onwards, although in restricted numbers. Even in April 1945 an attempt was made to set up a Hungarian tank hunter *Staffel*, which was to be equipped with Ju 87 Gs.

Because of the war situation and, above all, the lack of machines, this intention could no longer be realised.

4.4.8 The USSR

At least one Ju 87 A-1 was delivered, together with a few other combat aircraft, to the USSR in 1940 and served at the test centre, TsAGI, for a detailed investigation and performance testing.

The Red Army was also able to capture the wrecks of many abandoned or crashed Ju 87 Bs and Rs; initially, however, none of these machines came into the possession of the Russians in airworthy condition.

With the great Soviet offensives which began at the end of 1942, however, the opportunity presented itself to capture some of the Ju 87 Bs and Ds and subsequently to test them in order to evaluate their flying behaviour.

The majority of the first Ju 87 operational types to be captured in airworthy condition were on the airfield of Bolshaya Rossoshka and fell into the Red Army's hands at the beginning of 1943 after the Stalingrad operation, together with a few Bf 109s and He 111s – some completely undamaged.

Lieutenant Titov of the *Saratovskaya Voyenno-aviatsionnaya planernaya shkola vozdushno-deantnykh voisk* (SVAPsh VDM), the freight glider school of the ground troops, was entrusted with the transfer of the first captured Ju 87 D-1 to Saratov. He lost his way and landed with his machine at Rostov on Don, where no one among the German flying command paid any attention to his landing. Lieutenant Titov succeeded in taking off again unnoticed and landing safely on the bank of the Don that was occupied by the Red Army, with his fuel almost used up. After refuelling, he was able to continue his flight to Saratov. In the meantime a second machine had been transferred there by Aleksandr Auguls.

The Ju 87 D-1 (works no. 2754) was intensively tested from the beginning of 1943 onwards at the *Nauchno-ispytal'skiy institut Voyenno-vozdushnykh Sil* (NII WS), the research institute of the air forces. In the process bombs were dropped in dives with a bomb load up to 1,500 kg. A maximum speed of 382 kph was reached with a load of 500-kg bombs at an altitude of 3,500 metres. After one of the D-1s was briefly exhibited at a display of captured booty in Moscow in the summer of 1943, all trace of these machines has been lost.

Other than the captured D-1 machines, the Red Army succeeded in the spring of 1943 in getting their hands on a Ju 87 G-1 at Bryansk, together with the pilot Hans Trenkmann. From him they learned that an initial twenty-five Ju 87 Gs had been equipped with two 37-mm weapons each and had been transferred to the front in February 1943.

This Ju 87 G-2 captured by Soviet troops belonged to 10 (Pz)/SG 77 and was left behind near the Oder.

The fate of this machine, too, is not clear at present. The Red Army does not, however, seem to have taken a great interest in the Ju 87 D and G, as they themselves had sufficient ground attack aircraft – and they were well-armed.

4.4.9 Slovakia

On 24 November 1940 Slovakia joined the Three Power Pact. Seven months later, on 23 June 1941, Dr Josef Tiso proclaimed the entry of Slovakia into the war against the USSR. The 1st Slovakian Infantry Division took part in the campaign on the southern sector of the eastern front and was finally sent into action as a security division and involved in construction work. Several air formations were also set up with Slovakian personnel, which mostly received captured equipment from Bohemia, Moravia and Poland.

The Slovakian fighter forces, chiefly equipped with Bf 109 Es, G-2s, G-4s and G-6s, successfully attacked Allied machines over Slovakia between 1942 and 1944. When Soviet

One of the few airworthy Slovakian Ju 87 D-5s which survived the battles during the popular uprising.

units reached the eastern frontier of Germany's ally in the spring of 1944, apart from the 1st and 2nd *Zvedná letka* (Reconnaissance *Staffel*) and the 12th *Pozorovaci letka* (Fighter *Staffel*), a reinforcement unit was also available which consisted of three Letov S-328 light bombers and three Ju 87 D-5s. The machines were transferred to Poprad and Spisská Nová Ves and were to go into action mainly for ground attack.

The 11th *Letka* (*Staffel*) had five Ju 87 D-5s in June 1944 as well as seven used and partly unarmed Ju 87s (Bs and Ds) available. Most of the Ju 87 D-5s finally assembled and flight tested at Trencianske Biskupice were given over to the *Luftwaffe*. In August 1944, according to information from the Junkers works, eleven overhauled Ju 87s were delivered to the Slovakian air forces.

On 29 August 1944 units of the *Wehrmacht* began to occupy Slovakia, as the state was categorised as 'unreliable': in the countryside a popular uprising had begun. One of the *Kombinovaná Letka* (Combined Flying Units) formed from previous air forces flew more than 350 sorties during the uprising and gained six aerial victories. Several German machines, among them three Ju 87 Ds, were destroyed by the Slovakian pilots, one of them on 7 October 1944 at Hronská Brezinca and another on 18 October 1944 at Banská Bystrice.

At times only one of the Ju 87 D-5s of the Slovakian resistance movement was battleworthy; it was sent into action alone to bomb German columns.

Shortly afterwards, on 25 October 1944, the Slovakian airfield of Tri Duby, south of Banská Bystrice, had to be evacuated as the German Schill battle group was advancing on the field;

the threat to their own troops by aircraft of an underground army could not be countenanced.

As far as possible the Slovakian air forces, with their machines, joined forces with the Red Army in the Ukraine, and with Romania. Some went into the forests to join partisan groups. On 27 October 1944 Banská Bystrice and its surroundings were occupied, then a parade was held before President Dr Josef Tiso.

Of the five Ju 87 D-5s (OK-XAA to OK-XAE) which had been in the Slovakian air force inventory, in May 1945 there may have been only one (OK-XAC) available. It was operated with its identification letters painted over in grey and after the war was allegedly flown as B-37 with the registration OK-KAC.

5 Action on All Fronts

5.1 The Ju 87 – the Interim Solution

The use of combat machines capable of dive bombing was intended to provide rapid and decisive success in battle against all potential continental enemies. In addition, according to the *Luftwaffe* leadership, dive bombing would protect civilians in wartime because, at least part of the *Luftwaffe* leadership still wished to believe in the summer of 1939, that the civilian population would not be endangered at all, or only slightly, by the precision bombing involved.

By the spring of 1938, according to a requirement of the *Luftwaffe* General Staff, it was established that 'the main point of a bombing attack has shifted unambiguously from the area target to the point target'. But this included precision attacks on targets of small area.

As early as 20 May 1938, the leader of the Aerodynamic Institute of the Darmstadt Polytechnic, Professor Dr-Ing. Scheubel, had expressed the view that, in view of the relatively small payload of German bombers, stick bombing would be a waste of munitions. It also seemed to him that dive bombing attacks on important targets on and behind the front was the essential proviso for a rapid victory on the ground. He was to be proved right – at least in part and during the initial phase of the war.

In Vienna a large exhibition ran in 1941 under the title 'Victory in the West'. A Ju 87 A-2 was displayed there as an 'operational machine'.

Some Ju 87 B-1s of II/StG 77 were painted with sharks' teeth for propaganda purposes. At the controls of this machine sat Major Alfons Orthofer, later bearer of the Knight's Cross.

The leader of the Research Division in the RLM, assistant secretary Dr Rer. Nat. Adolf Georg Baeumker, expressed his views in a presentation before the German Academy for Aviation Research on the prospect of hits in dive bombing operations. Instead of relatively ineffective level bombing from great heights, it seemed to him – and to the majority of his listeners – that the diving attack was especially suited to operations against point targets. Even though the limited range and poor performance spectrum of the Ju 87 had been recognised at an early date, the replacement of the single-engined machine by one of Messerschmitt construction capable of dive bombing was already established in 1938.

The question of the tactical ability of the Ju 87 to fight its way through over the battlefield had already been raised before the beginning of the war. In view of the fact that there were German fighter machines which were faster than the Ju 87, it could only be a question of time before the enemy would produce equally fast combat types.

This was taken into account in the formation of *Luftwaffe* units which was ordered by General Field Marshal Hermann Göring on 26 October 1938. Besides fighter and bomber *Geschwader*, dive bomber units were also given the prospect of a new standard aircraft, in which great – but vain – hopes were placed. The Bf 210, at least in theory a potent combat type usable both offensively and defensively, was supposed to replace both the Bf 110 Destroyer and the Ju 87.

Only relatively few of the approximately 3,100 machines planned for this purpose were finally manufactured and delivered to the front-line units. They were battleworthy only to a limited degree, as their flight safety initially left much to be desired.

Ernst Udet departed this life voluntarily on 17 November 1941, after he had been unable to give an account of his omissions in the matter of the Bf 210. A committee of investigation was set up which in the end led to the whole development being shut down on the orders of the Imperial Marshal on 9 March 1942.

First the lengthening of the fuselage (in the Bf 210 V17) and then the installation of more powerful powerplants meant that the construction of the machine had to be reconsidered. A few test dives carried out on 21 December 1942 produced useful results but even so the 'dive bomber/destroyer' – referred to as such in the aircraft handbook – which had been the cause of much premature congratulation, proved a complete error of planning.

This led in the end to serious consequences at the Messerschmitt works. From 30 April 1942 onwards Prof. Willy Messerschmitt was allowed only to take on the task of a chief design engineer and lost – at least officially – his hitherto comprehensive influence on the destinies of the concern.

The conversion from the Ju 87 to the Bf 210, which had been trumpeted before the war, had to be regarded as wrecked. A long-lived combat type had arisen from the Ju 87 interim solution. The crews were to wait in vain for a more potent 'Stuka'.

5.2 Guideline: Close Air Support

We return to 1938. In order to ensure comprehensive close air support by the *Luftwaffe* for German ground troops, the formation of five ground attack *Gruppen* was begun in 1938.

The subordination of the dive bomber units, according to their armament, to the Inspector of Bomber and Reconnaissance Pilots took place on 1 January 1939. The offensive character of the new weapon was thereby underlined once more.

Six months later, on 1 July 1939, came the formation of the staff Air Leader for Special Applications under the former commander of the Condor Legion. From this arose, on 1 October 1939, as a result of experience gained during the Polish campaign, the Air Division for Special Applications, which after only a few days became the VIII (Close Combat) *Fliegerkorps*.

Thanks to the possibilities now offered to him, Major-General Dr-Ing. Wolfram von Richtofen could perfect the essence of tactical close support. It was unfortunate that, apart from the VIII *Fliegerkorps*, no other large units for close air support were set up. This led later to the enforced use of medium, twin-engined bombers to give close air support to the army groups engaged along the eastern front as an additional task.

As it was the only close combat corps, the VIII *Fliegerkorps* was from now on sent into

The crews of 9/StG 1 also took part in the French operation; this machine was a B-1 (G6+AT).

action at all the key points of battle and proved its excellence in the process, in spite of substantial losses.

The *Koluft* (commanders of the *Luftwaffe* in the army area), who were at first installed with the army groups, formed the liaison with the *Luftwaffe* and organised close air support. Thanks to their activities, the *Luftwaffe* operations over the eastern front were fundamentally better organised and optimised in their effect.

When the practice changed to assigning the close support air forces in each sector of the front to a *Luftflotte*, the *Koluft* liaison service was no longer needed.

It is worthwhile at this point to look at the tactical requirements of close air support with the Ju 87 in more detail. The operations of the ground attack air forces were coordinated and led by means of Air Liaison Officers (*Flievos*). As forward air control, there were so-called 'air guidance troops' with the army field divisions, which comprised one *Luftwaffe* officer and one army officer, as well as a radio unit, and were fully motorised. By this means it was ensured that the close air support could be carried out effectively and precisely as to targets. By the formation of key points and correct target selection it was thereby possible to use the close combat forces, equipped with the Ju 87 or other ground attack aircraft, in close proximity to the front. By this means, also, the danger to German troops through bombs dropped wide of their target was almost excluded.

As a rule the front-line troops requested close air support from the responsible *Fliegerkorps* through the air liaison command set up at division. From there the request would be forwarded to the appropriate *Luftflotte*. This ordered the operation and informed the liaison command which also received the report that the support forces had taken off. As soon as the Ju 87s were over the battlefield, the air guidance officer went into action and guided the ground attack operation locally. In this the German troops showed their own positions by marker cloths or other visual means, as far as possible.

In this role the robust Ju 87s, operating from badly constructed forward airfields, were irreplaceable even at the end of 1943.

The front-line *Geschwader* equipped with Ju 87s can, for reasons of space, only be briefly described here.

5.3 The Dive Bomber *Geschwader* (*Sturzkampfgeschwader* – StG)

5.3.1 Dive Bomber *Geschwader* 1

The ***Geschwader* staff** of Dive Bomber *Geschwader* (StG) 1 was formed in July 1940 from the staff of the Training *Geschwader* (LG) 2. The same was true for the staff *Staffel* of StG 1, the former staff *Staffel* LG 2 which was disbanded in September 1943 and then joined the Destroyer *Geschwader* (ZG) 3 as its third *Staffel*.

The staff of I ***Gruppe*** was formed from the earlier *Gruppe* staff of I/StG 160, which originated from parts of Ground Attack *Gruppe* 20 (with Hs 123s) at Tutow. In October 1943 the staff of Ground Attack *Geschwader* 1 came from it.

To the staff of I *Gruppe* were subordinated 1–3/StG 1, which formed the I *Gruppe* from May 1939 onwards. These *Staffeln* originated in the renaming of 1–3/StG 160. From I/StG 1 came II/StG 3 in January 1942, whereupon a new I/StG 1 was built up from June 1943 from I/StG 5 (formerly IV ('Stuka')/LG 1).

The *Gruppe* took part in the whole Polish campaign and was used from April 1940 in the occupation of Denmark and Norway. From August 1940 its crews attacked targets in southern England. In January 1941 the unit moved to Trapani in Sicily and from there achieved some hits on the British aircraft carrier HMS *Illustrious* on 10 and 11 January 1941. Further key points of operation were Malta and North Africa, to which the *Gruppe* moved briefly. In May 1941 the unit took part in the occupation of Crete and attacked maritime targets in the eastern Mediterranean from there. Up to the beginning of 1942 this area was I/StG 1's field of operations.

After the re-formation of the *Gruppe*, it was moved to the Army Group Centre area on the eastern front in the summer of 1943. In the autumn of 1943 it was finally renamed I/Ground Attack *Geschwader* (SG) 1.

II *Gruppe* was first formed in July 1940 from the staff of StG 51 as well as 7–9/StG 51. From this originated 4–6/SG 1 in October 1943 during the restructuring of the ground attack forces.

The later I *Gruppe* of StG 1 proceeded from the earlier III/StG 165, from which then was

Luftwaffe *Propaganda Company member Hauflein recorded this Ju 87 D-1 for posterity in the spring of 1943 in the area of the Army Group Centre.*

During operations over the Balkans, operational machines were given yellow engine cowlings and rudders.

Warming up the Jumo 211 of a Ju 87 B of 6/StG 77.

Briefing of crews before their next operation by a 2nd Lieutenant. The photograph originated with I/StG 1.

Training flight of three Ju 87 B-1s with under-slung cement bombs: a typical propaganda photograph of 'operations'.

These Ju 87 Bs of II/StG 77 were only painted with sharks' teeth for propaganda photographs for a Luftwaffe *war reporter's company.*

A Ju 87 D-5 of II/StG 1 which still carried the markings of III/StG 51 even in 1943.

War reporter Koltzenbaum took this photograph of two Ju 87 B-2s from a unit in action on the eastern front.

Numerous Ju 87 Bs, Rs and Ds were in action over the Balkans, the Mediterranean and North Africa with the Regia Aeronautica.

In North Africa as in Russia the maintenance of the Ju 87 demanded the utmost dedication from the groundcrews.

The crew of an early Ju 87 B-1 of II/StG 77 waits for the order for take-off during the campaign in France.

This Ju 87 B airframe, photographed at Zwischenahn in 1943, also belonged to 6/StG 77. It was used for the static testing of aero engines.

In spite of the severe hit in the fuselage, this machine of 7/StG 1 (previously 4 (St)/TrG 186) returned from the operation.

formed III/StG 51. The 'Stuka' *Gruppe* intervened effectively in September 1939 in the battles on the bend of the Vistula, at Warsaw and at Brest-Litovsk. The unit was tactically subordinate to StG 77 at that time. From May 1940, France provided a new field of activity for the 'Stuka' *Gruppe* operating in the unit of II/StG 1. On 9 July 1940 came the incorporation of III/StG 51 as II/StG 1, in order to fill out the *Geschwader*. Under the leadership of II *Fliegerkorps* there followed air attacks on Channel shipping and southern England. From 30 March 1941 the unit took part in the Balkan campaign and from 22 June 1941 attacked targets at Bialystok, Brest-Litovsk and Minsk. The hard fighting necessitated that the unit be rested in November, at Schwäbisch-Hall.

From February 1942 operations began over the central sector of the eastern front, and a continuation of operations over the southern sector began in May 1942. There followed attacks in the Taganrog area, in the bend of the Don and over Stalingrad. In February 1943 the *Gruppe* became a part of the Hozzel fighting unit; it participated fully in the hard defensive battles against the Red Army. A month later it was released to the central sector of the eastern front and took part in Operation *Citadel*. From August onwards numerous operations from Orsha followed in the central sector, some of which had to be carried out at night.

III *Gruppe* existed at first under the designation I/Carrier *Gruppe* 186 and was amalgamated into the *Gruppe* staff along with 1–3/TrG 186. The 'Stuka' *Gruppe* was intended for deployment on board the first German aircraft carrier. As this could not be completed in the foreseeable future, III/StG 1 with its 7th to 9th *Staffeln* was formed from the unit on 2 July 1940. In October 1943 it was renamed 7–9/SG 1.

Peacetime Bases of the Dive Bomber *Geschwader*

Unit	Base
I/StG 1	Insterburg
II/StG 1	Wertheim (as III/StG 41)
III/StG 1	Kiel-Holtenau (as I (Carrier *Gruppe*)/186)
I/StG 2	Cottbus
II/StG 2	Stolp-Reitz
III/StG 2	Langensalza
I/StG 3	Graz-Thalerhof (as I/StG 76)
II/StG 3	Insterburg (as I/StG 1)
III/StG 3	Stolp-Reitz (as II/StG 2)
I/StG 5	Greifswald (as IV ('Stuka')/LG 1)
III/StG 51	Wertheim
I/StG 76	Graz-Thalerhof
I/StG 77	Brieg
II/StG 77	Breslau-Schöngarten
III/StG 77	Wels (formerly II/KG 76)

In September 1939 I ('Stuka')/186 (T) went into action against targets on the Hela Peninsula. After the Polish campaign the unit moved to the vicinity of Danzig on 22 September 1939. Next, the *Gruppe* was prepared for operations in France at Hennweiler in the Hunsrück and supported the German advance up to 22 June 1940. From July 1940 the new III/StG 1 was brought into the attack on Channel convoys and in August 1940 attacked several southern English airfields. In November 1940 the attacks had to be abandoned because of the excessively strong British fighter opposition. The last operations followed over the Thames estuary. Only a special command, consisting of selected crews of the first two *Gruppen*, was entrusted with attacks on the southern English coast up to 13 February 1941.

Shortly thereafter III *Gruppe* moved to Sicily and followed I/StG 1 to Tripoli and Greece. After substantial losses the *Gruppe* had to be rested at Kitzingen in the summer of 1941. Then, from 22 June 1941, began the attack on the Soviet Union, in which the unit was chiefly able to show its capabilities in the encirclement battles (Bryansk-Viasma) in the area of VII *Fliegerkorps*. After attacks on the Moscow area the *Gruppe* had to be rested again and moved for that purpose to Neukuren in East Prussia.

From February 1942 onwards the attacks in the area of I *Fliegerkorps* were again taken up. In April 1943 the unit moved to the centre sector of the eastern front and attacked targets between Orel and Kursk. III/StG 1 also took part in the offensive on the Kursk salient in July 1943 and from August 1943 continued with attacks to relieve the army, among other things in the evacuation of Smolensk. After the defensive battles at Krivoi Rog, the *Gruppe* was renamed III/SG 1.

As a tank hunting *Staffel* in excess of planned establishment, from June 1943 onwards the 1/VersKdo belonged to the *Geschwader* for attacking tanks (see Chapter 10) .

5.3.2 Dive Bomber *Geschwader* 2

The second Dive Bomber *Geschwader* bore the traditional name StG 2 'Immelmann'. The ***Geschwader* staff** was formed in the spring of 1939 from personnel of the former StG 163. From April 1940 onwards there existed a staff *Staffel* which was still in existence when the unit was in action as SG 2.

To the *Gruppe* staff **I/StG 2** (previously Staff I/StG 163) were subordinated the former 1–3/StG 163, which were renamed 1–3/StG 2 in April 1939. From the *Gruppe* unit in October 1943 came the Staff *Staffel* and 1–3/SG 1.

After the Polish campaign I/StG 2 moved to the west into the area of VIII (Close Combat) *Fliegerkorps*, in order to be ready at Golzheim for operations against targets in France. The crews there forced the crossings of the Meuse and Oise

and made extremely effective attacks on targets at Calais, Dunkirk and Amiens. The *Gruppe* also played a decisive role in the air attacks on Channel shipping and southern England. In February 1941 the staff moved with the three *Staffeln* of I/StG 2 to Banesa and Optoni in Romania in order to be able to undertake operations from there over the Balkans. From March the *Gruppe* moved to the Sofia area where VIII *Fliegerkorps* had arrived in the meantime.

After attacks on the Metaxas Line and on Belgrade, the 'Stuka' crews bombarded the Greek airfields with great success and helped the German divisions in breaking through the Greek Thermopylae position. After supporting Operation *Mercury* (the occupation of Crete), the unit was rested and from June 1941 took part in the attack on the Soviet Union. Its initial successes there were the operations at Suvalki on 22 June 1941, in the encirclement battle at Grodno-Bialystok and in the Minsk area. After supporting the crossing of the Dnieper, the *Gruppe* was moved to the northern sector of the

ABOVE: *After a severe hit in the tail section, this crew were fortunate to make a landing at their home base.*

BELOW: *'Stuka' attacks caused a degree of chaos on the roads of northern France that can hardly be taken in at a single glance.*

Zeroing the guns of a Ju 87 B-2 of the staff of the II Gruppe *of StG 1 on one of the forward air bases shortly before the start of the French campaign.*

eastern front. There the region around Leningrad was one of the main objectives.

From November onwards, fighting against Russian counter-attacks became ever more important. After defending its own dispersal points against a tank attack, I/StG 2 moved to Böblingen for rest in December 1941. From the early summer of 1942 the unit was ordered to the support of the *Wehrmacht* in the Voronezh-Rostov area and also took part in the fateful attack on Stalingrad. After Stalingrad was encircled on 22 November 1942, the crews tried to cover the retreat of the stricken forces on the Don.

At the beginning of 1943 the second *Gruppe* was also ordered to the Hozzel fighting unit and next moved to Dniepropetrovsk South, in order to support a counter-attack from there. In May 1943 its operations were for the benefit of the German and Romanian forces fighting in the Kuban bridgehead. The 'Stuka' *Gruppe* also played a large part in the costly tank battle of Kursk as well as the defence against the major Soviet offensive against Army Group Centre in August 1943. The defence against enemy attacks still remained a decisive focus of operations after renaming as I/SG 2.

The second *Gruppe*, **II/StG 2**, was formed in April 1939 and consisted of the staff of the former II/StG 162 with the 4th to 6th *Staffeln* of this *Gruppe*. In January 1942 the staff of III/StG 3 were derived from the staff of II/StG 2, whereupon a new staff had to be formed for the II *Gruppe* of the 'Immelmann' *Geschwader*. The three former 'Immelmann' *Staffeln* next found themselves as 7–9/StG 3. In January 1942 came a new formation of 4–6/StG 2. From this the 4th *Staffel* became 10(Pz)/SG 3 in March 1944 and the 6th became 10(Pz)/SG 77. The weakened 5/SG 2 was completely disbanded.

II/StG 2 was at first used operationally in Poland and next in France. The unit's course led by way of airfields in Sicily to North Africa, where the second *Gruppe* supported the

In the Russian winter, the utmost dedication was required of the groundcrews.

operations of German and Italian units with decisive effect.

After the *Gruppe* had become a part of StG 3 at the beginning of 1942, it was re-formed and mainly operated in the area of *Luftflotte* 1 in the southern sector of the eastern front. When almost the whole of StG 2 was moved to Austria in May 1942 for rest, one *Staffel* of the *Geschwader* stayed behind for a time in the southern sector of the bitterly disputed eastern front.

Together with the forces that had been withdrawn in the meantime, its crews supported the advance on the Volga and intervened in the battles for Stalingrad. In covering the German retreat, the unit lost many of its crews and front-line machines. In spite of heavy losses, an attempt was made, with modest resources, to relieve the north-western part of the line within which the 6th Army was enclosed. Towards the end of the year the exhausted unit had to be taken off operations entirely and rested.

Under the command of the Don *Flieger-division* costly defensive battles followed, along with the Hozzel fighting unit. The *Gruppe* participated in the battles for the Kuban bridgehead as a part of the Kupfer 'Stuka' unit (II and III/StG 2, I/StG 3, II/StG 77 and III/JG 3). The attack on the Soviet landing at Novorossisk in April 1943 remained unsuccessful. In contrast, Operation *Citadel* brought some excellent scores, although the offensive was abandoned on

Three pilots of 10 (St)/LG 1 in the winter of 1941–2 on the airfield at Rovaniemi: 2nd Lieutenant Karl Arnold, Lieutenant Gerhard Agather and Lieutenant Karl Püls. In the background is an air heater, without which no flying was possible.

The arms of the unit's partner city, Breslau, served as an emblem for this Ju 87 B of 3/StG 1 as was usual with the Gruppe.

13 July 1943 as greater activity by the superior enemy had to be reckoned with in the Donetz Basin and on the Mius front. After the evacuation of the Kuban bridgehead, the unit was renamed II/SG 2.

The *Gruppe* staff of **III/StG 2** 'Immelmann' was formed in May 1939 out of the staff of the erstwhile II/StG 163. The 7th to 9th *Staffeln* had previously flown as 4–6/StG 163 and in October 1943 formed the third *Gruppe* of Ground Attack *Geschwader* 2.

III *Gruppe* flew massive attacks during the Polish campaign under the command of the 1st *Fliegerdivision* and by its precise bombing prepared the storming of the western plain. After the close air support it achieved at Lvov, the unit was sent into action over the Netherlands, Belgium and northern France with great success. The next operations were chiefly to do with the crossing of the Marne, Seine and Loire by German troops.

From July 1940 further operations followed, attacking Allied convoys as well as some RAF airfields in southern England. In February 1941 the *Gruppe* moved into the command area of VIII *Fliegerkorps* and then took part in the Balkan campaign. Of particular note were the hard-won successes against cruisers and destroyers of the Royal Navy in May 1941. After a thorough rest, the unit took part from August 1941 in the deployment against the Soviet Union and, after attacks on Russian troop concentrations, flew successful operations against the battleships *Marat* and *Oktjabrskaya-Revoluzia*.

From the northern sector III/SG 2 then moved to the centre sector, where it brought its weapons into action successfully in the encirclement battle of Bryansk-Viasma. Up to the end of November 1941 the German positions could to some extent be protected during enemy offensives by well placed attacks. At the beginning of December 1941 the weakened forces of

A machine of III/StG 2 was braked too sharply and stood on its nose. The Gruppe *emblem, the 'Hlinka Cross', was in memory of the leader of the Slovakian people's movement, Andrej Hlinka.*

A wrecked Ju 87 D-3 of 1/StG 2 which had to make an emergency landing as a result of enemy fire in the southern sector of the eastern front.

Lieutenant Hans-Ulrich Rudel receives the congratulations of Captain Martin Möbus after returning from his thousandth operational flight. Instead of champagne, there was a Cup of Honour full of fresh milk – how could it have been otherwise? The 'good luck pig' was there as well.

III *Gruppe* supported the advance on Tula, in which for a time II (Ground Attack)/LG 2 was subordinated to StG 2. After hard battles in the winter of 1941–2 the *Gruppe* was taken out of action for rest and did not return to the eastern front from the Graz-Wels-Markersdorf area until 22 June 1942.

In the area of *Luftflotte* 4 the *Gruppe* supported the advance on Rostov and took part in the battle for Stalingrad. At the beginning of 1943 the forces that had remained with the Hozzel fighting unit tried to further the German attack on Samara and Orel. The unit was also decisively engaged in the recapture of Belgorod on 21 March 1943. After the bulk of III/StG 2 with the Kupfer fighting unit had tried to disrupt the Soviet advance against the Kuban, came the move to Charkov North, together with I and II *Gruppen*, from which they were to be engaged in the battles in the Donetz Basin.

From 9 May 1942 onwards III/StG 2 moved to Kerch and from there intervened in the battles in the Kuban bridgehead. After Operation *Citadel* was prematurely abandoned in August 1943 the destruction of a Soviet armoured breakthrough succeeded. As a result of enemy superiority, the Kuban bridgehead had finally to be evacuated and German troops had to be pulled back to the west. On 18 October 1943 III/SG 2 was formed from III/StG 2; the main centres of operations remained the same.

Like StG 1, the second 'Stuka' *Geschwader* also possessed for a time a tank hunting *Staffel* in excess of establishment (see Chapter 10).

5.3.3 Dive Bomber *Geschwader* 3

The third Dive Bomber *Geschwader* was formed in the summer of 1940. The ***Geschwader* staff**, however, did not come into existence until October 1943 through renaming of the former staff of KG 28; the same was true for the staff *Staffel*.

The first of three *Gruppen*, **I/StG 3**, was formed with 1–3/StG 3 from July 1940 onwards and from October 1943 onwards formed the corresponding *Staffeln* of SG 3. The *Gruppe* came from I/StG 76. This had arisen from I/StG 167, which was previously known as II/StG 162. The *Gruppe* was at first stationed at Lübeck and from 1938 onwards at Graz.

The unit took part in the Polish campaign as I/StG 76 and went into action over western Europe in StG 2, before it took off for flights over southern England and the Channel as a part of StG 3. There followed operations over the Balkans and Crete. In July 1941 came a movement to Libya.

After six months' operations over North African deserts, there followed a rest at Herzogenaurach in January 1942. In February the *Gruppe* was moved to the southern sector of the eastern front and intervened in the attack on the Soviet landing at Novorossisk. In cooperation with the Kupfer 'Stuka' unit until the early summer of 1942, it operated in the fierce ground battles that took place in the Kerch peninsula. After the capture of the peninsula in May 1942 and the disbandment of the fighting unit led by Dr Jur. Kupfer, I/StG 3 was attached to X *Fliegerkorps* and occupied various operational bases in the eastern Mediterranean.

On 18 October 1943 the 'Stuka' unit was renamed I/SG 3 and was then rested at Markersdorf.

II/StG 3 originated in January 1942 by the renaming of I/StG 1. To it were subordinated

This photograph was taken of a Ju 87 B-2 (works no. 5413, S1+JK) of 2/StG 3 shortly before an operation.

4–6/StG 3. The *Gruppe* originated from Ground Attack Air Group 20, which was still equipped with Hs 123s. In the autumn of 1938 I/StG 160 originated from this Group, equipped with Ju 87s, and was renamed I/StG 1 in May 1939.

At the beginning of 1942 II/StG 3 was in action over North Africa before it went for rest at Bari in southern Italy in April 1942. From May 1942 the 'Stuka' unit went back to Africa in order to support the German-Italian offensive which began on 26 May 1942. At the beginning of November 1942 came a move to Sardinia to take part in the attack on Allied shipping targets in the X *Fliegerkorps* area. Next the crews flew air attacks from Tunis-Aouina on Allied troops who had landed in Morocco and Algeria. II/StG 3 went through the next months of the fading Africa campaign in the command area of the Tunis Air Leader. On 25 November 1942 twenty-four Ju 87 Bs and Rs of II/StG 3 were overrun by British tanks on the airfield of Djedeida.

It was possible to equip the *Gruppe* with new machines by the end of 1942, and so the last operations could be flown with limited means from small airfields in the Bone peninsula (Tunis bridgehead). The remnants of the unit then went to Herzogenaurach for rest.

In the autumn of 1943 the *Gruppe* was next stationed in the eastern Mediterranean. From October 1943 it became a part of the Ground Attack *Geschwader* SG 3 by renaming.

III/StG 3 first originated in January 1942 from II/StG 2. The former 4th to 6th *Staffeln* of StG 2 were at that time at Pancrazio, equipped with Ju 87 D-1s. In the summer of 1942 the *Gruppe* was in action in North Africa together with the *Staffeln* of I and II/StG 3. In spite of dive bombing and low-level attacks flown with the utmost determination against the Allied troop concentrations, the page of history could not be turned back.

In March and April 1943 III/StG 3 operated from Tunisia. The *Gruppe* was subordinate there to the Tunis Close Combat *Fliegerkorps* (*Luftflotte* 2). Shortly before the end of the battles on the African continent, the *Gruppe* moved to Yugoslavia in March 1943. In May 1943 III/StG 3 was to be found in the *Luftflotte* 6 area in the centre sector of the eastern front in defence against strong Soviet army units. In September 1943 the unit flew supporting attacks in the *Luftflotte* 4 area of the hard-fought southern sector of the eastern front.

The commander of II/StG 3, Major Kurt Kuhlmey, in the North African theatre of war.

From the III *Gruppe* with 7–9/StG 3 came the III *Gruppe* of SG 3 with its 7th to 9th *Staffeln* in October 1943.

5.3.4 Dive Bomber *Geschwader* 5

StG 5 did not get beyond the formation of a single 'Stuka' *Gruppe* with four *Staffeln*. At the beginning of 1942 **I/StG 5** came out of IV('Stuka')/LG 1. From the reinforcement *Staffel* of IV/LG 1 came the reinforcement unit of I/StG 5 and in June 1942 4/StG 5, whereupon a new reinforcement unit was formed.

In the early summer of 1942 I *Gruppe* had thirty Ju 87s at its disposal, of which twenty-four were reported as battleworthy. The unit was at that time equipped with Ju 87 Rs and Ds and flew in the northern sector of the eastern front as well as over Finland. The 'Stuka' unit received what had hitherto been the staff of IV('Stuka')/LG 2 as *Gruppe* staff. In June 1943 this became the new *Gruppe* staff of I/StG 1 and hence had to be set up anew. At the end of August 1943 thirty-four Ju 87 D-5s and two Ju 87 Rs were available to the unit. In September a few more Ju 87 D-5s were added, as well as eleven DFS-230 freight gliders for transport tasks. In October 1943 I/SG 5 came out of I/StG 5, in which thirty-six Ju 87 Ds were in operation. At the end of the year the number of Ju 87 Ds and DFS-230s sank noticeably. Meanwhile 14(Fighter Bomber)/JG 5 was renamed 4/SG 5. This could call upon fourteen Fw 190 A-2s and A-3s to carry out its tasks. Ju 87 D-5s continued

The German dive bombers stationed at Comiso until May 1942 being moved with the Staffel's *own DFS 230 freight glider. The freight gliders were used for the transport of ground equipment and ground personnel, and also for general transport flights for which the machines of the dive bomber units were brought in as tugs.*

to be flown by 1–3/SG 5 until March 1943. From April onwards conversion to Fw 190s began *Staffel* by *Staffel*, in the process of which the command of *Luftflotte* 5 disbanded the 4th *Staffel* and ordered that its machines be transferred to the three remaining *Staffeln*. Some of the personnel went into the formation of 2/NSGr 8, while the majority were distributed among the remaining units of SG 5.

Its operational debut as a ground attack *Gruppe* took place in the autumn of 1943 under the leadership of the Air Leader, North in the *Luftflotte* 5 area, mostly from Kirkenes. From December 1943 onwards the unit operated as a ground attack *Gruppe* from Allakurti and Kemiervi. Soviet positions on the Fischer peninsula and Murmansk harbour together with the Murman railway were attacked, but also shipping targets in the northern coastal waters.

On 31 May 1944 one Fw 190 A-3 and two Ju 87 D-5s were available with the *Gruppe* staff, and a total of eight Fw 190 As with the 1st *Staffel*, four Fw 190 A-3s and four Ju 87 D-5s with the 2nd *Staffel*, and two Fw 190 A/Fs and seven Ju 87 D-5s with the 3rd *Staffel*. By the end of June 1944 only Fw 190 A/Fs, totalling thirty-six machines, were still in operation with the *Gruppe* in the far north of Europe.

In September 1944 a move to Berlin-Staaken was ordered. There I/SG 5 was renamed III/KG 200, and the existing 'Eichhorn Special *Staffel*' of KG 200 was integrated into the *Gruppe*.

5.3.5 Dive Bomber *Geschwader* 51

StG 51 also did not get past its formation phase. Other than the *Gruppe* staff of I and II/StG 51, only six dive bomber *Staffeln* were formed, which were equipped with Ju 87s.

The staff of **I/StG 51** was first formed in May 1939 out of the *Gruppe* staff of I/StG 165. To it were subordinated 1–3/StG 165 from this *Gruppe*, which only a month later were renamed 1–3/StG 77 and so no longer belonged to StG 51.

The formation of a second *Gruppe* of StG 51 at first did not happen at all, as sufficient equipment could not be made available for the purpose.

III/StG 51 was the former III/StG 165, together with its *Gruppe* staff and its erstwhile 7th to 9th *Staffeln*. This unit was the first step towards the formation of StG 51 in June 1938.

In case of an emergency landing in water, the use of the rubber boat was periodically practised in the dive bomber Staffeln.

The *Gruppe* took part in the Polish campaign and after the end of the fighting was moved to the west. In July 1940 the unit was renamed as III/StG 77. With that StG 51 ceased to exist.

5.3.6 Dive Bomber *Geschwader* 76

The build-up of StG 76 began in April 1938. Except for one *Gruppe*, **I/StG 76**, which was formed between June 1938 and July 1940 together with its *Gruppe* staff, no other units were formed within the planned StG 76.

The *Gruppe* staff was the former staff of I/StG 168. The *Staffeln* 1–3/StG 76 came out of the three *Staffeln* of I/StG 168. After the Polish campaign, in which the unit had taken part, the *Gruppe* was moved to the west and placed under *Luftflotte* 3.

The *Gruppe* went through the French campaign from May 1940, subordinated to StG 2 for operations. In the western theatre of war the *Gruppe* was placed under II *Fliegerkorps* (*Luftflotte* 3). In July 1940 the complete *Gruppe* became III/StG 77 and so lost its erstwhile independence.

5.3.7 Dive Bomber *Geschwader* 77

After Dive Bomber *Geschwader* 1–3, StG 77 was the fourth and last completely formed dive bomber *Geschwader* of the *Luftwaffe*.

As ***Geschwader* staff** for StG 77 that of the existing StG 165 was chosen in April 1939. A staff *Staffel* of its own was, however, formed in February 1941 and retained until May 1943.

The *Gruppe* staff of **I/StG 77** was formed in May 1939 out of that of the existing StG 51. To it

A Ju 87 D-1 (S7+KS) of 8/StG 3 on its nose in North Africa.

Loading a Ju 87 D-5 of 1/StG 3 with high-explosive bombs.

were subordinated the former 1st to 3rd *Staffeln*. However, 3/StG 77 separated in July 1940 and became 2/Testing *Gruppe* 210. In the same month the re-formation of the third *Staffel* was begun in order to complete I *Gruppe* again.

The second *Gruppe*, **II/StG 77**, originated a month earlier than I/StG 77 and came out of II/StG 165. In October 1943 the staff of II/SG 77 came out of the *Gruppe* staff. The 4th to 6th *Staffeln* belonging to this *Gruppe* were previously part of II/StG 165 and there comprised the 4th to 6th *Staffeln*. From October 1943 onwards III/SG 10 came out of II/StG 77. The existing I/SG 1 then became the new II *Gruppe*.

III/StG 77 at first carried the designation I/StG 76. In July 1940 I/StG 76 was taken up into the *Geschwader* unit of StG 77 and continued to belong to it long after the 'Stuka' *Geschwader* had become a ground attack *Geschwader*. *Staffeln* 1–3/StG 76 were assigned to the *Gruppe*. From these came 7–9/StG 77 in 1940 as well as III *Gruppe* with its 7–9/SG 77 from 1943.

After the Polish campaign the *Geschwader* staff stayed with I and II 'Stuka' *Gruppen* in the east for a short time and were next assigned to *Luftflotte* 3 in the west. In the attack on France the whole *Geschwader* with three *Gruppen* was placed under VIII (Close Combat) *Fliegerkorps*. From August 1940 these 'Stuka' *Gruppen* also attacked targets in the English Channel and southern England under the command of *Luftflotte* 3. In January 1941 the attacks on England were continued to a significant extent after short interruptions caused by the weather.

Next came a move back to occupied Poland. Thereafter the *Geschwader* was assigned to the future centre sector of the eastern front as its operations area. In the attack on the Soviet Union StG 77 was subordinate to II *Fliegerkorps* (*Luftflotte* 2). In the autumn of 1941 the unit was added to IV *Fliegerkorps* (*Luftflotte* 4), in order to strengthen the forces there. In December 1941 the *Geschwader* staff, together with I and II *Gruppen* found themselves behind the Mius front, while III/StG 77 was being rested at Cracow after the hard battles, which practically amounted to a new formation.

In the next year of the war all three *Gruppen* found themselves together in the VIII *Fliegerkorps* area in the southern sector of the eastern front. In June 1942 the crews attacked numerous targets in the Crimea from Sarabus.

III *Gruppe* was assigned to StG 1 from September 1942 onwards and thus came under *Luftflotte* 1 (northern sector of the eastern front). After substantial losses, the unit was again rested at Bobruisk.

From January 1943 the *Geschwader* staff, together with I and II *Gruppen*, operated from Nikolaev (IV *Fliegerkorps* area). At that time III *Gruppe* was still stationed at Bobruisk, where the whole *Geschwader* was concentrated from May 1943. From 18 October 1943 the unit carried the designation SG 77.

5.3.8 'Stuka' Reinforcement *Staffeln*

In order to prepare personnel coming from the pilot schools for their future operations and to make up the inevitable omissions and training deficiencies, several reinforcement *Staffeln* were formed.

Thus from August 1939 StG 1 had its own reinforcement *Staffel* (Erg. St./StG 1). From this unit, from May 1941 onwards, the staff of the

The machines of III/StG 51 were parked far apart for protection against enemy attacks. The nearest Ju 87 B-2 bore the letters 6G+LR.

An unknown crew of II/StG 77, decorated with the Iron Cross, First Class.

first *Gruppe* of the Training *Geschwader* StG 151 was formed.

With StG 2, likewise, a reinforcement *Staffel* was formed in November 1940. From it came the *Gruppe* staff for II/StG 151 in July 1943.

In November 1940 the reinforcement *Staffel* was formed for StG 3, from which the third *Gruppe* staff for StG 151 was to be taken in June 1943.

The reinforcement *Staffel* of StG 5 was formed in January 1942 from parts of the reinforcement *Staffel* of LG 1, but three months later it became a regular *Staffel* (4/StG 5). From April 1942 onwards the reinforcement unit was therefore re-formed. This provided for the continuation training of new forces until the summer of 1943 and then became the staff of IV/StG 151.

6/StG 77 originated out of 6/StG 165.

This Ju 87 crew, just returned from an operation and reporting on it, belonged to 6/StG 77, recognisable by the bison, swelled up with power.

The Jericho sirens had already been removed from this Ju 87 B-1 of the 7th Staffel *of StG 77.*

View of the dispersal area of the 4th and 7th Staffeln *of StG 77. The SC 50s are fitted with Dinort rods to ignite the fuses at a distance. (In theory, the bomb burst above the ground by that distance, throwing splinters further than if the bomb exploded on direct contact with the ground. Tr.)*

Commanders of the German Dive Bomber *Geschwader*

Dive Bomber *Geschwader* 1

18 November 1939–21 June 1940	Major Eberhard Baier
22 June 1940–15 March 1943	Lieutenant-Colonel Walter Hagen
1 April 1943–18 October 1943	Lieutenant-Colonel Gustav Pressler

Dive Bomber *Geschwader* 2

15 October 1939–15 October 1941	Major Oskar Dinort
16 October 1941–13 February 1943	Major Paul-Werner Hozzel
13 February 1943–October 1943	Lieutenant-Colonel Dr Jur. Ernst Kupfer

Dive Bomber *Geschwader* 3

10 January 1940–3 July 1940	Colonel Karl Angerstein
3 July 1940–1 April 1941	Lieutenant-Colonel Georg Edert
1 April 1941–1 September 1941	Lieutenant-Colonel Karl Christ
1 September 1941–1 April 1943	Lieutenant-Colonel Walter Sigel
1 April 1943–18 October 1943	Colonel Kurt Kuhlmey (later SG 3)

I/Dive Bomber *Geschwader* 5

No *Geschwader* staff available, only one *Gruppe* formed

I and III/Dive Bomber *Geschwader* 51

No *Geschwader* staff available, for a short time only two *Gruppen* available

I/Dive Bomber *Geschwader* 76

No *Geschwader* staff available, only one *Gruppe* formed

Dive Bomber *Geschwader* 77

1 September 1939–14 May 1940	Lieutenant-Colonel (Colonel) Günter Schwartzkopf
15 May 1940–20 July 1942	Major (Lieutenant-Colonel) Clemens *Graf* von Schönborn
25 July 1942–12 October 1942	Lieutenant-Colonel Alfons Orthofer
13 October 1942–20 February 1943	Major Walter Enneccerus
20 February 1943–5 October 1943	Colonel Helmut Bruck

Dive Bomber *Geschwader* 101

1 June 1943–1 October 1943	Colonel Clemens *Graf* von Schönborn

Dive Bomber *Geschwader* 102

Unknown – 5 June 1943	Colonel Karl Christ
6 June 1943–18 October 1943	Major Bernhard Hamester

Dive Bomber *Geschwader* 151

5 June 1943 – unknown	Colonel Karl Christ

The Dive Bomber *Geschwader* 51 and 76, which existed for a relatively short time, had no reinforcement units of their own.

With StG 77 there was a reinforcement *Staffel* from November 1940, but it joined StG 151 in July 1943. That *Geschwader* formed a reinforcement *Staffel* of its own from parts of V/StG 151, although this existed for only two months and in October 1943 was disbanded. From 18 October 1943 onwards StG 151 became SG 151, whose history is reported in Chapter 8.

5.4 Operations as a Ground Attack Aircraft

5.4.1 Increased Firepower

The operational task of most of the dive bomber *Geschwader* that were renamed as ground attack *Geschwader* hardly changed as a result of the new designation. In spite of the improvement of tactical capability, in the face of a superior enemy in the east no miracles were to be expected from the ground attack units equipped with Ju 87 Ds.

In the tactical field the long-recognised problems of cooperation between the army and the *Luftwaffe* remained. Reports on surprise changes in the situation were often not passed on quickly enough. The *Luftwaffe* was often informed of centres of action late, sometimes much too late. The close support units of the *Luftwaffe* which were, in any case, far too meagre for the length of the front, could therefore not be assembled in time. Because of the Germans' numerical inferiority, the operational possibilities were, moreover, increasingly restricted.

All strategic operations, above all air attacks on distant industrial centres and armament plants, had to be ended from 1942, with a few exceptions. The hard-pressed army constantly needed more support in order to be able to some extent to withstand the continually growing enemy pressure.

From the early summer of 1943 it was finally decided that important targets in the hinterland of the eastern front should be attacked. As a result of the huge enemy offensives and the catastrophe of Stalingrad, suitable means of undertaking operations were in the end quite simply not available. The action did not therefore go beyond small attacks.

The daily business of the ground attack units consisted in preventing the army bleeding to death. Because of the ever more frequent deficiencies in resupply and the restrictions in the assignment of fuel, the ground attack forces could not intervene over the hard-pressed front in the numbers desired by the army.

Although the enemy had to submit to heavy defeats in the autumn of 1941, they continually became stronger after 1942. At the same time, not only could the Red Army and its air forces

The first Ju 87 D-5s went to III/StG 2 in June 1943. Because of the two MG 151/20 weapons, the offensive capacity was greatly enhanced.

The wreck of a Ju 87 D-3 (works no. 1221) belonging to SG 2. The VS 11 wooden propeller splintered during the emergency landing. (Federal Archives)

be assured of support from the western Allies; also, the armament plants lying beyond the Urals remained practically unreachable by the *Luftwaffe* bomber *Geschwader*. On 15 November 1943 the position of General of Close Combat Pilots was established and from then on was responsible for operational principles, training and the further development of armament. However, the close combat pilots and the ground attack units capable of dive bombing had increasingly to wait for the provision of new and, above all, more potent air equipment.

From the end of 1943 the defence of the *Reich*, including an increase in fighter production, received the highest priority. The operational strength of the close combat pilots had to suffer.

If an 'army air force' had been created, there would probably have been a decisive improvement in the situation of the close combat pilots. This, however, was not the intention of Imperial Marshal Hermann Göring. The creation of powerful air close support units – like the Allied Tactical Air Forces, as far as possible with their own fighter protection – did not take place on the German side.

A final attempt to build up such a formation with Ju 87 Ds failed at the end of 1944. The majority of the former Ju 87 units had for a long time been equipped with Fw 190 Fs; only a few of the units still flew the Junkers 'Stuka'.

The significance of the role played by the air close support units of the *Luftwaffe* up to the last years of the war was shown by the fact that shortly before the Allied invasion of Normandy, in the spring of 1944, about 45 per cent of the whole aircraft inventory of the *Luftwaffe* was employed in support of the army. In this phase came the replacement of the Ju 87 and the conversion to Fw 190 F-8 ground attack aircraft. The dive bombing attack already belonged in general to the distant past. Even for the Ju 87 units the main aim was in ground attack operations, especially in attacks on enemy troop concentrations or tank forces of the Red Army that had broken through the main battle line. Most of these operations were fought out in the area, about 50 km deep, behind the main battle line. Thanks to the firepower of the MG 151/20 cannon of the later Ju 87 Ds, unarmoured or partly armoured vehicles, especially if travelling in convoy, could be attacked relatively easily as long as no light flak was brought with them.

Against armoured targets the tank hunters equipped with 37-mm cannon (Flak 18) above all came into play.

Only when they had converted to Fw 190 F-8 single-seat ground attack aircraft, and with the increased equipment of these and similar construction series with modern anti-tank weapons such as 'Tank Lightning' (*Panzerblitz*) or 'Tank Terror' (*Panzerschreck*), did the anti-tank *Staffeln* receive a significant increase in combat value. (*Panzerblitz* and *Panzerschreck* were both anti-tank projectiles which could be fired from wooden launchers under the wings of the Fw 190 F-8, F-9 and D-9 or the Ju 87 D. The rockets were based on the R4M and had a hollow-charge explosive head.)

The AB 250 and AB 500 bomb containers, already long in service, effectively rounded out the Fw 190 F-8s equipped with anti-tank rockets or the Ju 87 G-2s equipped with 37-mm cannon – and not only during the transitional phase. They remained one of the most effective means of attacking enemy troop concentrations by reason of their area effect. They gave good service both against attacking infantry and against armoured vehicles.

Heavily armoured targets, especially superheavy battle tanks, could be attacked on the battlefield only with difficulty with the SC 50 bomb: here the hits were frequently not accurate enough. Apart from direct hits, which caused the destruction of the tank, near misses could damage the undercarriage or the tracks, so that the tank was left immobile.

Apart from this, the SC 50 bomb was not particularly efficient, as usually only four could be carried and they were quickly used up.

In complete contrast were the bomb containers AB 70, 250 and 500. These easily manufactured wooden containers, of which there were three different types, were especially suited to small armour-piercing munitions. Other than the folding shell form, bomb containers in framework or bundle form were in use in the anti-tank units.

In view of the numerous bombs in the bomb containers and their thin walls, they had to be

'Leni', a D-3 (T6+IIR). In front of the machine is the whole palette of free-fall weapons up to the SC 1000.

A5+EB belonged to the staff of I Gruppe *of SG 1 and was loaded with SC 250 bombs under the wings.* (Federal Archives)

handled extremely carefully. In particular, it was not advisable to drop them, roll them or throw them. Up-ending the containers was forbidden as the small bombs could come loose and detonate accidentally. For these reasons the bomb containers remained in their transport containers until immediately before they were loaded onto the aircraft. Being mostly made of wood, they had to be protected against wet or snow by tarpaulins. The following containers made up the bulk of this free-fall ordnance:

AB 70	with 23 SD 2 Bs with variable-delay fuses, total weight: 60 kg
AB 250-2	with 224 SD 1 bombs, total weight: 215 kg
	with 114 SD 2 bombs, total weight: 280 kg
	with 40 SD 4 Hl bombs, total weight: 210 kg
	with 17 SD 10 A bombs, total weight: 220 kg
	with 28 SD 10 C bombs, total weight: 270 kg
AB 500-1	with 392 SD 1 bombs, total weight: 415 kg
	with 74 SD 4 Hl bombs, total weight: 400 kg
	with 37 SD 10 A bombs, total weight: 470 kg
	with 28 French SD 10 bombs, total weight: 370 kg
AB 500-1D	with 24 SD 15 bombs, total weight: 430 kg
AB 500-3B	with 4 SD 70 bombs, total weight: 300 kg

According to munitions handbooks, point targets in an area of 30–50 metres × 30–40 metres could be attacked especially effectively with AB 250s and 500s with hollow-charge bombs – for example SD 4 Hl – in diving or shallow-dive attacks with a release height of 400–800 metres. The attacks could be flown with a speed of up to 540 kph.

With SD 1s to SD 15s the ground attack forces succeeded chiefly in destroying important railway targets, reinforcement areas and vehicle concentrations. With unprotected troop concentrations devastating results were achieved.

The rate of success was reduced from the end of 1943, with the ever more plentiful appearance of strong Soviet armoured flak forces which were sent out with the armoured formations, as well as the generally increasing flak concentrations which soon surrounded almost all targets that were worth protecting. Since the operational forces of the ground attack *Geschwader* that were equipped with Ju 87 Ds had to manoeuvre more slowly – compared to those with Fw 190 Fs and Gs – their losses were relatively higher. Their replacement by the single-engined Fw 190 was therefore advised and was undertaken as quickly as possible. In particular the F-8 series (as well as the F-9 planned for large-scale production) was supposed to be the standard equipment of the German ground attack *Geschwader* from 1944 onwards.

5.4.2 The Ground Attack *Geschwader* (*Schlachtgeschwader* – SG)

With effect from 18 October 1943 came a restructuring of the German close combat and ground attack units. From the existing dive bomber *Geschwader* (StG) came the ground attack *Geschwader* (SG). For reasons of space the individual ground attack *Geschwader* can be discussed only briefly.

5.4.2.1 Ground Attack *Geschwader* 1

Ground attack *Geschwader* 1, with its three *Gruppen*, operated exclusively in the east and between 1 April 1943 and 30 April 1944 was under the leadership of the bearer of the Knight's Cross, Lieutenant-Colonel Gustav Pressler. On 1 May 1944 Major Peter Gasmann took over the unit, to command it until it was disbanded in May 1945.

After the renaming of I/StG 1 as **I/SG 1**, which took place on 18 October 1943, the unit remained in operation with Ju 87 B-2s, D-1s and D-3s, first in the northern and then in the central sector of the eastern front. The main points of operation were, as before, the support of the offensive operations in the battle for Kursk and the defensive battles around Orel. The destinies of the unit were linked from 17 May 1943 – at first only provisionally – with Major Horst Kaubisch as *Gruppe* commander, who was decorated with the Knight's Cross on 16 November 1942. On 12 February 1945 he fell with his Fw 190 F-8 in aerial combat with Soviet fighters after more than 1,000 operational flights, the majority in the Ju 87.

The unit commanded by him until then operated in the winter of 1943–4 from Bobruisk, Mogilev and Luniniec in the 1st *Fliegerdivision* area, which belonged to the 6th *Luftflotte*. Between March and May 1944 the operations were mostly conducted from Biala-Podlaska. From June onwards the ground attack *Gruppe* was assigned to the 4th *Fliegerdivision* and briefly stationed at Tolotshin, whence it moved to Lida in July and then to Dubno and Kovno. At the beginning of September I/SG 1 flew its operations over the eastern front from Modlin in the area of *Luftflotte* 6. After the unit had operated for more than a month from Lubenstadt in Croatia, I/SG 1 moved to Schönfeld-Seifersdorf in Bavaria, where it was converted from the Ju 87 D to the Fw 190 F-8 from the end of November. With this aircraft operations in the east were resumed at the beginning of February 1945 from Cottbus. At the end of February 1945 the unit was at Fürstenwalde.

After numerous defensive operations over the middle sector of the eastern front, II/StG 1 was renamed **II/SG 1** on 18 October 1943 at Orsha. Previously, at Baranowice, twelve experienced crews were trained for night operations; after the renaming of the *Gruppe* they at times flew risky ground attack operations from both Mogilev and Bobruisk. The *Gruppe* was led from 16 April 1944 onwards by Major Karl Schrepfer, who on 28 April 1945 became the 850th soldier of the *Wehrmacht* to be decorated with the Oak Leaves to the Knight's Cross.

Up to January 1944 the attack on ground targets, especially armoured vehicles, in the middle sector of the eastern front, flying from Moledetshno, remained of the greatest importance. In mid-February 1944 the *Gruppe* was moved to Wesenburg in the northern sector and there was placed under the 3rd *Fliegerdivision* belonging to *Luftflotte* 1. In March 1944 the Ju 87 crews moved with their machines to Rovaniemi in Lapland and for a short time tried to destroy targets along the strategically important Muran railway. Next, from 25 April 1944, the crews intervened from Reval-Laksberg in the

Because of its size, the SC 1800 could be considered only as an overload for short operating distances This Ju 87 D-3 of 2/StG 2 was loaded with great effort by block and tackle.

With Ground Attack Geschwader *1 the Ju 87 D-5 was among the most popular versions of the 'Stuka' among the pilots. Fw 190 Fs with AB 500s were also operated from this snow-covered airfield.*

defensive battles in the Baltic. After that they operated in May 1944 from Idriza and Jakobstadt. Between 29 May 1944 and 28 June 1944 II/SG 1 also was retrained at Vilna on the inherently faster Fw 190 F-8.

With this equipment the unit was generally in operation over East Prussia up to the beginning of 1945, before it went to Mackfitz on 6 March 1945 after costly battles along the Oder front. After operational flights over the Berlin area, the ground attack *Gruppe* was disbanded at Flensburg at the beginning of May 1945.

III/StG 1 likewise became **III/SG 1** through renaming as a ground attack *Gruppe* in October 1943. Shortly before that the unit had been engaged in relief attacks in the evacuation of Smolensk (24 September 1943) and in the hard battles in the neighbourhood of Krivoi Rog south of Nikopol. After giving up its former aircraft, the *Gruppe* had been equipped solely with Ju 87 D-5s. Between April 1943 and April 1944 its leadership was in the hands of Major Friedrich Lang, who flew his thousandth operation with the Ju 87 against artillery positions south of Vitebsk on 7 March 1944.

At the beginning of 1944, the ground attack *Gruppe* was assigned the defence of the area around Vitebsk and the attack on enemy armour targets up to 70 km behind the main battle line.

This photograph of a Ju 87 D-5, with its Jumo 211 J engine just being started by two groundcrew members, originated with 1/SG 1 in the winter of 1943–4. (Federal Archives)

Major Friedrich Lang was decorated with the Knight's Cross and on 2 July 1944 received the Swords. He made 1,008 operational flights, of which only one was with the Fw 190 F; the others were all in Ju 87s.

In February the unit operated from Polotsk and at the beginning of March 1944 went to Orsha.

From March, III/SG 1 was also re-equipped with the Fw 190 F at Vilna. This was broadly completed by the middle of May 1944, and was followed by a move to Radzyn and from there to Baranovitshi, from where numerous operations were carried out over Russia and the north-eastern part of Poland. From the beginning of September 1944 operations over East Prussia followed from Insterburg. From Hexengrund, where the *Gruppe* was stationed between 9 and 27 February 1945, it went via Pomerania to the hard-pressed Oder front. In May 1945 the surviving parts of the *Gruppe* were disbanded at Flensburg-Weiche.

5.4.2.2 Ground Attack *Geschwader* 2

The legendary 'Immelmann' *Geschwader* was led from 1 October 1943 by Lieutenant-Colonel Hans-Karl Stepp, later to be awarded the Oak Leaves. From 1 September 1944 Lieutenant-Colonel Hans-Ulrich Rudel took over the unit, having previously led III/SG 2. After he was severely wounded, Kurt Kuhlmey temporarily took over (14 March 1945 to 20 April 1945).

From StG 2 'Immelmann' arose in mid-October 1943 the ground attack *Geschwader* SG 2 'Immelmann'. In the medium term SG 2 also had the prospect of conversion to the inherently faster, single-seat Fw 190 F-8 or F-9. After I/StG 2 had become **I/SG 2**, operations over the eastern front went on without noticeable change. Up to 15 October 1943 Major Bruno Dilley had led the *Gruppe*. He was followed by Captain Alwin Boerst, who undertook a total of 1,060 operations with the Ju 87 and was shot down with his Ju 87 G-2 in the attack on a concentration of armour at Parliti near Jassy on 30 March 1944.

Next the *Gruppe* was taken over by Captain Kurt Lau, who was decorated with the Knight's Cross by Colonel-General Otto Dessloch, chief of *Luftflotte* 4, on 22 April 1944 as a result of SG 2's 100,000th sortie. Kurt Lau undertook most of his 900 operations with the Ju 87 D-5. In the process he destroyed seventy to eighty tanks and in addition shot down two Russian aircraft. The last *Gruppe* commander was Captain Herbert Bauer, who destroyed more than fifty enemy tanks and could log eleven confirmed and twelve unconfirmed air victories.

The ground attack *Gruppe* led by these Knight's Cross bearers operated until June 1943 for the most part in the southern sector of the eastern front. Between 24 October 1943 and 10 November 1943 the crews also briefly flew operations in front of German positions on the Dnieper. At the beginning of 1944 the ground attack unit was located at Pervomaisk, in March at Uman, Nicolaev and Rauchovka. Starting on 1 April 1944, the crews attacked ground targets

Bomb containers, whose various fillings corresponded to the operations of the time, were increasingly used from 1943 onwards; here is a Ju 87 D-5 of StG 2.

Bomb containers lie ready for the Ju 87 D-5 of the Gruppe *commander of II/StG 2, Lieutenant-Colonel Ernst Kupfer.*

in the northern sector of the eastern front from Tiraspol for a few days, before the *Gruppe* moved to Husi in Romania, where it remained between 7 April 1944 and 26 June 1944. Small parts of it occasionally flew attacks from Pleso in Serbia against suspected partisan positions.

Only in June 1944 did the conversion of the unit, *Staffel* by *Staffel*, to the Fw 190 F-8 begin at Sächsisch-Regen. After the end of training with Fw 190 F-8s, the first parts of the unit were able to go into action until July 1944 against Soviet attacks in the Kovel area and later in the eastern regions of East Prussia.

Up to the capitulation the Fw 190 unit was in action in Hungary, Romania, Upper Silesia and Niederlausitz. Because of lack of fuel, the number of sorties had to be ever more reduced.

The second *Gruppe* of the *Geschwader*, II/StG 2 'Immelmann', had flown numerous combat operations between 7 September and 9 October 1943 to protect the evacuation of the Kuban bridgehead. Next the unit covered the further retreat in the area of Army Group South. After being renamed **II/SG 2** in the second half of October 1943, the relieving attacks on targets in the southern sector of the front were continued. The ground attack *Gruppe* was led successively by the Knight's Cross bearers Major Dr Jur. Ernst Kupfer, Major Heinz Frank and Major Karl Kennel. The latter was promoted Major on 30 January 1945 and undertook the last of his 957 operations on the morning of 8 May 1945.

Aircraft of III/StG 2 taxi for take-off. In the first machine, a D-5, is Captain Hans-Ulrich Rudel.

Between November 1943 and February 1944 the unit's Ju 87 D crews attacked targets behind the front given out by *Luftflotte* 4. Some of the attacks took place from Bagerovo. In February 1944 the unit operated from Pervomaisk and, from March, from Nicolaev. For a few days operational forces were moved to Romania and flew ground attack operations from Husi against advancing Soviet armoured divisions.

In March 1944 two *Staffeln* of II/SG 2 moved without their aircraft to Neisse-Stephansdorf and on 7 March 1944 became 10(Pz)/SG 3 as well as part of SG 77. At Markersdorf conversion to Ju 87 Gs took place. The remainder of the *Gruppe* remained at Karankut in the Crimea and from there attacked targets in the southern sector of the eastern front in April 1944. In the following weeks Chersonnese in the Crimea became the base for further ground attack operations. In June 1944 the remnants of the *Gruppe* moved to Zilistes and then further to Sächsisch-Regen, as the conversion to Fw 190s was imminent. After its conclusion in July 1944, the pilots were again sent into defensive action. The main points of these events were the defence of East Prussia and the battles east of Warsaw.

From the end of August 1944 onwards the unit attacked numerous individual targets in Romania and, from November onwards, in Hungary with its Fw 190 F-8s. In part the Fw 190s of II *Gruppe* were also drawn in as fighter protection for Hans-Ulrich Rudel and the tank hunting *Staffel* of the *Geschwader*. Relieving attacks in Silesia, on the Oder front and in the Bautzen-Görlitz area followed, as well as at Dresden.

III/SG 2 originated from III/StG 2 and at the beginning of October 1943 was in action in the withdrawal battles in the Army Group South area. Shortly before the change to III/SG 2 Captain Hans-Ulrich Rudel had taken over the

T6+CD belonged to the Gruppe *staff of III/StG 2. The SC 50 bombs were equipped with stand-off rods.*

Major Alwin Boerst, commander of I/StG 2, in the cockpit of his Ju 87 D-3; Russia in the winter of 1942–3.

leadership of the unit. At the end of August he passed it on to Major Lothar Lau who was shot down on 22 January 1945 in a low-level attack flown with Ju 87 Ds and went into captivity from which he did not return home until 18 January 1950. Major Müller, the former leader of the Pilot School (FFS) 7, with its home base at Görlitz, took over the unit. As he lacked the appropriate knowledge, III *Gruppe* was led into action by Captain Hendrik Stahl and Lieutenant Wilhelm Stähler alternately. Both had the appropriate experience thanks to their combined total of 2,300 operations.

III *Gruppe* found itself, like the other ground attack *Gruppen*, in continuous action along the eastern front. Between 24 October and 10 November 1943 the crews flew relieving attacks in front of the German positions along the Dnieper.

At the beginning of 1944 the ground attack unit operated together with 10(Pz)/SG 2 from Pervomaisk, where the operational forces were stationed in February. The flights were then continued with Ju 87 Ds from Jassy. There, from April 1944 onwards, the *Geschwader* staff followed with 10(Pz)/SG 2, in order to support the operations of III/SG 2 as far as possible. In May 1944 the crews flew their operations from Husi in Romania. As a result of enemy pressure,

Captain Karl Janke in the partly armoured cockpit of his Ju 87 D-3 (II/SG 2), with which he had just undertaken his 200th operational flight.

Company Sergeant of the staff of I/SG 2 in the cockpit of a Ju 87 D.

III/SG 2 moved to Dubno, Mielec and Zamosc in July, where the unit was under the command of VII *Fliegerkorps*. From there III/SG 2 briefly went into action over Hungary in September 1944 from Görgenyoroszfalu – together with the other parts of the *Geschwader*. A few weeks later, the Ju 87 Ds flew massive ground attack operations against Red Army tanks from Ferihagy together with Ju 87 D-5s and G-2s. After the operations by III/SG 2 from Sajo Kaza came the conversion to Fw 190 F-8s.

Only on 5 February 1945 were operations resumed in significant strength in the area of *Luftflotte* 6. The main areas of operations were Frankfurt an der Oder, Görlitz and Kamenz, north-east of Glatz. In the following weeks the crews of III/SG 2 attacked the enemy forces which had broken through in increased numbers. In March 1945 the *Gruppe* was at Prague-Kletzau, where the majority of the operational machines were set on fire in an American low-level attack. At the end of April 1945 desperate low-level attacks followed at Freiberg in Saxony and south-west of Dresden. At the beginning of May 1945 the *Gruppe* was at Milovic, 35 km north-east of Prague, from where it went to Niemes-South.

Among the final operations of the 'Immelmann' *Geschwader* were the flights of the three remaining Ju 87s and four Fw 190s against Soviet armoured forces. Then Colonel Hans-Ulrich Rudel led the crews to Kitzingen in Franconia after an unsuccessful attack, in order to surrender there to the American troops.

5.4.2.3 Ground Attack *Geschwader* 3

StG 3 was, in the same way, turned into a ground attack *Geschwader*, SG 3, on 18 October 1943. At the time of the renaming the unit was led by Major Kurt Kuhlmey, who was decorated with the Knight's Cross on 15 July 1942 and at the end of the war was active on the staff of the General of Ground Attack Pilots. From 15 February 1945 the commanding officer was Major Bernhard Hamester. This bearer of the Knight's Cross lost his life on 22 April 1945 in a low-level attack on super-heavy Stalin tanks, when his machine had received several flak hits and crashed from an altitude of 200 metres at Trebbin.

From I/StG 3 came **I/SG 3**, whose completely exhausted *Staffeln* had to be moved to Markersdorf at the beginning of 1944, after operating with *Luftflotte* South (in southern Russia), in order to rebuild the weakened units. In February 1944 I/SG 3 moved to the northern sector of the eastern front and there came under the command of the 3rd *Fliegerdivision* (*Luftflotte* 1).

Between February and June 1944 the main operations base was the relatively well-built Dorpat, before the *Gruppe* joined the 'Kuhlmey fighting unit' in June 1944. From July it was first

This Ju 87 D-5 belonged to 4/SG 3 and is just being fuelled for the next operation.

based at Lida and, after a return to Dorpat, moved from there to Pardubice. From 1 September 1944, the existing 'Stuka' unit was converted, *Staffel* by *Staffel*, to the faster Fw 190 ground attack aircraft. From Pardubice part of the ground attack *Gruppe* was transferred to Jesau in East Prussia from the beginning of 1945. On 6 February 1945 the unit supported ground troops at Heiligenbeil. The road led by way of Pinnow and Brüsterort to central Germany. On 21 March 1945 there were still twenty-one machines available in the *Gruppe*, of which, in spite of the catastrophic supply situation, seventeen Fw 190 F-8s were reported as airworthy.

II/StG 3 became **II/SG 3** on 18 October 1943. After the unit was withdrawn to Europe at the last minute from the collapsing Tunis bridgehead, to be rested at Herzogenaurach, in October 1943 operations began in the X *Fliegerkorps* area from Rhodes and Leros. Besides attacks on enemy maritime targets, attacks on partisans were also from time to time on the operations orders.

Between January and May 1944 there followed operations by II/SG 3 in the *Luftflotte* 1 area on the eastern front. Most of these were flown from the operational bases of Idriza, Petseri and Pleskau. In June the crews operated from Jakobstadt.

Shortly thereafter the *Gruppe* became a part of the 'Kuhlmey fighting unit', whose task was to support the relatively weak German forces in Finland.

From the end of August 1944 conversion of II *Gruppe* from Ju 87 Ds to Fw 190 F-8s began. Further operations from Dorpat followed against targets on the Neva. The unit moved in September to Riga-Splive and from there to Libau in October 1944. In February 1945 ground attack operations on the eastern front were flown from Sprottau. Among the unit's last stations were the airfields at Werneuchen and Finow, before the end of the war also reached II/SG 3. On 1 April 1945 the *Gruppe* still had thirty Fw 190 F-8s at its disposal, among them twelve battleworthy machines with 'Tank Lightning'.

III/SG 3 also originated from a dive bomber *Gruppe*, III/StG 3, which, in September 1943, was operating in the southern sector of the

S7+AS was a Ju 87 D-5 on the strength of III/SG 3 which flew ground attack operations along the eastern front.

This photographic memento was taken after the 300th operational flight of Corporal Qualo (left). On the right is Sergeant-Major Rainer Nossek (4/SG 2), who was later transferred to 10/SG 3 and was seriously wounded in an air battle on 30 April 1945.

eastern front under the command of *Luftflotte* 4. The *Gruppe* was at that time led by Captain Bernhard Hamester and, from 1 December 1943, by Captain Eberhardt Jacob, who received the Knight's Cross on 29 February 1944 and, from April 1944, was active in the OKL command staff. From May the commanding officer was Captain Siegfried Göbel. On 19 March 1945 he unexpectedly became a prisoner of war of the Russians during an operation near Plattensee. Captain Erich Bunge took over the ground attack *Gruppe* until the end of the war, which was then close.

After being renamed III/SG 3 on 18 October 1943, the unit remained in the southern sector of the eastern front and in the spring of 1944 flew numerous operations from Karankut, Petseri and Sevastopol-Chersonese under the command of I *Fliegerkorps*. At the beginning of May part of the unit operated from Foşcani in Romania.

On 5 May 1944, after a move to Pardubice, the conversion to Fw 190 Fs began. Then, from June 1944 the unit moved to the northern sector of the eastern front, where it received its operations orders from the 3rd *Fliegerdivision*. In July 1944 the crews flew air support, in spite of numerous losses, from Tilsit, Mitau and Wenden.

In September 1944 III/SG 3 was at Poltsama, in October at Skiotava and in November with *Luftflotte* 1 at Frauenburg. In 1945 the pilots with their Fw 190 F-8s intervened in the ground battles from airfields in the Courland. The unit

Loading a Ju 87 D-3 of 7/SG 3 with high-explosive bombs. (Federal Archives)

tried to support the 18th Army in the Courland battles from Zabeln. As a result of the rapidly deteriorating fuel situation, only a few sorties per day could be flown in the end.

5.4.2.4 Ground Attack *Geschwader* 4

Ground attack *Geschwader* SG 4, which was formed from parts of Ground Attack *Geschwader* 2 and the Fast Bomber *Geschwader* 10, was, because of its late formation, mainly equipped with Fw 190 Fs instead of Ju 87 Ds. The unit was led by the Knight's Cross bearers Major Georg Dörffel, Major Ewald Janssen, Colonel Alfred Druschel and Major Dörnbeck.

5.4.2.5 Ground Attack *Geschwader* 5

I/SG 5, which originated from the *Staffeln* of I/StG 5 (previously IV('Stuka')/LG 1), initially flew Ju 87 D-3s and D-5s, which were subsequently replaced by Fw 190 F-8s. As an additional fourth *Staffel*, 14(Jabo)/JG 5, with its Fw 190s, joined the ground attack *Gruppe* on 7 February 1944. From 1/SG 5 came 2/NSGr 5, whereupon the new first *Staffel* came out of 4/SG 5, which was renamed 9/KG 200 in January 1945. At the end of 1944 the former *Staffeln* of I/SG 5 were at Berlin-Staaken. The two other units, with their Fw 190 F-8s, formed the 11th and 12th *Staffeln* of KG 200 from 10 January 1945 onwards. On 15 February 1945 parts of the *Staffeln* were at Freiwaldau. The remnants which were still available at the end of the war were disbanded on 8 May 1945 in Schleswig-Holstein.

5.4.2.6 Ground Attack *Geschwader* 9

SG 9, with its two *Gruppen*, was an anti-tank *Geschwader* in the process of formation, whose equipment ranged from Ju 87s, through Hs 129s, to Fw 190s. At the beginning of 1945 the unit was led by Lieutenant-Colonel Hanscke. IV *Gruppe* was led by Captain Hans-Hermann Steinkamp, who had previously led 14(Pz)/SG 9 and had destroyed at least seventy enemy tanks and heavily damaged a further fifty. At the end of the war part of the *Gruppe* was on the air base at Wels near Linz. (For further information on SG 9 see Chapter 10.)

5.4.2.7 Ground Attack *Geschwader* 10

SG 10 came out of parts of Ground Attack *Geschwader* 1, IV/Fast Bomber *Geschwader* (SKG) and II/StG 77. Except for a relatively few Fiat CR 42s, only Fw 190s were flown. After numerous operations in the northern sector of the eastern front, I *Gruppe* was at Pistyan in Slovakia at the beginning of 1945 and next at Budweis. **II/SG 10** was then near Vienna and at the beginning of May 1945 was stationed at Wels. The last commandant was Lieutenant-Colonel Georg Jakob, who could boast 1,091 combat operations, the majority in Ju 87s with SG 77. On 12 April 1945 he was shot down at Tulln and was able to parachute to safety, although he was wounded. III *Gruppe* had previously been almost destroyed in the retreat from Hungary and at the beginning of May 1945 was at Prerau.

5.4.2.8 Ground Attack *Geschwader* 77

SG 77 consisted in 1943 of three ground attack *Gruppen* which were renamed on 18 October 1943 from the existing dive bomber *Geschwader* StG 77. Other than a few Ju 87 D-1s, most of the operational machines belonged to the Ju 87 D-3 series. The Ju 87 D-5 was in service in comparatively small numbers, for example with the 1st *Staffel*.

At the time of the renaming Major Helmut Bruck was the commanding officer of SG 77. As a captain, after 200 operations, he had been decorated with the Knight's Cross on 4 September 1941. On 19 February 1943, as commanding officer of I/StG 77, he received the coveted Oak Leaves to the Knight's Cross. The majority of his 973 combat operations were in Ju 87 Ds; he undertook only fifteen with Fw 190 F-8s. On 16 February 1945 Lieutenant-Colonel Manfred Mössinger replaced him as *Geschwader* commandant. As Colonel he served as the last General of Ground Attack Pilots (North) from April 1945.

The commander of I *Gruppe* was Karl Henze, who completed his thousandth combat operation on 26 February 1944 in a Ju 87 D at Uman and was promoted Major on 1 April 1944. When he took over SG 102 on 15 November 1944 Captain Hans-Joachim Brand followed him. This officer, who had been recommended for the Oak Leaves to the Knight's Cross, was hit by Soviet anti-aircraft fire on 18 April 1945 between

Colonel Alfred Heinrich Konrad Druschel

4 February 1917	Born in Bindsachen, District of Büdingen, Upper Hesse
1923–7	Primary school in Westerburg, Westerwald
1927–8	Secondary school in Westerburg, Westerwald
1 November 1928–December 1935	Upper secondary school at Dietzenburg
29 December 1935	Award of certificate of school completion
1 January 1936	Inducted into *Reich* Labour Service (to 1 April 1936)
6 April 1936	Entry as cadet into School of Air Warfare (LKS) at Berlin-Gatow (first semester)
31 July 1936	Call up to Rangsdorf (second semester)
1 October 1936	Promotion to Cadet Lance-Corporal
1 December 1936	Promotion to Cadet Corporal
20 April 1937	Promotion to Junior Under Officer
1 June 1937	Call up to third semester
1 May 1937	Ordered to I/JG 132
24 May 1937	Won military pilot licence
15 December 1937	Promotion to Senior Under Officer
24 February 1938	Commissioned as 2nd Lieutenant (seniority date 1 January 1938)
1 July 1938	Observer training at the Bomber School at Tutow; two-seat ground attack course, next *Fliegergruppe* 20
1 August 1938	For a short time with *Fliegergruppe* 40 and the Main Bomber School at Fassberg
1 September 1938	Posted from Fassberg to Regensburg
1 November 1938	Posted to I/KG 252 at Cottbus
1 January 1939	Posted to II (Ground Attack)/LG 2 as pilot
September 1939	Operations with 4 (Ground Attack)/LG 2 in Poland
27 September 1939	Decorated with the Iron Cross, Second Class
September 1939	Successful low-level attacks during the Polish campaign, especially during the encirclement battle on the River Bzura

21 May 1940	Decoration with the Iron Cross, First Class; ground attack operations (low-level attacks with the Hs 123) over France
1 June 1940	Promotion to Lieutenant
1 July 1940	Posting to *Luftflotte* Command 3 (staff officer)
20 September 1940	Posting to Fighter Reinforcement *Gruppe* Merseburg
11 December 1940	Posting to II (Ground Attack)/LG 2 as *Staffel* commander of 4 ('Stuka')/LG 2
1 February 1941	Posting StG 1 as *Staffel* commander of 2/StG 1
23 April 1941	Observation of the duties of the commander of I/StG 1
22 June 1941	First operations over Russia
21 August 1941	Decoration with the Knight's Cross to the Iron Cross, seven air victories to date in over 200 operational flights
21 August 1941	Promotion to Captain
October 1941	*Staffel* commander with I/SG 1
13 January 1942	Nomination as commander of I/SG 1
3 September 1942	Decoration with the Oak Leaves to the Knight's Cross of the Iron Cross as the 118th soldier of the *Wehrmacht* so decorated
4 September 1942	600th operational flight
19 November 1942	700th operational flight
19 February 1943	Decoration with the Swords to the Knight's Cross with Oak Leaves of the Iron Cross as the 24th soldier of the *Wehrmacht* so decorated
1 March 1943	Promotion to Major
1 March 1943	Nomination as commander of the Destroyer Reinforcement *Gruppe*
1 September 1943	Posting to the staff of Ground Attack *Geschwader* SG 1
13 September 1943	Posting to the staff of the Close Combat Pilots
1 October 1943	Promotion to Lieutenant-Colonel
11 October 1943	Inspector of Day Ground Attack Units with the General of Ground Attack Pilots
25 December 1944	Nomination as commander of Ground Attack *Geschwader* 4
1 January 1945	Missing in ground attack operations during Operation *Baseplate*; posthumously promoted Colonel with effect from 1 January 1945.

Colonel Druschel undertook more than 800 operational flights and, besides outstanding successes in the attack on point targets, could claim at least seven air victories.

Cottbus and Guben and crashed with his Fw 190 F-8. His successor was the bearer of the Knight's Cross, Captain Egon Stoll-Berberich, who had been shot down seven times in 460 combat operations. He survived the war and died in 1973 at Bensheim.

In October 1943 **I/SG 77** was in action in the southern sector of the eastern front with IV *Fliegerkorps* (*Luftflotte* 4). In February 1944 the unit was at Belaya-Zerkov, from where it went to Kalinovka and Proskurov a few weeks later and next to Bar and Tarnowitz. At the end of the month part of the unit arrived at Lezanie. In April the ground attack *Gruppe* took up its operational activities from Lysiatyce and a few months later operated from Stryj.

The conversion of I Gruppe to Fw 190s began at the beginning of July 1944 at Reichshof and was continued a few weeks later at Schönfeld-Seifersdorf in Bavaria.

At the beginning of September 1944 at least one *Staffel* moved to Cracow, where it was

Commanders of the German Ground Attack *Geschwader*

Ground Attack *Geschwader* 1

13 January1942–15 June 1942	Lieutenant-Colonel Otto Weiss
18 June 1942–10 June 1943	Lieutenant-Colonel Hubertus Hitschold
11 June 1943–November 1943	Major (Lieutenant-Colonel Alfred Druschel)

Ground Attack *Geschwader* 1 (ex-Dive Bomber *Geschwader* 1)

18 October 1943–30 April 1944	Lieutenant-Colonel Gustav Pressler
1 May 1944–8 May 1945	Major Peter Gasmann

Ground Attack Geschwader 2

20 December 1942–11 October 1943	Major Wolfgang Schenk

Ground Attack *Geschwader* 2 (ex-Dive Bomber *Geschwader* 2)

18 October 1943–31 July 1944	Lieutenant-Colonel Hans-Karl Stepp
1 August 1944–8 February 1945	Colonel Hans-Ulrich Rudel
8 February 1945–13 March 1945	Major Friedrich Lang
13 March 1945–20 April 1945	Colonel Kurt Kuhlmey
20 April 1945–8 May 1945	Colonel Hans-Ulrich Rudel

Ground Attack *Geschwader* 3 (ex-Dive Bomber *Geschwader* 3)

18 October 1943–15 December 1944	Colonel Kurt Kuhlmey
15 December 1944–28 April 1945	Major Bernhard Hamester

Ground Attack *Geschwader* 4 (ex-Ground Attack *Geschwader* 2)

5 May 1943–26 May 1944	Major Georg Dörffel
26 May 1944–20 July 1944	Major Werner Dörnbrack
20 July 1944–28 December 1944	Major Ewald Janssen
28 December 1944–1 January 1945	Colonel Alfred Druschel
3 January 1945–8 May 1945	Major Werner Dörnbeck

I/Ground Attack *Geschwader* 5

No *Geschwader* staff available, only one *Gruppe* formed.

I and IV/Ground Attack *Geschwader* 9

No *Geschwader* staff available, only two *Gruppen* formed.

Ground Attack *Geschwader* 10 (ex-Fast Bomber *Geschwader* 10)

18 October 1943–8 November 1943	Major Heinz Schumann
30 January 1944–8 May 1945	Major (Lieutenant-Colonel) Georg Jakob

Ground Attack *Geschwader* 77 (ex-Dive Bomber *Geschwader* 77)

18 October 1943–15 February 1945	Lieutenant-Colonel (Colonel) Helmut Bruck
15 February 1945–8 May 1945	Lieutenant-Colonel Manfred Mössinger

Ground Attack *Geschwader* 101

From November 1944	Lieutenant-Colonel (Colonel) Gustav Pressler

Ground Attack *Geschwader* 102

15 November 1944–8 May 1945	Major Karl Henze

Ground Attack *Geschwader* 151 (ex-Dive Bomber *Geschwader* 151)

18 October 1943–7 December 1944	Colonel Karl Christ
7 December 1944–8 February 1945	unknown
8 February 1945–1 April 1945	Colonel Helmut Bruck
1 April 1945–5 May 1945	Major Karl Henze

I/Ground Attack *Geschwader* 152

No *Geschwader* staff available, only one *Gruppe* formed.

drawn into costly ground attack operations on the hard-fought middle sector of the eastern front with the 1st *Fliegerdivision*. By about the end of September the unit had withdrawn to the neighbourhood of Krasno. In November the crews of I/SG 77 flew their operations in the area of the 1st *Fliegerdivision*, which belonged to *Luftflotte* 6, based at Zichenau. From the end of November 1944 onwards the whole *Geschwader* was again under the command of VIII *Fliegerkorps*. At the beginning of 1945 the unit operated from Sprottau. On 27 February 1945 it was at Bahrendt. On 21 March 1945 the *Gruppe* was at Alteno. There were still thirty-four Fw 190s with I *Gruppe* at the end of March 1945, of which thirty-two were still battleworthy. One of the last bases of the *Gruppe* was Niemes-South at the beginning of May 1945.

In October 1943, the second *Gruppe* of SG 77 was led by Captain Helmut Leicht, who failed to return from his 600th combat operation south-east of Vitebsk on 26 June 1944 and has remained missing. His successor was Captain Alexander Gläser, who carried out his thousandth operation in the spring of 1945 in the Breslau (Wroclaw) area. On 28 March 1945 he received the Oak Leaves to the Knight's Cross. Only thanks to his initiative was it possible to save a large part of **II/SG 77** from becoming prisoners of war of the Russians; the unit moved to the west.

The 5th and 6th *Staffeln* of II/SG 77 were previously a part of Ground Attack *Geschwader* 1. As the third *Staffel*, 1/SG 4 was added in November 1943. The aircraft equipment consisted of Ju 87 D-3s. Next, the *Gruppe* was transferred from IV to VIII *Fliegerkorps*. From February 1944 to the beginning of March 1944 the unit operated from Kalinovka.

From there II/SG 77 was near Lvov until June and in July moved to Krasno. Subsequent operational bases were Pinsk, Moderovka and Jasionka. Between August and October 1944 the *Staffeln* were at Naglovice. From there they went to Saslau in November 1944. The conversion to Fw 190 F-8s had by then been carried out at Schönfeld-Seifersdorf in all possible haste.

At the beginning of 1945 parts of the *Gruppe* were at Rudnicki. On 5 February 1945 the unit was ultimately, together with 10(Pz)/SG 77, at Aslau to support the defensive battles from there. As a result of fuel deficiencies, the number of daily operations had, however, noticeably declined. The last significant operational activities unfolded at the end of February 1945 before Cottbus, as well as in the Kamenz area, before the *Gruppe* had to withdraw further to the west. The *Gruppe* took part with decisive effect in the battle for the bridgehead at Steinau on the Oder. At the beginning of April 1945 twenty-three operational machines could still be reported, of which twelve Fw 190 F-8s were equipped with 'Tank Lightning'. On 3 May 1945 the *Gruppe* flew its last operations over the eastern front from Schweidnitz.

III/SG 77 was the former III/StG 77. The *Gruppe* was led in an exemplary manner up to 1 December 1943 by Captain Georg Jakob. This officer was named as commanding officer of SG 10 on 30 January 1944 and left SG 77. He was followed by Captain Franz Kieslich, who had been promoted from Sergeant-Major to Lieutenant (sic!) on 1 October 1941 and from 27 August 1943 onwards was *Staffel* leader and then *Staffel* captain of 7/SG 77. After his appointment as commanding officer of SG 148,

Captain Gerhard Stüdemann took over the leadership of the ground attack *Gruppe* on 20 February 1945.

At the end of October 1943 the ground attack unit had been in *Luftflotte* 4 with its Ju 87 D-3s and D-5s. In May 1944 the unit moved by way of Winniza and Lvov to Cuniov and in June 1944, in the context of the further withdrawal, to Grojec with the 1st *Fliegerdivision* (*Luftflotte* 6). In September the weakened forces of the ground attack *Gruppe* operated from Hüttenfelde and were re-formed at Schönfeld-Seifersdorf with Fw 190s. Next, the unit intervened in the extremely hard-fought ground battles along the eastern front with its Fw 190 F-8s from Sprottau. On 22 February 1945 it was near Cottbus with its thirty-one Fw 190 F-8s. At the end of the war the remnants of the *Gruppe* were at Pardubice.

5.4.2.9 Operational Forces of the Training *Geschwader*

In addition to these ground attack units, Ju 87 Ds were chiefly to be found with the training *Geschwader* SG 103 and SG 151. In these, under the impulse of war, operational *Staffeln* were formed; in particular, flying instructors could take off for ground attack sorties in addition to their instruction activities. As a result of the drastically deteriorating war situation, in February 1945 another massive air operation was being organised in the east by the 1st Fighter Division. For this purpose parts of SG 151 were made available by the General of Ground Attack Pilots. Besides seventeen Fw 190 Fs of 14/SG 151 from Berlin-Staaken and a total of fifty-two machines of II *Gruppe*, 15/SG 151 had available, shortly before the end of the war, twenty-seven Ju 87 crews with their Ju 87 D-5s, of which only nine were also capable of night attacks. There is no evidence that they went into operation as a unit.

5.5 Operations Over the Sea

5.5.1 Attacks on Shipping Targets

Precision air attacks on shipping represented a new type of maritime engagement in the conduct of war. The vulnerability of floating objects showed that a successful defence by the anti-aircraft guns of moving naval units against a fiercely pressed bombing attack was just as impossible as the protection of warships at anchor in a naval base by anti-aircraft defences on land.

As early as the mid-1930s costly war games had been carried out in France, Italy and Britain, with these and similar results. Deliberations in Germany came generally to this conclusion – although the German leadership tended all too easily to overestimate the possible operational successes.

The early expansion of the dive bombing concept led to the transfer of this form of attack to maritime targets, be they of the civilian or military kind. With bombs capable of breaking armour, the sinking of even the heaviest ships seemed possible and, according to the point target concept, also worthwhile without major air units. Even so, as the first operations over the sea showed, attacks on maritime targets with Ju 87 Bs and Rs was possible only in those regions in which German air superiority was assured. Indeed they were restricted even where the enemy did not have sufficiently strong fighter forces, as with the attacks on Channel shipping and the combat flights to the Thames estuary, and also in the Mediterranean and the Black Sea.

Even the higher-performance D version did not give Germany equality with the enemy forces in attacks on maritime targets. Basically, there were only a few elite crews who specialised in attacks on shipping and were later successful with their Ju 87 B-2s and R-2/R-4s. In view of the limited number of Ju 87 forces in action over the sea, the successes achieved were so much the greater. However, the Allies' superior economic capabilities made it increasingly easier for them to replace higher losses in the medium term.

In spite of the provision of heavy armour-breaking free-fall ordnance, such as the SD 500, the SD 1000 or the PC 1000, the peak of shipping attacks with free-fall weapons was already past by the beginning of 1942. The hopes of the *Luftwaffe* leadership in such weapons were to be fulfilled either only in certain conditions or not at all, as, for example, the heavy air attacks on the British aircraft carrier HMS *Illustrious* showed.

Guided weapons released from aircraft, such as the PC 1400 X (against warships) or the Hs 293 (against freighters), were at that time still in the future. The size and weight of these weapons, in any event, made it impossible to carry them under the fuselage of the Ju 87.

One thing the bombing, some of which was extremely precise, showed the Ju 87 crews, however, was that operations by naval units without continuous air cover would in the future lead to unbearably high losses.

5.5.2 Operations Over the Western Theatre of War

The first operation against shipping targets was not long in coming. Only one day after the German ship of the line *Schleswig-Holstein* had begun with the shelling of the Polish western plain, *Luftwaffe* forces belonging to the 1st *Fliegerdivision* succeeded in destroying the Polish torpedo boat *Mazur* with a single, well-aimed 'Stuka' bomb. This, the first sinking in the Second World War which had just broken out, was followed on 3 September 1939 by a second.

Lieutenants Lion and Rummel, both from 4('Stuka')/186, attacked several enemy warships in the Polish naval base on the Hela peninsula. The 1,550-ton destroyer *Wichr* sank as a result of a direct hit. In addition, Karl-Hermann Lion participated in the sinking of the modern 2,250-ton mine layer *Gryf* as well as the gunboat *General Haller* off Hela, which had been attacked in company with 3/KFlGr 506.

With this the massive operations against the Polish fleet came to an end; the surviving ships had succeeded in reaching British ports. Attacks on shipping in protected harbours was at that time still not allowed. Until the beginning of October 1939 air attacks were therefore possible only against enemy warships on the high seas.

Only on 4 October 1939 were 'unrestricted attacks' released against British armed freighters. Thirteen days later attacks on all enemy merchant ships was authorised by the German sea warfare leadership, except for passenger ships.

From 29 October 1939 passenger ships travelling in convoys could also be attacked.

During Operation *Weser Exercise*, the occupation of Denmark and Norway, the task of preventing enemy operations in fjords as well as

Loading a Ju 87 B with splinter bombs. The photograph was taken in April 1940 at Sousvannet near Vaernes.

their reinforcement by new troop landings fell to the Ju 87s of Dive Bomber *Geschwader* 1.

Between 9 April and 1 June 1940 crews of 3/StG 1 attacked ships of the Royal Navy and Allied naval forces and were able to log a few successes. In particular *Staffel* Captain Bruno Dilley scored hits. Lieutenant Martin Möbius was able to report several direct hits as well as a few near misses on ships of the Royal Navy in Namsos Fjord, for which he received the Knight's Cross on 8 May 1940. From June 1940, Britain had to withdraw from Norway with its forces which had been forced onto the defensive, whereupon Ju 87 units again went into action.

In the summer of 1940 Robert Georg *Freiherr* von Malapert-Neufville (II/StG 1) sank 35,000 tons of shipping off Dunkirk, including an enemy destroyer. For this, on 17 October 1940, the Lieutenant was the first *Wehrmacht* soldier to receive the German Gold Cross.

II/StG 2 under its commander, Captain Walter Enneccerus, was in action off Dunkirk; there and off Le Havre and La Rochelle the unit sank four major ships. Similarly, during the action in the west, Johannes Brandenburg, later Captain and bearer of the Knight's Cross, proved himself and, together with the crews of 2/StG 2, was able to sink one cruiser, three destroyers and two transport vessels and freighters. Of these, one destroyer and one freighter were to his sole account.

After Ju 87 B-equipped 'Stuka' *Gruppen* had participated decisively in the victory over the French forces, and the armistice of 22 June 1940, it was possible to mount massive attacks on the whole enemy fleet from forward operations bases on the Channel coast. On 9 July 1940 Friedrich Karl *Freiherr* von Dalwigk zu Lichtenfels, who was posthumously promoted Major, attacked shipping targets in the English Channel with several crews of I/StG 76, in which he was fiercely attacked by British fighters. According to British sources, the Major and his gunner were shot down by Flying Officer

This Ju 87 R-2 of III/StG 1 was loaded with an SC 1000 high-explosive bomb; North Africa, July 1942.

D. M. Crook (609 Squadron). On 25 and 26 July 1940 II/StG 1, led by Captain Paul-Werner Hozzel, together with IV('Stuka')/LG 1 (Captain Bernd von Brauchitsch), attacked the British convoy CW 8 and sank five of the total of twenty-one ships. In addition, two destroyers and five other freighters were damaged. In the summer of 1940 Helmut Mahlke of III/StG 1, later Lieutenant-Colonel, distinguished himself. Several crews of II/StG 77 also achieved particular success in the assault on Channel shipping.

On 1 November 1940 I/StG 1 attacked several shipping targets off Margate in the Thames estuary. On 8 November 1940 crews of 3/StG 3 went into action there, as did 9/StG 1 on 11 November 1940. These attacks resulted in the sinking of a total of seven ships. The end of this phase of the attack left a further three substantially damaged.

Off the Thames estuary and at the eastern entrance to the Channel Ju 87 *Staffeln* seldom scored hits because of the presence of the RAF.

On 14 November 1940 a further 'Stuka' operation took place there. Captain Helmut Mahlke, with his crews of III/StG 1, succeeded in destroying or damaging some warships and merchant vessels. The Ju 87 forces ran into several Spitfire squadrons in the process, which attacked immediately. In this engagement one Ju 87 B of the 7th *Staffel* and one B-1 and one B-2 of the 9th *Staffel* were shot down. Numerous Ju 87 Bs returned with gunfire damage. It rapidly became clear that, without massive support from German fighters, almost unbearable losses would soon follow.

Among the especially successful pilots who operated over the Channel and southern English coast were Lieutenant Joachim Rieger, who was named as *Staffel* Captain of 5/StG 1 on 1 July 1940. Together with his *Staffel*, he was able to sink more than 30,000 tons of enemy shipping in twenty-five operations up to 19 February 1941.

5.5.3 Operations Over the Southern Theatre of War

When the British air defences became too strong for Ju 87 operations, further action in the west had to be abandoned. New theatres of war, especially the Mediterranean area, opened up. From December 1940 most of the dive bomber *Gruppen* were moved from northern France to southern Italy and Sicily, into the X *Fliegerkorps* area. In addition, on 10 December 1940 the *Luftwaffe* command staff ordered the movement of a combat unit consisting of sixty He 111s and further Ju 87s into the Mediterranean area. On 14 December I/StG 1 and II/StG 2 with thirty-nine Ju 87 Rs were available as 'Stuka' forces.

The task assigned to them was to attack the Royal Navy in the Mediterranean and to neutralise the 'unsinkable aircraft carrier' – the island of Malta, which belonged to Britain. In addition they were to attack the Royal Navy covering forces protecting resupply transports on their way through the Mediterranean. The seaways were of overwhelming importance for the resupply of Malta, Greece and Egypt.

After British troops landed on Crete on 31 October 1940, a further field of operations for the *Luftwaffe* developed there. It was clear, moreover, that in the near future an essentially stronger involvement of the *Wehrmacht* in the whole Balkan area and North Africa would be required.

From 1 January 1941 I/StG 1 attacked enemy shipping in the Mediterranean area for the first time. Then, with other forces from X *Fliegerkorps*, the unit attacked shipping off the coast of Sicily. Next, the crews turned to the immediate vicinity of Malta.

A few days later, on 10 January, picked crews of I/StG 1 under the leadership of Captain Paul-Werner Hozzel, together with II/StG 2 led by Major Walter Enneccerus, tried to sink the one-year-old British aircraft carrier HMS *Illustrious*. In spite of six heavy direct hits and three additional near misses, the ship was able to be saved.

One of the hits was scored by Lieutenant Ernst Fick. Slight damage was also inflicted on the battleship HMS *Warspite* by 'Stuka' bombs.

In total the Ju 87 action against the Royal Navy Force A lasted just six minutes. The attack on HMS *Illustrious* showed, however, that to sink a 23,000-ton carrier, even with PC-1000 armour-piercing bombs, was not as simple as the crews had expected.

On 11 January 1941 Force B left the Malta naval base, whereupon strong Ju 87 forces of X *Fliegerkorps* took off once again to the attack. On this day a combat unit of II/StG 2 led by Walter Enneccerus succeeded, about 400 km east of Sicily – just at the limit of their range – in hitting the British cruiser HMS *Southampton* so hard that it had to be abandoned by its crew. A crew of II/StG 2 scored a direct hit on the cruiser HMS *Gloucester* with an anti-armour bomb which, however, failed to explode.

Five days later, on 16 January 1941, a massive air attack on Malta took place and HMS *Illustrious*, which had been brought there in the meantime, was again damaged. In a 'Stuka' attack three days later the aircraft carrier again suffered along with the island. On 23 January 1941 it entered Alexandria; it was subsequently repaired in a naval dockyard at Norfolk, USA.

Meanwhile the *Wehrmacht* had marched into Yugoslavia and Greece from several directions. Soon after the beginning of the Balkan campaign on 6 April 1941, Lieutenant Hendrik Stahl of III/StG 2 sank a destroyer. This experienced pilot participated in the destruction of another warship with a direct hit.

In February 1941 6/StG 1 went into action from Sicily against convoys and British warships in the western Mediterranean. In addition, the existing objectives on and around Malta stayed on the target list. In this action Captain Johann Zemsky proved himself and for this and other operational successes was decorated with the Knight's Cross on 4 February 1942. Between 1 and 11 April 1942 heavy air attacks were carried out by II *Fliegerkorps* led by General of Pilots Bruno Loerzer. Together with Italian units, a major attack on Malta took place. Losses on both sides mounted rapidly. More reinforcements were necessary for the RAF forces stationed on Malta, so that further attacks could be repulsed.

On 18 April 1941 the British Mediterranean fleet, under the leadership of Admiral J. H. D. Cunningham left Alexandria. In this unit were the three battleships, HMS *Warspite*, HMS *Barham* and HMS *Valiant*, the aircraft carrier HMS *Formidable*, the light cruiser HMS *Phoebe* and the anti-aircraft cruiser HMS *Calcutta*, together with several escort destroyers.

The aim of the operation, to be achieved at all costs, was the resupply of the island of Malta which was under continuous attack by Axis

This Ju 87 D-1 of 7/StG 1 was loaded with an SC 500. In exceptional cases an SC 250 bomb was hung under each wing.

The crew of this Ju 87 R-4 (I/StG 1) attacked targets in Tobruk harbour with a 1,000-kg armour-piercing bomb.

forces. The attacks by the German and Italian air forces at that time represented the high point of a series of attacks which was never reached again. In April 1942 alone these came to 4,082 sorties by day and 256 by night.

Meanwhile the battles for the Greek mainland had been concluded. Between 24 and 29 April 1941 Greece was evacuated with the help of the Royal Navy in Operation *Demon*. VIII *Fliegerkorps* sent all available Ju 87s into action against it.

Shortly before that, on 22 April 1941, Sergeant Horst Hermann of 5/StG 2 'Immelmann', the bearer of the Knight's Cross, sank a tanker in the Gulf of Corinth. In addition, Götzpeter Vollmer and Johann Waldhauser reported successes in shipping attacks.

By 30 April 1941 the whole Greek mainland and the Peloponnese had been occupied by the *Wehrmacht*.

At the same time the Royal Navy reinforced its heavy units for the resupply of Malta and the forces operating in North Africa with HMS *Gloucester* and three destroyers, which were diverted to the protection of a convoy with important reinforcements for Malta at the beginning of May 1941.

The German landing on Crete (20 May 1941 to 1 June 1941) inflicted heavy casualties on the paratroops, air landing troops and mountain rifle troops. The 'Stuka' *Gruppen* sent into action against the Royal Navy in the seas around Crete and off the Greek coast also took losses. I/StG 2 was particularly involved in the fierce air-sea battles. During the fighting Captain Hubertus Hitschold was able to sink the modern British destroyers HMS *Kelly* and HMS *Kashmir* on 23 May 1941. Two days later, on 25 May 1941, the crews of II/StG 2, led by Captain Walter Enneccerus, scored well-placed hits on the deck of the British aircraft carrier, HMS *Formidable*. Besides this, the destroyer, HMS *Nubian*, sailing as convoy protection, was severely damaged. On that day also the destroyer HMS *Greyhound*

This Ju 87 D-3 of I/StG 1 probably had only scrap value after an emergency landing on the Italian island of Pantelleria.

was attacked by eight Ju 87s of II/StG 2. The direct hit by a 250-kg bomb, as well as two other hits, caused the British warship to sink in four minutes. Heavy losses resulted among the crew.

II/StG 2, led by Captain Heinrich Brückner, was also in action off Crete in May and June 1941. About 125,000 tons of merchant shipping was sunk and a further 70,000 tons severely damaged. Lieutenant Friedrich Platzer, flying with I *Gruppe* of StG 2 'Immelmann' as a *Staffel* leader, was able to sink four enemy transports during the battles over the sea. In addition, he damaged a battleship and two destroyers and set fire to an British cruiser. In total he took off on 160 operations during the air-sea battle in the early summer of 1941.

Lieutenant Robert Georg *Freiherr* von Malapert-Neufville was also among the successful Ju 87 pilots. As *Staffel* captain of 5/StG 1, he sank 100,000 tons of shipping, among which were four minor warships. In this combat area III/StG 77 destroyed a total of 46,000 tons of shipping and heavily damaged a further 86,000 tons. The *Staffel* captain of 1/StG 3, Lieutenant Heinrich Eppen, alone sank a destroyer and ten merchant ships in the summer of 1941, a total of 50,000 enemy tons.

In the X *Fliegerkorps* area on 7 June 1941 there were, besides the *Geschwader* staff of StG 3 with three Ju 87s, I/StG 1 with thirty-five machines, of which only twenty-six were battleworthy, and I/StG 3 with its thirty-one Ju 87 Rs. Of these, likewise, twenty-six machines were battleworthy, which resulted in a total of sixty-six Ju 87 Rs. As protection only 7/JG 26, III/JG 52 and III/ZG 26 were in place. At the same time thirty Ju 87s of the Dive Bomber *Geschwader* StG 1 and StG 2 could be sent into action against maritime targets from Africa.

Up to 21 July 1941 the crews of I/StG 2 sank at least 164,000 tons of shipping in the eastern Mediterranean.

In spite of these successes, the Royal Navy was still not to be underestimated as an opponent of the *Luftwaffe*. The number of operationally ready Ju 87s of X *Fliegerkorps* and of the

Air Leader, Africa had declined further by 15 November 1941. Measured against the size of the theatre of war, the available forces were basically far too small to fulfil the offensive tasks that were assigned to them. At the beginning of 1942 in southern Europe there were only the combat forces of I/StG 3 with twenty-six Ju 87 Rs as well as another sixty-eight machines stationed in Africa. Bf 109 F-4s of JG 27 took over the direct protection of these. Unfortunately there were too few Messerschmitt fighters available for the purpose. The number of Ju 87 Rs fell until the beginning of April 1942 in spite of numerous demands from the area of the Air Leader, Africa for forty-five machines.

With the X *Fliegerkorps* no more Ju 87s were available, but thirty-five Ju 87 Rs were available with II *Fliegerkorps*. Up to the summer of 1942 there was no reinforcement to the German forces. Meanwhile, the war against the USSR had turned out to be a bottomless pit for Ju 87 production. Hence, there remained only a limited allowance of new dive bombers to replace the losses suffered by the Ju 87 units in action in the Mediterranean area. Operation *Pedestal*, carried out by the Royal Navy between 10 and 15 August 1942, was again intended to resupply the island of Malta, pressed hard by the Axis forces. After several relatively unsuccessful attacks by Ju 88 As, as well as Savoia S 79 three-engined, medium bombers, on the late afternoon of 12 August 1942 a total of twenty-nine Ju 87s of StG 3, with imposing fighter protection, attacked the British aircraft carrier HMS *Indomitable*. The Ju 87 crews scored three severe hits, and the modern carrier was completely out of action for flying.

This Ju 87 D (A5+FL) of 3/StG 1 was captured as war booty by the British in North Africa. The sign indicates its new owners.

After several E-boat attacks on 13 August 1942, and air torpedo operations by He 111 Hs of KG 26, some of the eight Italian Ju 87 crews scored several hits on the transport ships *Dorset* and *Port Chalmers* as well as on the tanker *Ohio*. A combined attack by twenty Ju 87s and Ju 88s resulted in further hits. Apart from the *Dorset* and the *Ohio*, which were hit again, the *Rochester* also received a bomb.

On 13 and 14 August 1942 the British Operation *Agreement* took place against Tobruk. After the RAF had carried out a heavy attack on the night of 14 August, marines shipped in two destroyers, as well as 150 landing troops, were supposed to neutralise Tobruk harbour. The attack failed completely after the destroyer HMS *Sikh* was shot to pieces by the Ist *Abteilung* (8.8) of 43 Flak Regiment and sank.

A portion of the smaller craft was lost as a result of an Italian fighter-bomber attack. Lieutenant (later Captain), and bearer of the Knight's Cross, Siegfried Göbel of StG 3 had the good fortune, on 14 September 1942, to sink the powerful English anti-aircraft cruiser HMS *Coventry* off Tobruk. Lieutenant Kurt Walter, who had already sunk a destroyer and 20,000 tons of shipping, also participated in this successful operation. On 18 May 1943 he received the Knight's Cross to the Iron Cross.

Lieutenant Hans-Adolf Meyer, a pilot of III/StG 3, not only destroyed twelve British tanks during the battle of Sollum but also sank two freighters. On 14 September 1942 he damaged another British destroyer by means of a direct hit, also off Tobruk.

When the retreat in North Africa could not be stopped, and when the bridgehead formed in Tunisia from 9 November 1942 was hardly defensible any longer, Army Group Africa capitulated on 13 May 1943. The last defenders withdrew to Sicily where the first Allied units landed on 10 July 1943.

On 25 July 1943 the Duce was deposed, whereupon Marshal Badoglio concluded an armistice with the Allies on 3 September 1943. British troops landed on some of the Aegean islands hitherto occupied by the Italians.

Among the last Ju 87 operations in the Mediterranean area was therefore a German counter-attack on these islands. After Ju 88 A 4 crews of Training *Geschwader* 1 had sunk two British destroyers in the harbour of the island of Leros on 26 September 1943, the *Luftwaffe* carried out Operation *Polar Bear.* German troops landed on the island of Kos and took the British and Italian troops there prisoner. After the Royal Navy had destroyed a German supply convoy on the way to Kos, Ju 88s of LG 1 and II/KG 51 attacked, together with Ju 87s of II/StG 3. The cruiser HMS *Penelope* on the way from Scarpanto was heavily damaged. When the cruiser HMS *Carlisle*, together with two destroyers, had advanced to a point south of Piraeus, Ju 87s of II/StG 3 attacked and sank HMS *Panther*, a destroyer. The cruiser was also so heavily damaged that it had to be towed back to Alexandria by the second destroyer, HMS *Rockwood*. The damage turned out to be so severe that a subsequent rebuilding was abandoned.

In November 1943 the battle for the islands of Leros and Samos broke out. The attacking Royal Navy destroyers were fought by 5/KG 100 guided weapons, in the process of which HMS *Rockwood* was substantially damaged. After heavy battles on Leros, the British commander surrendered on 17 November 1943 and went into captivity with 8,500 of his comrades. After II/StG 3 had attacked the town and harbour of Tigani on Samos, the occupying forces there also surrendered on 22 November 1943. With that the reconquest of the Dodecanese was concluded.

5.5.4 Operations Over the Eastern Theatre of War

On 22 June 1941 the German attack on the Soviet Union began.

At first the support of the rapidly advancing *Wehrmacht* remained the prime task of the Ju 87 *Gruppen*. Not until a few months later, in September 1941, did numerous Ju 87s of I/StG 2 attack the Russian fleet in Kronstadt. In spite of all the efforts of the crews involved, only one light hit was scored on a heavy cruiser.

On 12 September 1941 air attacks on ships of the Russian Black Sea fleet, in particular on the cruiser *Krasny Pereslnec,* took place without success. In operations between 16 and 21 September 1941 the crews involved also scored no effective hits.

From 21 September 1941 crews of II and

This Ju 87 D-3 of 5/SG 77 operated without wheel fairings to guard against problems with muddy airstrips.

III *Gruppen* of StG 2 (Lieutenant-Colonel Oskar Dinort) attacked units of the Baltic fleet. Here Hans-Ulrich Rudel hit the Soviet battleship *Marat* with an SD 1000 bomb. The armoured ship at once took on water and sank to the bottom of the harbour near the mole. In these attacks Captain Egbert Jaekel, who achieved more than ten air victories with Ju 87s, distinguished himself; in addition he scored two direct hits on ships of the Red Fleet.

On 23 September 1941 Captain Ernst-Siegfried Steen, commander of III/StG 2, in the course of his 301st combat operation, led a dive bombing attack on the Russian cruiser *Kirov* in which he received a direct flak hit at more than 1,500 metres; his elevator tore off. With his machine barely controllable, the *Gruppe* commander nevertheless tried to destroy the heavy cruiser. The 1,000-kg high-explosive bomb, released shortly before he crashed into the water, severely damaged the ship. With Ernst-Siegfried Steen, who received the Knight's Cross posthumously on 17 October 1941, went his radio operator, Corporal Alfred Scharnovski.

During the operations the battleship *Oktyabrskaya Revolyutsia* was damaged by six hits. In addition, the destroyer *Stereguskiy* capsised after a direct hit and three other destroyers were substantially damaged. Lieutenant Hans-Joachim Lehmann of 8/StG 2 also took part in the attacks on Kronstadt. On 23 September 1941 he participated in further hits on the cruiser *Kirov* as well as on the destroyer *Grosyaskiy*.

By 10 November 1941 StG 2 had already sunk 210,000 tons of enemy shipping. Captain Walter Hagen, who from 1944 was commander of the 17th *Fliegerdivision* in the Balkans, led the *Geschwader* at that time.

By the end of November 1941 II/StG 77, under the leadership of the Captain, later Lieutenant-Colonel, Alfons Orthofer, had sunk ten enemy warships, among them a Russian cruiser, as well as twenty-seven merchant ships totalling 50,000 tons.

On 12 November 1941 the *Staffeln* of the II *Gruppe* of StG 77 also participated in the operations against Russian naval forces. Two

Russian cruisers and two destroyers were at that time intervening effectively with their heavy artillery in the fierce land battles against the German advance on the fortress of Sevastopol. IV *Fliegerkorps* sent chiefly I/StG 77 with its Ju 87s into action against them. Under the leadership of Captain Orthofer, the *Gruppe* scored three severe hits on the cruiser *Servona Ukraina*, which sank a little later close to the shore. Warships in the extensive dock installations of Sevastopol, among them two destroyers whose damage was later repaired, again received heavy hits.

On 4 April 1942 sixty-two Ju 87s of III/StG 1 (Lieutenant-Colonel Walter Hagen), I and II/StG 2, as well as thirty-three Ju 88 A-4s of KG 1 'Hindenburg', attacked. JG 54 with fifty-nine Bf 109 Fs provided fighter protection. In this and the subsequent attacks the *Oktyabrskaya Revolyutsia* was hit by three bombs. The *Maksim Gorki*, a cruiser, received seven moderately severe hits. At the same time one heavy hit could be observed on each of the cruisers *Kirov* – for the third time – and *Petropavlovsk*. Several smaller units were damaged. On 24 April 1942 Lieutenant Herbert Bauer scored a direct hit on the Soviet battleship *Oktyabrskaya Revolyutsia* lying in Kronstadt harbour as well as another on the heavy cruiser *Kirov*. By 30 April 1942 these units, under the command of *Luftflotte* 1, had flown a total of 596 sorties on targets in Leningrad.

On 15 May 1942 Ju 87s of I/StG 5 attacked targets in Murmansk. The Soviet submarine SC 403, as well as the American freighter *Yaka* (6,200 tons), were heavily hit.

A little later, on 1 June 1942, crews of I/StG 5 succeeded in sinking the British freighter *Empire Starlight* (6,850 tons) in Murmansk harbour.

Between 8 and 30 June 1942 the major attack of the 11th Army (Colonel-General von Manstein) on Sevastopol took place with the support of VIII *Fliegerkorps*. Several hits were scored in the extensive harbour installations.

In the northern sector of the eastern front on 24 June 1942 several Ju 87 Ds of I/StG 5 attacked the British minesweeper HMS *Gossamer* in the Kola Bight and sank her. From 1943 the defence of German land positions in the Army Group North area and in the Finnish area took priority. Shipping targets were scarcely attacked any more with Ju 87s.

In the southern sector of the eastern front the situation appeared somewhat different. Although the Soviet fleet operated within the combat area of Ju 87s, apparently no major attacks on shipping took place until the spring of 1943.

In April 1943 Hans-Ulrich Rudel then succeeded in sinking seventy Russian landing craft with his Ju 87 G. During a Russian landing attempt he attacked the boats on the water with his 37-mm cannon.

On 5 October 1943 a Soviet destroyer flotilla attacked the German evacuation transports off the Crimean coast. After shelling the coast at Yalta and after a fight with the 1st E-boat Flotilla, the destroyers were found again by a German long-range reconnaissance aircraft, whereupon a *Staffel* of StG 77 went into action. In the first attack the *Charkov* received a hit and had to be taken in tow by the *Sposobny*. In the second dive bombing attack all three destroyers received hits. During the third attack the *Besposkadniy* sank and a little later the *Charkov*. While rescuing the survivors, the *Sposobny* was again hit and sank. After the loss of the entire flotilla Stalin forbade the use of warships from destroyer size upwards without his express agreement. Captain Hubert Pölz had a large share in the success of the attack with the sinking of the *Charkov*. Among the participants were the crew of Lieutenant Hans-Adolf Meyer, who had already sunk several freighters off the North African coast with his Ju 87 R-4.

In the following months the 'Stuka' forces in the southern sector were of necessity used in applying the brakes to the Soviet advances on land. For this reason further maritime operations were initially put in abeyance. With the fall of Sevastopol on 12 May 1944 and the retreat of the German forces, which were in any event small, any significant operation against maritime targets on the Black Sea was impossible.

The Ju 87 had served its purpose as a means of combat against maritime targets. Attempts to make a comeback with the machine as a torpedo bomber were not very successful.

6 Night Ground Attack Aircraft and Units

6.1 Development Guidelines

Ju 87 B-2s, R-2s and R-4s were offered to the RLM with flame-eliminator pipes as early as the summer of 1942.

The construction office of the Junkers works sent in a proposal on this subject on 23 July 1942, from which resulted the application of exhaust gas mixing tubes (later, flame eliminators, abbreviated FlaV – *Flammenvernichter*). On 10 November 1943 the RLM, Division GL/C-E2, authorized the suggested change instruction No. 1117 for existing Ju 87 dive bombers of the B and R series. The units projected for night ground attack operations could easily install the flame eliminators themselves. The tubes were to be ordered from the air equipment bureau at Kölleda by way of the resupply route.

Apart from the Ju 87 B and R, a further suggestion, which was also submitted in July 1942, envisaged some of the Ju 87 D-1s and D-3s assembled at the Weser Aircraft Works at Bremen (from works no. 087 2926 onwards)

One of the production prototypes for the Ju 87 D-5 'N', a night ground attack aircraft with improved flame eliminators (C version) and MG 151/20 armament.

being retrofitted with flame eliminators.

The additional equipment meant that the Ju 87 was less easily spotted by the enemy ground defences during the approach flight to its target. Even so, without an inherently more comprehensive change to the existing equipment, the outlook for a safe return from night operations at low altitude was not particularly good. Even with the additional equipment which was completed later, operations at night often demanded more than good piloting ability.

For operations as a night ground attacker the Blind Flying Certificate 3 was specially introduced, which could be obtained at Stubendorf, near Oppeln. During this special training numerous flights were made using the rate of climb indicator, altimeter and turn indicator; navigation exercises were flown at night over unfamiliar terrain.

In July and August 1944 equipment which had hitherto been used mostly for auxiliary purposes was rigorously tested by the Rechlin Test Centre for Ju 87 night ground attack operations. This went back to a suggestion by the General of Ground Attack Pilots (GdS). According to his requirements the Junkers Aircraft and Engine Works Co. manufactured a special aircraft equipment for night ground attack operations with the Ju 87 D-1, D-3 and D-5 as well as for the tank hunters of the G-1 and G-2 versions.

The recommendation of the Junkers works envisaged a new, pneumatically operated artificial horizon for the Ju 87 D-1s, D-3s and G-1s equipped with the FuG VII C radio. For that purpose the existing fuel consumption instrumentation was omitted for reasons of space.

In all other Ju 87 ground attack and tank hunting aircraft equipped with the FuG VII C, the existing reflector sight (Revi) C12D was in addition exchanged for a night reflector sight (Nachtrevi) C12N or the already installed Revi 16D was exchanged for the Nachtrevi 16D/N. After installation of the night sights supplied by the optics works at Osterode in the Harz, the fixed armament was zeroed afresh.

An ultra-violet light in front of the instrument panel provided better working conditions for the pilot, and various control lights in the instrument panel were dimmed. The high-altitude breathing gear was omitted, as only low-altitude operations were envisaged.

On the underside of the aircraft two additional recognition lights were installed and the hitherto fixed direction-finding loop was exchanged for one which could be swivelled through 90°. By this means a safe landing was made possible, even under the worst conditions of visibility. Ju 87 D-5s, which were already equipped with a FuG 16Z(S) radio, did not have this change.

The two fixed MG 151/20 cannon received flash eliminators; the MG 81 Z operated by the radio operator was retrofitted with similar equipment. The flash eliminators were supplied through the resupply line and could be mounted without problems by the armourers. The exhaust system was equipped with the flame eliminator, which was already mature from a construction point of view.

The equipment order, already modified again by the RLM, went back to Dessau on 2 September 1944 and was authorised by the RLM on 12 September 1944. For the conversion of a machine, between fifty-nine and seventy-four working hours were required, depending on the version of the Ju 87 D or G, as long as two or three trained technicians were available.

6.2 The Formation of Night Ground Attack *Gruppen*

On 7 October 1942, at the suggestion of the *Luftflotten* engaged in the east, the formation of the first auxiliary bomber *Staffeln* was set in motion. These had the task of not allowing the enemy any rest at night. The first unit was the 1st Auxiliary Bomber *Staffel* with *Luftflotte* 1. The *Staffel* was stationed at Orsha and was led by Captain Müller.

From 15 November 1942 the existing Auxiliary Bomber *Staffeln* were renamed as Harassment Bomber *Staffeln*. In the spring of 1943 there were already twelve of these independent *Staffeln* available. By the summer there were four with *Luftflotte* 1, six with *Luftflotte* 4 and another two with *Luftwaffe* Command East. Besides Ar 66s and Go 145s, the equipment consisted of all apparently suitable types. The spectrum reached from Hs 126s and Fw 158s, through He 46s and He 50s to Fiat CR 42s. Their service – mostly over the eastern front – demanded a high level of flying capability from all the crews engaged, as sorties often had to be flown at night and, in addition, in almost any weather conditions.

All in all, the operations of the Harassment Bomber *Staffeln* led to a noticeable relief for the German ground troops, even though the auxiliary equipment made decisive victories impossible. By day the *Staffeln* attacked the infrastructure of partisan-occupied sectors behind the German lines with bombs and on-board weapons.

From 1942, the operations of the various close combat forces required a unified and technically equipped leadership. For this reason the post of Inspector of Ground Attack Pilots was set up and occupied by Colonel Dr Jur. Ernst Kupfer, the former commander of StG 2 'Immelmann'. Previously the dive bombers were placed under the Inspectorate of Bomber Pilots and the ground attack pilots were under the Inspectorate of Fighter Pilots. There was also a Leader of Tank Hunters.

In order to put an end to the confusion of authority, from October 1943 the newly-named General of Ground Attack Pilots was responsible for all dive bomber and ground attack *Geschwader* as well as the night ground attack units. Dr Ernst Kupfer crashed on 6 November 1943 on an inspection flight over Greece and on 11 April 1944 posthumously received the Swords to the Oak Leaves of the Knight's Cross.

On 18 October 1943, all dive bomber units, with the exception of two *Gruppen*, I/StG 2 and II/StG 77, became ground attack *Geschwader*. At the same time the existing Harassment Bomber *Staffeln* were consolidated into six night ground attack *Gruppen* (NSGr), which as a rule had two, but often three, *Staffeln*. Seven more night ground attack *Gruppen* were also set up, which operated from Finland to Italy.

Colonel Hubertus Hitschold, whose primary task from 12 November 1943 was that of the General of Ground Attack Pilots, was responsible for the subsequent intensification of night ground attack operations. He took over this position on 1 January 1944. Promoted Major-General on 1 January 1945, he had previously led Ground Attack *Geschwader* 1 in the fierce battles on the Don and Volga and had, as a Major, received the Oak Leaves to the Knight's Cross on 31 December 1941.

Colonel Hitschold continued the reorganisation and modernisation of the *Geschwader*, which had been begun by Kupfer, with great enthusiasm. He appointed Colonel Alfred Druschel, who later flew at the head of his ground attack pilots (SG 4) on 1 January 1945 in Operation *Baseplate* and went missing, as Inspector of Day Ground Attack Pilots. Major Boris von Maubeuge became the last Inspector of all ground attack pilots.

The work of these officers bore its first fruit chiefly in the equipment of the night ground attack *Gruppen* with the Ju 87 D. But not until the beginning of 1944 were the *Staffeln* of the individual night ground attack *Gruppen* extensively equipped with this aircraft. Only in individual cases, as with NSGr 20 in the west, did Fw 190 Fs also come into service. Through the conversion of the greater part of the ground attack *Geschwader* from the slow Ju 87 to the much faster Fw 190, the existing inventory of machines became available and could be passed on to the night ground attack units. Thanks to the Ju 87 D-1s, D-3s and D-5s which were now assigned to them, their firepower was significantly increased: at last heavy free-fall ordnance could be carried. Moreover, the late D versions possessed an offensive armament consisting of two 20-mm weapons (MG 151/20), which were extremely effective. Thanks to this equipment, it was increasingly possible to attack enemy infantry and artillery positions successfully.

In addition, the harassing effect of the night ground attack *Gruppen* remained important in all sectors of the front. Even though only pinpricks were possible, even these led to the temporary relief of the German ground troops.

On 11 January 1944 a discussion of the future equipment of the *Luftwaffe* night ground attack units took place under the chairmanship of Major-General Dipl.-Ing. Walter Vorwald, chief of the RLM Technical Bureau. Major Boris von Maubeuge, Inspector of the night ground attack units, reported on the current front-line operations of his forces and indicated, further, that greater importance was to be given to the night ground attack *Staffeln* because ever-stronger partisan units were forming, chiefly in Croatia and northern Italy. 'Bands', however, were also appearing ever more frequently in the eastern theatre of war and were interrupting the

Major-General Hubertus Hitschold

Major-General Hubertus Hitschold, one of the best known dive bomber pilot personalities.

7 July 1912	Born at Kurwin, District of Johannisburg
1 April 1930	Pre-military flight training at the German Transport Pilot School and abroad at the expense of the *Reich* (to 30 September 1931)
1 October 1931	Entry into the 6th Squadron of Cavalry Regiment 2
1 December 1931	Promotion to Lance-Corporal
1 April 1933	Promotion to Corporal
1 June 1933	Promotion to Junior Under Officer
1 February 1934	Promotion to Senior Under Officer
1 March 1934	Promotion to 2nd Lieutenant
1 January 1935	Departure from the army as 2nd Lieutenant and transfer to the *Luftwaffe*
September 1934	Pilot and *Staffel* officer with StG 2 'Immelmann'
1 October 1935	Promotion to Lieutenant
1 October 1936	*Staffel* commander in StG 2 'Immelmann'
1 January 1939	Promotion to Captain
1 October 1939	Nomination as *Gruppe* commander of I/StG 2
19 July 1940	Promotion to Major
23 May 1941	Sinking of the English destroyers HMS *Kelly* and HMS *Kashmir*
15 October 1941	Handover of I/StG 2 to Major Bruno Dilley
16 October 1941	Nomination as commander of 'Stuka' School 1 at Wertheim
18 June 1942	Nomination as commander of Ground Attack *Geschwader* SG 1
1 February 1943	Promotion to Lieutenant-Colonel
12 June 1943	Nomination as Air Leader Sardinia (until 11 November 1943)
1 July 1943	Promotion to Colonel
12 November 1943	Assigned to observe the duties of the General of Ground Attack Pilots
1 January 1945	Promotion to Major-General
1 January 1945	Nomination as General of Ground Attack Pilots
8 May 1945	Prisoner of war of the Allies until June 1947
10 March 1966	Died at Söcking on Lake Starnberg

As the last General of Ground Attack Pilots, Major-General Hitschold was also entrusted with the conversion from the piston-engined to the jet-propelled ground attack aircraft. During his time with StG 2 and SG 1 he undertook a total of 300–400 operations.

rearward connections of the *Wehrmacht*. Besides the assignment of Fiat CR 42s, which were no longer needed and were therefore available for conversion, the Inspector demanded above all Ju 87 Ds, which were no longer needed as ground attack aircraft as their role had been extensively taken over by Fw 190 F-8s. As the production of the Ju 87 was to be closed down in the forthcoming months, however – that much was certain, although a binding decision had still not been taken – the Siebel Si 204 was to come into action as a ground attack aircraft. Major Boris von Maubeuge demanded twenty to thirty of these machines each month from

July 1944 onwards. Whether the 120 machines required each month would be produced at all, however, was still unclear at the beginning of 1944 because of the tense situation. In the middle of the year it became apparent that the Si 204 could only be counted on to a limited extent and that Fw 190s, like Ju 87s would form the majority of all ground attackers, at least until the beginning of 1945.

6.3 Night Ground Attack Units of the *Luftwaffe* (*Nachtschlachtgruppen* – NSGr)

6.3.1 Night Ground Attack *Gruppe* 1 (Fuselage Marking V8+)

On 7 October 1942 the 1st Auxiliary Bomber *Staffel* of *Luftflotte* 1 was formed; on 18 October 1943 it became Night Ground Attack *Gruppe* 1 with two flying *Staffeln*. In 27 December 1943 a third *Staffel* was added, 3/NSGr 1. The aircraft consisted at first of Go 145 two-seater auxiliary bombers as well as a few improvised converted Ju W 34s. Their combat value was hence very slight.

From May 1943 the slow conversion to Ju 87 Ds began, and continued until September. The conversion of the *Staffeln* of the unit at Kovno was, until June 1944, accompanied by type conversion to the Ju 87 and intensive blind flying training.

In February 1944 the three *Staffeln* of the night ground attack *Gruppe* were at Idriza; from there they went by way of the Kovno area to East Prussia, where part of the unit was stationed for several months from July 1944.

As a result of the rapid advance of the Western Allies, a first section of the unit was moved to Krefeld from 6 September 1944, and a further section was moved from mid-October 1944 to Störmede near Lippstadt and to Bönninghardt near Wesel. By 16 October 1944 the unit was entirely in the west and first went into action under the command of the 'Hallensleben fighting unit' in the Aachen and Venlo battle area. The unit was finally stationed on the Bönninghardt airfield. The leadership of the unit was still in the hands of Captain Herbert Hilberg. At the beginning of February 1945 the majority of the operations were flown from Kirchhellen near Gladbeck and from the Krefeld area.

When the fighting unit was disbanded again on 26 February 1945, the units were placed under the command of the 15th *Fliegerdivision* led by Major-General Karl-Eduard Wilke. At the end of February 1945, in the context of the general collapse, the *Luftwaffe* High Command divided NSGr 1 into NSGr 1 (North) and NSGr 1 (South). From the Kirchhellen airfield Ju 87 D-5s of the northern *Gruppe* continued to attack numerous ground targets in the west. Between 10 February 1945 and 8 March 1945 alone, ten Ju 87 Ds of NSGr 1 were lost. The majority of the crews were shot down by Allied flak units or for the time being went missing. On 8 March 1945 the *Gruppe* possessed only twenty battleworthy machines; forty-two of the nominal inventory of sixty-two Ju 87s had meanwhile been lost or laid aside, damaged.

On 8 March 1945 the Remagen railway bridge was attacked by ten Ju 87 D-5s of NSGr 1 (North). Take-off was from Kirchhellen. *Gruppe* commander Captain Herbert Hilberg had refused to carry out suicidal attacks. As appropriate bomb fuses were not available, the SC 500 bombs with a charge of enhanced explosive, released from 150 metres altitude, all failed.

The machine of the *Gruppe* commander, followed by three Ju 87s of the 1st to 3rd *Staffeln*, returned from this operation badly damaged. After the initial surprise was over, the American flak gunners opened with well-placed fire. Of the crews, only four came back with their Ju 87 Ds. The machines of 2nd Lieutenant Wolfram Hölzel, Corporal Eberhard Berg, both of 1/NSGr 1, Sergeant Zbyrowsky (2/NSGr 1) and Sergeant Johannes Debel (3/NSGr 1) did not return from this combat flight. A further Ju 87 D-5 hit by flak was 35 per cent damaged in an emergency landing near Grevenbroich. The machine of Junior Under Officer Erich Päch crashed in the immediate neighbourhood of the target, hit by flak, before it could release its SD 1000 bomb with its charge of enhanced explosive. Most of the remaining crews succeeded in making emergency landings in German territory.

The attacks by Fw 190 F-8 pilots of 2/NSGr 20 were equally unsuccessful. Even the suicide operation which was called up on 8 March 1945, as well as attacks with Ar 234 B-2s, Me 262 A-2s and fighter pilots of JG 2 were unsuccessful. The bridge collapsed on 17 March 1945 because of near misses, but chiefly because of overloading. At the end of the month the northern *Gruppe*, instead of the sixty-two machines assigned to it, possessed only thirty-two, of which twenty-eight were battleworthy. Of forty-four crews, only twenty-three were fully trained, so that on 30 March 1945 only twenty-three ground attack sorties took place over the front.

With NSGr 1 on 1 April 1945 only ten out of sixty-two machines were still available with crews, who daily flew between eight and fifteen sorties. By mid-April 1945 the number of Ju 87 Ds rose again to twenty-six, of which, however, only fourteen were battleworthy. Some of the thirty-four crews took off daily for hardly more than fifteen sorties. Because of low-level attacks the number of machines declined, also because of several crash landings. A few days later, on 9 April 1945, the northern operational *Gruppe* possessed only one battleworthy Ju 87 D-5; all of the other eight were reported as unserviceable.

Because of the rapid advance of the Western Allies, NSGr 1 with its Ju 87 D-3s and D-5s was continually forced to move. The retreat of the night ground attackers led by way of the Düsseldorf area to Wunstorf near Hannover and from there to Celle. The hard-hit unit then went into Schleswig-Holstein and shortly afterwards moved to Hagenow. From there it went to the vicinity of Schwerin before the last machines finally went to Husum.

On 4 May 1945 a few crews of NSGr 1 (North) flew their last ground attack operation against the continually advancing British ground troops.

NSGr 1 (South), on the other hand, was driven by way of an interim station at Wertheim to

This Ju 87 D-5 'N' used two 0.5-cubic metre wooden containers during a positioning flight.

Upper Bavaria. On 26 April 1945 eleven Ju 87 Ds were available, of which only six were in airworthy condition. Although thirty-three trained crews were available, action was prevented by lack of fuel. On 3 May 1945 the flying sections were at Aibling, while the ground sections were already in unaccustomed ground combat. The path of NSGr 1 (South) ended on 9 May 1945 in the vicinity of Bad Reichenhall. The remaining machines awaited scrapping on the airfield of Aibling which had become a gathering point for air equipment.

6.3.2 Night Ground Attack *Gruppe* 2 (D3+)

NSGr 2 was formed on 7 October 1942 at the Orsha airfield as the 1st Auxiliary Bomber *Staffel* of *Luftwaffe* Command East. From this came the Harassment Bomber *Gruppe* of *Luftwaffe* Command East, which was equipped with a number of different types and from May 1943 onwards was surprisingly renamed as the Harassment Bomber *Gruppe* of *Luftflotte* 6.

From 18 October 1943 this became Night Ground Attack *Gruppe* 2, which had three ground attack *Staffeln*.

In November 1943 the conversion to Ju 87 Ds began, followed by the formation of 4/NSGr 2 in January 1944. This unit, however, was not equipped with Ju 87 Ds, but received Ar 66 biplanes which had become available.

From the beginning of 1944 operations began in the middle sector of the eastern front. As with NSGr 1, road and rail connections and enemy artillery positions, together with rear supply depots, were among the chief targets. Even though the majority of the operations took place at dusk or at night, there were from to time also daylight attacks. Because of enemy air superiority these were for the most part relatively costly.

At the beginning of 1944 the *Staffeln* were in action at Baranovitshi, Terespol (1/2), Lida (2/2)

This Go 145, captured by the enemy, belonged to 2/NSGr 2, which for a time went into action under the command of the 15th Fliegerdivision.

Picked crews of the dive bomber and ground attack Geschwader *were already flying night ground attack operations from the end of 1942 onwards.*

and Uretshye and Borissov (3/2). 2/NSGr 2 left the *Gruppe* as early as March 1944 and was transferred to the command area of *Luftflotte* 2 (Italy). Operations of the remaining parts of the *Gruppe* took place on the eastern front up to the summer of 1944. Important places in the unit's operational history were Baranovitshi, Pinsk, Terespol, Orsha and Mogilev.

On 26 June 1944 the staff of NSGr 2 was at Lida, where fourteen Ju 87s were available. The 1st *Staffel* was stationed at Bobruisk and could summon up twenty-one Ju 87 Ds. With 3/NSGr 2 at Lida seventeen Ju 87s and Ar 66s were in operation. At Mogilev several Ar 66s, Go 145s and captured U-2s flew with the 4th *Staffel* of the ground attack unit.

From the end of August 1944 the 1st *Staffel* and parts of 3/NSGr 2 moved from the eastern front to Vörden on the Aller. In the end the night ground attackers went to Cologne-Butzweiler, while part of the 3rd *Staffel* and 4/NSGr 2 stayed longer in the east.

On 23 September 1944 1 and 3/NSGr 2 became part of the 'Hallensleben fighting unit'. From September 1944, part of NSGr 2 was diverted to Eudenbach in the Westerwald, while the bulk of NSGr 2, together with forces of NSGr 20, remained stationed at Hangelar, Ostheim and on the airfield at Wahn near Cologne. As a result of numerous air attacks on the Cologne area there were some losses of personnel and operational machines there in 1944. The operations room of NSGr 2, meanwhile, was in the nearby Röttgen castle. With the disbandment of the 'Hallensleben fighting unit' these parts of NSGr 2 became independent once more.

Owing to the weak state of their opponents, the massive attack of the 6th, 12th and 21st

Allied Army Groups led relatively quickly to large gains of territory. The Rhine was reached at Cologne on 7 February 1945. Strong enemy units everywhere pushed surprisingly quickly towards the west. The air bases at Ostheim and Wahn in the neighbourhood of Cologne soon had to be evacuated under heavy enemy pressure. For that reason, in the first days of March 1945 NSGr 2 moved into the nearby Westerwald. On 7 March 1945 the Remagen railway bridge fell into American hands; in a short time the well-known and well-consolidated bridgehead was established with a correspondingly strong concentration of flak.

The *Staffeln* were initially well received at the airfields of Ailertchen, Breitscheid and Lippe in the command area of Air District Command XIV. The 1st and 2nd *Staffeln* arrived at Lippe on 7 March 1945 while 3/NSGr 2 landed on an airstrip near Breitscheid only two days later. On 8 March 1945 the Ju 87 forces led by Captain Gustav Weber also went there from Eudenbach.

From the middle of March 1945 crews of NSGr 2 flew operations from Breitscheid, Ettinghausen and Lippe. Their targets were the Remagen bridgehead as well as several Allied troop concentrations west of the Rhine. As a lengthy stay in the Westerwald was unthinkable, it was necessary to look for new operations bases further east in Thuringia. In the process the commander of NSGr 2, Major Robert, was stopped by a Hitler Youth patrol on 12 March 1945 and accidentally shot. He died on 8 May 1945 in the Bad Hersfeld hospital.

On 13 March 1945 NSGr 2 was attacked with bombs and guns on the Breitscheid and Lippe airfields by B-26s and P-47s of the 9th Air Force. In the process the Thunderbolt and Marauder crews destroyed twenty-two out of twenty-six Ju 87 D-5s which were standing ready for take-off, loaded with bombs. With that the already hard-hit ground attack *Gruppe* almost ceased to exist.

On 17 March 1945 the damaged Remagen bridge, which had been attacked many times, collapsed – without any direct action by the *Luftwaffe* – and took many American soldiers with it to the depths.

The situation of NSGr 2 at the end of March became ever more difficult as part of the fuel supply had been burnt in the American attack of 13 March 1945. More and more often a lack of fuel, which was issued first to the fighter units, prevented a higher state of operational readiness. The delivery of free-fall ordnance was also more and more problematical because of the rapidly deteriorating war situation. In addition, the losses caused by enemy fighters and fighter-bombers could barely be replaced. By 28 March 1945 the Allies had taken Marburg, Giessen and Limburg and advanced by way of Hanau and Aschaffenburg. During those days the *Gruppe* could summon up only fifteen out of twenty-eight (nominally sixty-two) Ju 87s for operations. In total fifty-four crews were available, of which only thirty-three had the necessary operational experience. With scarcely a dozen machines, the night ground attack *Gruppe* moved by way of Altenkirchen, near Montabaur, to Kirchdorf and finally to Eschwege. Small remnants retreated further to southern Germany. The next station for NSGr 2 was the well-built airfield at Bayreuth at the end of March 1945. On 1 April there were only five operational machines with the night ground attack *Gruppe* which then belonged to the 16th *Fliegerdivision*. The number of crews also declined to five. Even on 9 April 1945, according to a strength report, five battleworthy machines were still available. In the days that followed, the number of Ju 87 Ds still available with NSGr 2 remained as low as at the beginning of the month.

Finally, at the end of April 1945, a few ground attack operations followed from the Straubing airfield, where the *Gruppe* had been stationed since 19 April 1945. The low-level attacks were on enemy tanks which were moving towards Regensburg on the autobahn.

As a result of other units giving up their Ju 87s, NSGr 2 was again brought up to twenty-six aircraft on 26 April 1945, of which only a small number were airworthy. For twelve battleworthy Ju 87s at the last, fifty-six crews were available. Operations did not, however, take place every day.

A little later, on 2 May 1945, the last crews retreated with their Ju 87 D-5s to Aibling. Others had flown to Holzkirchen, where almost all machines were destroyed by German troops on 8 May 1945. Next, the pilots went to Miesbach with the bulk of the remaining maintenance personnel, where the unit, still 450 men strong, finally surrendered.

6.3.3 Night Ground Attack *Gruppe* 4 (1K+)

Beginning in October 1942, so-called Auxiliary Bomber *Staffeln* were set up in the *Luftflotte* 4 area, which formed two *Gruppen* on 17 November 1942 and were sent into action in the *Luftflotte* 4 and *Luftwaffe* Command Don areas. A little later, on 1 March 1943, these *Staffeln* became the 1–6/Harrassment Bomber *Staffel Luftflotte* 4; at first only a few Ju 87s were available with the 4th *Staffel*. Later the first two *Staffeln* also received a few Ju 87s. The other aircraft equipment consisted mainly of Ar 66s, Go 145s, He 46s and a menagerie of different types. The main area of operations of these units was in the southern sector of the eastern front. Often the crews – singly and with inadequate navigation equipment – were sent on harassment operations far behind the front. Tactical tasks were also carried out individually at the *Staffel* level. Particularly significant were the costly operations in the summer of 1943 in the Kursk salient during Operation *Citadel*. From September 1943 came numerous low-level attacks against Soviet supply formations on the Dnieper and on the advancing divisions of the Red Army.

After the battles on the southern sector of the front, from the summer of 1943 onwards, the conversion of the night ground attack *Gruppe* to Ju 87 Ds took place at Lodz and Brunnstadt. In the context of the restructuring of the close combat units, on 18 October 1943 all Ju 87s which were with the 1st, 2nd and 4th *Staffeln* were pulled together into the 1st and 2nd *Staffeln* of the newly formed Night Ground Attack *Gruppe* 4. From October 1943 parts of *Staffeln* were in continuous action over the northern Balkans and the eastern part of Hungary with bombs and guns against the advancing enemy forces. Because of the low-level attacks and ground attack sorties which were ordered, ever more numerous losses occurred among the insufficiently trained replacement crews.

In May 1944 alone, sixteen Ju 87 D 'N's were manufactured; in July thirty-three followed and in September forty-two conversions. On 26 June 1944 NSGr 4 had a *Gruppe* staff and three *Staffeln*. Of these 1/NSGr 4 at Hordinia possessed a total of twenty-eight Go 145s, while the 2nd and 3rd *Staffeln* were still being trained on Ju 87s. By summer both *Staffeln* were ready for action and carried out numerous low-level attacks and ground attack sorties against the Red Army. On 15 October 1944 1/NSGr 4 was at Lübben.

In December the former 2/NSGr 6 became the new 1/NSGr 4. Major operations took place from Balice, Malacky and Fünfkirchen.

At the beginning of 1945 the second *Staffel* of NSGr 4 was mostly equipped with Ju 87 D-3 'N's and D-5 'N's and was especially well equipped for night operations, thanks to the flame eliminator installations and additional navigational equipment. On 1 February 1945 one extra Ju 87 D-5 was with the *Gruppe* staff of NSGr 4 as well as five Si 204 D-1s. Of these, however, only three machines were battleworthy.

The 1st *Staffel* possessed seventeen Ju 87 D-3s and D-5s, of which the maintenance staff reported ten ready for action each day. The 2nd *Staffel* still had fifteen aircraft at that time, of which ten could have been sent into action. The aircraft inventory of 3/NSGr 4 amounted to fourteen machines. In total the *Gruppe* had forty-seven ground attack machines at its disposal and had thirty Ju 87 Ds available. In January and February 1945 the third *Staffel* lost at least four crews at Oberglogau, Stephansdorf, Neisse-Möckendorf and Böhmischdorf, of which one went down to enemy flak on 25 February 1945. Senior Under Officer Hermann Robel, on the other hand, crashed immediately after take-off and Senior Under Officer Franz Vogel crashed in action; Cadet Corporal Harry Ahlers fell at Glogau.

Until 27 February 1945 the 3rd *Staffel* was near Bautzen and operated from the Kamenz airfield south-east of Dresden. There, on 3 March 1945, the unit lost two of its Ju 87 D-5s by hitting the ground and crash landing.

Other almost intact ground attack machines were blown up by German troops during the retreat, for example D-5, works no. 142873, at Komin.

In the first days of March Ju 87 Ds of 1/NSGr 4 flew a heavy ground attack operation in the Kolberg area, but achieved little success because of bad weather: the majority of the AB 250s and AB 500s released missed. The Red Army had meanwhile been able to concentrate its flak units as the length of the front decreased. As the mobile units were now assigned to the tank regiments, attacks on troop concentrations behind the main battle line also became increasingly dangerous for the Ju 87 crews.

The equipment of NSGr 4 on 21 March 1945 comprised two Ju 87 Ds and three Si 204s with the *Gruppe* staff. Another sixteen Ju 87s were to be found with the 1st *Staffel*, twelve with the 2nd and nineteen with the 3rd. On that day thirty-three Ju 87 D-3s and D-5s were reported as battleworthy. On 29 March 1945 crews of 3/NSGr 4 – operating simultaneously from Kamenz near Dresden and Hirschberg in Silesia – took part in defensive operations against the Red Army. The 2nd *Staffel* was meanwhile stationed at Brno. By 31 March 1945 the number of ground attack aircraft had dwindled to forty-four. Among the losses was one Ju 87 D-5 of the *Gruppe* staff.

In 1945 NSGr 4, under the command of the 4th *Fliegerdivision*, flew only 199 operations, in the course of which 25,750 kg of bombs and 129,640 kg of bomb containers were released over enemy positions and supply columns. In the process two machines were a total loss, and a further two went missing. The enemy shot down one Ju 87 D, and four aircraft were more or less damaged as a result of crashes. On 30 March 1945 2/NSGr 4 was subordinated to the 3rd *Fliegerdivision*, whose jurisdiction also contained parts of SG 9 and JG 77. NAGr 2 provided short-range reconnaissance. The third *Staffel* was under VII *Fliegerkorps*, to which forces of JG 52, 8/JG 6 and three *Rotten* of NAGr 15 were also assigned.

The experience report of 1/NSGr 4 of 1 April 1945 concerning the operations of the *Staffel* in the month of March indicated mainly attacks on Soviet lines of communication behind the eastern front. The enemy defences, so the report stated, had adapted astonishingly well to the nocturnal threat. Particularly around the bridge targets and river crossings attacked by the *Staffel*, a powerful concentration of Soviet flak units had been assembled which could provide massive defence of the target areas against the threat from the air.

On 1 April 1945 four machines were in action with the staff of NSGr 4 in the area of the 3rd *Fliegerdivision*, *Luftflotte* Command 6, of which at least two or three were Si 204 D-1s with bomb release mechanisms.

With the 3rd *Staffel* eighteen Ju 87 Ds were available at the beginning of the month, of which fourteen were ready for action. In total

British troops captured these four Go 145 training aircraft of NSGr 6 in northern Germany in the spring of 1945.

Heavy demands in service made necessary numerous changes of the Jumo 211 J in-line engine under field conditions. Thanks to plentiful practice, engine mechanics of NSGr 7 could do this with relatively few men.

eighteen crews awaited the take-off order, although there was generally insufficient fuel available. Besides their ground attack operations, on the night of 8 April 1945 crews of 3/NSGr 4 flew to Breslau with six Ju 87s loaded with 2,040 kg of ammunition in bomb containers with parachutes. Three of the machines, however, diverted because of adverse weather conditions before reaching the target. At almost the same time sixteen Ju 87 Ds, together with eight piston-engined fighters assigned as escort, attacked in the Rathstock area and at Küstrin. Shortly afterwards twenty-nine Ju 87 D-3s and D-5s of the unit bombarded targets on the autobahn between Breslau and Liegnitz. In addition 40,000 leaflets were dropped over the Soviet columns.

On 9 April 1945 forty-five Ju 87 Ds and Si 204s were still available with the fourth Night Ground Attack *Gruppe*, which was at that time among the most powerful, but only thirty-six machines were battleworthy.

On the night of 11–12 April 1945 ten Ju 87 Ds of the 1st *Staffel* flew an operation over the Stargard area. On the following night eight of the machines again sought worthwhile ground targets on the autobahn to Breslau. On 14 April 1945 thirty ground attack machines bombarded the Soviet ground units advancing in Silesia. One day later 3/NSGr 4 once again had thirty Ju 87 D-3s and D-5s in action at Steinau-Neisse and along the autobahn, mainly in the Haynau Forest. On 16 April 1945 twenty-three Ju 87 Ds of 2 and 3/NSGr 4 attacked targets at Ratibor. One Si 204 D-1 of the unit flew against a target at Brno with two AB 250s and eight SD 70s.

On the night of 23–4 April 1945 sixteen

Ju 87 Ds of the ground attack unit bombarded the vicinity of Rathstock with the support of Ju 88 A-4s and A-14s as illuminators, and mainly AB 250s and AB 500s were dropped. On 29 April the 3rd *Staffel*, now reduced to three *Schwärme*, was at Kamenz. The *Gruppe* staff, together with the 2nd *Staffel* and the seconded command of the 3rd *Staffel*, was at Schweidnitz.

On 3 May 2/NSGr 4 was at Olmütz-South and 3/NSGr 4 was at Ludwigsdorf. The third *Staffel* was at that time a part of the 'Weiss *Luftwaffe* fighting unit' led by Otto Weiss, which was assigned to Army High Command 17 for direct air support.

Otherwise NSGr 4, II/SG 77 and III/JG 52 belonged to the fighting unit. The important operational bases of the unit were Glatz, Schweidnitz and Ludwigsdorf.

Shortly before the end of the war ground attack operations were scarcely to be considered, as the supply of fuel had collapsed. In the first days of May 1945 NSGr 4 was disbanded by the OKL.

6.3.4 Night Ground Attack *Gruppe* 6

Night Ground Attack *Gruppe* 6 originated on 18 October 1943 from the 3rd and 6th Harassment Bomber *Staffeln* of *Luftflotte* 4. As early as 17 April 1944 the *Gruppe* staff was disbanded, 1/NSGr 6 was renamed 3/NSGr 4 and 2/NSGr 6 was renamed 3/NSGr 5. From 27 September 1944 1/NSGr 6 was re-formed at Hohensalza and now received Ju 87 D-3s. At the same time 2/NSGr 6 was equipped with the robust Junkers ground attack aircraft at Grieslienen. Both *Staffeln* were mainly in action with I *Fliegerkorps* in the southern sector of the eastern front. At the beginning of November 1944, 1 and 2/NSGr 6 were at Grieslienen and flew their operations over the weakened eastern front from there. On 5 December 1944, 1/NSGr 6 was renamed 2/NSGr 2 and, after moving to Hangelar near Cologne, became part of the 'Hallensleben fighting unit'. On 17 December 1944, 1/NSGr 4 was formed out of 2/NSGr 6.

Among the last Ju 87 D-5s of NSGr 6 to be lost on the eastern front was the machine with works no. 140727 which failed to return from an operation on 2 March 1945 in which NSGr 8 was also engaged.

6.3.5 Night Ground Attack *Gruppe* 7 (4X+)

NSGr 7 originated at the beginning of 1944 from Harassment Bomber *Staffel* South-east and was mainly equipped with He 46s and Hs 126s. Later Fiat CR 42s were added with 3/NSGr 7.

After the unit was placed under *Luftwaffe* Command South-east in 1943, there was vigorous operational activity in the next year in the area of the Air Leader Croatia (*Luftwaffe* Command South-east) and the Air Leader North Balkans in the Agram (Zagreb) and Pless areas. As a result of the release of machines from the Italian theatre of war, in the middle of July 1944 six Ju 87 Ds of NSGr 9 together with eleven Fw 190s of SG 4 went to Tirana in order to fly ground attack operations from there for NSGr 7. At the beginning of March 1945 NSGr 7, which had meanwhile been partly equipped with Ju 87s, was again at Agram.

On 13 March 1945 NSGr 7, which belonged to *Luftflotte* 4, including its staff and three *Staffeln*, was disbanded.

6.3.6 Night Ground Attack *Gruppe* 8 (6J+)

The 1st *Staffel* of NSGr 8 went into action in the northern sector of the eastern front from 28 February 1944 onwards. Under the leadership of the Air Leader North (Kirkenes, Norway), the unit had initially to be content with the low-performance Ar 66. From 17 May 1944 onwards 2/NSGr 8 was equipped with Ju 87 Ds, in which the majority of the aircrews came from the ranks of the released 4th *Staffel* of SG 5. In the early summer of 1944 the unit was in action over Finland. Meanwhile, the exhausted 1st *Staffel* was taken out of action and began to convert to Ju 87 Ds. From July 1944 the *Gruppe* staff also received Ju 87 Ds, while all Ar 66s that were still operational were concentrated in the newly formed 3/NSG 8. As early as August 1944 the whole unit was in action with both types over Finland.

To 1/NSGr 8 fell the task at the end of August of interrupting the railway line leading to Murmansk. The fuel made available for this purpose did not, however, suffice for the planned bombing operations

In the winter of 1942–3 it was mostly Ju 87 D-3s, later also a few Ju 87 D-5s, which flew with the night ground attack Gruppen *equipped with the Junkers machines.*

from Pontsalenjoki. At the beginning of September 1944 the 2nd *Staffel* possessed about fifteen Ju 87s at Kemijärvi. A further sixteen were available to 1/NSGr 8 on the airfield at Kemi. On 1 September 1944 twenty-nine Ju 87s were available for service with this night ground attack *Gruppe*. All operations by the unit were coordinated by Air Leader 3, who was subordinate to *Luftflotte* 5.

Finland broke off relations with the German *Reich* on 2 September 1944, having signed a separate armistice with the Soviet Union. This made it necessary to withdraw NSGr 8 with its Ar 66s and Ju 87s from the far north by 15 September 1944. Until January 1945 the *Gruppe* was then subordinated to the commanding general of the *Luftwaffe* in Norway. Up to the beginning of October 1944 Finland was again its main centre of operations, as was northern Norway (*Luftflotte* 5) from December 1944. Next, the unit moved from Norway to the area of Frankfurt an der Oder and was there placed under *Luftflotte* 6. The *Staffeln* operated mostly from Werneuchen. They were particularly important on the Oder front and in the battles for Berlin. A Ju 87 D-5 was shot down by flak at Kienitz on 31 January 1945; the crew succeeded in making a smooth emergency landing. Several other machines went missing in the first days of March near Görlitz on the Neisse. Two of the crews, among them that of Sergeant-Major Schumann, were missing after ground attack operations against the Red Army. Further losses affected the staff of NSGr 8, when crews which had only recently been assigned did not return with their Ju 87 D-5s. The machines with works nos. 130522 and 141295 were damaged; both crews survived uninjured. On 1 February 1945 mostly Ju 87 D-5s, but also a few Ar 66s and Go 145s, were in action with the three flying *Staffeln* of NSGr 8. The 4th *Staffel* at that time mostly

A Ju 87 D-5 of NSGr 9 over Italy in the late summer of 1944.

flew the long-obsolete Ar 66 and Go 145 auxiliary bombers, which had been in service since 1943 and of which there were still just thirty on the inventory.

From 6 to 27 February 1945 the three night ground attack *Staffeln* operated from the well-built airfield at Werneuchen.

On the night of 23 March 1945 forty-eight Ju 87s of NSGr 8 flew against the enemy bridgehead at Görlitz in order to provide the greatest possible support to the German ground troops. Also on the night of 23–4 March 1945 fourteen Ju 87 Ds of the night ground attack *Gruppen* attacked targets near Görlitz with visible success.

On 23 March 1945 the unit scored a decisive success in front of the positions of the 712th Infantry Regiment in the Lebus area: almost all free-fall ordnance landed precisely on target, so that the German troops were given a short respite.

On 31 March 1945 thirty-four Ju 87 Ds were still available with the 1st to 3rd *Staffeln*, of which twenty-nine machines were reported airworthy by the maintenance personnel. In seven days of operations in March 1945 a total of 178 Ju 87s and two Go 145s were in action in the east. The operations were often accompanied by Ju 88s or Ju 188s which functioned as guide aircraft and illuminators with LC 50 flare bombs. In the operations a total of 37 LC 50s were dropped, which provided sufficient aiming light for the Ju 87s, averaging fifteen in number.

If visibility was more than 5 km, the crews could usually find their targets. The conduct of the operational task was facilitated if the ground troops in the relevant part of the front fired white recognition signals so that the line of the front became more easily recognisable. On 1 April 1945 there was a total of only thirty-seven sorties, although forty-nine crews were available – there was not enough fuel for more.

By way of free-fall ordnance, a total of sixty-one AB 500s, 143 AB 250s filled with SD 10s, 262 AB 250s filled with SD 1s and two AB 70s were dropped in April by NSGr 8 alone. In addition the crews dropped six SC 500s, nineteen SD 250s and 250 SD 70s. The targets were either troop concentrations, artillery positions or vehicle concentrations. On the night of 8–9 April 1945 eight Ju 87 D-5s of the unit, together with a Ju 88 A-4, attacked several targets at Aurinth and Ziebingen. In the process the crews dropped an additional two SC 250s and two SD 70s. On 11 April an attack by thirty-two Ar 66s, Go 145s and a few Ju 87s took place against targets in the Görlitz area.

The Ju 87 D-5s of the ground attack unit next moved to northern Germany where they could intervene in the ground battles only sporadically as a result of the dwindling fuel and munitions supply.

In the first days of May the *Gruppe* was disbanded at Schleswig.

6.3.7 Night Ground Attack *Gruppe* 9 (E8+)

NSGr 9 was formed on 30 November 1943 from parts of NSGr 3. It was at Udine at the end of

Because of Allied air superiority the operational machines of NSGr 9 in Italy always had to be pushed under cover quickly. (Federal Archives)

1943 and was equipped with Caproni Ca 314s and Ar 66s. In January 1944 the *Gruppe* moved to Casella, where it gave up the unusable Ca 314s, and from 28 January 1944 received Fiat CR 42s. Next, the night ground attack *Gruppe*, led by Captain Rupert Frost, moved to Cantocelle near Rome, where it took significant losses among the parked machines in a massive P-47 attack on 21 April 1944. Previously ten machines of NSGr 9 had attacked targets in the hard-fought battle of Anzio, in which three crews went missing as a result of night fighters or flak.

At the end of May 1944 the 1st and 2nd *Staffeln* of NSGr 9 already had thirty-seven Ju 87 D-3s and D-5s. After a move via Lago to Forli-Ravenna and then to Florence, there were hardly any operations with Ju 87 Ds by the 1st *Staffel*; but most operations were with CR 42s, as the conversion to the new type had not been completed. With the 2nd *Staffel*, retraining had only just begun in the summer of 1944. There, on 31 May 1944, eighteen Fiat CR 42s were still in action as night ground attack aircraft.

In June 1944 the night attacks were continued; in the course of these operations E8+RH, a Ju 87 D-5 of 1/NSGr 9, attacked enemy positions and supply columns at Frascati and Grottoferrata on 5 June 1944. On 13 June 1944 nine Ju 87s and Fiat CR 42s of the unit were in action over the Viterbo area. Other operations were carried out as part of the fight against partisans.

On 1 July 1944 alone thirty-three night sorties took place in the area of Lake Trasimene and the Tiber valley in which 2/NSGr 9 also took part. On 3 July 1944 there followed thirty-three Ju 87 attacks against supply targets in the

Loreto-Macerata area and north-west of Lake Trasimene. In the following days too, NSGr 9 developed its activities chiefly by night. Some losses were incurred, caused by Beaufighter operations. On 15 July 1944 six Ju 87 Ds, together with eleven Fw 190s of SG 4, were moved to Tirana in order to fly ground attack operations from there. In the middle of the month the number of night ground attack flights declined for a short time. Not until 26 July 1944 did Ju 87 D-5s from Cavariago attack Livorno harbour.

In August 1944 almost all operations with Ju 87 D-3s and D-5s took place on the first and last days of the month. In these the free-fall ordnance was mostly released from heights of 1,000–2,000 metres – but some in low-level attacks about 100 metres above ground. The three *Staffeln* of NSGr 9, stationed at Ravenna and Rimini, still had thirty-four Ju 87 Ds available after six machines had been released and at least ten had been lost on operations or damaged. On 28 August 1944 six Ju 87 Ds of 3/NSGr 9, with one AB 250 and four AB 70s each, attacked targets at Arezzo. In this operation two crews were shot down by Beaufighters of 600 Squadron north-west of Florence. By 31 August 1944 the number of Ju 87 Ds – in spite of a few newly supplied Ju 87 D-5s – had declined to thirty-three, of which twenty-four were battleworthy.

At the beginning of September 1944 the *Gruppe* staff and 1/NSGr 9 were stationed at Ferrara, the 2nd and 3rd *Staffeln* at Cavariago. From there 2/NSGr 9 moved to Ghedi and on 16 September 1944 3/NSGr 9 moved to Villafranca, where the majority of the remaining crews followed from Aviano and Piacenza. As a result of moves and advanced training of new crews, relatively few operations took place in September. On 30 September 1944 thirty-four aircraft were operational. Of these seventeen were Ju 87 D-3s, the rest D-5s.

In October 1944 there were only a few attacks against enemy supply targets in the Bologna area, as the weather was not conducive to night operations. At the beginning of November the staff and 1st *Staffel* were at Bovolone, while 2/NSGr 9 was still at Ghedi and 3/NSGr 9 at Aviano. Supply lines were the main targets, for example the road between Florence and Bologna which led through the Appenines. In the middle of November eight Ju 87s of Night

Removal of the engine cowling of a Ju 87 D-5 of 1/NSGr 9; summer 1944.

Ground Attack *Gruppe* 9 from Villafranca successfully attacked targets in the area of the front.

On 30 November 1944 NSGr 9 had only seven Ju 87 D-3s and eighteen D-5s, as insufficient replacements had arrived in Italy. Correspondingly the number of operations declined severely; the deliveries of fuel in particular were further restricted. Even so, on 25 December 1944 there were fourteen operational flights from Ghedi and a further seventeen from Villafranca. Two days later five night ground attackers attacked targets at Faenza. A few days later the number of battleworthy Ju 87s fell to twelve; a further nine machines had to be parked for lack of spare parts or due to operational damage and for the time being were not available for operations.

In January 1945 all the machines in the staff, 2nd and 3rd *Staffeln* were consolidated. With these the crews flew a total of ninety operational sorties in six nights.

On 2 February 1945 the *Gruppe* staff was moved from Bovolone to Villafranca, where the first *Staffel* was to be equipped with Fw 190 F-8s for better combat capability. By the end of February twelve of the faster fighter bombers had come to 1/NSGr 9. The two other *Staffeln* and the staff stayed with Ju 87 Ds, of which twenty-six were still on hand on 1 March 1945. In spite of the approaching collapse, the number of Ju 87 D night ground attack aircraft rose again until the end of March 1945. At that time there were twenty-seven machines with NSGr 9, of which about ten Ju 87 Ds were on the airfields of Ghedi and Villafranca in April.

On 1 April 1945 the number of machines credited to NSGr 9 was sixty, of which forty-two were Ju 87 Ds; of those, however, only twenty-seven were available. Due to a lack of crews, there were only sixteen low-level attacks on that day.

The strength reports of the OKL, GenQ 6 Division, show thirty-eight Fw 190s and Ju 87 Ds with NSGr 9 on 9 April 1945, of which thirty-five were battleworthy. As a result of enemy action and missing spare parts, their number was halved in the following two weeks. The last operations were flown on 22 and 23 April 1945; at least twenty Fw 190s and Ju 87s attacked the Modena area in a dusk attack.

On the morning of 27 April 1945 NSGr 9 moved off in the direction of Innsbruck with the last five Fw 190 F-8s as well as thirteen Ju 87 D-3s and D-5s. Most of the Ju 87 ground attack aircraft were parked there with the last Me 262s of Fighter Unit 44.

6.3.8 Night Ground Attack *Gruppe* 10 (5B+)

Part of NSGr 10 was already stationed at Werneuchen between 14 February 1944 and 31 July 1944 and took part in testing there until the end of November 1944.

Various Ju 87 D-5 'Ns' were equipped with A-version flame eliminators.

The bulk of NSGr 10 was in the South-east Area of the eastern front from 17 September 1944. The two *Staffeln* of this night ground attack *Gruppe* had been formed from part of the staff of II/Training *Geschwader* 1 at Agram (Zagreb). The unit was subordinated to II *Fliegerkorps* and in the late summer of 1944 was at Mayar Mecska, Neusatz and Skoplje, where the unit was equipped with the Ju 87 D in October 1944.

The majority of the machines of NSGr 9 and the remnants of training units stationed in Italy were moved further north in 1944.

For moving Ju 87 D-3 'Ns' and D-5 'Ns' were fitted with large wooden containers. Often the groundcrew leader was carried in the narrow cockpit.

As early as 17 November 1944 the 2nd *Staffel* was probably disbanded at Stubendorf and in its place the 1st *Staffel* of NSGr 5 was taken into the *Gruppe*.

From the second half of November the ground attack unit was in action over the northern Balkans as well as in the *Luftflotte* 4 area in Hungary. Among the last losses, reported on 11 and 22 February 1945, were the crews of Lieutenant Kosemund and Sergeant-Major Wedall, whose machines had to be written off as a total loss at Balatonpuszta after crash landings. In the process three crew members were killed; one radio operator survived, injured.

An unidentified crew of the staff of NSGr 10 was involved in a flying accident caused by tyre damage on 5 March 1945. The pilot, however, succeeded in making an emergency landing at Novy-Dvor without problems, with the result that he and his radio operator got away uninjured.

At the end of March 1945 two Ju 87 D-5s were battleworthy with the staff of NSGr 10, which took part on 30 March 1945 in one of the last major operations. One day later, 1/NSGr 10 could even take off for ground attack sorties with seventeen out of eighteen Ju 87 Ds. During the following days a few aircraft fell out, so that on 9 April 1945 only fourteen were still available. Of these the maintenance crews could get just nine into airworthy condition.

As a result of enemy pressure, the night ground attack *Gruppe* had to be withdrawn; in the process numerous unserviceable machines were blown up by German troops.

On 3 May 1945 2/NSGr 10 was at Wels in Austria. A little later the *Staffel*, along with the whole *Gruppe*, which was barely capable of any further operations, was disbanded by OKL.

6.3.9 The 'Hallensleben Fighting Unit'

On 16 September 1944 the General of Bomber Pilots decided to disband KG 2 'Holzhammer' with the consent of OKL, with effect from 18 September 1944.

The *Geschwader* staff of KG 2 was then appointed to the leadership of the powerful 'Hallensleben Fighting Unit', which was led by Lieutenant-Colonel Rudolf Hallensleben from 23 September 1944. The unit consisted initially of the following units, although the *Gruppe* of KG 3 soon left.

- III/KG 51 (later NSGr 20) at Bonn-Hangelar
- 1 and 3/NSGr 2 at Cologne-Ostheim and Ailertchen
- 3/KG 51 as the 'Schenk Command' at Rheine
- III/KG 3 at Alhorn, Münster-Handorf and Varelbusch

A machine of NSGr 10 was abandoned on the airfield at Fürth in April 1945. Two AB 250 bomb containers were still hanging under the wings.

The 'Hallensleben Fighting Unit' was briefly subordinated to *Luftflotte* Command 3 (Colonel-General Otto Dessloch) and from 26 September 1944 to Air Command West, which was led by Lieutenant General Alexander Holle and then by Lieutenant-General Josef Schmidt. From 26 November 1944 the unit came under the command of Major-General Dietrich Peltz and thus II Fighter Corps.

When this was disbanded on 26 February 1945, the three night ground attack *Gruppen* joined the 15th *Fliegerdivision*.

The identification of the individual targets to be attacked, as well as the whole operational planning in Army Group B, was done through the 7th Army until 22 October 1944, through the 5th Panzer Army until 29 October 1944 and through the 1st Parachute Army until 29 November 1944.

The use of night ground attack units began on 23 September 1944 with the assignment of the 1st and 3rd *Staffeln* of NSGr 2. On 16 October 1944 1–3/NSGr 1 were added. In addition, it was possible to bring NSGr 2 up to three full operational *Staffeln* with 1/NSGr 6. The conversion of III/KG 51 into NSGr 20 (Fw 190) on 14 November 1944, as well as the assignment of 11/KG 200 (Special *Staffel* 'Eichhorn') on 23 December 1944, strengthened the structure of the unit. This was chiefly intended to fight the Allied advance in the area of the American 12th Army Group (General Bradley) and the British 21st Army Group (Field Marshal Montgomery) to a standstill. Before the gates of Aachen in the middle of September 1944 a unit of NSGr 2, together with parts of NSGr 1 and 20, even succeeded in delaying the Allied assault by means of a concentrated attack. On 15 September 1944 the Allied units were only 3 km from Aachen, where the German resistance stiffened.

On 22 September 1944 an operation by KG 51 and NSGr 2 took place. On that day thirty-five machines were available with the night ground attack *Gruppe*, of which twenty-one could be sent out. Up to 30 September 1944 the number of Ju 87 Ds increased to forty-three, of which twenty-six were available at the end of the month.

The fighting unit was able to score important operational successes between mid-September 1944 and the beginning of October 1944 in the Aachen area and, from the end of the month, around Geilenkirchen as well as in the bitterly disputed Hürtgen Forest. On the night of 3 October 1944 eighteen Ju 87 Ds attacked several targets in the rear areas of the western front. On the nights of 7, 8 and 12 October 1944 the Ju 87 crews also dropped mostly AB 250s, but also several SC 500s on the assigned targets. At times AB 500s with various contents were also used.

Two waves of twenty-three and twenty-one Ju 87 D-3s and D-5s, with a total of nineteen

This Ju 87 D-3 'N' with C-version flame eliminators also belonged to NSGr 10. The Gruppe *operated in February 1945 under the command of* Luftflotte 4.

AB 250s and thirteen AB 500s, attacked Allied positions in the early evening of 13 October 1944. In spite of enemy flak, only one machine was lost in September. In addition to its forty-three Ju 87 D-3s and D-5s which were available on 1 October 1944, NSGr 2 received a further nine operational machines by the end of the month. Ten machines were lost to enemy action, especially to reinforced flak, and five were lost as a result of accidents and crash landings. Thus, the number of operational machines with NSGr 2 was thirty-seven ground attack aircraft, of which only twenty-two were reported as serviceable on 31 October 1944.

On 22 October 1944 NSGr 1 with its twenty-five Ju 87 D-5s also joined the 'Hallensleben Fighting Unit'. After the *Gruppe* had lost one of its operational machines, the number of its Ju 87 D-5s amounted to twenty-four.

At the beginning of November 1944 NSGr 1 had fifty-eight Ju 87s at its disposal and NSGr 2 a further thirty-seven. Thirteen Ju 87s were assigned to both *Gruppen* up to 30 November 1944, so that the serviceable roster was eighty-nine Ju 87 D-3s and D-5s after seven losses due to enemy action and twelve to causes other than enemy action, according to memoranda of the staff officer Ic of the fighting unit. Of these, however, seventy-four were reported serviceable. The operating losses to both NSGr were mainly due to night fighters. Five crews probably failed to return from operations from this cause alone. Two Ju 87 Ds collided on take-off for an operation; a further machine struck the ground on 19 November 1944.

In the Maastricht-Liège-Nijmegen area the night ground attack pilots scored some successes against Allied troop concentrations up to 12 December 1944. Because of bad weather and the resultant limited enemy fighter action, the night ground attack *Gruppen* were able to score some noticeable successes. Between September and December, mainly SD 50s, SC 500s with charges of enhanced explosive and AB 250s and AB 500s were dropped over Allied positions and troop concentrations. After KG 3 and KG 51 left the fighting unit, it consisted of Night Ground Attack *Gruppen* 1, 2 and 20 which together had eighty-nine Ju 87 D fighter bombers as well as forty-five Fw 190 Fs.

In December the unit received a further thirty-one Ju 87 D-5s as well as three Fw 190 F-8s. With the unit staff only one machine was available, which went missing in December. NSGr 1 lost five machines on operations, NSGr 2 eight and NSGr 20 five. Even without enemy action twenty-eight machines were lost solely on

At the end of the war this Ju 87 D-5 'N' of an unknown night ground attack Gruppe *was ownerless; in the autumn of 1945 it was scrapped.*

This Ju 87 D-5 with the FuG 16 antenna on the Morane mast, captured by British troops in northern Germany, was among the most modern of the night ground attack aircraft. It may have been an operational machine of NSGr 1 (North).

take-off and landing or due to taxiing damage. The cause often lay with bad airfields but also lack of experience on the part of the pilots.

Captain Kösel of NSGr 1 crashed on the night of 6 December 1944 after striking the ground. Another crew parachuted out after the bomb container had failed to release. In the middle of the month the number of operations was significantly reduced in view of the forthcoming final German offensive in the west.

At 5.35 a.m. on 16 December 1944 strong forces of the 5th to 7th Panzer Armies, in part without artillery preparation, attacked as part of the Ardennes offensive ('Watch on the Rhine'). The centre of the attack was between the High Venn (at Monschau) and the north of Luxembourg (towards Echternach) and covered

This Ju 87 D-3 of NSGr 9 stayed behind near Innsbruck at the end of the war.

the whole area of Army Group B led by General Field Marshal Walter Model.

In spite of a shortage of ammunition, an increasing shortage of fuel and only 446 serviceable battle tanks, the last offensive in the west was begun. The reconquest of the Antwerp-Brussels-Namur-Dinant area was planned. Night Ground Attack *Gruppen* 1, 2 and 20 attacked in the framework of the 'Hallensleben Fighting Unit'. To these three powerful night ground attack units fell above all the task of attacking the enemy supply traffic, important traffic nodes and railway traffic in the immediate enemy hinterland. From 24 December 1944 strong forces of the RAF attacked several airfields, for example in the Düsseldorf and Cologne areas, from which several night ground attack units were taking off for their attacks in the west.

After operational losses which were at first relatively light at the beginning of the last major German offensive, on the night of 25 December 1944 several pilots did not return from combat flights. Only one of the radio operators succeeded in parachuting from a low altitude after the machine was attacked by an enemy night fighter at an altitude of about 150 metres. Most of the twelve crews of NSGr 2 that went missing at the end of December 1944 did so after their machines had been hit by flak. On the night of 28 December 1944 three crews of NSGr 2 became lost and made emergency landings after their fuel ran out.

On 31 December 1944 eighty-seven Ju 87 D-3s and D-5s were still available with the 'Hallensleben Fighting Unit', although more enemy night fighters were in action than previously and the operational bases of the fighting unit were increasingly attacked.

Apart from the usual traffic targets, individual crews also attacked ships on the Meuse with some success. After the Ardennes offensive had finally failed at the end of 1944, Allied troops fought their way forward again to the positions from which it had been launched. The battles continued around the Bastogne pocket at the beginning of January 1945, until the enemy was able to push through more and more in the area of the 5th Panzer Army and the front moved relatively quickly to the east.

The air attacks on the encircled town of Bastogne, which was desperately defended by American troops, had begun in December, and were continued by the Ju 87s and Fw 190s of the fighting unit. Bottlenecks in the supply of fuel and ammunition, however, limited these operations.

At the beginning of January 1945 forty-nine machines were still airworthy with the night ground attackers of the fighting unit. In total the unit possessed eighty-six Ju 87s. In spite of the war situation, in January 1945 another twenty-nine ground attack aircraft were issued, so that on 31 January 1945 a total of ninety Ju 87 D-3s and D-5s were available. About thirty-one machines were lost shortly after, of which thirteen resulted from enemy action. Of these seventeen were lost from NSGr 1 and fourteen from NSGr 2. On 7 February 1945 German and American troops stood once again opposite each other on the former front line.

As a result of the rapidly increasing losses, as well as the steadily increasing presence of Allied night fighters, the number of night ground attack operations carried out by the 'Hallensleben Fighting Unit' declined significantly up to the middle of February 1945.

On 21 February the fighting unit was officially disbanded. In almost 3,100 sorties more than 140 operational machines had been lost, thirty alone due to enemy air attacks. NSGr 1 and 2 went to the 15th *Fliegerdivision*, NSGr 20 to the 14th. Besides their Fw 190s, a few Ju 87s also remained to this night ground attack *Gruppe*.

6.3.10 Night Ground Attack *Staffel* of I *Fliegerkorps*

I *Fliegerkorps*, which was in action on the eastern front under the command of *Luftflotte* Command 4, maintained its own night ground attack *Staffel* at the beginning of 1945, which had been formed from parts of disbanded *Staffeln*.

The *Staffel* was in fact supposed to have been equipped with twenty Ju 87 D-3s and D-5s, but in the last days of March 1945 it possessed only twelve ground attack aircraft, of which only six were in operational condition due to war conditions. Six out of thirteen crews took off to attack their assigned targets on 31 March 1945. The unit was disbanded in April 1945 without any particular operational success.

7 Carrier Aircraft and Torpedo Bombers

7.1 Development Guidelines

On 18 June 1935 the German-British fleet agreement was signed, according to which the German *Reich* was allowed to build two 19,250-ton aircraft carriers.

As early as 16 November 1935 an order went to the German Works Kiel Ltd, concerning the laying down of the keels for the aircraft carriers 'A' (later *Graf Zeppelin*) and 'B' (initially unnamed). They were to have extremely modern designs with powerful armament and equipment. The keel of carrier 'A' was laid down at Kiel on 28 December 1936.

On 21 June 1937 an order was issued to the Aerodynamics Experimental Institute (AVA – *Aerodynamischer Versuchsanstalt*) for comprehensive wind tunnel studies for carrier 'A'. The experiments took place between 17 and 30 September 1937 at Göttingen on a 1:100 scale model of the carrier, which was altered many times.

In the presence of Adolf Hitler, Hermann Göring and more than 15,000 spectators, the first German aircraft carrier, *Graf Zeppelin* (carrier 'A'), was launched on 8 December 1938. Göring made the dedication speech; the dedication itself was carried out by Helene, Countess of Brandenburg-Zeppelin. By 1 September 1939 carrier 'A' was almost 85 per cent complete.

On 2 October 1939 the Sea War Leadership (Skl – *Seekriegsleitung*) war diary contained the entry: 'The operational capability of the aircraft carrier *Graf Zeppelin* has not yet been identified in the current war. Its further construction must cease.'

Ernst Udet visits the Travemünde Test Centre. Behind a Bf 109 T-1 the nose of the Ju 87 V10, prototype of the 'carrier Stuka', can be recognised.

However, Grand Admiral Erich Raeder, as Commander in Chief of the Navy (ObdM – *Oberbefehlshaber der Marine*) applied to Adolf Hitler on 10 October 1939 for the construction of aircraft carriers to continue in the near future, for use, for example, in the commerce war in the Atlantic.

In spite of all arguments, Hitler agreed only to the continued construction of carrier 'A'. The construction of carrier 'B' was to be stopped immediately. The Sea War Leadership also spoke in favour of the completion of carrier 'A' on 8 February 1940 at a conference with their chief, also seeing it as being useful in the Atlantic. The Sea War Leadership could not, however, convince Adolf Hitler. On 29 February 1940 the decision stood to dismantle carrier 'B'.

On 28 April 1940 the Sea War Leadership again took the view that further work on carrier 'A' was unneccessary. The opinion was that the military and gunnery conditions for its use were not in place and would not be so before the end of 1941. One day later the High Command of the Navy (OKM – *Oberkommando der Marine*) decided to halt construction. The 150-mm guns were initially to go to strengthen the defences of the Norwegian coast.

Construction nevertheless continued until the beginning of July 1940, and by 15 July 1940 the carrier was largely complete.

Because of the excessive concentration of shipping in Kiel, the danger of enemy air attacks was expressly discussed on 5 July 1940. It was decided to move the *Graf Zeppelin* to a harbour further east. The carrier was therefore moved from Kiel to Gotenhafen near Gdynia on 6 July, to remove it from attacks by the RAF. The powerplant was to be 'broadly' completed at Gotenhafen. The *Graf Zeppelin* arrived there on 12 July. During the journey the construction stoppage was extended to the autumn of 1940. On 8 November 1940 there was an examination of whether and how construction work should be resumed.

The aircraft carrier continued to lie in a 'preserved condition' at Gotenhafen. Meanwhile a profound change in the war situation had taken place. The *Wehrmacht* was in France. The operational possibilities thus opened up allowed a wide-ranging commercial war.

On 5 March 1941, therefore, a detailed memorandum was prepared on future flight operations on the *Graf Zeppelin*: twenty Fi 167 A-1 multi-purpose aircraft, ten Bf 109 T-1 fighters and thirteen Ju 87 C-1 maritime dive bombers were to be housed onboard the carrier in the upper hangar between the middle and forward lift platforms.

It was quickly recognised that, because of its greater wing span compared to the C version, the Ju 87 D envisaged for the purpose fitted rather tightly in the lifts and that problems were to be expected with the flight operations.

At the end of the month, on 31 March 1941, the Sea War Leadership renewed its pressure for the aircraft carrier *Graf Zeppelin* to be completed for the conduct of war in the Atlantic. They required completion of the ship by all possible means within six months.

On 14 May 1941 Adolf Hitler named the date for the operational debut of the carrier *Graf Zeppelin* as the beginning of 1943. Shortly thereafter, on 22 May 1941, Grand Admiral Erich Raeder, the Commander in Chief of the *Kriegsmarine*, reported to his supreme war lord that the construction could still take another eight months and that a complete year would then be needed for the testing phase.

The conference of 31 May 1941 on the further construction brought no definite result as it had become clear that equipping the ship would take far more than eight months. A few days later the need for aircraft carrier operations in the Atlantic became clearer to Hitler as a result of the loss of the battleship *Bismarck*.

The initiation of a separate flight deck cruiser development was also discussed at a presentation of the war situation by the ObdM before the *Führer* on the Obersalzberg on 11 July 1941. From this resulted a flood of different projects, some of which were built as scale models and tested in the wind tunnel.

The only carrier, the *Graf Zeppelin*, was incomplete and therefore not usable, and it was clear on 23 July 1941 that it could hardly be completed before October 1942 because of labour and materials bottlenecks. On 25 May 1941, Adolf Hitler expressly instructed that the further construction of armoured ships and carriers was not to continue until the eastern campaign had been completed successfully. Thus, as early as 25 July 1941, an instruction was issued against further work on of the carrier.

On 12 March 1942 a total of sixty-seven

Side view of the Ju 87 C-0 with folded wings.

operational machines were planned for the initial equipment of the *Graf Zeppelin*. Fifty Bf 109 Ts, four Ju 87 Cs and thirteen Fi 167 As were to be provided by the *Luftwaffe* for the whole testing and training. The further construction of the existing types did not seem sensible in the opinion of the *Luftwaffe* leadership, as they no longer met the performance requirements of 1942–3.

Moreover, several accidents during the initial testing of the Ju 87 C-0 and C-1 meant that not all of the C series were completely battleworthy. The *Luftwaffe* saw that the only option that could be put into effect relatively quickly was to take over already available types for carrier operations, or otherwise to create completely new types. The latter possibility was fully supported by Adolf Hitler during a presentation by the ObdM in the 'Wolf's Redoubt' headquarters.

Another presentation by Grand Admiral Erich Raeder on 13 April 1942 at the *Führer's* 'Wolf's Redoubt' headquarters stated that about two years would be necessary for the conversion to other carrier aircraft (for example the Ju 87 D and Bf 109 F). The increase to a take-off weight of 6,000 kg would demand the construction of fundamentally stronger catapult installations, which could not be done in a few months. As to the construction of carrier aircraft, these would not be available before 1946. If Bf 109 Fs and Ju 87 Ds were used the number of fighters would be limited to ten Bf 109s and twenty-one to twenty-three Ju 87 Ds (previously thirty-three). Of these six would be carried only in dismantled form and would therefore not be immediately ready for operations. As the enemy defences had increased strongly, multi-purpose and torpedo aircraft would be omitted because of the unsatisfactory performance of the Fi 167.

Later, the operational basis of attack with air torpedoes was considered; possibilities were investigated of attacking in diving flight and then spending only a short time in level flight for aiming and release, in order to remain in the

The aircraft carrier Graf Zeppelin *at Swinemünde.*

area of the enemy air defences for as short a time as possible.

For that reason, experiments began into bringing torpedoes as close as possible to the target in diving flight. The normal air torpedo release was now scarcely possible with any prospect of success because of the strong enemy air defences. On 16 April 1942 Adolf Hitler personally ordered that the work on the hull and powerplant was to be concluded by the summer of 1943 at the latest.

From May 1942 the carrier was laid out for twelve Bf 109s and thirty-eight (instead of twenty-two hitherto) Ju 87 dive bombers. At the same time the alteration of the flak armament and the addition of a bulge on both sides of the hull against enemy underwater weapons was ordered.

On 9 June air staff engineer Friebel reviewed the number of machines still available for the aircraft carrier at a development conference in Berlin. Fifteen to twenty Bf 109 Ts, twelve Fi 167s and three Ju 87 Cs were on hand. The machines had their full equipment and could be made ready in a relatively short space of time for the instruction of carrier crews.

On 21 August 1942 the intention to bring the *Graf Zeppelin* into service in October 1942 was announced internally. The carrier may thus have been almost ready to move. What was missing were effective carrier aircraft. Even on 25 September 1942 the number of carrier aircraft on hand was was still far from sufficient for equipping of the *Graf Zeppelin* completely.

But on 1 October 1942 the planned commissioning of the carrier could not take place. The date of 1 March 1943 for the provision of adequate training machines also had to be shelved. On 30 November 1942 the *Graf Zeppelin* left Gotenhafen and entered Kiel once more on 5 December 1942, in order to go into the 40,000-ton dock there. The ship was supposed to be completed by autumn 1943 and then begin sea trials, but because of delays in its conversion, its commissioning was expected in five months at the earliest, thus on 1 April 1944.

While the completion of the *Graf Zeppelin* was postponed again and again, the further development of the existing on-board aircraft progressed unexpectedly quickly. For carrier operations the Ju 87 C series was now no longer to be used, but a version of the Ju 87 D. Junkers wanted to deliver a first production prototype by March 1943 at the latest. By the summer of 1943 a further ten machines were promised. General Field Marshal Erhard Milch immediately informed the management of the Junkers works that this date was to be absolutely adhered to.

In the course of 1944 the overall situation developed so badly, however, that the completion could no longer be counted on at all.

Finally, on 25 April 1945 the still unfinished aircraft carrier was blown up in the naval harbour at Stettin.

It was raised in March 1947, and served the Soviet navy as an object of study. It was said to have been sunk on 18 June 1947. The exact course of events and reasons for sinking are not known.

7.2 Carrier-Based 'Stuka' and Air Torpedo Forces

The necessary preliminary work for the formation of carrier-borne Ju 87 units at first progressed well in the mid-1930s. Thus, as early as 30 January 1936 the decision was taken to set up a total of sixteen *Staffeln* for carrier operations by 1942.

For each aircraft carrier one reconnaissance, one fighter/dive bomber and one multi-purpose *Staffel* was planned. This division, which in its initial form was already in place in 1935, was changed at the beginning of 1936 by the proposed formation of a unified carrier *Geschwader*.

On 29 July 1937 the Commander in Chief of the *Luftwaffe* (ObdL *Oberbefehlshaber der Luftwaffe*) issued the formation order for the first carrier *Geschwader*. The unit was to be set up by 1 October 1938 in the Bremerhaven area and, besides three multi-purpose *Staffeln*, was to

Catapult launch of the Ju 87 V10 (TK+HD) in May 1940.

consist of a dive bomber and a fighter *Staffel*. For each *Staffel* eight operational aircraft and four reserves were envisaged. The first results of the plan, however, showed that the number of machines per carrier would have to be reduced from sixty to forty-eight because of the reduced hangar space which was ultimately available.

At the beginning of 1938 the new organisation of the flying forces envisaged for each carrier was established at one multi-purpose, one fighter and one dive bomber *Staffel* of an average of nine machines each. The Ju 87 Cs with folded wings were to be set on a launching carriage, prepared and brought on deck by means of a large lift before the operation. The machines were then to be fuelled and their arming completed.

On the forward flying deck of carrier 'A' two catapults were available in order to launch a *Staffel* of fighters and a *Staffel* of dive bombers within a short time. A minimum take-off separation of one minute was envisaged. The Ju 87 C was to be launched at about 135 kph at maximum take-off weight. The launching carriages returned below deck by means of a retrieval arrangement and could then be loaded with fresh aircraft. The preparations for this type of operation progressed according to plan in the summer of 1938.

On 1 August 1938 Carrier Bomber *Gruppe* I/186 was formed with the 1st to 3rd *Staffeln* at Bug on the island of Rügen. But on 22 October 1938 it was disbanded in its existing form and was to be sent into action as a land-based 'Stuka' *Gruppe* with Ju 87 Bs. A little later, on 1 November 1938, the formation of Carrier *Staffel* 4/186 with Ju 87 C dive bombers was ordered.

On 6 February 1939 came the re-formation of Carrier 'Stuka' *Staffeln* 1, 2 and 3/186 as well as the Carrier Fighter *Staffel* 5/186, to start from November 1939. In addition, on 4 April 1939 it was arranged that a motorised airfield operations company be formed for the *Graf Zeppelin*.

Because of a lack of air torpedoes for the multi-purpose units, the *Luftwaffe* leadership ordered that Carrier *Geschwader* 186 initially comprise only four dive bomber *Staffeln* and two fighter *Staffeln*.

On 16 May 1939 it was ordered that Carrier *Geschwader* 186 should support the formation of I *Gruppe* with the staff of Carrier *Gruppe* II/186 at Kiel-Holtenau and 4 and 6/186. Shortly before that, during the last weeks of peace, the carrier *Staffeln* of II/Dive Bomber *Gruppe* 186 had moved from Kiel-Holtenau to Brüsterort in East Prussia and Stolp in Pomerania and thus found themselves on the western frontier of Poland.

At the outbreak of war part of the 'Stuka' crews of Dive Bomber *Gruppe* 186 attacked several anchorages of the Polish fleet, among others the submarine base on the Hela Peninsula. On 10 September 1939 the formation order was issued for the staff of I/Dive Bomber *Gruppe* 186 (T) with two *Staffeln* which later received the designation 1 and 2/186 (T). From 20 September 1939 3/186 also started operations against targets in Poland. Five days later the *Staffel* (3/186) was placed under command of *Luftflotte* 2.

On 25 September 1939 General Field Marshal Hermann Göring instigated the removal of all carrier units from the naval air forces and their consolidation under the command of *Luftflotte* 2 until the first carrier was put into service. As it was not clear when the *Graf Zeppelin* would actually begin trials, on 24 October 1939 the concentration of all the carrier *Staffeln* was suggested, in order at least to use the personnel and their experience.

At the beginning of the relatively quick campaigns in western Europe, in May 1940, I(St)/186 T had thirty-nine Ju 87 Bs at its disposal. The operations of the *Gruppe* took place mainly over northern France and the Channel ports. The *Gruppe* was placed under the command of StG 1.

On the eve of 10 May 1940 the Dive Bomber *Gruppe* received its first operational target assignment: the well constructed airfield of Metz-Frescaty. The machines moved for the purpose from their concentration point at Hennweiler in the Hunsrück to Ferschweiler, an airstrip near Bitburg in the Eifel.

The 2nd *Staffel* alone flew sixty dive bombing attacks on targets in France. From 30 June 1940 several operations followed against shipping targets near the south coast of England, among others off the Thames estuary and in the Channel.

As it became clear that the *Graf Zeppelin* would not be completed on time, I(St)/186 (T) was renamed III/StG 1 on 9 July 1940. Captain

Helmut Mahlke, formerly the *Staffel* captain of 2/Dive Bomber *Geschwader* 186, was installed as *Gruppe* commander.

It then appeared that the *Graf Zeppelin* would be finally completed in 1941, so from May the training of maritime observers for the carrier-based 'Stuka' forces began. For this purpose thirty naval officer cadets were detailed and, after basic training at the torpedo school at Mürwick, and next at Sassnitz on Rügen, they were trained at Swinemünde and Kiel. Between 2 September and 9 October 1942 the naval ensigns went through an abbreviated training as 'observer students for special purposes' at Air Signals School 6 (Maritime) at Dievenow. Next followed a period at the Air Weapons School (Maritime) at Parow, in order to gain a basic knowledge as radio operators and gunners. The Ju 87 D or E were the operational aircraft envisaged.

When the construction of carriers was halted, they were returned to the *Kriegsmarine*.

7.3 The Ju 87 as Carrier Aircraft and Torpedo Bomber

7.3.1 Production Versions

The decision about which machine would be best for use on a modern aircraft carrier was extremely difficult from the outset as all the guidelines had, themselves, first to be obtained and verified.

Even before the end of 1935, Major Ernst August Roth (an expert in the RLM), Corvette Captain Hans-Armin Czecj and Dipl.-Ing. Ohlerich of the Marine Construction Board formed a study commission for the development of German aircraft carriers. Previously Major Roth had inspected the Japanese *Akagi* on 8 October 1935, where landings by day and by night were demonstrated to him.

On October 1936 the acceptance trials for the future carrier dive bomber began. The RLM Technical Bureau began with the examination of the Ar 81, Ju 87 and He 118 (He P 1030).

When the construction of carrier 'A' began in Kiel on 28 December 1936, the preparations for the necessary combat machines for it were already going ahead at full speed. The Junkers works had already planned two B-0 aircraft – the Ju 87 V10 and V11 – for carrier use, in order to collect data. From the late summer of 1937 both machines were cleared for flight. Other competitors, like the Ar 81 and the He 118, could not make headway. Machines like the Ar 195

The production prototype for the D-4 construction series (works no. 2292) was tested at Travemünde. An F-5 practice torpedo hung under the fuselage of the machine by way of an aerial torpedo.

The long-planned equipment of the Carrier Gruppe *186 with the 'carrier Stuka' could not be undertaken. The aircraft therefore remained Ju 87 B-1s and B-2s.*

and Ar 197 A-0 were already obsolete and had no chance from the outset.

7.3.2 The Ju 87 C-0 and C-1

On 18 August 1937 the RLM decided that only the Ju 87 Tr(C) would be introduced. Greater importance was therefore attached to the manufacture of the production prototype.

A mock-up of the carrier 'Stuka' had already been produced at Junkers in June 1937. According to instructions from the RLM, the first production prototypes were to be available for practical testing in January 1938. The flying evaluation was to begin at the Travemünde test centre in February 1938 and the testing of the prototype was to end in April 1938.

According to a Junkers works monthly report for September 1937, the prototype Ju 87 V10 (D-IHFH, later TK+HD) was to be tested as the forerunner of the carrier 'Stuka' with fixed wings and the V11 with folding wings. Both prototypes were first mentioned in the Aircraft Development Programme of 1 October 1937.

The production prototypes were taken from the zero series Ju 87 B-0 and were equipped with Jumo 211-A aero engines. Because of slippage in the procurement of equipment, the Ju 87 V10 was not completed until the middle of March 1938. On 17 March 1938 the first flight of the

The Ju 87 V10 (D-IHFH, later TK+HD) was equipped with fixed wings, catapult fittings and an arrester hook. In spite of lengthy attempts, only production prototypes could be produced.

production prototype, designated C-1, took place. Two months later, on 12 May 1938, came the first take-off of the Ju 87 V11. With both machines performance testing was next carried out. This included arrested landings on dry land, which had begun on 10 March 1938 with another machine. By 15 December 1939 a total of 915 of these arrested landings had been carried out. After the first series of numerous simulated deck landings, initially with a Ju 87 A-1, it became apparent that the existing DEMAG winch for the arrester rope installation was too weak, and it had to be replaced by a stronger Atlas winch.

The Ju 87 V10 was put out of action for some time on 5 May 1938. The landing hook sprang up too quickly in an arrested landing and severely damaged the rear fuselage of the aircraft. The installation was therefore converted to a tail hook.

Between 28 May and 20 August 1938 a machine was arrested on landing by means of an Atlas arrester rope winch 219 times. The installation proved itself with heavier machines, but not with lighter types. This led to another reconstruction in August 1938. Between 5 September and 15 December a third series of arrested landing experiments took place at the test centre. The average braking distance was as a rule 20–35 metres.

As the first production prototype of the future Ju 87 C-1, which was to be equipped with folding wings, the Ju 87 V11 was inspected by representatives of the Technical Bureau (TA) and the Test Centre Command (KdE) in September 1938. Next came the transfer of the machine to Travemünde near Lübeck. On 8 October the Ju 87 V11 was transferred to Dessau in order to be converted to the Ju 87 C-0 equipment standard there. In this the

The Ju 87 C-1 was the production prototype of the 'carrier Stuka' with an arrester hook.

installation of an improved wing-folding mechanism was important.

A month later, on 11 November, a series of arrested landings with an Ar 195, an Ar 197 and a Ju 87 C was conducted before Lieutenant-General Ernst Udet.

The testing of sequential arrested landings with two He 50s resulted in twenty-four landings in thirty-eight minutes. On average the four arrester ropes were missed only every tenth landing. This led, later, to the use of five ropes to increase the safety of deck landings.

The testing of the Ju 87 C production prototypes meanwhile produced useful results, so in January 1939 it was decided to start the series production of the carrier 'Stuka' (Ju 87 C) at the Weser Aircraft Co. Ltd in Bremen. On 1 April it was agreed to manufacture the zero series of the Ju 87 Tr(C) between April and July 1940. Between July 1940 and August 1941 120 Ju 87 C-1s were to come off the production line at Weser as part of Aircraft Procurement Programme No. 11. At first ten Ju 87 C-0s were ordered, but then five were considered sufficient to carry out a thorough examination, since the Ju 87 airframe was already considered to have been sufficiently tested. In fact only the special equipment specific to carriers had to be completed and thoroughly tested. This was a two-seat rubber dinghy with signal ammunition and emergency rations, which was housed in the rear fuselage. The undercarriage was to be mechanically jetissonable. Two inflatable rubber bags of 750 litres air capacity each in the wing leading edges and a further two of 500-litres capacity in the fuselage, together with a fuel quick-dump, provided for the machine to be capable of floating for up to three days in a calm sea.

The zero series programme of 26 April 1939 envisaged as prototypes for carrier use the Ju 87 V10 (flight clearance date: March 1939) and the Ju 87 V11 (flight clearance date: April 1939). The five machines of the zero series were to be manufactured as follows: one in April 1940, one

The Ju 87 V11 (D-ILGM, later TV+OV) possessed folding wings for the first time.

in May, two in June and one in July.

The plan for the series production of the Ju 87 C-1 in the framework established on 1 April 1939 was still in effect on 6 August 1939. Because carrier operations were still uncertain, for safety's sake, on 6 October 1939, ninety Ju 87 Tr(C) s of the 120 planned were cancelled.

The cancellation issued in July 1941 according to the procurement programme was based on the cessation of work on the carrier 'B' as far as Junkers was concerned. But the testing of the aircraft equipment continued almost undisturbed. On 11 and 12 April 1940 the production prototype of the catapult was tested with six trial shots, launching water-filled metal containers. Between 18 April and 6 May 1940 there were thirty-six successful take-offs by aircraft with the FL 24 catapult (German Works, Kiel). Of these, seventeen were with Ar 197s, four with Bf 109 Ds and fifteen with Ju 87 Cs. The greatest weight was reached with the Ju 87 C with a take-off weight of 5,300 kg. The Junkers machine usually reached a speed of 133 kph in the process. One of the Ju 87 launches took place with an SC 500 under the fuselage and four SC 50s under the wings. This equipment was expressly envisaged in the data sheet for the C-1. In addition, it was planned to equip the machines with two 300-litre drop tanks to extend their penetration range. All C machines were to have an armament of two fixed MG 17s and a movable MG 15 – exclusively as a defensive weapon.

More than ninety-eight machines were on hand at the Travemünde test centre on 7 May 1940, of which two were Ju 87 A-1s. These were D-IEXC (TK+HC, works no. 870013) and D-IAGR (TK+HE, works no. 5000). In the spring of 1940 the machines served chiefly for testing the VS30 propeller, evaluating the most diverse camouflage coats and testing weapons.

On 23 August 1940 several arrested landings were demonstrated to Colonel-General Ernst Udet at Travemünde with Ar 197s, Fi 167s, Bf 109s and the Ju 87 V10 (TK+HD) by aircraft master builder Kursch. Further, a 'Hermann' SC 1000 bomb was released in a dive from a height of 2,000 metres by Dipl.-Ing. Nolte in the Ju 87 V11 (TV+OV) onto a bombing target.

The manufacture of the first zero series aircraft (C-0) had meanwhile been postponed once again. On 18 May 1940 therefore the series production of the Ju 87 C-1 was switched to the Ju 87 R-1.

On the instructions of the *Luftwaffe* General Staff the Ju 87 C-0 remained for the time being as a carrier 'Stuka'. Of the originally planned C types, however, only one machine came into being as the C-0. All other machines were to be completed to Ju 87 C-1 standards. The C-Bureau programme of 1 October 1940 still envisaged a zero series of five machines. Of these two were to be completed in December 1940, one in January and two in February 1941. The machines, meanwhile, had Jumo 211 D engines and VS-5 or VS-11 Junkers propellers.

In the Aircraft Procurement Programme of January 1941 the completion dates for these machines were again put back. The five Ju 87 C-1s were to be manufactured as 'zero-series aircraft' and were to be made ready as follows:

March 1941: works no. 0570, registration unknown
March 1941: works no. 0571, registration unknown
April 1941: works no. 0569, GD+FB
April 1941: works no. 0572, GD+FC
June 1941: works no. 0573, SH+DB

The Ju 87 V11 (works no. 4929) originated from the conversion of a Ju 87 B-0 and set the C-0 construction standard. Testing began in May 1938.

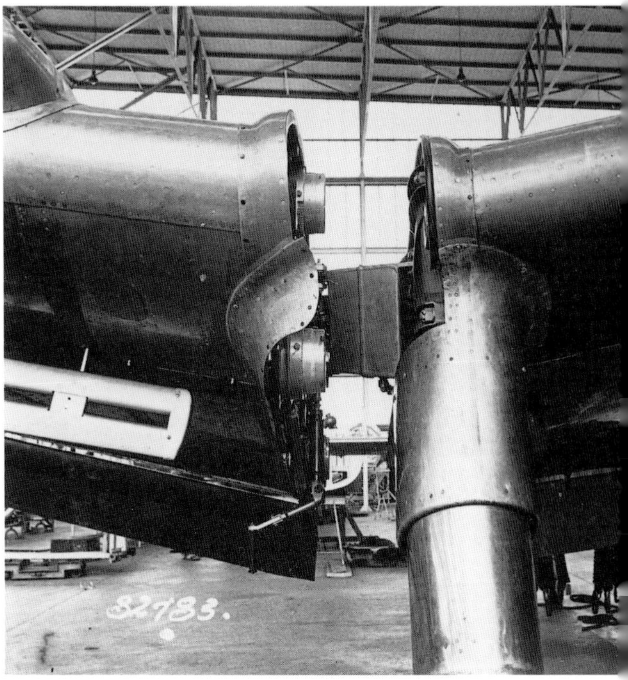

The production prototype for the 'carrier Stuka' was equipped with dive brakes.

The initially planned first series version of the projected carrier 'Stuka', the Ju 87 C-1, was exhibited to the RLM at Dessau as a sample of the C-0 version on 22 January 1941.

There followed quick-dump and pumping experiments on a prototype airframe; no objections resulted. The Patin compass installation built into the fuselage was easily accessible, a point on which the pilot engineers who had travelled from Berlin had placed special emphasis. The Ju 87 C-1 was generally envisaged for catapult launching, although a normal take-off on the carrier deck or on an airfield on land was possible if necessary. The machine was laid out solely for carrying bombs, not torpedoes.

At the test centre at Travemünde, a first production prototype was planned for the end of January 1941; the completion was meanwhile significantly delayed. Not only the remaining armour plate, but also the Jumo 211 H in-line

Separation point of the folding wings of the Ju 87 V11.

Ju 87 D und G
Bed.Vorschr.-Fl

Flugbetrieb **II 3**

Motor Jumo 211 J
Luftschraube VS 11
3,46 m

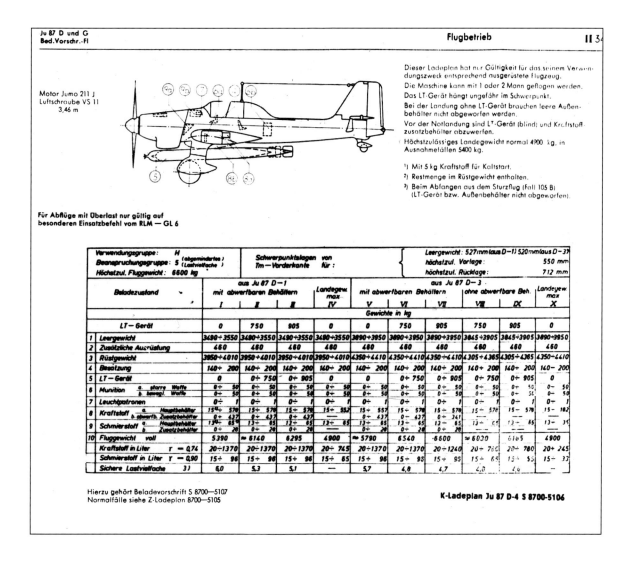

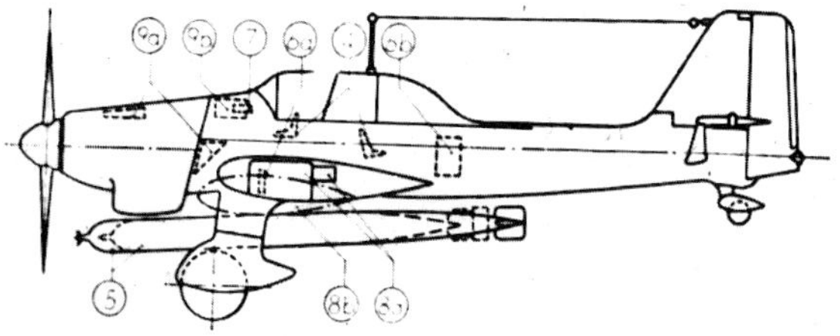

Dieser Ladeplan hat nur Gültigkeit für das seinem Verwendungszweck entsprechend ausgerüstete Flugzeug.

Die Maschine kann mit 1 oder 2 Mann geflogen werden.

Das LT-Gerät hängt ungefähr im Schwerpunkt.

Bei der Landung ohne LT-Gerät brauchen leere Außenbehälter nicht abgeworfen werden.

Vor der Notlandung sind LT-Gerät (blind) und Kraftstoffzusatzbehälter abzuwerfen.

Höchstzulässiges Landegewicht normal 4900 kg, in Ausnahmefällen 5400 kg.

[1]) Mit 5 kg Kraftstoff für Kaltstart.

[2]) Restmenge im Rüstgewicht enthalten.

[3]) Beim Abfangen aus dem Sturzflug (Fall 105 B) (LT-Gerät bzw. Außenbehälter nicht abgeworfen).

Für Abflüge mit Überlast nur gültig auf besonderen Einsatzbefehl vom RLM — GL 6

Verwendungsgruppe: H *Beanspruchungsgruppe:* 5 (abgemindertes Lastvielfache) *Höchstzul. Fluggewicht:* 6600 kg	*Schwerpunktslagen von Tm—Vorderkante für:* *Leergewicht:* 527 mm (aus D-1) 520 mm (aus D-3) *höchstzul. Vorlage:* 550 mm *höchstzul. Rücklage:* 712 mm

	Beladezustand	aus Ju 87 D-1 mit abwerfbaren Behältern			Landegew. max	aus Ju 87 D-3 mit abwerfbaren Behältern			ohne abwerfbare Beh.		Landegew. max
		I	II	III	IV	V	VI	VII	VIII	IX	X
		Gewichte in kg									
	LT-Gerät	0	750	905	0	0	750	905	750	905	0
1	Leergewicht	3490÷3550	3490÷3550	3490÷3550	3490÷3550	3890÷3950	3890÷3950	3890÷3950	3845÷3905	3845÷3905	3890÷3950
2	Zusätzliche Ausrüstung	460	460	460	460	460	460	460	460	460	460
3	Rüstgewicht	3950÷4010	3950÷4010	3950÷4010	3950÷4010	4350÷4410	4350÷4410	4350÷4410	4305÷4365	4305÷4365	4350÷4410
4	Besatzung	140÷ 200	140÷ 200	140÷ 200	140÷ 200	140÷ 200	140÷ 200	140÷ 200	140÷ 200	140÷ 200	140— 200
5	LT-Gerät	0	0÷ 750	0÷ 905	0	0	0÷ 750	0÷ 905	0÷ 750	0÷ 905	0
6	Munition a. starre Waffe	0÷ 50	0÷ 50	0÷ 50	0÷ 50	0÷ 50	0÷ 50	0÷ 50	0÷ 50	0÷ 50	0— 50
	b. bewegl. Waffe	0÷ 50	0÷ 50	0÷ 50	0÷ 50	0÷ 50	0÷ 50	0÷ 50	0÷ 50	0÷ 50	0— 50
7	Leuchtpatronen	0÷ 1	0÷ 1	0÷ 1	0÷ 1	0÷ 1	0÷ 1	0÷ 1	0÷ 1	0÷ 1	0÷ 1
8	Kraftstoff a. Hauptbehälter	15[1]÷ 570	15÷ 570	15÷ 570	15÷ 552	15÷ 557	15÷ 570	15÷ 570	15÷ 570	15— 570	15— 182
	b. abwerfb. Zusatzbehälter	0÷ 437	0÷ 437	0÷ 437	—	0÷ 437	0— 437	0÷ 341	—	—	—
9	Schmierstoff a. Hauptbehälter	13[2]÷ 65[2]	13÷ 65	13÷ 65	13÷ 65	13÷ 65	13÷ 65	13— 65	13÷ 65	13÷ 65	13÷ 35
	b. Zusatzbehälter	0÷ 20	0÷ 20	0÷ 20	—	0÷ 20	0÷ 20	0÷ 20	—	—	—
10	Fluggewicht voll	5390	≈ 6140	6295	4900	≈ 5790	6540	6600	≈ 6030	6165	4900
	Kraftstoff in Liter γ = 0,74	20÷1370	20÷1370	20÷1370	20÷ 745	20÷1370	20÷1370	20÷1240	20÷ 780	20÷ 780	20÷ 245
	Schmierstoff in Liter γ = 0,90	15÷ 96	15÷ 96	15÷ 96	15÷ 65	15÷ 96	15÷ 95	15÷ 95	15÷ 65	15÷ 55	15÷ 33
	Sichere Lastvielfache [3])	6,0	5,3	5,1	—	5,7	4,8	4,7	4,8	4,6	—

Hierzu gehört Beladevorschrift S 8700—5107
Normalfälle siehe Z-Ladeplan 8700—5105

K-Ladeplan Ju 87 D-4 S 8700-5106

Loading plan for the Ju 87 D-4 two-seat torpedo bomber.

engine and the VS-11 propeller were still not available. Moreover, the delivery of a few minor pieces of equipment in the area of the radio installation was still awaited.

Flights for range began at the beginning of March 1941 with the first Ju 87 C to arrive at Travemünde. The resulting flight range table for the Ju 87 C-1 was determined at the Travemünde test centre by 21 March 1941.

The construction acceptance of the first Ju 87 C (works no. 0569, GD+FB) took place on 5 April 1941, and the machine with works no. 0572 on 16 April 1941.

The Travemünde test centre was still waiting for the long-promised Ju 87 C-1 series aircraft. Not until 25 April 1941 did the first two Ju 87 C-1s arrive at the Maritime Test Centre and go through their entrance inspection.

On 18 June 1941 the centre of gravity weighing took place with another Ju 87 C-1 at the JFM works at Dessau. On 8 August the powerplant testing was continued with Ju 87 C-1 works no. 0569. Works no. 0573, destined for Travemünde, was however still not available. The machine was still not cleared for flight on 17 September 1941 because of a defective propeller and only on 18 September could it undertake four arrested landings. Because of a breakage on the fifth landing due to an arrester rope which tore out of the coupling, the aircraft was swung out of the landing direction and substantially damaged. With the fifth Ju 87 C-1, manufactured in June 1941, all machines of this version were accepted.

Only on 26 September 1941 was Ju 87 C-1, works no. 0569, again cleared for flight. Only two days later the machine was unserviceable again due to damage to the hydraulic system. The Ju 87 C-1 works no. 0572 (GD+FC) could still not be flown as the firmly promised new propeller had not been delivered.

On 3 October 1941 works no. 0572 went to Travemünde as a replacement for the damaged machine. Works no. 0569 was still not airworthy on 10 October 1941; works no. 0573 was still not available and was replaced by works no. 0572 (GD+FC), after a new propeller had finally arrived at Travemünde.

At the end of 1941, according to an inventory report by the Quartermaster General of the *Luftwaffe* (GenQu.), four of the original five machines were on hand in airworthy condition. Of these, one was with Junkers at Dessau and three with the Air Equipment Bureau (LZA – *Luftzeugamt*) at Travemünde, which was responsible for resupplying the maritime air forces. The fifth machine was parked in an unairworthy condition.

In March 1942 it was decided to repair works no. 0573, again. Thereafter the machine was once more ready for experimental purposes. Two of the machines, works nos. 0570 and 0571, were stored at the LZA at Travemünde and served then as a reserve.

From 5 May 1942 to 15 April 1943 a fourth series of arrested landings was simulated on the experimental installation of the Travemünde test centre. Four Ar 96s, one Ar 195 and one Ar 197, two He 50s, three Fi 167s, three Bf 109s and four Ju 87s took part. At the same time work was done with these machines on the fulfilment of future carrier operations. The Ju 87 (VD+LA) landed at 130 kph at 4,200 kg landing weight and 140 kph at 4,850 kg without major difficulty. The Ju 87 C-1, works no. 0569, was slightly damaged as a result of an accident to the undercarriage. In May 1942 works no. 0573 was also transferred to the test centre for the testing of a jetissonable undercarriage, in order to be better equipped for emergency landings on sea or land: in landing on a smooth belly the crew had a greater chance of survival, as the danger that the machine would overturn due to the undercarriage was minimised.

The arrested landings with the Ju 87 constituted the last part of the prototype testing which ended on 10 June 1942. By way of conclusion a comprehensive aircraft data sheet was produced by pilot engineer Steinkopf, Division E2 of the Travemünde test centre.

In July 1942 the two Ju 87 Cs, works nos. 0570 and 0571, were still stored at the Air Equipment Bureau. With at least one machine preparatory works were continued for the next generation of carrier aircraft based on the Ju 87.

According to a task summary of the Travemünde test centre dated 1 September 1942, the testing of the Ju 87 C-1 had been completed, with the exception of the tail hook, in the summer of 1942. The latter had been rebuilt and tested previously. It was possible to achieve an improvement of the cooling system and subsequently test it. The cold starting characteristics had also been optimised: from engine start to take-off was only one minute.

An adequate equipping of the *Graf Zeppelin* was no longer possible at the end of September 1942 because of a lack of carrier aircraft, as the few carrier aircraft which were stored at the Air Equipment Bureau (Sea) at Pillau were not sufficient.

On 3 March 1943 one Ju 87 C-1 (works no. 0573, SH+DB) was at Perugia, Italy, and was used there for the testing and adjustment of an arrester gear which came into question for Italian aircraft carriers. The machine was then to be taken onboard the Italian carrier *Aquila* for experimental arrested landings. Two months later, on 14 May 1943, the Ju 87 V10 (works no. 4928) and the Ju 87 C-1s, works nos. 0571 and 0572, were transferred to XI *Fliegerkorps*. A third Ju 87 C-1, SH+DB, works no. 0573, was operated in test condition at the Travemünde test centre until the beginning of 1944. The machine was next assigned to I/SG 103 and was 35 per cent damaged on the Metz-Frescaty airfield on 25 April 1944 in an Allied air attack. The Ju 87 C-1, works no. 0570, was likewise in the inventory of I/SG 103 after the conclusion of the carrier experiments. The machine crashed on

Mock-up of the Ju 87 D-4 with underslung aerial torpedo.

24 March 1944 with Senior Under Officer Hans Moskopf; the pilot was killed.

The fate of the last Ju 87 C-1, works no. 0569, is not clear; the machine was probably scrapped.

7.3.3 The Ju 87 D-4 and D-5 with Aerial Torpedo

The Ju 87 V24 (DJ+YC, works no. 0544) originated in the spring of 1941 from the conversion of a Ju 87 B-1 airframe to the construction standards of the new D-1 version. In August 1941 the V24 was being discussed as the production prototype for the further development of a carrier aircraft. For the sake of a greater performance spectrum, work was referred back as quickly as possible to the Ju 87 D airframe with the Jumo 211 J.

At a project meeting at the Junkers works at Dessau on 14 August 1941, the existing planning guidelines were finally defined precisely.

Because of the necessary limitation of gross weight in carrier operations, limits were set to the Ju 87 as a torpedo bomber. The reason lay in the unsatisfactory performance of the catapult, which was designed for a maximum take-off weight of only 6,000 kg. Apparently the existing concept was abandoned for that reason – albeit temporarily – with the result that the Ju 87 V24 fuselage had already been used in a Ju 87 R by November 1941. The carrier-based torpedo bomber based on the Ju 87 D in its existing form was abandoned for the time being.

In the JFM monthly report of December 1941 a new test programme was mentioned: the Ju 87

D-1 with a tail hook. This was a torpedo bomber, which was to carry the F-5w aerial torpedo. As the first of these, a Ju 87 D-1/torp., BK+EF, was transferred to the Travemünde test centre on 16 December 1941.

After a detailed entry inspection, there followed, among other things, load tests with an Italian F-5w aerial torpedo. Because of bad weather, the flight testing had to be postponed to the end of 1941.

The Ju 87 V25, forerunner of the Ju 87 E, was tested by the Travemünde test centre with an F-5 practice torpedo.

The Ju 87 V25 was equipped with two 300-litre capacity drop tanks besides the aerial torpedo, and the gross weight increased to its maximum permissible value.

In addition to Travemünde, numerous tests with the Ju 87 as a torpedo bomber also took place at the Grosseto airfield in Tuscany. Apparently these went very well, so that there was further interest in the use of the Ju 87 D with an aerial torpedo on the part of the *Luftwaffe* leadership.

On 4 August 1942 Engineer Colonel Georg-Bernhard Alpers reported during a bureau chiefs' conference that a total of 200 aerial torpedo equipment sets had already been ordered for the Ju 87 D and thirty sets a month would be manufactured between October 1942 and February 1943. The first of these were tested at Hexengrund on the torpedo weapons site (TWP – *Torpedowaffenplatz*) and released for operational use.

As the Ju 87 D-3 was meanwhile more and more displacing the Ju 87 D-1 in the units, the new torpedo bomber version was increasingly considered for the third construction series of the 'Dora' version. On 15 April 1943 came the delivery of the first two Ju 87 D-3s that were envisaged for retrofitting with aerial torpedoes. Interest centred on the land-based, short-range, dusk attack with an underslung torpedo, i.e. in the coastal area. According to the torpedo used, the take-off weight was between 5,750 and 6,400 kg. Operations from aircraft carriers were therefore excluded in practical terms, not only because the machine did not have folding wings and thus would not have fitted the lift, but also because the take-off weight was far too great.

The Ju 87 D-4 was to be manufactured as a potent dive bomber and torpedo bomber. The Junkers works tried to deliver a first production prototype equipped as for the series by March 1943.

For torpedo bomber operations the dive brakes under both wings were omitted. A further ten of the new Junkers machines were promised to the RLM by the summer of 1943. General Field Marshal Erhard Milch gave Junkers unmistakable instructions that the completion date was to be met without fail, in order to assure the necessary equipment for the aircraft carrier *Graf Zeppelin*. It is not known whether Milch knew that the dimensions of the D-4 precluded operations from a carrier.

Of the Ju 87 D-4 version, for which the series construction programme was finally cancelled, probably only one or two machines were produced and tested. The machines were subsequently modified back and issued to the front-line units.

One of these production prototypes – works no. 131104 – was lost from the staff of SG 103 on 6 June 1944. After being heavily shot up by another aircraft, the pilot succeeded in making an emergency landing on the airfield at Voves, in which the machine was 60 per cent destroyed. The radio operator was slightly wounded in the attack.

According to the aircraft construction series sheet for the Ju 87 of 19 August 1944, a total of three basic versions was envisaged for the planned Ju 87 D-4, powered by a Jumo 211 J engine:

Equipment set A: dive bomber
Equipment set B: torpedo bomber
Equipment set C: dive bomber with skis

The gun armament consisted of two fixed MG 151/20 cannon in the wings for offensive use as well as MG 81 Z twin machine-guns as rearward defensive weapons. The bomb release mechanism could comprise one of the following:

- Lock mounting ETC 1000/500 XIB with 500 XII lock, or 1000 XI lock, or 2000 XIII
- 2 ETC 50 VIIIe
- PVC 1006 B (aerial torpedo)

For fuel the Ju 87 D-4 could carry a total of

Suspension of the aerial torpedo on the planned Ju 87 E version. The machine was the V25, BK+EF.

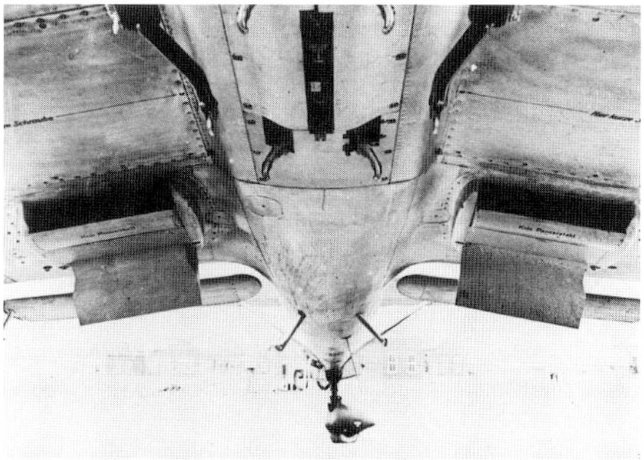

1,370 litres, of which 590 litres were carried in two 295-litre drop tanks, as was the case with the R-1 and R-4.

As the majority of operations had to be flown at dusk or in darkness because of enemy capabilities, consideration was given to using a flame eliminator, version 5.

The second D version to be laid out with torpedo bombing as a subsidiary mission was the D-5. Like all D-5 machines, it had lengthened wings. Otherwise, equipment and armament were the same as the D-3.

In the end only three Ju 87 D-3s were rebuilt with the aerial torpedo installation (ETC 2000/XII), which were delivered to the Gotenhafen torpedo weapons site (TWP). All other efforts to bring out the Ju 87 D as a potent torpedo bomber in noteworthy quantities came to nothing. After the completion of testing, the machines were reconverted back to their original condition and transferred to a front-line unit.

7.3.4 The Ju 87 E

The Ju 87 E-1 was a two-seat dive bomber built on the airframe of the Ju 87 D-1. It was not capable of taking off on its own, but needed a catapult installation.

The machines were intended to carry either free-fall bombs or an aerial torpedo (F-5w) as offensive load. The reason for this development lay in the fact that the Ju 87 C-1 had shown itself to be obsolete and the Ju 87 D without folding wings was not only too cumbersome but also too heavy for carrier operations. Basically, the new E-1 constituted a more potent new version of the Ju 87 C-1, with folding wings and catapult fittings. In addition, there were safety arrangements for maritime operations for the crew, which still consisted of two men.

The construction of the Ju 87 E-0 and E-1 went on simultaneously at Junkers (JFM) and Weser (WFG). According to an agreement between the Hexengrund torpedo weapons site (TWP) and the maritime test centre at Travemünde, the ETC 2000 XII release mechanism was to be used on the Ju 87 torpedo aircraft. For aiming, a torpedo reflector sight was installed so that a torpedo attack could be carried out from a dive.

The Ju 87 V19 (VN+EN, works no. 4930), a B-0, was already used experimentally for aerial torpedo drops by pilots of the Travemünde test centre before the end of 1941. The prototype served as the starting point for the development of the fifth construction series (E) of the Ju 87. From the summer of 1942 VN+EN flew as the production prototype for the planned Ju 87 E-0 version.

The Ju 87 V19, as well as a second E production prototype with the Jumo 211 J, a converted Ju 87 D (VD+LB), was tested at the Travemünde test centre. On 27 July 1942 the test pilot K.-F. Königs carried out one of the arrester hook experiments at the Travemünde test centre with VD+LB. The machine served further for the testing of a 4.9-kilonewton take-off booster rocket, which had a burning time of only six seconds. Even after the first rocket-assisted take-off, which took place at Peenemünde West, this take-off assistance for the Ju 87 E was rejected by both the *Kriegsmarine* and the Test Centre Command (KdE) at Rechlin, instead, they voted for a medium-term increase in the catapult performance.

By 1942 another two Ju 87 Ds with the callsigns VD+LA and SF+TW, whose exact construction version and prototype designation remain unknown, were in test service. One was the production prototype for the radio installation planned for the Ju 87 E. With the second the catapult fittings, which had been strengthened in the meantime, were thoroughly tested in practice.

The C Bureau Programme of 1 November 1942, on the subject of prototypes, referred to ten Ju 87 E-1s with Jumo 211 J-1 in-line engines. Of these the first production prototype was to be manufactured from November 1942 onwards. The Test Centre Command wanted to begin flight testing as a carrier aircraft in the early summer of 1943.

Study 1013 of 10 February 1943 on the future aircraft programme envisaged the completion of the first series Ju 87 E-1 in November 1943. In December three machines were to come off the production line, between January and March 1944 twenty-one and, from April 1944 onwards, fifteen a month. Production was to continue at this level at least until September 1946.

New considerations led to these guidelines being reviewed in the middle of 1943, as the

Ju 87 D und G
Bed.Vorschr.-Fl

Flugbetrieb **II 36**

Motor Jumo 211 J
Luftschraube VS 11
3,46 m

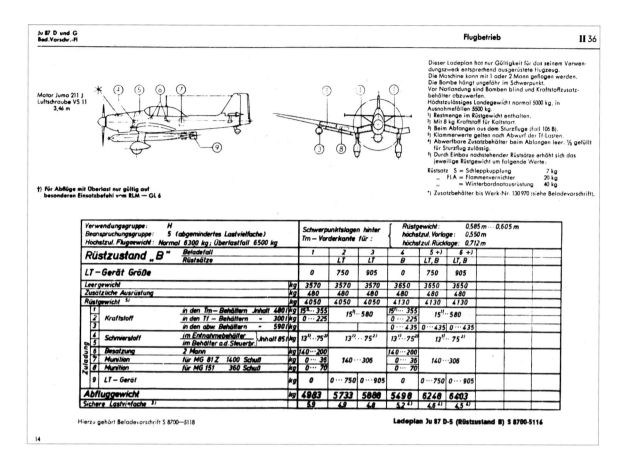

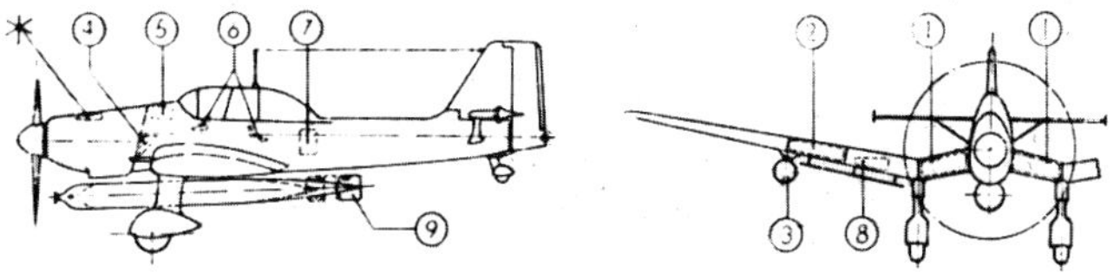

†) Für Abflüge mit Überlast nur gültig auf besonderen Einsatzbefehl vom RLM — GL 6

Dieser Ladeplan hat nur Gültigkeit für das seinem Verwendungszweck entsprechend ausgerüstete Flugzeug.
Die Maschine kann mit 1 oder 2 Mann geflogen werden.
Die Bombe hängt ungefähr im Schwerpunkt.
Vor Notlandung sind Bomben blind und Kraftstoffzusatzbehälter abzuwerfen.
Höchstzulässiges Landegewicht normal 5000 kg, in Ausnahmefällen 5500 kg.

1) Restmenge im Rüstgewicht enthalten.
2) Mit 8 kg Kraftstoff für Kaltstart.
3) Beim Abfangen aus dem Sturzfluge (Fall 106 B).
5) Klammerwerte gelten nach Abwurf der Tf-Lasten.
4) Abwerfbare Zusatzbehälter beim Abfangen leer. ⅓ gefüllt für Sturzflug zulässig.
5) Durch Einbau nachstehender Rüstsätze erhöht sich das jeweilige Rüstgewicht um folgende Werte:

Rüstsatz S = Schleppkupplung 7 kg
„ FLA = Flammenvernichter 20 kg
„ = Winterbordnotausrüstung 40 kg

*) Zusatzbehälter bis Werk-Nr. 130 970 (siehe Beladevorschrift).

Verwendungsgruppe: H
Beanspruchungsgruppe: 5 (abgemindertes Lastvielfache)
Höchstzul. Flugaewicht: Normal 6300 kg; Überlastfall 6500 kg

Schwerpunktslagen hinter Tm – Vorderkante für: Rüstgewicht: 0,585 m ··· 0,605 m; höchstzul. Vorlage: 0,550 m; höchstzul. Rücklage: 0,712 m

Rüstzustand „B"				1	2	3	4	5 +)	6 +)
Beladefall / Rüstsätze					LT	LT	B	LT, B	LT, B
LT-Gerät Größe				0	750	905	0	750	905
Leergewicht			kg	3570	3570	3570	3650	3650	3650
Zusätzliche Ausrüstung			kg	480	480	480	480	480	480
Rüstgewicht 5)			kg	4050	4050	4050	4130	4130	4130
Zuladung 1	Kraftstoff	in den Tm-Behältern Inhalt 480 l	kg	15¹⁾ ··· 355	15¹⁾ ··· 580		15¹⁾ ··· 355	15¹⁾ ··· 580	
2		in den Tf-Behältern „ 300 l	kg	0 ··· 225			0 ··· 225		
3		in den abw. Behältern „ 590 l	kg				0 ··· 435	0 ··· 435	0 ··· 435
4	Schmierstoff	im Entnahmebehälter } Inhalt 85 l	kg	13¹⁾ ··· 75²⁾	13¹⁾ ··· 75²⁾		13¹⁾ ··· 75²⁾	13¹⁾ ··· 75²⁾	
5		im Behälter a.d. Steuerbr.							
6	Besatzung	2 Mann	kg	140 ··· 200	140 ··· 306		140 ··· 200	140 ··· 306	
7	Munition	für MG 81 Z 1400 Schuß	kg	0 ··· 36			0 ··· 36		
8	Munition	für MG 151 360 Schuß	kg	0 ··· 70			0 ··· 70		
9	LT-Gerät		kg	0	0 ··· 750	0 ··· 905	0	0 ··· 750	0 ··· 905
Abfluggewicht			kg	4983	5733	5888	5498	6248	6403
Sichere Lastvielfache 3)				5,9	4,9	4,8	5,2 4)	4,6 4)	4,5 4)

Hierzu gehört Beladevorschrift S 8700—5118

Ladeplan Ju 87 D-5 (Rüstzustand B) S 8700-5116

14

Supplementary drop tanks were also considered in the deployment of the Ju 87 D-5 as a torpedo bomber, as the loading plan shows.

completion of the first aircraft carrier was once again being considered. By November 1943 ten machines were to have begun flight testing as quickly as possible. Because of the requirements for the aircraft carrier, only ninety-five machines were ordered instead of 250 previously. But the production of these Ju 87 Es was also cancelled, mainly because the tactical problems of a Ju 87 E-1 which was not capable of taking off unassisted had shown them to be extremely troublesome for operations.

8 Training Aircraft and Units

8.1 Development Guidelines

The Ju 87 A to R for a time comprised the bulk of the aircraft available for dive bomber training with the initial training schools, dive bomber schools and, naturally, with training units in the framework of the *Geschwader*. It turned out to be a disadvantage that a version with dual controls remained the exception. Only with the H conversion variant was this to change.

8.1.1 The Ju 87 A-1 to R-4

The Ju 87 A-1 already showed significant performance deficiencies shortly before its introduction. The machines were therefore quickly released by the dive bomber *Gruppen* to several training units after the first of the better-performing Ju 87 B-1 and B-2 versions had entered the operational units.

In order to acquaint new crews with the specifics of the enlarged tankage, from 1940 onwards not only B versions but also the diverse versions of the Ju 87 R were flown with numerous schools and training units. The same was true for the various versions of the Ju 87 D, which differed from the B and R in numerous improvements. The use of series operational machines as two-seater training aircraft, however, presented a major problem: the machines as a rule had no dual controls. This disadvantage was to be overcome with the conversion variant Ju 87 H, in order to shorten the existing training time.

8.1.2 The Ju 87 H

The Ju 87 H versions were conversions of the Ju 87 D-1 as well as of the D-3, D-5, D-7 and D-8 versions which arose from it. The first training version, the Ju 87 H-1, was a two-seat training aircraft with dual controls, capable of blind flight, which originated in the series conversions of used D-1 machines and, according to choice, could be equipped with wheel or ski undercarriage.

The H machines had a second instrument panel instead of the normal controls for the radio installation. The movable, rearward pointing defensive armament had to be omitted

One of the Ju 87 B-2s on the strength of 'Stuka' School 2; compared to the B-1, it had an improved exhaust installation.

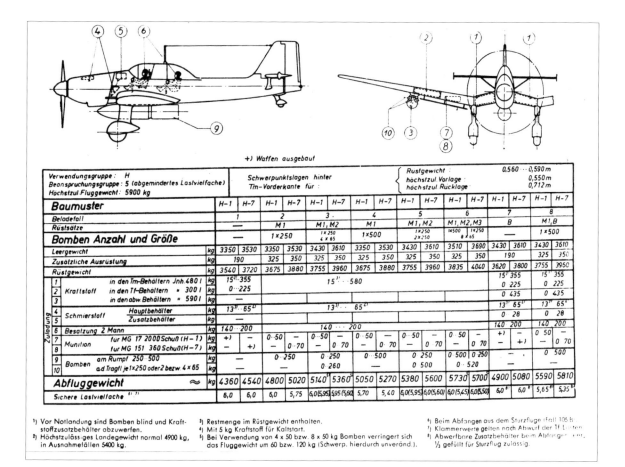

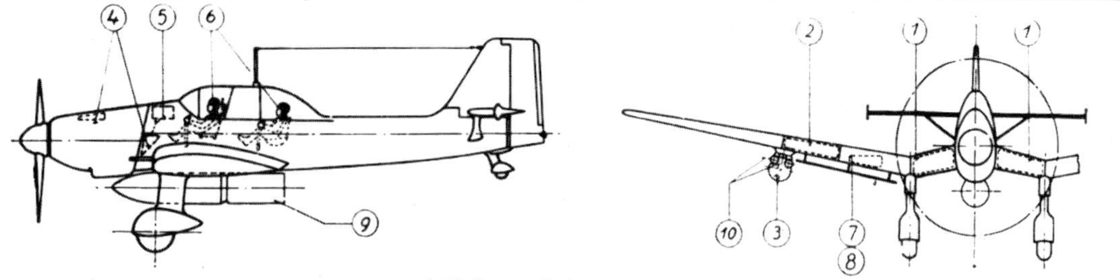

+) Waffen ausgebaut

Verwendungsgruppe: H Beanspruchungsgruppe: 5 (abgemindertes Lastvielfache) Höchstzul. Fluggewicht: 5900 kg		Schwerpunktslagen hinter Tm-Vorderkante für:								Rüstgewicht: 0,560 … 0,590 m höchstzul. Vorlage: 0,550 m höchstzul. Rücklage: 0,712 m							
Baumuster		H-1	H-7	H-1	H-7	H-1	H-7	H-1	H-7	H-1	H-7	H-1	H-7	H-1	H-7	H-1	H-7
Beladefall		1		2		3		4		5		6		7		8	
Rüstsätze		—		M1		M1, M2		M1		M1, M2		M1, M2, M3		B		M1, B	
Bomben Anzahl und Größe		—		1×250		1×250 4×65		1×500		1×250 2×250		1×500	1×250 8×65	—		1×500	
Leergewicht	kg	3350	3530	3350	3530	3430	3610	3350	3530	3430	3610	3510	3690	3430	3610	3430	3610
Zusätzliche Ausrüstung	kg	190		325	350	325	350	325	350	325	350	325	350	190		325	350
Rüstgewicht	kg	3540	3720	3675	3880	3755	3960	3675	3880	3755	3960	3835	4040	3620	3800	3755	3960
Zuladung 1 Kraftstoff in den Tm-Behältern Jnh. 480 l	kg	15[3] … 355		15[3] … 580										15[3] 355		15[3] 355	
2 Kraftstoff in den Tf-Behältern " 300 l	kg	0 … 225												0 225		0 225	
3 Kraftstoff in den abw. Behältern " 590 l	kg	—												0 435		0 435	
4 Schmierstoff Hauptbehälter	kg	13[3] … 65[4]		13[3] … 65[4]										13[3] 65[4]		13[3] 65[4]	
5 Schmierstoff Zusatzbehälter	kg	—												0 28		0 28	
6 Besatzung 2 Mann	kg	140 … 200		140 … 200										140 200		140 200	
7 Munition für MG 17 2000 Schuß (H-1)	kg	+)	—	0 … 50	—	0 … 50	—	0 … 50	—	0 … 50	—	0 … 50	—	+)	—	0 50	—
8 Munition für MG 151 360 Schuß (H-7)	kg	—	+)	—	0 … 70	—	0 70	—	0 70	—	0 70	—	0 70	—	+)	—	0 70
9 Bomben am Rumpf 250 … 500	kg	—		0 … 250		0 … 250		0 … 500		0 250		0 500	0 250	—		0 500	
10 Bomben a.d. Tragfl. je 1×250 oder 2 bzw. 4×65	kg	—		—		0 … 260		—		0 500		0 … 520		—		—	
Abfluggewicht ≈	kg	4360	4540	4800	5020	5140[5]	5360[5]	5050	5270	5380	5600	5730[5]	5700[5]	4900	5080	5590	5810
Sichere Lastvielfache [6, 7]		6,0	6,0	6,0	5,75	6,0 (5,95)	5,95 (5,60)	5,70	5,40	6,0 (5,95)	6,0 (5,60)	6,0 (5,45)	6,0 (5,50)	6,0[8]	6,0[8]	5,65[8]	5,35[8]

1) Vor Notlandung sind Bomben blind und Kraftstoffzusatzbehälter abzuwerfen.
2) Höchstzulässiges Landegewicht normal 4900 kg, in Ausnahmefällen 5400 kg.
3) Restmenge im Rüstgewicht enthalten.
4) Mit 5 kg Kraftstoff für Kaltstart.
5) Bei Verwendung von 4 x 50 bzw. 8 x 50 kg Bomben verringert sich das Fluggewicht um 60 bzw. 120 kg (Schwerp. hierdurch unveränd.).
6) Beim Abfangen aus dem Sturzfluge (Fall 105 b).
7) Klammerwerte gelten nach Abwurf der Tf.-Lasten.
8) Abwerfbare Zusatzbehälter beim Abfangen leer, ⅓ gefüllt für Sturzflug zulässig.

Loading plan for the two-seat training aircraft of the Ju 87 H-1 and H-7 construction series.

for reasons of space. The dual controls were taken over in their basic characteristics from the Ar 96. In order to give the flying instructor a better view in the direction of flight, the glazing of the rear cockpit was changed so that it had bulges on the left and right sides.

The second H version bore the designation Ju 87 H-3 and, except for the modified controls, corresponded to the ground attack aircraft of the D-3 version. The Ju 87 H-5 was also designed as a training machine, but possessed the airframe of the D-5 which differed from the D-3 in having larger wings.

The Ju 87 H-7 was a training machine with dual controls which originated in the conversion of the D-1 but, in contrast to the H-1, had the larger wings of the D-5.

The Ju 87 H-8 was also to be a two-seat training type with dual controls, fully capable of blind flight. It was converted from repaired aircraft of the Ju 87 D-3 series, but had the wings of the D-5. The additional armour was omitted.

Two fixed MG 151/20 cannon could be built into the wings for training purposes in the H-5, H-7 and H-8.

The operating instructions for the Ju 87 H-1 to H-7 (and possibly the H-8 version) described the training machine with a two-man crew facing in the direction of flight. The bomb load was limited to 500 kg, although up to eight 50-kg loads could be carried. The machines had an empty weight between 3,430 kg and 3,610 kg. The gross weight was a maximum of 5,810 kg.

The loss data of the schools mention only two Ju 87 Hs for the time between the autumn of 1940 to the late summer of 1944. Whether the converted machines still carried their former series designations or whether only individual

Walter Enneccerus in the cockpit of a Ju 87 A, probably equipped with dual controls as a training machine. This officer rose to be the commander of II/StG 2 and received the Knight's Cross on 21 July 1940.

machines were produced remains uncertain. The first machine to be lost was an H-3 (works no. 3486) of the ground attack *Geschwader* SG 111, which crashed on 8 June 1944 at Stubendorf. In the process the pilot, Sergeant Fritz Klügel, lost his life. The second Ju 87 H was a training machine designated as an H-6, which made an emergency landing on the airfield at Voves on 6 June 1944 and belonged to the staff of SG 103.

Unfortunately no photographs of a Ju 87 H, showing the altered cockpit arrangement, have appeared to date. It may be that, with the machines with dual controls, the rear part of the cockpit was simply retained.

8.2 Dive Bomber Initial Training Schools

8.2.1 Overview

Some Ju 87 A-1s and A-2s were put into service mainly for selecting suitable pilots from those who had applied for the 'Stuka' force. In the dive bomber pilot initial training schools the pre-selection of future 'Stuka' pilots was carried out in four-month classes. The pilot's suitability was also tested in about fifteen dives under the supervision of a flying instructor. Fifteen dives were allowed in a day so that crews would not sustain bodily damage. Pilots who were not judged suitable for the Ju 87, but were still suitable for service as pilots were mostly posted to transport units. Pilots who were considered suitable were posted to one of the dive bomber pilot schools.

8.2.1.1 Dive Bomber Pilot Initial Training School 1

'Stuka' Initial Training School 1 was at Aibling near Bad Reichenhall in 1940 to 1941 and, besides a few Ju 87s, had numerous Ar 68s, Ar 96s, Bü 131s, Bü 133s and Na 64s. As early as 17 November 1942 it was disbanded again; its tasks were transferred to other 'Stuka' schools.

8.2.1.2 Dive Bomber Pilot Initial Training School 2

'Stuka' Initial Training School 2 was at the Thalerhof airfield near Graz in 1940 and in 1942 moved to the northern Italian airfield at Piacenza. Aircraft equipment and tasks corresponded to 'Stuka' Initial Training School 1. This training unit was also disbanded in November 1942.

8.2.1.3 Dive Bomber Pilot Initial Training School 3

A third initial training school was to have been formed at San Damiano, but was cancelled.

8.3 Dive Bomber Pilot Schools

8.3.1 Overview

The dive bomber pilot schools served for the training of the pilots transferred from the initial training schools as well as for providing the crews with the necessary basic technical and tactical knowledge. The main points of the training were dependent on the current main points of operations. In addition to the execution of the diving attack, in particular

A Ju 87 A-2 (CB+KF) of 'Stuka' Initial Training School 1 shortly before the start of a workshop flight.

the improvement of bombing, the theoretical basis of air equipment and armament was deepened. The two-man crews also had to carry out navigation tasks, simulate the use of weapons with cement bombs and on-board weapons, and create a 'tactical unit'. After the completion of training, the personnel were moved to one of the three training *Geschwader* (StG 101–103 and 151) in order to acquire training in tactics, up to the *Gruppe* framework.

8.3.1.1 Dive Bomber Pilot School 1

The first dive bomber pilot class was carried out at Kitzingen in the summer of 1936 with I *Gruppe* of StG 165. As training machines, which at the same time helped in the perfection of the diving attack, a few Ar 65s, He 50s, He 51s and Hs 123s were used. At that time service as ground attack pilots, i.e. low-level attacks, was equated with dive bombing operations.

Further classes took place on 1 November 1938 with I/StG 162 at the Barth airfield in Vorpommern, where the unit was stationed from 15 March 1937 and from the spring of 1937 onwards was assigned to the training *Geschwader* as IV ('Stuka') *Gruppe*. Most of the training crews were transferred from StG 165. The two permanent courses of instruction were at first the only training available to fill the dive bomber units with suitable crews.

From the spring of 1939 both units were combined in the Kitzingen dive bomber pilot school in Franconia and were then moved to Insterburg in East Prussia. In the summer of 1939 the school received the designation Dive Bomber Pilot School 1. In spite of all its efforts, however, it was not possible to supply enough Ju 87 crews to the front-line units. In August 1939, one month before the attack on Poland, the *Luftwaffe* was still thirty-six crews short to man all its operational aircraft.

The first 'Stuka' school next moved to Regensburg, where at first Ju 87 A-1s, and to a small extent also A-2s, and later B-1s in larger numbers were put into service. Machines can be identified with the registrations D-IDJU and

This Ju 87 A-2 belonged to a 'Stuka' school.

D-IDFS as well as the Ju 87 A-1s with the works numbers 5006, 5011, 5036, 5047–5049, 5052 and 5053.

At Regensburg several losses were reported between 1939 and April 1941. Corporal A. Schmidt suffered a serious accident, hitting the ground and the two-man crew lost their lives. As a result of a collision with an Hs 123, Lieutenant K. Toppier also crashed at Regensburg with his Ju 87 A-1 (works no. 0018). Two other A-1s (work nos. 0187 and 5050) collided in flight, while a Ju 87 B-1 of 'Stuka' School 1 rammed an Ar 68. In this accident the 'Stuka' was 35 per cent damaged.

In addition, a few early A-1s and numerous B-1s were on hand at Wertheim, which were no longer fit for front-line service because of damage.

By 1941 the Wertheim airfield had become the training centre for 'Stuka' School 1. Because of engine failure and engine damage, in the Wertheim area alone five Ju 87 A-1s and B-1s were wrecked in emergency landings. A few pilots wrote off their aircraft by hitting obstructions, or because of technical failures or premature landings. In total the loss data indicate fifteen Ju 87s damaged or – in one case – completely lost between the summer of 1940 and August 1942 alone. In addition to the Ju 87 machines, various Ar 68s, Ar 96s, He 51s and Hs 123s were to be found at Wertheim.

From January 1941 the training operations of 'Stuka' School 1 were to an increasing extent carried out at the Kitzingen airfield. At the beginning of 1943 there were at least eight losses in training. Two machines were damaged by hitting the ground. Two others crashed after they had collided in mid-air. While the first accident was a slight one, in the second only one member of the crews was able to parachute to safety. The pilot of the Ju 87 B-1 (works no. 0421), 2nd Lieutenant Pritzner, was killed in parachuting out.

Dive Bomber Pilot School 1 was led between 1 August 1940 and 31 July 1941 by Colonel (later Lieutenant-General) Eberhard Baier. He was followed, between 31 July 1941 and September 1941, by Major Paul-Werner Hozzel. In

September and October 1941 Major Bruno Dilley took over command.

Between 16 October 1941 and 17 June 1942, Major Hubertus Hitschold was apppointed leader of the school. In the summer of 1942 he was followed for two months by Lieutenant-Colonel Alfons Osthofer and, from July 1942, by Colonel *Graf* Schönborn. He was still leading the unit when it was renamed Dive Bomber *Geschwader* 101 on 8 December 1942.

8.3.1.2 Dive Bomber Pilot School 2

'Stuka' School 2 was at Graz-Thalerhof from 1939 and carried out the flight training of new 'Stuka' crews there until October 1942. Apart from Ju 87s, the school had at its disposal a few He 51s as well as several Hs 123s. The leadership was in the hands of Major Karl Christ from 31 July 1940.

At Graz, for a time, the Ju 87 As with works numbers 5023, 5038, 5039, 5049, 5062, 5065 and 5069 were available for training purposes. During training at Graz, 'Stuka' School 2 lost six Ju 87 A-1s and one Ju 87 B-1 (works no. 0249) between the late summer of 1940 and July 1942. Of these the A-1s, works nos. 0009 and 0089, collided near the airfield and crashed. One pilot lost his life; the second was injured.

Near Hasslach the school also lost five Ju 87 B-1s as a result of crashes or through contact with the ground after an unsuccessful dive. Only two crews succeeded in making emergency landings; all the others lost their lives. In October 1942, the training operation was moved to Foggia in southern Italy. Loss data indicate numerous Ju 87 crashes and wrecks there for the period October–November 1942. Apart from Ju 87 A-1s and B-1/B-2s, at least six A-2s were still flying, recognisable by the large numbers painted on the voluminous undercarriage fairing. In the autumn of 1942 'Stuka' School 2 was disbanded.

8.4 Würzburg Reinforcement Dive Bomber *Gruppe*

As a reinforcement unit for the two dive bomber pilot schools, the Würzburg Reinforcement Dive Bomber *Gruppe* was formed at the beginning of

This Ju 87 A-1 was almost completely destroyed except for the fuselage mid-section.

7/'Stuka' School 2 (later 7/SG 102) was at Foggia in southern Italy; because of the mostly sunny weather, flight training could be carried out without major losses among the crews.

A massive observation bunker was erected on the Kitzingen bombing range, so as to be able to observe bombing results.

This photograph was taken in the spring of 1944 on the satellite airfield of Sbralovice at Deutsch-Brod. Part of the undercarriage fairing of this Ju 87 A-1 was removed for safety reasons.

1941, but it existed only until the spring of 1941. During this time four Ju 87 B-1s were lost as a result of ground strikes, because of engine damage and as a result of unforeseeable deterioration in the weather.

8.5 Dive Bomber Training *Geschwader*

8.5.1 Overview

Crews who had gone through the dive bomber pilot initial training school as well as the dive bomber pilot school were next schooled in tactics at one of the training *Geschwader*. Their airmanship as a dive bomber pilot was thoroughly tested and weak points that might still be present addressed through further training. The training at a training *Geschwader*, as at all schools, served the current war picture, in which ground attack operations naturally displaced the pure diving attack more and more.

8.5.1.1 Dive Bomber *Geschwader* 101

Dive Bomber *Geschwader* 101 arose from 'Stuka' School 1 in November 1942. As early as the beginning of 1943 the training of new 'Stuka' crews began there. Training proceeded with I/StG 101 at St Raphael in southern France and with II/StG 101 at Cuers north-east of Toulon.

The equipment of StG 101 in southern France consisted mainly of Ju 87 A-1s, A-2s, B-1s and B-2s. Between April and September 1943 StG 101 lost just ten of these machines there. Mostly crash landings and emergency landings were the main cause of damage which amounted to between 20 and 55 per cent. According to loss data they were mostly harmless; in only a few cases were the crews injured. Among these was Corporal Hans Kosutenelk who had to make an emergency landing near the training airfield after an engine failure, in which the machine was severely damaged. Due to an operating error, the Ju 87 B-2 (works no. 5735), piloted by Corporal Gustav Gerndt, was lost in a crash landing. The pilot as well as his radio operator were slightly injured in the accident.

On 18 October 1943 Training *Geschwader* StG 101 was renamed Ground Attack *Geschwader* (SG) 103.

These crews have assembled for a briefing before a flight by the unit.

This Ju 87 B-2 (works no. 5378) was in training service with StG 102 at Graz-Thalerhof in the Steiermark.

8.5.1.2 Dive Bomber *Geschwader* 102

StG 102 was formed from parts of 'Stuka' School 2, which was still based at Graz-Thalerhof, in the summer of 1942. This affected only one *Gruppe* with a staff and three training *Staffeln* – 1–3/StG 102. At the end of 1942 Ground Attack Training *Geschwader* SG 102 arose out of StG 102.

8.6 Ground Attack Training *Geschwader*

8.6.1 Overview

With the conversion of the dive bomber *Geschwader* into ground attack *Geschwader* on 18 October 1943, the training *Geschwader* were also renamed. Apart from the four units that arose from the existing dive bomber pilot training *Geschwader*, more units were formed. SG 101–104, and SG 111, 151 and 152 provided for the continuing tactical training of the future crews of the *Luftwaffe* ground attack *Gruppen*, which for the time being were still almost entirely equipped with Ju 87 Ds. In the course of the forthcoming year of the war training on the Fw 190 A and F received ever more importance.

8.6.1.1 Ground Attack *Geschwader* 101

SG 101, formed in October 1943 from IV *Gruppe* of Destroyer School 2 (Rheims) and III/Destroyer School 2 (Orly), as well as parts of 'Stuka' School 1, initially had its staff at Metz. From 24 September 1943 Major Fritz Thran led the unit. In June 1944 he was replaced by Major Friedrich Lang, in whose hands the fortunes of SG 101 lay until his replacement in February 1945.

The first of two training *Gruppen* was located at the airfields of Cuers and at St Raphael in southern France from the beginning of 1944.

Junior Under Officer Josef Reitinger went through dive bomber training at Deutsch-Brod with the Ju 87 B-1.

According to loss data, training was carried out at Cuers between April and September 1944, while at St Raphael, it took place only until October 1943. Apart from Ju 87s, the unit had Ar 96s as well as numerous Fw 190s, but also a few Hs 129s.

Part of the training with II/SG 101 was carried out at Otrokovitz in Moravia. There the training unit had mostly Fw 190s and Ju 87s at its disposal. Losses show evidence of intensive training between February and August 1944. The Ju 87 A-1s originally put into service there, with works numbers 5001, 5017, 5021, 5029, 5033, 5034, 5043, 5060 and 5065, were no longer on hand at the beginning of 1944. They were increasingly exchanged for Ju 87 B-1s and B-2s and, from the spring of 1944 onwards, Ju 87 D-3s and D-5s. Between May and August 1944 three Ju 87 Ds were lost in crashes and two in crash landings. In the process three pilots died: Sergeant Otto Grosse, Junior Under Officer Eberhard Schulze and Corporal H. Hattei.

In Moravia, too, training on the Ju 87 was reduced because of the ever more widespread use of the Fw 190 in the ground attack *Geschwader* of the *Luftwaffe*. At the end of 1944 I/SG 101 with its Ar 96 training aircraft for initial training was at Wirschau. The II and III *Gruppen* were at Brno and Hörsching near Linz with their Fw 190s. On 27 December 1944 SG 101 was disbanded; remnants were still in existence, however, at the beginning of February 1945.

8.6.1.2 Ground Attack *Geschwader* 102

SG 102 arose out of StG 102 in the autumn of 1943. The training operation took place with I and II/SG 102 between February 1944 and the early autumn of 1944 on the airfield at Deutsch-Brod. About thirty Ju 87 B-1s, B-2s, R-1s, R-2s, D-1s, D-3s and D-5s were lost in crashes and crash landings. Of the B series, seven B-1s and three B-2s were lost; four of the aircraft were of various R versions. The bulk of the losses were Ju 87 D-3s; there were also one D-1 and one D-5. Almost half the crashes of the flight trainees were fatal. Operating errors, and also engine failures, were the main cause of the accidents. A few of the crews in training hit the ground unintentionally, for example Corporal Hans Kehle on 10 June 1944 and Corporal Karl Schimmer on 14 August 1944, both of whom were killed near the airfield.

Up to October 1944 the unit was led by Major Bernhard Hamester and, besides Ju 87s, also had Fw 190s and Si 204s. The second *Gruppe* possessed similar aircraft and had been formed from parts of StG 103. This training *Gruppe* was also based at Deutsch-Brod in 1944.

Part of the two training *Gruppen* went into action under the leadership of the 2nd Training *Fliegerdivision* on the eastern front against forces of the Red Army that had broken through, from February 1944 from Baranovitshi and from April 1944 from Borissov.

The operational *Gruppe* of the 2nd Training *Fliegerdivision* also had to attack the advancing Red Army under the command of the 1st *Fliegerdivision* (*Luftflotte* 6 area) from July 1944. In the process seven Ju 87 D-3s and D-5s

Loading of a Ju 87 B-2 of SG 102 with a 500-kg load, also at Deutsch-Brod.

were lost, of which the majority were shot down by Russian flak and fighters. The pilots, as a rule Junior and Senior Under Officers, often lost their lives in the low-level attacks. The last operations took place in August 1944.

At the beginning of 1945 the remnants of SG 102 were on the airfield at Grossenhain. Major Karl Henze was the commander from November 1944. On 4 February 1945 SG 102 was disbanded.

8.6.1.3 Ground Attack *Geschwader* 103

I/StG 101 arose out of Ground Attack Pilot School 1 at Wertheim and from it, in turn, arose I/SG 103 on 18 October 1943. The training unit was formed into the staff of SG 103 at Metz-Frescaty and two training *Gruppen*, of which II *Gruppe* formed II/StG 101, previously renamed II/SG 103. The aircraft consisted of Ar 96s, Fw 190s and Ju 87s. At the beginning of 1944 the machines were stationed on the airfield at Frescaty near Metz and at Thionville (Diedenhofen). The leader was Colonel Clemens *Graf* Schönborn, who commanded the unit at least until the middle of 1944. Previously he had been the commander of Dive Bomber Pilot School 1.

At the end of 1943 there were some losses during the training of new 'Stuka' crews at the Thionville airfield and its surroundings. On 18 November 1943 a Ju 87 B-1, works no. 5180, of I/SG 103 crashed near the airfield because of technical defects – the crew, however, made a successful parachute jump.

In April 1944 several losses occurred due to enemy action. Senior Under Officers Günther Frohne and Wolfgang Vreden were shot down by Allied fighters in their Ju 87 D-3s (works nos. 110013 and 131205) with their radio operators during a training flight on 12 April 1944. Low-level attacks on the bases of SG 103 took place on 12, 14, 24 and 27 April 1944. In the process eight Ju 87 B-1s, B-2s, R-4s, D-1s and D-3s were

Gunner Karl-Heinz Rapp, here with SG 102, was in training at Deutsch-Brod in October 1943.

damaged. Another five Ju 87s, mainly the D version, were lost in training through crashes resulting from engine failures or the sudden formation of fog. In total I *Gruppe* of SG 103 lost more than twenty of its Ju 87s at Thionville.

Between March 1943 and September 1943 there were twenty-six losses to II/SG 103 in the Metz area, in which eight Ju 87 A-1s, sixteen B-1s, one R-4 and one D-1 were lost. Eighteen emergency and crash landings and three crashes happened on the Frescaty airfield alone, the rest mostly in the immediate vicinity. In a collision between two Ju 87 B training machines (works nos. 0270 and 5661) of SG 103 both pilots died and their machines had to be written off as total losses.

With II/SG 103 at Metz-Frescaty it was not only in practice operations that numerous losses occurred: from 1944 onwards enemy activities hindered the training. The low-level attack on 1 April 1944, in which two Ju 87 B-1s were lightly damaged, was followed on 25 April 1944 and 14 August 1944 by two heavy air attacks. In these a total of twenty-six Ju 87s were damaged by bombing or had to be written off as total losses on 25 April 1944 alone. Mainly Ju 87 B-1s and B-2s and a few R machines were hit, but a few modern D-3s also suffered significant damage. Apart from these machines, one Ju 87 C-1 (works no. 0573) was 35 per cent damaged.

The attack in August 1944 hit the training unit less hard, but even so a few Ju 87 D-3s and D-5s were put permanently out of action. More than a dozen training machines suffered damage in excess of 75 per cent in the two attacks.

From the spring of 1944 substantial parts of SG 103 moved to Biblis, east of Worms on the Rhine, as their existing base no longer permitted undisturbed training due to its proximity to the enemy. In the area of the Biblis airfield between May and September 1944 there were at least eight total losses with fatal consequences, mainly attributable to operating errors. Apart from a few Ju 87 B-1s, R-1s and R-2s, it was mostly Ju 87 D-3s that went missing with SG 103 in the Biblis area as well as a few Ju 87 D-5s from the summer of 1944. One of the last crashes was caused by Leading Aircraftsman Christoph Rödel on 4 September 1944.

In the west in 1944 there remained only one operational *Staffel* of SG 103, consisting of twelve instructor crews and advanced trainees, which was to be sent into action against the Allied troops that had landed in Normandy. On 6 June 1944 it was on the airfield at Voves. According to loss data, nine Ju 87s, mainly D-1s and D-3s, were lost on that day as a result of enemy action. Five of the machines crashed after being shot up by aircraft guns, and the majority of the crews were wounded. Four pilots succeeded in making emergency landings at Voves. The crews were, as far as is known, those of Lieutenant Skupin and Flight Sergeants

Fw 190 As and Fs increasingly displaced the existing two-seat dive bombers with the front-line and training units.

Genrich, Klunth, Rachau, Uhlhans and Wirner. The loss reports describe one of the damaged machines (works no. 1289) as a Ju 87 C-3, works no. 1104 as a Ju 87 C-4 and one of the machines, without giving the works no., as an H-6. What is hidden behind the designations C-3, C-4 and H-6 is not clear. Only one Ju 87 D of the operational *Staffel* finally arrived at the forward air base in northern France.

By the end of 1944 all the sections of SG 103 stationed in occupied France had to withdraw to Fassberg and Jüterbog-Damm, where training on Ju 87 Ds, and increasingly on Fw 190 Fs and Gs, was carried out. Next, the remnants withdrew to Hörsching near Linz. In February 1945 SG 103 was placed under the 3rd Training *Fliegerdivision*.

With effect from 1 April 1945 the personnel were transferred to Paderborn, to the SS brigade 'Westphalia', as there was no possibility of further training.

8.6.1.4 Ground Attack *Geschwader* 111

In the late summer of 1943 the new Ground Attack *Geschwader* SG 111 arose from Blind Flying School 11 (previously Pilot School FFS A/B 10) and from then on was responsible for the training of all night ground attack aircrew. On 15 October 1943 the unit consisted of three *Gruppen*: Majors Kraus, Zahn and H. Müller were the commanders.

At the end of 1943 the training was carried out at Stubendorf and Oppeln. For this purpose, besides Ar 66s, Go 145s, Ju W 34s, Fw 190s,

This photograph of a Ju 87 B-2 (trop.) (works no. 5322) of StG 151 was taken during dive bomber training at Agram (Zagreb).

Ju 88s and Hs 129s, several Ju 87 Bs and Ds were available and also individual Ju 87 Hs. A Ju 87 D-3 (works no. 131146) and a Ju 87 H-3 (works no. 3486) crashed in the immediate vicinity of Stubendorf; both pilots, Sergeant Fritz Klügel and Corporal Hans Ludwig, died and one of the radio operators was injured. In 1944 the training unit moved via Oppeln and Ludwigslust to Denmark. In February 1945 the training of new crews with SG 111 on the Aalborg was slowed because of fuel shortages. In April 1945 SG 111 was disbanded.

8.6.1.5 Dive Bomber/Ground Attack *Geschwader* 151

StG 151 originated at Agram (Zagreb) on 17 May 1943 from the consolidation of several reinforcement *Gruppen* belonging to active dive bomber units. With effect from 18 October 1943 the training *Geschwader* was renamed as the Ground Attack *Geschwader* SG 151, consisting of ten *Staffeln*:

I/SG 151	with the 1st and 2nd *Staffeln*	(previously IV/StG 1)
II/SG 151	with the 3rd and 4th *Staffeln*	(previously IV/StG 2)
III/SG 151	with the 5th and 6th *Staffeln*	(previously IV/StG 3)
IV/SG 151	with the 7th and 8th *Staffeln*	(previously IV/StG 77)
V/SG 151	with the 9th and 10th *Staffeln*	(previously IV/StG 5)

On 27 December 1943 it was again reorganised; besides the staff, three *Gruppen* – I–III/SG 151 – were formed. At that time there was already an Operational *Staffel*/SG 101 which went into action at the end of 1943 with its Ju 87s

This Ju 87 D-3 with the wheel fairings removed also belonged to SG 151 at Agram as a training machine.

Targets in the northern part of the eastern front were attacked by the crews of IV ('Stuka')/Training Geschwader *1. A devil riding on a bomb can be recognised as the emblem of the 12th* Staffel.

in the northern Balkan area under the command of *Luftwaffe* Staff Croatia as 13/SG 151. The operational airfields were, among others, Vel Gorica and Bihac. In the summer of 1944 the surviving Ju 87s were transferred to other training units: the *Staffel* received the more potent Fw 190 F.

On 7 June 1944 the existing 3/Night Ground Attack *Gruppe* (NSGr) 3 joined SG 151 and was taken on as the 15th *Staffel*. Just a month later, on 17 July 1944, the former *Staffel* 'Ritter' was likewise added to the training unit as 9/SG 151. On 7 August 1944 I/SG 152 became the new I/SG 151. At the same time the existing I/SG 151 became the new IV *Gruppe* of SG 151.

Due to war conditions, in December 1944, an additional operational *Staffel* was formed from forces of I/SG 151, but was equipped with Fw 190s.

This unit, like all the other operational *Staffeln* of the ground attack training *Geschwader*, was taken out of action on 11 February 1945 on the orders of *Luftflotte* Command 6 and two days later was disbanded on the orders of the

Starting a Ju 87 A-2 by means of a hand crank.

ObdL. The operational *Staffel* – together with the remains of SG 151 – was disbanded at Grove near Karup in Denmark on 4 May 1945.

At the beginning of 1945 training had been carried out at Grossenbrode and on the airfield of Lübeck-Blankensee, although it was severely restricted.

8.6.1.6 Ground Attack *Geschwader* 152

Ground Attack *Geschwader* 152 formed the basis for the I *Gruppe* of SG 151 on 7 August 1944.

8.7 Training *Geschwader* (*Lehrgeschwader* – LG)

8.7.1 Training *Geschwader* LG 1

In the later Training *Geschwader* 1 the IV *Gruppe* functioned as the training *Gruppe* for dive bomber crews. Between the beginning of 1940 and February 1942 at least sixteen Ju 87 B-1s, B-2s, R-1s and R-2s were lost in flying accidents with the 10th to 12th *Staffeln*. The first losses – mostly Ju 87 B-1s – took place during operations in the west, for example off the Kent coast. Then, IV *Gruppe* was moved to Finland. There IV/LG 1 was stationed at Kirkenes in the *Luftflotte* 5 area from the summer of 1941. In August 1941 two Ju 87 *Staffeln* were in action over the eastern front. On 9 August five Ju 87s were destroyed in an air attack. In December 1941 two of the *Staffeln* were moved to Rovaniemi, the third to Kiestins. In the area of Air Leader North-East at the beginning of January 1942 there were about twenty-five to thirty Ju 87s. Eight of them went into action in the occupation of the island of Suursaari (27–8 March 1942). In April 1942 ten Ju 87s were lost. The weak fighter forces gave no effective protection to the machines of LG 1 in action in the far north. In July 1942 crews and machines became I/StG 5 and, with that, left Training *Geschwader* 1.

8.7.2 Training *Geschwader* LG 2

According to log-books covering the period from the summer of 1938 to the spring of 1939, 2 (Maritime)/Training *Geschwader* 2 had at least three Ju 87 As at Travemünde. Losses are not known. Besides Ju 87s, a few He 60s, He 114s, He 111s, one Do 18 and one Ar 196 were on hand.

Apparently the machines of 2/LG 1 were transferred to LG 2, which had its own training *Gruppe*.

8.8 Other Schools

8.8.1 Pilot Schools

Ju 87s were also in service at Pilot School FFS (C) 12 set up at Prague-Ruzyn in January 1940. Further Ju 87s were with FFS (A) 4, which arose out of FFS (A/B) 4 in October 1943; individual aircraft were still flying up to October 1944.

On 14 September 1944 one of these machines, a Ju 87 D-3 (works no. 131494) was lost at Thorn as a result of technical failure. The crew were uninjured in the crash landing. The school was disbanded on 15 October 1944.

8.8.2 Blind Flying School 11

Blind Flying School 11 was formed in June 1943 from Pilot School FFS (A/B) 110. In the late summer of 1943 a few Ju 87 D-1s and D-3s were on hand there for practice purposes. Two of the machines were wrecked in crashes at Oppeln and in the vicinity of Kattern. They were Ju 87 Ds with works nos. 2103 and 2346; the crews lost their lives. The pilots were Corporals Leonhard Heid and Karl Klaus.

From 15 October 1943, the blind flying school became I/SG 111.

8.8.3 Air Signals Schools

Other schools that flew a few Ju 87 B-1s were the Air Signals School (LNS – *Luftnachrichtenschule*) 5 at Erfurt-Bindersleben and Air Signals School 6 (Maritime) at Dievenow. With the LNS (Maritime) one of the machines was wrecked at Raschnitz in a forced landing caused by engine failure on 13 December 1941. It is doubtful whether the severity of the damage made a subsequent repair advisable. The majority of the air signals schools were disbanded in 1944: the Ju 87s still on hand were transferred to SG 103 and SG 151.

8.8.4 Bomber Observer School 2

In the late summer of 1944 Ju 87 D-3s and D-5s were in practice service with *Luftwaffe* Bomber Observer School 2 at Hörsching near Linz. Here a D-5 (works no. 666020) crashed in an emergency landing at Lezani on 4 September 1944 after being shot up by air-to-air gunfire. The pilot, Senior Under Officer Ludwig Süss, and his radio operator were missing, according to loss data.

Other than Ju 87s, the school possessed several Fw 189s, He 111s and Ju 88s. The unit was disbanded in December 1944.

8.8.5 The *Luftwaffe* Air Medical School

At least one Ju 87 A was in service with the *Luftwaffe* Air Medical School. The machine was used for medical purposes, to give medical personnel who were not from the dive bomber area an impression of the forces generated during the dive and recovery.

8.8.6 Bomber *Geschwader* KG 101

Training Bomber *Geschwader* KG 101, which functioned as the main bomber school until 1 February 1943, received dive bombers only in very small numbers. At the end of 1943 the unit possessed a few Ju 87 B-1s and B-2s as well as several D-1s and D-3s. KG 101 at Tours (and Foggia) was a unit leader school which was responsible for the training of officers who would later take over bomber units. KG 101, also designated Unit Leader School 101, lost one of its Ju 87 D-1s on 29 July 1942 in the vicinity of Foggia as a result of an undercarriage defect. Another Ju 87 B-1 crashed at Tours after an engine defect and was completely wrecked. One of the crew members was slightly injured in a parachute jump. One Ju 87 B-1 (works no. 0407) was lost to bombing in an air attack on the Tours airfield on 31 December 1943. A second loss struck KG 101 on 8 May 1944 in the course of a cross-country flight; the machine, a B-2 (works no. 5815), swerved on landing on the airfield at Neuburg an der Donau and was 10 per cent damaged – the crew got away with a fright.

9 Reconnaissance and Other Purposes

9.1 The Ju 87 as a Reconnaissance Aircraft

On 11 February 1942 General Field Marshal Erhard Milch ordered that the use of the Ju 87 as a reconnaissance aircraft with normal armour, but without a bomb load, was to be tested thoroughly. It can be assumed that the work was begun, but there is no proof to date whether this led to the conversion of such machines. As the machines were in any case too slow, the 'reconnaissance' use may have been filed away after testing for suitability.

According to the Aircraft Assignment Reports of the Quartermaster General (6th Division III C) for the period from May to September 1944, fifteen Ju 87 Ds were assigned to the jurisdiction of the General of Reconnaissance Pilots (GdA – *General der Aufklärer*); of these two were delivered in May 1944, a further one in July and twelve in August. They were, however, mostly used as glider tugs for the DFS 230 freight gliders built by the German Gliding Research Institute in Darmstadt, with which they transported important materials for the short-range reconnaissance units, particularly in the case of short-term movements.

The short-range reconnaissance units were increasingly equipped with the Bf 109 G in the last two years of the war, and these had shown themselves insufficiently powerful for towing the DFS 230. As the Ju 87s were replaced by the Fw 190 F, from 1944 a new field of activity opened up.

9.2 The Ju 87 as a Communications Aircraft

Sundry Ju 87s were with various staffs and headquarters. The two-seater machines were frequently used as a communications aircraft because of their robustness. A Ju 87 B-1 (works no. 5213) even flew for a short time with the personal flight of the Chief of Development and Testing (GLZ). The machine was shot down by flak south of Lvov on 21 June 1944; the airframe was substantially damaged in the emergency landing, but the crew survived uninjured.

The increase in the performance of Jumo 210 and 211 engines led to ever more powerful engines.

Reconnaissance and Guide Aircraft with Dive Bomber and Ground Attack *Geschwader*

Time	Unit	Type	Quantity
August 1940	StG 1	Do 17	4
	StG 2	Do 17	5
	StG 3	Do 17	5
		He 111	1
	StG 77	Do 17	6
June 1941	StG 1	Bf 110	6
	StG 2	Bf 110	6
	StG 3	Bf 110	4
	StG 77	Bf 110	6
July 1942	StG 1	–	0
	StG 2	Bf 110	6
	StG 3	Bf 110	4
	StG 77	Bf 110	6
March 1943	StG 1	Bf 110	6
	StG 2	Ju 88	6
	StG 3	–	0
	StG 77	Ju 88	6
May 1944	SG 1	–	0
	SG 2	He 111	1
	SG 3	–	0
	SG 77	–	0

A few of the aircraft control stations also had one or two Ju 87s, for example the control station with *Luftflotte* 5, whose Ju 87 B-1 (works no. 5252) was 75 per cent damaged on 15 May 1943.

Ju 87s served extensively with the air service commands (LD-Kdo – *Luftdienstkommando*). Three of these units usually formed an air service unit. Their main tasks were service and courier flights, target towing, photographic flights and a number of other tasks.

One of these commands was LD-Kdo 1/12. It had moved from Mannheim to Chartres and from there serviced the surrounding *Luftwaffe* forces. The command lost one Ju 87 B-1 (works no. 5529) on 19 June 1941 during flying operations at the Nantes airfield after an engine failure; the machine was 90 per cent destroyed in the crash. A second Ju 87 B-1 (works no. 5499) was lost with LD-Kdo 1/12 on 2 March 1944 as a result of an air attack on the airfield at Chartres. The machine was 45 per cent damaged.

With Air Service Command, Western France, two Ju 87 B-1s were lost. The first machine (works no. 5498) on 4 February 1941 made an emergency landing which led to damage of moderate severity. The second one (works no. 5315) was forced into an emergency landing at Rennes as a result of fuel shortage. Both crews got away with a fright.

At least one Ju 87 R-2 (works no. 5832) was used with Air Service Command, Finland, for communications and light transport tasks. The machine was lost on 5 March 1944. The pilot was Corporal Werner Stache.

At Stuttgart-Ruit a Ju 87 D-3 was experimentally fitted with two supplementary containers. An older model of the Ju 87 was reused for wind tunnel tests.

This Ju 87 B-2 (trop.), CE+EN, together with DN+ZT, received a voluminous freight container.

The presence of other Ju 87s can be confirmed at the beginning of 1943 with the *Luftwaffe* Pilot Testing Centre at Prenzlau. Here a Ju 87 B-1 (works no. 5330) was slightly damaged on 1 April 1943 in a crash landing, but could be repaired.

In addition, one Ju 87 was on hand for a time with the Heavy Field Workshop Division IV/50 in November 1943, and one with the Central Administration for Air Equipment at Berlin-Adlershof in the summer of 1944.

At the Jüterbog air park at least five or six Ju 87 R-2s and D-3s were in use. Of these one Ju 87 R-2 (works no. 5937) was lost after hitting the ground, and Leading Aircraftman Erich Hommel, who was flying the machine, lost his life. The second R-2 (works no. 5912) crashed on 22 December 1940 at Delmenhorst as a result of pilot error; Sergeant W. Reks was killed. Corporal Specht crashed with the Ju 87 D-1, works no. 2071, which was also at the Jüterbog air park, on 13 December 1941; he was killed on impact. The Jüterbog air park lost a Ju 87 D-3 (works no. 2378) on 12 May 1942 in a landing accident. Although the machine was 45 per cent destroyed, the pilot was uninjured.

Ju 87s of all series which were no longer capable of front-line service were from time to time used in the administration of the air bases for communications tasks. With the Air Base Headquarters, Erfurt, a Ju 87 B-1 (works no. 5239, BA+KY) was lost in a crash landing with an unidentified crew on 29 October 1940 at Erfurt-North.

10 Tank-Hunting Aircraft and Units

10.1 Development Guidelines

Soon after the beginning of the campaign in Russia it became clear that machines were needed for the express purpose of low-level attack in order to bring effective support to the hard-fighting ground troops. This was necessary because, with the size of the theatre of war, their own armoured units were not always available.

It was hoped that a reworked Ju 87 B, the Ju 87 D version, would improve the situation comprehensively from 1943 as a potent ground attack aircraft and also as a tank hunter – like the Hs 129.

At first the focus was on operations with new, armour-piercing free-fall ordnance. Discussions centred mainly around the thick-walled high-explosive bombs of the SD 2, SD 4, SD 4 Hl and SD 10 versions, and for a time also the SD 50. In addition to operations against field positions and the enemy's resupply arrangements, attacks on enemy armour concentrations or tanks that had broken through gained increasing importance.

At the beginning of the campaign, in June 1941, many Ju 87 Bs, as well as numerous

One of the first production prototypes of the G-1 construction standard, which was tested with the experimental unit for attacking tanks.

Bf 109 Es, but also eight bomber *Gruppen* equipped with Ju 88 As and Do 17 Zs, were already equipped with the SD 2 bomb which was suitable for attacking tanks. The twin-engined machines carried up to 360 bombs, a much greater quantity than Ju 87s or Bf 109s.

The first Hs 129 Bs had quickly shown themselves to be very vulnerable to gunfire, although their main problem was that they were completely underpowered. In particular the large wing tanks were an easily inflammable target for enemy flak. The crew could only be protected against ground fire by fundamentally strengthened armour. Hence the rapid introduction of a faster, but also well-armoured, combat aircraft against Soviet tanks took on immense importance. At the same time, large-calibre airborne guns were intended to come into service.

These were the essential factors which were to determine the layout of the new ground attack aircraft. It was foreseeable that the Red Army would expand its superiority in armoured fighting vehicles of all kinds, which would force the German armoured divisions to become overworked fire-fighters along the far-flung front. Air support was urgently necessary. As early as 1942 the Technical Bureau announced, with the agreement of the OKL, 'that in the shortest possible time a replacement of the Hs 129 type must take place'. The question was whether to use a more potent Ju 87 or a completely new development.

Moreover, it could already be foreseen in 1942 that, by reason of the reinforced enemy defences, the time would come for the use of fast, single-seat fighter bombers (Bf 109 and Fw 190).

In addition to the need to clarify how the new ground attack aircraft was to be procured, the question of armament also arose. The development of hard-core ammunition for the 37-mm Flak 18 gun had already begun in the spring of 1942. By 30 June the first results of firing experiments were available. The weapons specialists were, however, not satisfied with the penetrations achieved. Within a 60° impact angle the shells could penetrate only 120 mm thick steel. A final solution had still not been found.

On 3 November 1942 General Field Marshal Erhard Milch, at a bureau chiefs' conference, again raised the question of the replacement of the Ju 87 in its existing form as well as its future equipment. The participants reached the conclusion that an armament of at least two 30-mm weapons, if possible MK 108s, and an effective free-fall load of up to 500 kg seemed to be required. Besides this, a more powerful

This Ju 87 G-2 of 10 (Pz)/SG 3 was fitted with additional armour to give the crew better protection against ground fire. (Federal Archives)

powerplant than the Jumo 211 J was regarded as necessary for a successor to the Ju 87 D. This was emphasised by the fact that operations by the Ju 87 B/R in the west were possible only by accepting substantial losses to the superior Allied fighters. In comparison with the types sent into action on the enemy side from 1943 onwards, the Junkers machines could only be described as 'lame ducks'.

The call therefore came loudly from the dive bomber units to exchange the Ju 87 as soon as possible for a modern, single-seat fighter bomber with an air-cooled powerplant.

At a development conference on 18 December 1942, Milch established that the decision on a successor type for the Ju 87 had to be reached by the beginning of 1943 at the latest. The losses that had occurred over the eastern front had also shown that haste was required. Meanwhile, the General of Fighter Pilots, Major-General Adolf Galland, had also intervened in this discussion. On 9 February 1943 he demanded that, besides the Hs 129, a new 'armoured aircraft' – at once a ground attack and reconnaissance machine – had to be created. The machine should borrow its layout and armament from the Soviet Il-2. Massive armour protection should offer the crew sufficient protection against both ground and fighter gunfire. Instead of MK 108s, the new machines should have a fixed armament of at least two MK 103s for use against armoured targets. He also demanded the ability to carry up to 1,000 kg of free-fall loads.

With such equipment, according to the General of Ground Attack Pilots, all the necessary tactical capability would initially be available, both for ground attack operations in direct support of the fighting troops and for offensive tank hunting.

The decision on the replacement of the Ju 87 by the fundamentally more effective aircraft type was, however, once more postponed. To avoid having to enter into the risks of a new development, the OKL initially wanted to hold onto the Ju 87 D and to await the development of new machines.

As the interim solution – the Ju 87 F with a Jumo 213 powerplant – was not to be become the new standard version, the planned 'cannon birds' stayed with the Jumo 211 in-line engine.

By 10 March 1943 the first twenty-five Ju 87 G-1s had been completed and most had been delivered to the front-line units. From the starting point of suitability as a tank hunter, the Technical Bureau GL/C turned to the *Luftwaffe* General Staff in March 1943, in order to obtain the further requirements of the front-line units.

The defensive capability of the Soviet Union had meanwhile grown considerably, not least thanks to the generous support of the United States. The armaments industries which had been moved to the east soon after the German attack had now taken up their work and were producing, almost without threat of any kind from the *Luftwaffe*, tank after tank and aircraft after aircraft.

Hence, in the medium term, Germany had to expect far stronger major attacks than had been the case hitherto.

For this reason, between May and July 1943 the *Luftwaffe* leadership staff considered all aspects of attacks on tanks for the period from the winter of 1943–4 onwards. Most of the army divisions engaged along the eastern front were insufficiently equipped with anti-tank weapons.

Enemy tanks that had broken through, individually or in groups, could not be stopped in the rear areas away from the main battle line and quickly inflicted severe damage on the German infrastructure.

Especially in winter, the situation of the anti-tank forces on the ground was made still more difficult by the fact that the movement of heavy anti-tank guns was possible to only a restricted degree because of insufficient road connections or poor road conditions. It became clear to the *Wehrmacht* high command that, without air support, a catastrophe could easily result. In order to be able to support the army directly, the *Luftwaffe* General Staff therefore spoke up for an increase in tank-hunter production in the near future as well as for the formation of new tank-hunting units.

In the summer of 1943 only the following five *Staffeln* had been specially equipped for tank hunting and had been spread over continually changing operational airfields behind the eastern front:

4 and 8/(Pz)/SG 1	with Hs 129s
4 and 8/(Pz)/SG 2	with Hs 129s
Tank Hunter *Staffel* 51	with Hs 129s
Tank Hunter *Staffel* StG 1	with Ju 87 Gs
Tank Hunter *Staffel* StG 2	with Ju 87 Gs

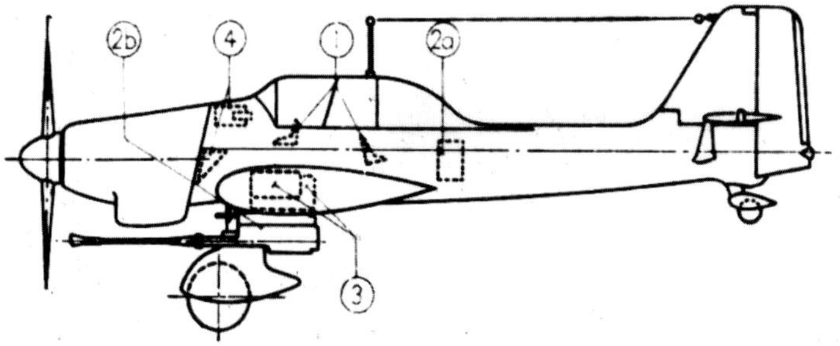

Dieser Ladeplan hat nur Gültigkeit für das seinem Verwendungszweck entsprechend ausgerüstete Flugzeug.
Die Besatzung ist stets 2 Mann.

1) Restmenge im Rüstgewicht enthalten.
2) Mit 5 kg Kraftstoff für Kaltstart.
3) Fall 105 B. Abfangradius bei Va = 600 km/h mindestens 700 m.
4) Höchstzulässiges Landegewicht in Ausnahmefällen 5400 kg. Das entspricht (für Beladefall 3) Betriebsstoff 60% ausgeflogen.
5) Höchstzulässige Sturzfluggeschwindigkeiten
Va = 600 km/h bis 2 km Höhe.
Va = 550 km/h über 2 km Höhe
6) Beim Fliegen ohne Funkerschützen und Abwehrbewaffnung sind aus Schwerpunktsgründen insgesamt 70—100 kg Ballast im 2. Sitz erforderlich.

Achtung!
Bedienungsvorschrift-Fl Ju 87 G-1 beachten!

Verwendungsgruppe: H Beanspruchungsgruppe: 5 (abgeminderter Lastvielfache) Höchstzul. Fluggewicht: 5750 kg		Schwerpunktslagen von Flügelvorderkante für:	Rüstgewicht: 0,560 m höchstzul. Vorlage: 0,550 m höchstzul. Rücklage: 0,712 m
Beladefall		1 mit 2 Tm-Beh.	2 mit 2 Tm-Beh u. 1 Tf-Beh.	3 mit 2 Tm-Beh u. 2 Tf-Beh.
		Gewichte in kg		
	Rüstgewicht	4800 ··· 4835	4800 ··· 4835	4800 ··· 4835
1	Besatzung	140 ··· 200	140 ··· 200	140 ··· 200
2	Munition a. für MG 81 Z (2000 Schuß)	0 ··· 50	0 ··· 50	0 ··· 50
	Munition b. für 2 x 3,7 cm BK (2 x 12 Schuß)	0 ··· 50	0 ··· 50	0 ··· 50
3	Kraftstoff	15[1] ··· 355	15[1] ··· 465	15[1] ··· 575
4	Schmierstoff	13[1] ··· 68[2]	13[1] ··· 68[2]	13[1] ··· 68[2]
	Fluggewicht voll	5530	5640	5750
	Kraftstoff in Liter	20 ··· 480	20 ··· 630	20 ··· 780
	Schmierstoff in Liter	15 ··· 76	15 ··· 76	15 ··· 76
	Sicheres Lastvielfache [3]	5,0	5,0	5,0

Ladeplan Ju 87 G-1 mit 2 x 3,7 cm BK (S 8700-5111 c)

Excerpt from the operating instructions for Ju 87 Ds and Gs, to which the loading plan for the Ju 87 G-1 belonged.

For this reason the *Luftwaffe* leadership staff (Ia) suggested in a secret command document (No. 3300/43 g.Kdos. –op-) that a first tank hunter *Geschwader* be formed with three *Gruppen*. This powerful unit should be organised as follows:

Geschwader staff	
I *Gruppe*	five *Staffeln* with Hs 129s
II *Gruppe*	two *Staffeln* with Ju 87 Gs
III *Gruppe*	two to three *Staffeln* with Ju 88 Ps.

The I and II *Gruppen* should consist of the tank hunting *Staffeln* already in action in the east in the summer of 1943. The III *Gruppe* was planned as a new formation by re-equipping the existing III *Gruppe* of KG 1 'Hindenburg' with twin-engined Ju 88 P-1 tank hunters.

The use of the Ju 87 G, however, was only effective as an interim solution, as the machines, according to combat experience to date, had been found to be insufficiently manouevrable and insufficiently resistant to gunfire. There would, however, be no unambiguous vote against the retention of the Ju 87 G as there had been individual successes. Moreover, because of the tight material situation, the *Luftwaffe* leadership had no real choice other than to leave the Junkers machine in service for the time being.

So that their use could be continued as effectively as possible, General Field Marshal Erhard Milch ordered a little later that, from then on, twenty Ju 87 Gs a month were to be manufactured. For this purpose already available Ju 87 D machines were to be converted.

In view of the immense capability of the Russian enemy the limited conversion order offered no certainty of bringing the advance of

Colonel Dr Jur. Ernst Kupfer

Colonel Ernst Kupfer, who was killed in a crash in the Belasia Mountains, Greece, and was not found until 17 November 1943 by a search team. This outstanding officer was finally laid to rest in the military cemetery at Salonika.

2 July 1907	Born at Coburg, Bavaria
1913–16	Primary school at Coburg
1917–26	High school at Coburg, certificate of completion
1926–8	University at Heidelberg, law (five semesters) and at the University of Erlangen (three semesters)
1 October 1928	Recruit with the 5th Squadron of the 17th Bavarian Cavalry Regiment
1 April 1929	Nominated as officer candidate
1 July 1930	Cadet Lance-Corporal (Nomination as Cadet and promotion to Lance-Corporal)
1 October 1930	Promotion to Cadet Corporal
3 October 1930	Posting to the first course at the Infantry School
1 August 1931	Promotion to Junior Under Officer
1 August 1932	Promotion to Senior Under Officer
15 October 1932	Nomination as 2nd Lieutenant
18 January 1934	Marriage leave granted
12 February 1934	Marriage to Annemarie Vögler
1 December 1934	Promotion to Lieutenant
1 May 1936	Left active service and transferred to officer corps of Bavarian Cavalry Regiment 17 as Reserve Lieutenant; preparation for degree
4 March 1937	Awarded Dr Jur. degree
5 March 1937	Active in father-in-law's business
1 October 1937	Return to Bavarian Cavalry Regiment 17
12 October 1937	Nomination as chief of 8th (Mechanised) Squadron
12 March 1938	Service in Austria (until 27 March 1938)
1 May 1939	Promotion to Cavalry Captain
30 September 1939	Transfer to *Luftwaffe*; posted as Captain to Reconnaissance School at Jüterbog
13 June 1940	Posted to dive bomber training as Officer, Special Duties ('Stuka' School 2)
1 August 1940	Posting to 'Stuka' Reinforcement *Staffel* at Gross-Lippstadt
7 September 1940	Posting to StG 2 'Immelmann' on the Channel coast
23 November 1941	Knight's Cross to the Iron Cross after 260 operational flights
22 May 1941	Participation in the sinking of HMS *Gloucester* as *Staffel* commander
22 June 1941	Start of operational activity over Russia
14 October 1941	Award of the cup of honour for special achievements in air warfare
27 February 1942	Nomination as commander of II/StG 2 'Immelmann'
1 April 1942	Promotion to Major
30 October 1942	500th operational flight
2 November 1942	Decoration with the German Gold Cross
8 January 1943	Oak Leaves to the Knight's Cross of the Iron Cross
13 February 1943	Assigned to observe the duties of the commander of StG 2 'Immelmann'
July 1943	Formation of the 'Kupfer fighting unit'
2 July 1943	600th operational flight
1 September 1943	Promotion to Lieutenant-Colonel
1 September 1943	Nomination as Fighting General of Ground Attack Pilots
10 September 1943	Assignment to the so-called Officer Reserve (for officers temporarily unavailable for front-line duty because of wounds or illness)
6 November 1943	Fatal crash during a tour of inspection in Greece

Colonel Dr Jur. Kupfer was the first leader of a *Luftwaffe* unit which succeeded in destroying an enemy armoured unit from the air. He was posthumously promoted Colonel, with effect from 1 November 1943. In a total of 636 operational flights he was shot down by flak three times and once severely wounded in the process. He was the first Fighting General of Ground Attack Pilots.

the Soviet guards tank armies and motorised rifle divisions to a standstill. The increased production of the modern SD 4 Hl hollow-charge bomb, an extremely effective weapon, was therefore initially the most effective means of supporting tank hunting.

Extensive experimental drops on captured Russian tanks in the *Luftflotte* 4 and 6 areas at times gave useful results. The use of this free-fall ordnance was, however, not planned against enemy tanks that had broken through. These were to be stopped as far as possible by 'cannon birds'. The main application for the hollow-charge bombs was against stationary armoured fighting vehicles of the Red Army, or those which were just being concentrated for action. Only with a development conference on 10 September 1943 was the scene set for an essentially better support of the German ground troops. Lieutenant-Colonel Dr Jur. Ernst Kupfer, the General of Close Support Pilots, could only speak for the dive bomber, ground attack and fighter bomber units belonging to his inspectorate. The flying tank hunters, as well as the harassment bomber units and the long-range fighter bombers, still fell under the jurisdiction of the General of Bomber Pilots.

Only a complete reorganisation, and therefore, an end to jurisdictional disputes, made sense in the long term. Lieutenant-Colonel Ernst Kupfer hence outlined clearly the future tactical and technical requirements for an effective close combat aircraft.

In his opinion the new single-seat machine would have to be not only small, fast and manouevrable, but as a rule capable of operating without fighter protection. The armament of the close combat aircraft should not be heavier than the 20-mm cannon. As free-fall weapons, AB 500s filled with small hollow-charge, incendiary or shrapnel bombs were the best for operations against both armoured and unarmoured targets. By contrast, for individual bombs he wanted to limit the weight to a maximum of 250 kg, to use them in attacking stationary targets.

The general foresaw an average approach altitude hardly greater than 5,000 metres. As a rule the pilots would operate from an altitude of about 700–800 metres or lower. The return flight would be at low altitude from purely tactical considerations. In addition, a good climb performance at low altitude as well as suitability as an auxiliary fighter for attacking enemy low-level attack aircraft would be very useful. The armouring of the airframe must not have a noticeable effect on the speed.

Not until the beginning of September 1943 were all close combat pilots subordinated to the General of Close Support Pilots, Lieutenant-Colonel Ernst Kupfer. Besides the dive bombers, this included ground attack pilots and fighter bombers ('fast bomber units') as well as all harassment bomber units – and, not least, the tank hunters.

Operational flight with the 'Weiss Tank Hunting Command', which was decisively involved in putting together the future operational guidelines for tank hunting.

Operations against ground targets, according to Kupfer on 10 September 1943, were mainly carried out as shallow diving attacks, rather than in almost vertical dives – as happened with the Ju 87 B and R.

The best solution, the general then said, would be to use an already adequately proven type of aircraft for these ground attack operations. The Fw 190 F and G, of which 400 machines a month were desired as fighter bombers, were the most suitable aircraft, and not only in his opinion.

As a tank hunter, both the Ju 88 P-1 with a KWK 75-mm cannon and the armoured Ju 87 and Hs 129 (with improved equipment) were useful in his opinion, and he spoke also for the General of Bomber Pilots. General Field Marshal Erhard Milch again indicated on 10 September 1943, with reference to an order from the Chief of the Technical Bureau, that Ju 87 production was to be run down only slowly. The obsolete machines would be progressively replaced by Fw 190 Fs and Gs, corresponding to an order already issued by the OKL in the summer. The Ju 87, as well as being a flying tank hunter, was also to be used as a night ground attacker. For this suitable radio equipment was required (FuG 101 and FuG 7A).

Meanwhile the war situation had developed to the further disadvantage of Germany. As a result of the superiority of the Allied air fleets, the defence of the *Reich* had continually to be reinforced. The call for ever more powerful fighter machines went out again.

In order to impede the ability of the American and British bomber units to operate over the *Reich* and occupied areas almost without opposition, the bulk of aircraft production had to be assigned to the defence of the *Reich* at the expense of offensive capability. For that reason, the available Ju 87 Ds and Gs were as far as possible to be used up and progressively replaced at the units by the faster Fw 190 fighter bombers and ground attack aircraft. To increase their offensive capability as many Fw 190s as possible were to be equipped with 'Tank Lightning' or 'Tank Terror' projectiles. Only the new types of anti-tank rockets, it was believed, could to some extent stop the heavy battle tanks of the Red Army.

The number of Ju 87s continually declined as a result, so that by the end of the war only a few *Staffeln* and *Gruppen* were equipped with them.

Most of these machines, in any event, served as tank hunters or anti-tank ground attack aircraft and were to carry out this task until the conversion to Fw 190s and Ta 152s equipped with spin-stabilised anti-tank rockets.

10.2 Construction Versions (Ju 87 G-1 and G-2)

The history of the Ju 87 G-1 and G-2 actually began at the end of 1941, when the quick end to the campaign in the east expected by Adolf Hitler did not materialise.

At the beginning of January 1942 Junkers and the RLM had numerous studies and developed plans before them for a Ju 87 equipped with two heavy cannon; it was supposed to go into action chiefly over the eastern front as a flying tank hunter.

In a presentation to engineers and officers of the RLM in March 1942 Dipl.-Ing. Günther Voss spoke for the introduction of heavy onboard weapons for attacking tanks:

> We absolutely must produce stronger onboard weapons, if we do not wish to give up altogether on attacking armoured fighting vehicles from the air. Giving up in this way would undoubtedly make the defence of the Russian front much more difficult, even after the annihilation of the main Soviet forces, because only the aircraft has the necessary mobility to fight off an enemy armoured break-through at any point of the more than 1,000-km front. A 50-mm weapon would probably suffice for the armoured fighting vehicles that will be sent into action by the enemy in the future; by using extremely light explosive shells with an armour-piercing hollow charge, these weapons would probably be feasible, even in smaller aircraft, without anti-recoil devices.

The enemy superiority in tank production, bolstered by deliveries from the United States, made action imperative. Even near misses often immobilised enemy tanks for a time. Only a 45° diving attack onto the target offered some assurance of success with practice, but even these results were usually modest.

In any case, with cannon, chance hits with both MG 151/20s sufficed to put the vehicle out

Colonel Hans-Ulrich Rudel

The most successful of the flying tank busters, Colonel Hans-Ulrich Rudel, who was the only soldier of the *Wehrmacht* to receive the Golden Oak Leaf to the Swords and Diamonds of the Iron Cross.

2 July 1916	Born at Konradswaldau, District of Landshut, Silesia
1922–6	Primary school at Seiferdau
1926–7	Secondary school at Schweidnitz
1927–8	High school at Sagan
1928–31	Niesky school
1931–4	High school at Görlitz
16 February 1932	Won German Association for Air and Space Flight basic licence at Breslau
1935–6	High school at Lauban, Lower Silesia
22 September 1936	Completion certificate at Lauban high school
4 December 1936	Start of basic training at the Air Warfare School at Wildpark-Werder (first semester) as Cadet
1 May 1937	Start of second semester at Wildpark-Werder
1 June 1937	Promotion to Cadet Lance-Corporal
1 August 1937	Promotion to Cadet Corporal
1 December 1937	Promotion to Junior Under Officer
7 February 1938	Award of military pilot licence
1 April 1938	Start of third semester at Wildpark-Werder (until 31 December 1938)
13 September 1938	Promotion to Senior Under Officer
1 December 1938	Posting to Reconnaissance School, Hildesheim for observer training
1 January 1939	Promotion to 2nd Lieutenant (seniority date 1 January 1939)
8–27 February 1939	Participation in the ski championships at Kitzbühl
1 June 1939	Posting as Officer, Special Duties (Training Establishment) to Long-Range Reconnaissance *Gruppe* (F)/121 at Prenzlau, Uckermark; move to Schneidemühl
2 September 1939	Service on long-range reconnaissance in the Polish campaign (operations to Brest-Litovsk and Kovel)
10 November 1939	Decoration with the Iron Cross, Second Class, for successful reconnaissance operations over Poland
2 March 1940	Posting to Pilot Training Regiment 43 (for a short time at

	Vienna-Stammersdorf) then to Crailsheim, Jagst
9 July 1940	Posting to I/StG 3 at Caen in northern France
1 September 1940	Promotion to Lieutenant (seniority date 1 September 1940)
14 November 1940	Posting to I/StG 2 'Immelmann'
21 February 1941	Posting to Reinforcement *Staffel* of StG 2 at Graz-Thalerhof
20 May 1941	Transfer to I/StG 2 at Molai in Greece (no combat operations)
22 June 1941	First operations with 1/StG 2 over Suvalki on the eastern front
28 June 1941	Successful operation against Grodno (with I/StG 2)
18 July 1941	Decoration with the Iron Cross, First Class, with the Combat Flying clasp
23 July 1941	Posting to to II/StG 2, service as *Gruppe* Technical Officer
18 August 1941	Hit the ground without serious results in an operation near Chudovo
29 August 1941	Posting to III/StG 2 in the northern sector (Leningrad front)
10 September 1941	Direct hit on bunkers on the Duderhofer Heights
21 September 1941	Successful dive bombing attack by III/StG 2 on the Cronstadt naval harbour (hits on the battleship *Marat*, belonging to the Baltic Fleet, with SD 500s)
23 September 1941	SD 1000 direct hit destroys the battleship *Marat* near the Cronstadt mole
1 October 1941	Sinking of a Soviet cruiser and a destroyer
20 October 1941	Decoration with the
	Cup of Honour for special achievements in air warfare
2 December 1941	Decoration with the German Gold Cross
6 January 1942	Decoration with the the Knight's Cross to the Iron Cross, awarded by General of Pilots Dr-Ing. Wolfram *Freiherr* von Richthofen (VIII *Fliegerkorps*); meanwhile more than 400 operational flights
18 February 1942	Defensive operation near own airfield at Dugino, south-west of Rchev
20 March 1942	Marriage to Ursula Bergmann at Alt-Kohlfurt
25 April 1942	*Staffel* leader of the 'Stuka' reinforcement *Staffel* at Graz-Thalerhof
August 1942	Move of the 'Stuka' reinforcement *Staffel* from Graz to Sarabus in the Crimea
15 August 1942	Nomination as *Staffel* commander of the 9th *Staffel* of StG 2 'Immelmann'
1 September 1942	Decoration with the Winter Battle in the East 1941–42 medal (Eastern Medal)
24 September 1942	500th operational flight over the southern sector of the eastern front
12 November 1942	Posting to I/StG 2 'Immelmann'
10 February 1943	1,000th operational flight over the southern sector of the eastern front against targets in the area of the 57th Army
April 1943	Sinking of seventy landing craft
1 April 1943	Promotion to Captain (because of his decorations for bravery and his position, with seniority date 1 April 1942)

14 April 1943	Oak Leaves to the Knight's Cross of the Iron Cross as the 229th soldier of the *Wehrmacht*
16 April 1943	Takeover of 1/StG 2 'Immelmann' at Kerch, operations over the Kuban bridgehead
2 July 1943	Visit by Imperial Minister Speer to StG 2
5 July 1943	Participation in the battle of Kursk
19 July 1943	Assigned to observe the duties of the commander of III/StG 2, handover of 1/StG 2
12 August 1943	1,300th operational flight
9 October 1943	1,500th operational flight (with Sergeant-Major Erwin Henschel as gunner) against the Dnieper bridge near Romankovo
October 1943	Attacks on enemy armoured units from Kirovograd
28 October 1943	100th tank victory with the Ju 87 G: a T-34 at Nova Praga east of Kirovograd
23 November 1943	Destruction of seven Russian tanks in one day
25 November 1943	Decoration with the Swords to the Knight's Cross of the Iron Cross as 42nd soldier of the *Wehrmacht* by Adolf Hitler at the 'Wolf's Redoubt'
January 1944	Defence against the 67th Russian Armoured Brigade in the battles for Kirovograd
11 January 1944	150th tank victory
16 January 1944	1,700th operational flight
22 February 1944	Nomination as commander of III *Gruppe* of Ground Attack *Geschwader* 2 'Immelmann'
1 March 1944	Promotion to Major (seniority date 1 October 1942) because of the highest decorations for bravery
21 March 1944	Wounded in an attack on the Dnieper bridge at Yambol (emergency landing in enemy territory and fought his way back to the German lines on 22 March 1944)
24 March 1944	1,800th operational flight
26 March 1944	Destruction of seventeen enemy tanks in one day
29 March 1944	Diamonds to the Knight's Cross with Swords. Decoration by Adolf Hitler on the Obersalzburg, followed by award of the Combat Flying clasp in gold with diamonds and a '2,000' pendant by Imperial Marshal Hermann Göring
9 May 1944	100,000th sortie by SG 2 'Immelmann'
1 June 1944	2,000th operational flight from Husi in Romania
5 August 1944	Eleven tank victories in one day, making 300 enemy tanks put out of action to date
18 August 1944	325th tank victory in the Courland
1 September 1944	Promotion to Lieutenant-Colonel (seniority date 1 September 1944) and nomination as commander of Ground Attack *Geschwader* SG 2 (handover of III *Gruppe* to the bearer of the Knight's Cross, Captain Kurt Lau)
17 November 1944	Wounded (shot through the left thigh) in action

	over the eastern front
23 December 1944	2,400th operational flight and 463rd tank victory
29 December 1944	Golden Oak Leaf with Swords and Diamonds to the Knight's Cross of the Iron Cross (the only soldier) with simultaneous nomination as Colonel with effect from 1 January 1945
3 January 1945	125,000th sortie by SG 2 under leadership of Hans-Ulrich Rudel
12 January 1945	Attack on the Soviet offensive along the Weichsel
16 January 1945	Award of the Hungarian Gold Medal for Bravery, the only award to a foreigner
18 January 1945	481st tank victory
25 January 1945	500th tank victory
31 January 1945	505th tank victory
2 February 1945	Destruction of fifteen Russian tanks in one day by Colonel Rudel and the tank hunter *Staffel* of SG 2
8 February 1945	Destruction of thirteen enemy tanks in the Lebus, Oder, area (516 tank victories); severely wounded, resulting in amputation of the shin bone at the SS main dressing station at Seelow, west of Küstrin
27 March 1945	Return after hospitalisation in Berlin
17 April 1945	Move of the *Geschwader* staff and III/SG 2 to Kummer at Niemes in the Sudetenland
20 April 1945	Entry in Rank List A: Colonel Rudel, commander of SG 'Immelmann' No. 2
8 May 1945	Landing after 2,530th operational flight at the Kitzingen airfield occupied by American troops
April 1946	Release from captivity, next, haulage contractor at Coesfeld, Westphalia, followed by emigration to Argentina as 'consultant'
August 1949	Participation in the Argentinian ski championships (fourth place in the downhill races)
31 December 1951	Climbed the 7,020-metre Aconcagua in the Argentinian Andes
10 January 1960	First in the Riesentor run of the Austrian Ski Federation at Kitzbühl
31 March 1963	First ascent of Llullay-Yacu (6,920 metres)
22 May 1965	Memorial speech by Colonel Hans-Ulrich Rudel at the dedication of the memorial to the fallen of the 'Immelmann' *Geschwader* at Staufenberg castle
18 December 1982	Hans-Ulrich Rudel died at the age of 66
22 December 1982	Burial of Colonel Hans-Ulrich Rudel at Dornhausen in central Franconia in the presence of more than 2,000 mourners

of action by fire if the small ventilation slits or fuel tanks carried on the vehicle were hit.

However, the unpromising use of MG 151/20s induced Lieutenant Hans-Ulrich Rudel to suggest to his *Gruppe* Technical Officer that a Ju 87 D be provisionally fitted with modified and remote-operated 37-mm Flak 18 guns. The two large-calibre guns were to fire outside the propeller arc and therefore did not need to be synchronised.

The full-scale evaluation of the cannon installation from a weapons-technical point of

Captain Andreas Kuffner among his comrades of 10 (Pz)/SG 3 in front of a Ju 87 G-2.

view took place at the beginning of 1943 at the *Luftwaffe* test centre at Tarnewitz, where the 37-mm weapons were first measured and fired from a static position.

At a bureau chiefs' conference on 5 January 1943 Staff Colonel G. Wolfgang Vorwald stated that these experiments had not gone particularly well. He therefore suggested that this armament should be expedited with greater emphasis, not on the Hs 129 as actually planned, but on the Me 410. Initially there was no discussion of the Ju 87 as a 'cannon bird'.

Only the provisional conversion of two production prototypes at the end of 1942 and the beginning of 1943 led to practical results, based on the Ju 87 D-3. After addition of the appropriate fittings, a Flak 18 gun was hung under each wing.

The first flight of a Ju 87 D-1 (works no. 2552) as 'Gustav the tank killer' took place on 31 January 1943. The first production prototype was tested by Captain Hans-Karl Stepp, who had received the Knight's Cross on 4 February 1942, first at Rechlin and then, at the beginning of 1943, on the Briansk training area. In the process it was verified that, as a result of the increased air resistance, the speed of the machine was 270 kph at best and that it was less agile than the existing 'Dora'.

Because of the relatively low speed and approach altitude, the anticipated danger to crew and machine in future operations was by no means slight. At the same time it was a disadvantage that the two weapons could not be reloaded in flight and had only six rounds per magazine. Although this was quickly changed by welding two six-round magazines together, the amount of ammunition that could be carried was still unsatisfactory.

In April 1943 there followed the first Ju 87 G-1s equipped with the 37-mm Flak gun, which soon afterwards were delivered to the front-line units. The machines were mostly former Ju 87 D-1s or D-3s which, as Ju 87 G-1s, were put through rigorous tactical testing in attacking tanks by an experimental command within the testing unit.

In February 1943 the testing unit was led by Lieutenant-Colonel Otto Weiss, who was also Inspector of Ground Attack and Destroyer Pilots between July 1942 and November 1943.

The actual testing work was assigned to Captains Hans-Karl Stepp and Hans-Ulrich Rudel. As the problems with the Ju 88 P-1 continued, the importance of the single-engined Ju 87 G increased. When the 75-mm weapon was fired, cracks continually appeared in the propeller blades, so that the Ju 88 P-1 had to be taken out of action from time to time.

On 18 March 1943 the first tank-hunting operation with the G-1 production prototype took place, albeit only experimentally. Within a

At the end of the war numerous operational machines were blown up by German troops. This Ju 87 G-2 of 10 (Pz)/SG 2 made it as far as Zeltweg in Styria.

short time a second machine was added which, after the completion of testing at Briansk (*Luftflotte* Command East area) in May 1943, was transferred, together with the first one, by Hans-Ulrich Rudel to the forward airstrip Kerch 4 in the Crimea. From there he succeeded in destroying at least seventy Soviet landing craft one after another with his 'cannon bird' between the Temryusk and Achtarski Bays.

The experience report of *Luftflotte* 4, which Captain Haller presented at a development conference on 4 June 1943, concerned the use of the Ju 87 on the eastern front. Apart from the usual undercarriage defects and propeller failures, the Ju 87 D had proved itself in attacking tanks and positions with SD 1 and SD 2 bombs. In addition the operational availability of the rugged ground attack aircraft was described as good. Attacks on tanks with SD 1s and SD 2s, however, were hindered more seriously than hitherto from the beginning of 1943 onwards by the light flak assigned to the armoured units. The small bombs worked with devastating effect against infantry advancing with the tanks or riding on them, provided hits were scored.

Often two AB 70s were released in a dive from 1,800–2,000 metres, which forced infantry and flak crews to take cover immediately. Next, the aircraft, covering each other, attacked battle tanks with individually aimed single bombs. In this it was shown that the development of the SD 70 with a hollow charge must be given greater importance than hitherto.

The Ju 87 Gs with heavy cannon armament had not previously made any special appearance, although the general suitability of the Ju 87 as a tank hunter was already established. Besides Hans-Ulrich Rudel, this was chiefly thanks to Hans-Karl Stepp, who returned to StG 2 in June 1943. There he was nominated as commander of II *Gruppe* on 17 June 1943, before he rose to be commander of the 'Immelmann'

Fuelling the 'cannon birds' of 10 (Pz)/SG 2 'Immelmann'. In the background (right) an Fw 190 of the staff of SG 2 can be seen.

Geschwader on 10 September 1943.

The first successes led, after the manufacture of production prototypes in June 1943, to the RLM issuing an order in June 1943 for, initially, twenty Ju 87 tank hunters. In order to keep the 37-mm weapons operable even in cold weather, they were equipped with a heater installation which took only five minutes to warm the cannon before firing.

As a rule, in the first variants of the new tank hunter, the Ju 87 G-1, the original MG 17s were removed and the openings closed off with linen. In the following conversion series, the Ju 87 G-2, with a few exceptions the two MG 151 weapons were also dispensed with. As defensive armament one MG 81 Z remained with an ammunition supply of 1,000 rounds. Both in the G-1 and in the G-2 the dive brakes were omitted, as these were not needed in operations against armoured targets. In the series-converted tank hunters, oxygen equipment and bomb racks, as well as the additional fuel tanks, were omitted.

With StG 2 'Immelmann', tank hunting operations were first flown with the Ju 87 G-1 in the Bielgorod-Charkov area on 5 July 1943, in the central sector of the eastern front. In this operation Hans-Ulrich Rudel, who in addition flew the only airworthy 'cannon bird', shot up the surprising number of twelve T-34 tanks. After the operation he reported:

We dived on the steel colossus, sometimes from behind, sometimes from the side. The approach angle is not too steep to make the approach quite close to the ground, and thus in the pull-out to have no difficulties with stalling the machine.

We must try always to hit the tank at its weaker points. Those are the sides and the rear. At the rear are the engine and cooling system. Here only thin armour plate could be installed and there are also holes set into the armour plate to assure the cooling of the engine. It is worth holding out for this point.

It had been shown, however, that the Ju 87 G-1 lagged behind the D-5, which meanwhile had become the standard, and which, besides, had a greater wingspan than the D-1 and D-3, because of the noticeably increased gross weight and the greater air resistance. It was therefore a good idea to go over to the G-2 construction series as quickly as possible. This had the airframe of the D-5 and also had its wings.

By August 1943 operations with the Ju 87 equipped with the 37-mm cannon had shown within a few weeks that, in spite of their relative slowness, the machines had proved themselves as tank hunters. The basic precondition was precise preparation for the operation and the right element of surprise.

The production of the Ju 87 G was once again scheduled to cease in September 1943 because of the Ju 88 P, but the Chief of Development and Testing, General Erhard Milch, immediately tried to ensure its further production.

From now on at least twenty Ju 87 G-2s a month were to be made ready for operations over the eastern front. In the middle of August 1943 he implored the leadership staff of the *Luftwaffe* to agree. They did, but the conversion of the Flak 18 to the BK 3.7 cannon could not keep up with the demand from the front-line units. At times only half the monthly requirement of seventy cannon was completed.

The use of the Hs 129, according to the conference held by the *Luftwaffe* leadership staff on 1 August 1943, had not received unrestricted approval because of the poor destructive power of the MK 103 cannon. The Ju 87 G-2 was described as 'not manoeuvrable enough' but had 'proved itself well' according to a marginal note in the conference minutes. This was, above all, because of the operational successes that the tank hunters scored in the *Luftflotte* 6 area around Briansk and Orel.

Colonel-General Walter Model was able to telegraph to the army and *Luftwaffe* High Command on 12 July 1943:

For the first time in military history the air force has destroyed an armoured brigade that had broken through, successfully and without the support of ground troops.

Luftflotte 4 could also assure the crews of the Ju 87 G-2s that their machines had far exceeded what had been expected of them.

The direct danger of ground fire had meanwhile increased sharply, which inflicted corresponding losses on the *Staffeln* assigned to tank hunting. Because of light flak, but also due to massed infantry fire, there were numerous cases of damage to the machines, resulting in a rapid decline in operational strength.

In spite of this the Ju 87 Ds and Gs, according to the General of Close Combat Pilots on 10 September 1943, remained capable of use as a night ground attack aircraft. General Field Marshal Erhard Milch therefore tried to convince the *Luftwaffe* leadership to give precedence to attacks on tanks on the eastern front from the winter of 1943–4. In his opinion, at least two *Geschwader* should be prepared for the purpose.

The first of these tank hunter *Geschwader* was to consist of three, later four, *Gruppen*, to be equipped as follows in the late summer of 1943:

I *Gruppe* with five *Staffeln* of Hs 129s with MK 101 cannon (machines available)
II *Gruppe* with two *Staffeln* of Ju 87s with BK 3.7 cannon (machines available)
III *Gruppe* with two *Staffeln* of Ju 88s (in process of formation from III/KG 1)
IV *Gruppe* (still without machines, planned as a reinforcement *Gruppe*)

The tank hunter *Staffeln* and their scattered operations remained, however; an opportunity was wasted.

On 16 August 1943, at a conference chaired by Lieutenant-Colonel Eschenauer (General Staff 6th Division), the measures necessary for the defence of the *Reich* were established.

It was decided that that, apart from the Ju 88

P with a 75-mm Pak 40 cannon, a 50-mm KWK 39/I armoured car gun or two 37-mm Flak 18 cannon, Ju 87 G-2s with two of these weapons would be especially important.

As a result of the tense war situation and the continually increasing demands of the defence of the *Reich*, it was to be expected that the production of anti-tank aircraft would have to be pushed into the background. Thus, all that was demanded was that at least twenty Ju 87 G-2s per month be produced, instead of only five. Within the conversion planning, the Ju 87 G ranked behind the Ju 88 P-2, but in front of the Bf 110 with its 37 mm armament. The Ju 87 G-1s on order were to be completed as quickly as possible and assigned to the front-line units.

In addition to the gun armament, the use of high-explosive bombs for attacking tanks was still regarded as extremely important. Thus, in September 1943 for the first time, the SD 50 was successfully equipped with a strengthened explosive head for attacking tanks. The bomb could, however, be made available only in limited quantities. The same was true of the SD 10 Hl (with hollow charge), whose penetration had been increased to 200 mm of steel.

Moreover, the Test Centre Command was to test as quickly as possible whether arming with spin-stabilised rocket shells was possible in the medium term.

The necessary experiments turned out to be extremely expensive, which led to the Ju 87 G-2 remaining in the production programme longer.

Initially the relatively few Ju 87 G-1s and G-2s were called on to attack tanks at the main points of action. Together with conversions by front-line units, the first ten machines of the first conversion series went to the two Ju 87-equipped tank hunter *Staffeln* of the dive bomber *Geschwader* StG 1 and 2 by September 1943.

By 30 October 1943 the first fifteen of the twenty Ju 87 G-1s ordered had been equipped with Flak 18 cannon at the Weser aircraft works. The remaining five tank hunters (G-1) could not be completed until the end of 1943. The machines were taken from the D-3 series, as was supposed to be the case with the additional forty Ju 87 G-2s to be converted at Weser, whose production was planned for by 31 December 1943. As people had meanwhile become convinced that the use of the D-5 was better, however, those airframes were used for the subsequent conversions.

Unfortunately, in December 1943 the production of the Flak 3.7 collapsed almost completely due to enemy action, resulting in substantial delays. In the previous months continual delivery bottlenecks had already occurred, although the most urgent needs could mostly be satisfied. Only from mid-April 1944 was it again possible to equip the completed machines with BK 3.7 cannon.

Free-fall weapons continued to be important because of the lack of heavy cannon. The available experience reports on these means of attacking tanks showed in the spring of 1944 that the Experimental Command of the General of Ground Attack Pilots had reported that the SD 4 Hl was superior to all larger free-fall weapons in attacking tanks. The Ju 87 crews scored seven hits with SD 4 Hls to every one with all other free-fall loads combined. For this reason the Chief of Development and Testing made a proposal to Adolf Hitler on the release of the SD 4 Hl, which was finally authorised by him.

The importance of this free-fall load was based purely on the fact that the Ju 87 G was available only in relatively small numbers for anti-tank ground attack operations, considering the length of the eastern front. By contrast, the number of enemy tanks increased continually. At the Chief of Development and Testing's conference of 14 April 1944 Erhard Milch was again concerned with the introduction of heavy cannon, which was only half-hearted, and immediately communicated this to Edgar Petersen who summed up the situation regarding attacks on tanks quickly and precisely:

> A year and a half ago came the order to equip the Ju 88 with the 75. Twenty aircraft were built. Today seventeen still exist. The aircraft have been in action for a short time and have been withdrawn from action because of difficulties with the gun mount and the propellers. In approximately 300 flights the propellers flew off. This has caused very great expense: conversion at Merseburg and in the Volkswagen works when the aircraft should have been in action. Then, again, an application of the 75 in the Hs 129 is currently possible as a single-loader with single

shots and not with a magazine. The magazine requires a colossal amount of development work and may not be in production before the middle of 1945.

In spite of all efforts, the expected results had not been achieved with the Ju 88 P-1 and the Hs 129 as, from March 1943, the Ju 88 P-1s delivered had proved to be insufficiently agile and offered far too large a target for the enemy defences. With the Hs 129, by contrast, a lengthy struggle had been necessary with diverse technical problems of the weapon installation. What, then, was the situation with the Ju 87?

With his Ju 87 G-2 Hans-Ulrich Rudel had shot up his 200th tank from the air. The weapons installation with its two BK 3.7s had developed into an outstanding means of defence against tanks, especially in the hands of experts – of which, however, there were far too few.

The threat to the German divisions which were on the defensive demanded an increase in Ju 87 G production from the beginning of 1944 in order to bring relief to the troops. Thus, in May 1944 alone, a total of eighty-seven Ju 87 Ds were converted to Gs. Of these *Luftflotte* 3 received eight, *Luftflotte* 6 five and the General of Pilot Training four; the majority – seventy Ju 87 G-2s – were assigned to the OKL reserve.

Of the fifty-seven Ju 87 G-2s manufactured in July 1944, fifty-three were new constructions in the framework of series conversion, while four were repaired aircraft which were converted to 'cannon birds'. Of these *Luftflotte* 6 received a total of twenty-one; thirty-six machines went to the OKL aircraft reserve. The report on aircraft assignments in September 1944, issued on 2 October 1944, indicated only twenty Ju 87 G-2s from the OKL reserve.

A total of twenty Ju 87 G-1s and 210 Ju 87 G-2s were delivered to the *Luftwaffe*, of which 174 can be shown to have been from the Weser aircraft works at Bremen.

Tank hunters in action over Hungary. On the left below a vehicle can be seen, hit and on fire.

10.3 Anti-Tank Ground Attack Units

On 17 December 1942 the reorganisation of the *Luftwaffe* ground attack units into *Gruppen*, each with three Fw 190 fighter bomber *Staffeln* and one Hs 129 tank hunter *Staffel* was ordered. However, operations mostly went on with individual *Staffeln* which were moved from one 'fire' to another, in order to be sent into action against local breakthroughs as 'flying firemen'.

Only at the end of 1944 was the attempt again made to form a complete and extremely powerful anti-tank defence *Geschwader* – SG 9 – whose first *Gruppe* comprised two *Staffeln* with Ju 87 Ds and Gs. The equipment of the Fw 190 F-8 with spin-stabilised anti-tank rockets, such as 'Tank Lightning' or 'Tank Terror', had made great progress from 1944 onwards and led to the Ju 87 G remaining in service only with relatively few tank hunter *Staffeln*.

StG 5 and StG 76, as well as the training *Geschwader* StG 101 to StG 186, had no tank

In the winter of 1944–5 some of the Ju 87 G-2s in action in Hungary were painted with winter camouflage.

hunter *Staffeln* of their own. The same was also true of the training units SG 101 to SG 152, although there individual Ju 87 G-1s and a few Ju 87 G-2s were on hand for training purposes.

10.3.1 10 (Pz)/StG (SG) 1

One tank hunter *Staffel* was assigned above planned establishment to some of the dive bomber *Geschwader*. A 10th *Staffel* for attacking tanks was added to StG 1 on 17 June 1943 from the former 1/Experimental Command. The *Staffel* was soon removed from the *Geschwader* unit once more and assigned to StG 77. On 18 October 1943, in the course of unit standardisation, the unit was renamed 10(Pz)/SG 77, but stayed with SG 77 only until the middle of October and then, on 18 October 1943 as 10 (Pz)/SG 1, returned to Ground Attack *Geschwader* 1 which had arisen out of StG 1.

With the Ju 87 G-1s and G-2s of the ground attack *Geschwader* tank-hunting operations were chiefly carried out. In February and March 1944 the *Staffel* was at Orsha, then moved to Bobruisk and at the beginning of April returned to Orsha. It received its operations orders from the 1st *Fliegerdivision*. In May 1944 the 10th *Staffel* had moved to Biala-Podlaska, where the staff and I *Gruppe* of SG 1 were. At that time the unit, with twelve machines, possessed more Ju 87 Ds and Gs than trained crews.

In June 1944 the unit moved to Tolotshin. On

The machine of the commander of SG 2, Colonel Hans-Ulrich Rudel, in the final phase of the Second World War.

26 June the tank hunter *Staffel*, with twenty machines, of which fourteen were battleworthy, was at Bojari. The remaining Ju 87s and Fw 190s with I and II/SG 1 were meanwhile at Tolotshin and near Vilna. In July 1944 the tank hunter *Staffel* withdrew by way of Matshulitshe, Lida and Kovno to Dubno, where it stayed for several weeks. After the withdrawal battles in the east between the beginning of September and the middle of October 1944, 10 (Pz)/SG 1 was at Hüttenfelde near Tilsit and was under the command of the 4th *Fliegerdivision*.

In November 1944 the *Gruppe* was at Schippenbeil, south-east of Königsberg, and flew further tank-hunting operations over the eastern front. From Schippenbeil, the unit moved to Gutenfeld.

While a part of the *Geschwader* was taken out of action for re-equipping with the Fw 190, the anti-tank ground attack operations went on for the 10th *Staffel*.

On 7 January 1945 the existing 10 (Pz)/SG 1 became a part of the newly formed first tank hunter *Gruppe* of SG 9, I(Pz)/SG 9, and therefore left SG 1.

10.3.2 10 (Pz)/StG 2 (SG) 2

In the same way a tank hunting *Staffel* of StG 2 in excess of planned establishment was formed from the former 2nd *Staffel* of the Anti-Tank Experimental Command on 17 June 1943 as the 10th Tank Hunting *Staffel*. The first *Staffel* captain was Lieutenant Helmut Schübel, who played a decisive part in the later operations of the tank hunting *Staffel*.

The unit received the designation 10 (Pz)/StG 2 and became 10 (Pz)/SG 2 on 18 October 1943, after the 'Immelmann' 'Stuka' *Geschwader* had become a ground attack *Geschwader* as part of the reorganisation of all ground attack forces.

In the autumn of 1943 enemy tanks that had crossed the Dnieper were attacked from the air. At the beginning of 1944 forces of 10 (Pz)/SG 2 supported the breakout of the 5th 'Viking' SS Armoured Division from the Cherkassy pocket. The *Staffel* at that time was at Pervomaisk, as well as at Uman and Rauchovka for a short time.

Up to the end of March the retreat to the Bug was effectively covered from Rauchovka; several armoured units that had broken through were successfully attacked from the air. On 29 March 1944 Captain Hans-Herbert Thienel was decorated with the German Gold Cross after he had shot up several Russian tanks. In April 1944 the

Staffel was at Jassy and from there moved to Husi in May 1944. There, on 31 May 1944, fourteen battleworthy Ju 87 Ds and Gs were still ready for take-off.

On 26 June 1944 the tank hunter *Staffel* possessed sixteen Ju 87s which were stationed at Husi and in the summer of 1944 had to take part in further retreat battles over Romania. The battles in the north of the eastern front forced the leadership to find new operational bases for the *Staffel*. At the beginning of July 1944 it operated from Husi, then from Poland (Dub, Jaroslavice, Zamosc and Mielec). From there the unit moved to East Prussia.

On 29 July 1944 10 (Pz)/SG 2 was at Insterburg and from there intervened in the battles in the northern sector of the eastern front. In August 1944 Reserve 2nd Lieutenant Anton Korol took over the 10th *Staffel* from Helmut Schübel, who was posthumously promoted Captain after losing his life in his burning Ju 87 G. Anton Korol brought his score to over seventy-five tanks in a few months. His radio operator was Sergeant-Major Karl Müller. At the beginning of August 1944 the 'cannon birds' intervened repeatedly in the ground battles between Weichsel and Memel, in which they destroyed twenty-seven Russian tanks. In the process, Major Hans-Ulrich Rudel scored his 300th tank victory. Meanwhile, the Red Army had pushed forward into East Prussia.

The staff machine of Colonel Rudel after the 'landing' at Kitzingen on 8 May 1945, in which American P-47 Thunderbolts were damaged.

In the following months the crews of 10 (Pz)/SG 2 tried – as far as resupply permitted – to bring relief to the German divisions from the air. Soon afterwards, the Soviet advance in the southern part of the eastern front made a further move necessary. In September 1944 the unit went to Görgenyoroszfalu in Hungary and next moved to Tasnad, Budak and Zilah.

In October 1944 the tank hunters moved to Ferihagy and further to Böngönd. From there it went a month later to Tanis St Marton and from there back to Böngönd in Hungary.

In December 1944 operational forces of the 10th *Staffel* with their Ju 87 G-2s attacked enemy armoured units in the area of the Red Army Ukrainian front before a further major offensive in January 1945 broke through the German main battle line in numerous places and opened the way to the Oder.

After 10 (Pz)/SG 2 had moved to Märkisch-Friedland to hinder the advance of enemy armoured forces there, the Soviet gains in territory enforced further moves. On 10 January 1945 there were still ten operational machines with the unit, of which all except one were reported serviceable.

The low-level attacks which were often undertaken against Russian tanks involved numerous losses. For example the bearer of the Knight's Cross, Sergeant-Major Hans Ludwig, died on 20 January 1945, when his Ju 87 G-2 was rammed by a Russian Il-2 at Dorf Loben in Upper Silesia, and a part of the right wing broke off. With him fell Lieutenant Herbert Weissbach, the operations officer of SG 2, who was flying with him as gunner. Hans Ludwig had 750 operations behind him and, although shot down many times, had destroyed eighty-five enemy tanks.

At the beginning of 1945 the *Staffel* flew its operations from Furstenwalde, east of Berlin. Between 12 and 15 February 1945 the unit was at

Major Karl Kennel (right), commander of II/SG 2, and Captain Kurt Lau, commander of II/SG 103, also surrendered on 8 May 1945 after attacking Allied armoured units right to the end.

Freiwaldau (between Sagan and Görlitz) and from the middle of the month was at Kamenz near Dresden. On 4 February 1945 the *Staffel* lost the crew of Siegfried Reinfeldt, whose Ju 87 G-2 (works no. 141074) crashed at the Fürstenwalde airfield. On 14 February 1945 a Ju 87 G-2 (works no. 494016) was shot down by flak south of Goldbach; the crew succeeded in making an emergency landing. Two days later another Ju 87 G-2 was badly shot up by the enemy ground defences and was completely wrecked in the emergency landing east of Hammerfeld. Meanwhile many Soviet units took self-propelled turrets with quadruple weapons with them in order to protect their own armoured forces effectively against attacks by Ju 87 Gs and Fw 190 Fs.

On 12 March 1945 Reserve 2nd Lieutenant Anton Korol was decorated with the Knight's Cross and at the same time – as one of the few reservists to bear the Knight's Cross – was named commander of the *Staffel*.

At the end of March 1945 the *Staffel* had twenty Ju 87 Ds and Gs, which were all reported airworthy on 31 March 1945. The unit was at that time north-west of Bautzen and from time to time operated in the same area as the operational forces of II/SG 2.

On 6 April 1945 came the move to Niemes-South (near Böhmisch-Leipa), from where it went to Budweis on 10 April 1945. At that time the *Staffel* had twenty-one Ju 87s instead of the establishment number of twelve, although there was often not enough fuel to send all the machines into action at the same time. Hence, only twelve of the twenty airworthy machines took off. The *Staffel* had at that time sixteen

This Ju 87 G-2 of 10 (Pz)/SG 3 is equipped with provisional camouflage paint.

crews at its disposal, of whom eleven had completed their training in tank hunting.

On 17 April 1945 the *Staffel* moved to Prossnitz. From there eighteen Ju 87 Ds and Gs of 10 (Pz)/SG 2 attacked tanks in the Brno area on 18 April 1945 and destroyed ten enemy battle tanks, six heavy self-propelled guns, one self-propelled quadruple flak vehicle, a tanker truck, seventeen lorries and fifty-five teams of horses. Sergeant-Major Fehdler distinguished himself by shooting up four tanks and two self-propelled guns. This brought his total number of victories of this kind to sixty-five.

On 19 April 1945 10 (Pz)/SG 2, together with 10 (Pz)/SG 77, attacked the Soviet advance on Bautzen with four Ju 87 Gs. On 20 April 1945 only part of the Oder front was still held. The attack tore the German positions to pieces and strong Russian units made their way irresistibly towards Berlin. Only three days later the battle for the *Reich* capital burst out in all its fury.

Soon afterwards 10 (Pz)/SG 2 was forced to move off to the south-east; next, it moved to Niemes-South near Böhmisch-Leipa. Many Ju 87 Ds and Gs of the unit were left behind, damaged, or were blown up by German troops so that they would not fall into enemy hands. From the surviving operational forces of II/SG 2, 10 (Pz)/SG 2, I *Gruppe* of SG 77 and II/JG 6, arose the 'Rudel fighting unit', in which all machines still airworthy were combined at the beginning of May 1945.

Reserve 2nd Lieutenant Anton Korol brought his score by the end of the war to ninety-nine confirmed tank victories and a further 200 immobilised through hits on the tracks or engines.

Second Lieutenant Jakob Jenster, who had received the Knight's Cross on 29 February 1944, also flew his operations over the eastern front to the end. His total was 960 operational flights, most of them in Ju 87s. In the process he succeeded, in more than 350 anti-tank ground attack operations, in destroying more than 100 tanks.

The last low-level attacks on armour concentrations and units that had broken through followed, before the cessation of hostilities.

10.3.3 10 (Pz)/SG 3

II/StG 2 was in action with Ju 87 Ds in the summer of 1943 in the *Luftflotte* 4 area. The personnel of its fourth *Staffel* were moved to Stephansdorf – albeit without machines – in September 1943 and on 18 October 1943 the unit was renamed as the 4th *Staffel* of SG 2. Next, the unit received a new complement of aircraft, consisting of Ju 87 G-2s, at Markersdorf near St Pölten. In March 1944 10 (Pz)/SG 3 arose out of the previous 4th *Staffel* of SG 2.

From 1 March 1944 onwards the unit moved to Danzig by way of Neudorf near Oppeln and further to Birzi near Jakobstadt, in order to go into action in the northern sector of the eastern front from there, but they waited in vain. On 24 March 1944 the *Staffel* flew under the leadership of Lieutenant Andreas Kuffner to Insterburg in East Prussia, where three out of twelve Ju 87 Gs sank into soft ground after landing and could be dragged out only with difficulty.

At the end of March 1944 the unit was at Krosno. Next, it went by way of Warsaw to Reichshof and then to the operational base at Jassy which was commanded by I *Fliegerkorps*.

In the first operational flight on 29 March 1944 Corporal Walter Eisenhardt died. His radio operator, Corporal Günther Neitzel, also failed to return from this first combat operation north of Jassy. As Russian forces already stood a short distance from the town, the unit was moved to Tiraspol, where the 'Boerst fighting unit' was formed, together with parts of I/SG 2, under the command of Captain Alwin Boerst. Several of the heavy T34/85 tanks were hit with two to four shots each with 37-mm weapons from 200–300 metres range by this unit. The approach flight was mostly from behind.

Senior Under Officer Josef Reitinger, promoted 2nd Lieutenant, flew numerous anti-tank ground attack operations up to the end of the war.

Between 29 March 1944 and 1 April 1944 two tanks, three lorries, ten horse-drawn vehicles and an anti-tank position were destroyed. As the enemy were pressing, the crews of 10 (Pz)/SG 3, led by Senior Under Officer Josef Reitinger, together with the Ju 87 D-5s of 1/SG 2, moved to Husi. From there five more tanks and two self-propelled guns were destroyed south of Stelly, at Carpiti, Targ and Grossulovo.

Next, the *Staffel* moved to Karankut in the Crimea by way of Mamaia with twelve tank hunters on 9 April 1944. An He 111 H-6 flew ahead as the 'Lotse' guide aircraft. The technical personnel were loaded into six He 111 Hs that were made available.

From 10 April 1944 the first operations took place. Under enemy pressure the unit moved to

Captain Andreas Kuffner, commander of 10/SG 3, was shot down by a Spitfire near Schwerin in the last days of the war.

Chersonese. Further tank hunting operations followed up to 16 April, in which at least fifteen Soviet tanks were hit.

After three weeks of operations in the Crimea, the unit was withdrawn to Roma in Romania at midday on 21 April 1944. North of Jassy, forces of 10 (Pz)/SG 3 attacked a breakthrough by enemy armoured units. From 2 May 1944 strong Russian units attacked the 'Grossdeutschland' Armoured Division and the 3rd SS Armoured Division at Targul-Frumos with more than 200 tanks and crushed the German positions. Against this, the 'cannon birds' took off for several attacks in which about twenty-five enemy tanks were shot up; others remained immobile on the battlefield. On 10 May 1944 SS-*Gruppenführer* Priess sent a telegram to I *Fliegerkorps* which was intended for the 3rd *Staffel*:

> In the past days of battle heavy losses in personnel and material were inflicted by the sharp attacks flown by the Roman numerals one *Fliegerkorps* and thereby much of our own troops' blood was saved. The Division thanks the *Korps* for the outstanding support carried out for the most part in the face of strong enemy defences.

In June 1944 10 (Pz)/SG 3 was engaged in the direct defence of Vilna, where the *Staffel* shot up thirty-two tanks as well as various other Red Army vehicles in low-level operations in three days. In this the crew of Sergeant Alfred Reimers was reported missing.

On 2 July 1944 the operations base of the *Staffel* was at Chotzov; Lida and Kovno followed. By 3 July 1944 10 (Pz)/SG 3 had already shot up its hundredth tank. In July, however, the *Staffel* lost several crews. Part of the unit moved to Sudauen for a few days and on 22 July 1944 moved further to Jürgenfelde in East Prussia.

At that time the 'cannon birds' of III/SG 3 had been assigned and constituted the only tank hunter *Staffel* in the northern sector of the eastern front. After a few days the *Staffel* made a surprise move to Gospori, south of Lievenhof, in order to bring relief to the hard-fighting army from there. In the process the *Staffel* destroyed twenty-one out of twenty-five attacking tanks at Mietau on 28 July 1944. By the end of July 1944 the 200th tank victory could be reported; Corporal Josef Bluemel (previously of 5/SG 151) shot up his thirty-fourth battle tank. During the last days of July two *Schwärme* were on the airfield near Jakobstadt.

After low-level attacks along the Narva front, the unit moved to Riga-Spilve on 7 August 1944. A few days later it succeeded in destroying eight tanks in one day south of Verro. The *Staffel* flew its operations against the Red Army, further subdivided into individual *Schwärme*, from Dorpat, Wesenberg and Oberpahlen.

On 1 September 1944 Andreas Kuffner was promoted Captain; a little later, on 25 September 1944, his *Staffel*, in spite of the ever increasing flak defences of the enemy, could report the destruction of its 300th enemy tank. Because of the strong fighter and flak defence, the operations of the slow tank hunters became ever more dangerous. At that time the unit operated mostly with four to six operational machines from Walmar. During these defensive battles a crew, consisting of Josef Bluemel, promoted Sergeant, and his trusted radio operator, Lance-Corporal Hermann Schwärzel, were shot in the back of the neck by Russian soldiers after an emergency landing at Kekava near Riga. Their Ju 87 G-2 (works no. 494231) had been shot down by enemy flak near the main battle line. The pilot, who had destroyed sixty Russian tanks, was decorated posthumously with the Knight's Cross on 28 January 1945.

At the beginning of October 1944 the *Staffel* moved to Hüttenfelde near Tilsit, where it remained until the middle of the month. *Staffel* commander Andreas Kuffner shot up his fiftieth tank on 22 October 1944. On 2 November 1944 the unit was at Schippenbeil, East Prussia. For two days Imperial Marshal Hermann Göring visited the *Staffel*. He promoted 2nd Lieutenant Rainer Nossek to Lieutenant and Senior Under Officer Josef Reitinger to 2nd Lieutenant. After issuing some decorations, he vanished as suddenly as he had arrived.

In December 1944 the unit was finally allowed a few weeks' rest after operations lasting several months. On 20 December 1944 the *Staffel* commander, after 600 operational flights, received the Oak Leaves to the Knight's Cross that he had received on 10 April 1943. In operations from East Prussia the unit was subordinate to the 4th *Fliegerdivision* belonging to *Luftflotte* 6. One of the main operating bases, besides Schippenbeil, was the airfield at Gerdauen.

The *Staffel* was in further action over the eastern front in SG 3 under the leadership of Captain Andreas Kuffner up to 7 January 1945 and on 25 December 1944 moved to Wormditt. At the beginning of 1945, the 10th *Staffel* joined the I Tank Hunter *Gruppe* of SG 9; the enthusiastic Captain Andreas Kuffner rose to be its *Gruppe* commander.

10.3.4 10 (Pz)/SG 77

On 18 October 1943 the former 10 (Pz)/StG 1 became 10 (Pz)/SG 77 (fuselage marking S2+). The *Staffel* therefore left its current *Geschwader* but on 27 January 1944 was again subordinated to SG 1. The aircraft consisted of Ju 87 D-3s, D-5s, G-1s and G-2s. Among the most successful pilots at that time was Corporal Leopold Schweizer, who received the German Gold Cross on 5 February 1944.

In March and April 1944 the *Staffel* intervened in the ground battles in the Army Group

Taxiing from a woodland clearing, this crew takes off on its next tank hunting operation.

This 'cannon bird' belonged to 10 (Pz)/SG 3 and went into action over the eastern front.

Centre area from Lvov. In May 1944 the 10th *Staffel* also operated from Lvov, together with the staff and II *Gruppe* of SG 77. At the end of the month twelve machines were on hand with 10 (Pz)/SG 77. In June the tank hunter unit was at Starzeva.

When the long-awaited major Russian offensive against Army Group Centre broke out on 22 June 1944, the few 'cannon birds' brought for the most part only temporary relief for the German divisions in their fighting withdrawal.

The 10th *Staffel*, which was still under the command of SG 1, was also caught up in the vortex of the withdrawal battles. Numerous unairworthy operational machines of the *Staffel* had to be blown up on their erstwhile operations bases.

In addition, the number of 'cannon birds' shot down by the Russian flak rose sharply. Nevertheless, the *Staffel*, separated from the *Geschwader*, still had nineteen Ju 87 Ds and Gs at Starzava on 26 June 1944, but only a few were battleworthy.

In July and August 1944 the unit operated from Pruzana, Terespol, Minsk and Grojek, before it had to retreat to Krakow in September. At the end of the month the *Geschwader* was again assembled under the command of VIII *Fliegerkorps*. In November and December 1944 the flying tank hunters were on the airfield at Balice and from there undertook numerous operations against Soviet armoured forces.

With the 10th *Staffel* ten Ju 87 G-2s were lost between 14 January 1945 and 18 February 1945 alone. Of these losses, almost all fell to the well situated defensive fire of the Red Army. On 17 January 1945 one of the operational machines, Ju 87 G-2 (works no. 490196, S2+KC), was blown up on the Balice airfield which had become threatened by the enemy. Four days later another Ju 87 G-2 (works no. 491299, S2+HX) went the same way under enemy pressure at Stubendorf and had to be written off after destruction by German forces shortly

A shot-up Russian T-34 in the northern sector of the eastern front.

The emblem of 10 (Pz)/SG 3 shows the aim of the Staffel*'s operations.*

before withdrawal. At the end of January S2+FX crashed after a direct flak hit. S2+CX was substantially damaged after an emergency landing which had become necessary as a result of engine damage.

On 1 February 1945 a total of fifteen Ju 87 Ds and Gs were on hand with 10 (Pz)/SG 77, of which eleven were reported serviceable. On 5 February 1945 the 'cannon birds' were at Aslau. The 10th *Staffel* lost Ju 87 G-2 works no. 490191 on 9 February 1945 after a landing accident.

Meanwhile, further moves had become necessary under enemy pressure. The *Staffel* was at Gahro between 12 and 21 February 1945. During the phase of operations there, enemy fighters shot down Corporal Werner Witeckim with his gunner on 18 February 1945. On the same day the *Staffel* lost a second 'cannon bird', Ju 87 G-2 works no. 494017 in an air battle with single-engined enemy fighters. At the end of the month the tank hunter *Staffel* was at Fürstenwalde.

Although further losses occurred to 10(Pz)/SG 77 at the beginning of March 1945, the maintenance forces were able to report between seven and twelve Ju 87 G-2s serviceable each day. Spare parts were removed from damaged Ju 87 Gs, and machines returning out of action with hits were thus repaired. The number of operations was from time to time severely reduced by the acute lack of fuel.

On 21 March 1945 in spite of everything, strength reports indicated fourteen Ju 87 G-2s available for the next tank hunting operations. This number was maintained until the end of the month, when the unit was north of Bautzen.

At the beginning of April, fourteen aircraft, two in excess of establishment, and a total of sixteen crews were available with the *Staffel*. With these, eleven ground attack sorties were flown on 1 April 1945. On 6 April 1945 the *Staffel* moved to Kamenz.

From there the bearer of the Knight's Cross, Lieutenant Max Diepold, was able to shoot up one more Russian tank during the last of his 150 tank-hunting operations. He ended the hostilities with eighty-seven acknowledged tank victories.

In spite of severe deficiencies in spare parts and numerous cases of damage by enemy defensive fire, the number of 'cannon birds' did not fall. The ground personnel organised the necessary spare parts or built them from damaged machines. Even on 16 April 1945,

A machine of 2 (Pz)/SG 9 in the winter of 1944–5.

fourteen Ju 87 G-2s were still on hand, but only nine were airworthy. On 18 April 1945 10 (Pz)/SG 77 attacked a concentration behind the eastern front with seven Ju 87 G-2s, together with nineteen other Ju 87s, mostly D-5s.

In this attack nineteen Russian tanks were shot up; the enemy also lost two personnel transport vehicles with anti-tank guns in tow as well as 108 motor vehicles. The 'Stuka' crews also succeeded in damaging twelve tanks, two personnel transport vehicles and twenty-one lorries. On 19 April 1945 several low-level attacks followed in the vicinity of Görlitz on the Neisse, before the sorely reduced *Staffel* had to move further to the west.

At the beginning of May 1945 the tank hunter *Staffel* began to disband.

10.3.5 Ground Attack *Geschwader* SG 9

After the formation of IV (Pz)/SG 9, into which the Hs 129 tank hunter *Staffeln* were incorporated, the formation of a tank hunter *Gruppe* with Ju 87 Ds and Gs was planned for the beginning of January 1945. This decision was changed to the extent that one of the *Staffeln* was to receive Fw 190 F-8s instead of Ju 87s.

I (Pz)/SG 9 originated on 7 January 1945 from 1 (Pz)/ SG 9 which was converted from Ju 87 Ds to Fw 190 Fs with 'Tank Lightning' projectiles at Perleberg near Wittenberge. In February 1945 the unit was at Freiwaldau and next at Grossenhain. Until the middle of March 1945 seventeen Fw 190 F-8s with 'Tank Lightning' were battleworthy with the 1st tank hunter *Staffel*.

A second unit was formed in I (Pz)/SG 9, namely 2 (Pz)/SG 9 which originated from the former 10 (Pz)/SG 1, as well as from

This machine flew operations on the eastern front with 2 (Pz)/SG 9 in the winter of 1944–5.

10 (Pz)/SG 3 which had been renamed 3 (Pz)/SG 9. Both *Staffeln* flew both Ju 87 D-5s and G-2s.

Until the middle of January 1945 the 3rd (previously 10th) *Staffel* was at Wormditt and was to be equipped with Fw 190 F-8s as quickly as possible. This did not happen, however, as the *Staffel* was renamed 3 (Pz)/SG 3 and received further Ju 87 Ds and Gs to fill out its inventory.

Otherwise, the 2nd and 3rd *Staffeln* possessed a few Fw 190 Fs each; the ground attack operations were, however, flown only with Ju 87s. The Fw 190s were used as accompanying fighters and as fighter bombers.

Because of the ever more dangerous low-level attacks, more and more experienced crews did not return from operational flights. Others fell victim to flying accidents. This happened to Sergeant-Major Ulrich Mundt, who took off with his Ju 87 G-2 in spite of bad weather. He lost his life in an emergency landing at Bützow in Vorpommern during a positioning flight. He was among the best combat pilots in SG 9, with forty tanks and twenty-five bridges to his name. The radio operator, as well as a third occupant of the Ju 87 G-2, was severely injured.

On 1 February 1945 the 2nd *Staffel* had only one Ju 87 D and one Ju 87 G. The decimated forces were stationed on the Finsterwalde airfield in the *Luftflotte Reich* area. In 3 (Pz)/SG 9 on the airfield at Berent, the number of available machines had also fallen drastically; it now had only five Ju 87 Ds and Gs. Unlike the first two *Staffeln*, the 3rd *Staffel* was for a time subordinate to *Luftflotte* 6.

At the beginning of February 1945, the three *Staffeln* of I *Gruppe* were placed under the 1st *Fliegerdivision* and were sent into action in the area of Army High Commands (AOK – *Armeeoberkommando*) 2 and 4. From 5 February

1945 the number of Ju 87 Ds and Gs assigned grew astonishingly and on 7 February 1945 was eighteen.

Between 12 and 15 February the 2nd *Staffel* was at Altdamm near Stettin and on 6 March 1945 was stationed at Mackfitz. On 18 February 1945 the unit lost another Ju 87 G-2 (works no. 494084), which was flown by Sergeant Hans Matthes, to flak fire. The wounded crew succeeded in making an emergency landing in friendly territory. In a second emergency landing on that day a Ju 87 G-2 (works no. 494219) was 60 per cent damaged; the crew, however, remained uninjured in the crash landing.

The 3rd *Staffel* with its Ju 87s was at Perleberg between the beginning of February and 27 February 1945, landed at Altdamm and at the beginning of March was stationed at Mackfitz.

On 5 March 1945 numerous Fw 190 F-8s of 1 (Pz)/SG 9, together with twenty-three Ju 87s of the unit, attacked Soviet tanks on the road from Stargard to Moritzfelde, in the course of which two of the combat vehicles exploded after direct hits, six others caught fire and three were left immobile. On five others, hits were scored on the turrets. One day later eighteen Fw 190s of II/SG 1 attacked at Stargard; another twelve from III/SG 1 as well as twenty-two Ju 87 Ds and Gs of 2 and 3 (Pz)/SG 9 joined them. More than eight enemy tanks were destroyed, together with two flak batteries. The pilot of a Fw 190 of III/SG 1, in addition, reported shooting down a Yak 3 fighter. On 7 March 1945 thirteen Ju 87s of I/SG 9 attacked south-east of Stettin, in which one machine was seriously damaged by flak. Six tanks were destroyed; some others and a self-propelled gun were damaged.

One day later a telegraphed order from the General of Ground Attack Pilots reached the tank hunter *Gruppe*, to the effect that the *Staffeln* equipped with Ju 87s were to be converted to Fw 190s with 'Tank Lightning' or 'Tank Terror'. But initially the action along the eastern front went on with undiminished ferocity. In the vicinity of Altdamm near Stettin on 8 March 1945, seventeen Fw 190 Fs of the staff of SG 3 and II *Gruppe*, together with five Ju 87s of 2 and 3 (Pz)/SG 9, flew a ground attack operation in which the crews of two 'cannon birds' were able to report one victory each.

Between 21 and 30 March 1945 the number of Ju 87 Ds and Gs on hand with the two *Staffeln* rose again to nineteen, of which twelve to fifteen were airworthy. The small amount of fuel assigned, however, hindered operations to a significant degree. On 22 March 1945 the battles were chiefly in the Schaumberg-Golzow-Gorgast area, and seventeen tanks were put out of action, mostly by the rocket shells of the Fw 190 pilots.

At the end of the month nineteen machines were still on hand with the 2nd and 3rd *Staffeln*. Of these fourteen Ju 87 D-5s and G-2s were battleworthy.

One of the last awards of the Knight's Cross to a ground attack pilot took place on 1 April 1945 with I (Pz)/SG 9: 2nd Lieutenant Karl Spreitzer had completed 652 operational flights and destroyed eleven tanks in the process; in addition, he had sunk an 8,000-ton tanker.

On 1 April 1945 2 (Pz)/SG 9 possessed a total of nineteen Ju 87 G-2s instead of the establishment twelve. Fourteen crews were available, for whom fifteen machines stood ready. By 3 April 1945 the number of Ju 87s with the second *Staffel* had fallen to eighteen. On 12 April 1945 seventeen machines were battleworthy, of which only thirteen could take off because of fuel limitations. In the middle of April 1945 the second *Staffel* was assigned to *Luftflotte* Command North-East and from then on was under the jurisdiction of the 1st *Fliegerdivision*.

At the same time sixteen ground attack aircraft were on hand with 3 (Pz)/SG 9. The *Staffel* was at Roggenthin near Rechlin until 29 April 1945 and only one day later moved under enemy pressure to Sülte, a small hamlet south of Schwerin, where the unit remained until 2 May 1945.

The *Gruppe* commander and bearer of the Oak Leaves, Captain Andreas Kuffner, had shot up a further ten Russian armoured fighting vehicles in the previous weeks, so that shortly before the end of the war he could look back on sixty tank victories. On 30 April 1945 he was shot down by British Spitfires on landing at the Sülte airfield. On that day the tank hunter *Gruppe* tragically lost two more highly decorated *Staffel* commanders, both bearers of the Knight's Cross, Lieutenants Rainer Nossek (3 (Pz)/SG 9) and Wilhelm Bromen (1 (Pz)/SG 9). According to information from Josef

Thanks to tungsten-cored shells, the guns of the Ju 87 G-2 could attack even the heaviest armoured vehicles effectively.

Reitinger, some relief operations were flown during the battle for the *Reich* capital by Fw 190 F-8s equipped with 'Tank Lightning'.

Because supplies of fuel were limited, combat operations to relieve German ground troops could hardly be flown at all at the beginning of May 1945. The remnants of the tank hunter unit moved, to the extent that the fuel situation permitted, to northern Germany from 2 May 1945, where a few machines landed in the vicinity of Schleswig.

10.3.6 NSGr 1 (North)

Ju 87 G-2s came into operation with only one night ground attack *Gruppe* – NSGr 1. Because of the advance of the Allies, this unit had to be divided into two *Gruppen* (see Chapter 6).

In March and April 1945 the northern *Gruppe* was in defensive action in the Gütersloh area under the command of the 15th *Fliegerdivision*. On 12 March it retreated from Kirchhellen on the River Ruhr to Störmede near Lippstadt, about 30 km south of Gütersloh.

The Ju 87 D-5, which was suitable for night ground attack, formed the bulk of the Ju 87s which were still available there. In addition, individual daylight operations were flown against Allied troop concentrations and columns of march between 13 March and 7 April 1945. The Ju 87 G-2s assigned to the unit went into action with the Ju 87 D-5s, which were equipped with bomb dispensers. At Gütersloh the Allies captured at least three Ju 87s of NSGr 1 in the last days of the war. The tactical markings of two of the Ju 87 G-2s are known: V8+FH and V8+KH. A few days later the last crews gave up the struggle in north-western Germany, which had become hopeless, and went into captivity.

11 The Ju 87 F – the Last Version

After the operations over southern England, it was already certain that the chances of successful sorties with Ju 87 Bs were becoming limited. The existing generation of aircraft could not hold its own in terms of performance with the enemy potential, as its powerplant, the Jumo 211 J, was not powerful enough.

The calculations carried out in the project office of the Junkers works, which were based on data supplied by the Junkers Engine Works for projected aero engines of the Jumo 211 type, did not show a decisive increase in the performance spectrum.

The only sensible further development of the Ju 87 would have been to equip it with the much more powerful Jumo 213 A.

2nd Lieutenant Anton Korol, the last commander of 10 (Pz)/SG 2, surrendered with his gunner and groundcrew leader on 8 May 1945 on the airfield at Kitzingen, after he had flown his last operations with the Ju 87 G-2 over Bohemia.

This prototype may have been a preliminary experiment for the installation of the Jumo 213 E in-line engine. The machine landed on the airfield at Kirchheim, Teck, near the Hirth aircraft works.

The new development received the construction series designation Ju 87 F. As early as the spring of 1941 the project office of the Junkers works presented a construction description of the planned F-1 version to the Technical Bureau. The variant, powered by a Jumo 213 A-1 in-line engine, could not reach the speed of normal piston-engined fighters but a noticeable advance in performance was nevertheless to be expected.

The power output of the Jumo 213 A-1 was 1,370 kW (1,775 horsepower), which would have led to a relatively large reserve of power in combat operations. Without a noticeable increase in performance, the Ju 87 B would have fallen behind far sooner than the *Luftwaffe* leadership expected. Even in areas where the *Luftwaffe* almost had control of the air, heavy losses to enemy fighters had to be expected.

As the series production of the Jumo 213 A was ever more delayed in 1941 due to technical problems, however, prototypes of a new variant of the 'Stuka' could not be expected before the end of 1942.

It nevertheless became clear in the early summer of 1942 that production would take place in the coming year, although the production rate of the new in-line engine was limited. The bulk of the more powerful powerplants would be required just to cover the most urgent needs of Ju 88 A production – only a limited capacity would be left for the Ju 87.

The production of the Ju 87 F was referred to in the aircraft programme of 19 August 1942 – Delivery Plan 22; the first machines, however, were expected more than a year later.

Series production was planned to begin in September 1944 with a single machine. According to Delivery Programme 22, three

Fw 190 Fs of III/SG 2 'Immelmann', led by Colonel Hans–Ulrich Rudel, attacked targets on the eastern front. The time of the Ju 87 as a ground attack aircraft was over.

aircraft were planned for October, six in November and in December another fourteen aircraft. In January 1945 twenty-five were to leave the production line at the Weser Aircraft Co. Ltd (WFG), in February 1945 forty and, from March 1945 sixty-five per month.

Significant production of the Jumo 213 A-1 had first begun at the end of 1942. Works testing had progressed only slowly; even at the beginning of 1943, there were severe delays.

After seventy-five Jumo 213 A-0s, the first thirty A-1 powerplants were completed; of these, the last ten had still not passed their 100 hours' running by the middle of February 1943.

The establishment of the necessary safety in operation of the Jumo 213 had mainly come to grief on the fact that the Junkers Engine Works had faced problems with the connecting rod bearing and the oil circulation.

By the middle of February 1943 there was still no reliable in-flight experience. Series production was therefore not expected until October 1943, so that the timing of the series installation in both the Fw 190 and in the Ju 87 was for the time being uncertain.

The Test Centre Command came to the conclusion that flight testing – at least on a broad basis – could not be expected before May 1943, as the first series powerplants would not leave final assembly until April. Meanwhile, the earlier priorities were overtaken. The search for fundamentally more powerful fighter aircraft, especially the development of jet aircraft but also an improvement in the combat value of types already on hand, such as the Bf 109 or the Fw 190, was more important in the production programme in the medium term in face of the Allied potential.

Hence, on 16 January 1943 Major-General Adolf Galland had already made the suggestion to the leader of the Technical Bureau of the RLM, Staff Colonel Wolfgang Vorwald, that at least 100 of the powerplant sets envisaged for the Ju 87 F be withdrawn from this area and that the engines be made available for the Fw 190 D. Only in that way would the series introduction of the Fw 190 D be possible.

Imperial Marshal Hermann Göring therefore decided that enough Jumo 213s were to be made available from the Ju 188 area for the Ju 87 F.

This did not happen, however, as the variants of the Ju 87 planned with the Jumo 213 could not be produced without affecting fighter production and the completion of the Fw 190 F.

In March 1943, therefore, the order for the whole Ju 87 F development was withdrawn and accounts to date were settled with the Junkers works.

Instead, discussions began as to whether an entirely new ground attack aircraft – perhaps the Ju 187, a belated new version of the Ju 87 F – should be built, whether to turn to a concept submitted by Blohm & Voss, or whether, instead of all these, to change the single-engined fighter bomber with an air-cooled powerplant.

In view of the war situation in the early summer of 1943, the construction series of the Fw 190 F was the only alternative to the Ju 87 which could be produced quickly.

Illustration Acknowledgements

Aders	5
Arena	2
Balss	3
Bernád	9
Borzutzki	1
German Federal Archives	26
Creek	28
Crow	3
Dabrowski	2
DASA	12
German Aero Club	3
Deutsche Lufthansa	2
German Museum	3
Dressel	15
Finnish Air Force Museum	4
Frankfurt Airport	4
Gliss	1
Griehl	21
Herwig	4
Höfling	5
Knobloch	1
Dr Koos	1
Krieg	1
Kroll	1
Lang	1
Lauck	5
Lutz	5
Maliza	1
Marschall	2
Martinez	9
Michulec	2
Morin	3
Müller	7
Müller-Rominger	2
NASM	8
Nowarra	20
Obernaier	1
Peter	1
Petrick	35
Punka	4
Radinger	5
Reitinger	12
Rosch	2
Salvati	2
Sauer	1
Schenk	1
Schlaug	1
Schliephake	1
Schmeelke	2
Schmitt	2
Selinger	6
Sengfelder	3
Smith	3
Stapfer	2
USAF	4
Weber	1

Index

Page numbers in *italics* refer to illustrations.